AN INTRODUCTION TO REVENUE MANAGEMENT FOR THE HOSPITALITY INDUSTRY

Principles and Practices for the Real World

Kimberly A. Tranter, MBA, CHE
Johnson & Wales University, Denver

Trevor Stuart-Hill, CRME, CPP
SynXis

Juston Parker
Parker Hospitality Group

PEARSON

Prentice Hall

Upper Saddle River, New Jersey 07458

Library of Congress Cataloging-in-Publication Data

Tranter, Kimberly A.
    An introduction to revenue management: principles and practices for the real world /
    Kimberly A. Tranter, Trevor Stuart-Hill, Juston Parker.—1st ed.
        p. cm.
    Includes bibliographical references and index.
    ISBN-13: 978-0-13-188589-9 (alk. paper)
    ISBN-10: 0-13-188589-8 (alk. paper)
    1. Hospitality industry—Management.   2. Revenue management.   I. Stuart-Hill, Trevor.
II. Parker, Juston.   III. Title.
TX911.3.M27T737 2008
647.94'068—dc22

                                                                        2007044388

Vice President and Executive Publisher: Vernon R. Anthony
Acquisitions Editor: William Lawrensen
Editorial Assistant: Lara Dimmick
Director of Marketing: David Gesell
Marketing Manager: Thomas Hayward
Marketing Assistant: Les Roberts
Production Manager: Wanda Rockwell
Creative Director: Jayne Conte
Cover Design: Bruce Kenselaar
Cover Illustration/Photo: Getty Images, Inc.
Full-Service Project Management/Composition: Integra
Printer/Binder: R.R. Donnelley/Harrisonburg

Credits and acknowledgments borrowed from other sources and reproduced, with permission, in this textbook appear on appropriate page within text.

Pearson Education LTD.
Pearson Education Australia PTY, Limited
Pearson Education Singapore, Pte. Ltd
Pearson Education North Asia Ltd
Pearson Education, Canada, Ltd
Pearson Educación de Mexico, S.A. de C.V.
Pearson Education–Japan
Pearson Education Malaysia, Pte. Ltd

20 19 18 17 16 15 14 13 12 11
ISBN-13: 978-0-13-188589-9
ISBN-10:   0-13-188589-8

Contents

Preface

You are about to embark upon a journey into an exciting new dimension in the field of hospitality management. Inside the pages of *An Introduction to Revenue Management: Principles and Practices for the Real World*, you will find a map, a RevMAP, which will lead you to your ultimate destination. A winding path containing eight very important steps, called fundamental elements, will deliver you to the four cornerstones of the strategic revenue management planning process. Here you will encounter the four building blocks that create the IDEA. The first building block is the identification of goals and objectives. The second building block is the development of strategies and tactics. The third building block is the execution of strategies and tactics. And the fourth building block is the analysis, evaluation, and adjustment of strategies and tactics to enable you to continue your journey. For once you have reached your final destination, the achievement of enhanced revenues, it is time for you to depart once again to continue your journey and explore new environments and experience new revenue-producing adventures.

An Introduction to Revenue Management: Principles and Practices for the Real World was written to fill a void in the marketplace. Being assigned the task of teaching an entry-level revenue management course in the Hospitality College at Johnson & Wales University's new Denver campus, I quickly discovered that no textbook covering this subject existed. After checking with all major textbook publishers and coming up empty, I decided to venture out into cyberspace to see what had been written and was available there. Again to my surprise, there existed no appropriate text from which to create an introductory course in revenue management. I had searched the major bookstore websites and also researched the availability of material in each of the online bookstores of colleges and universities offering degrees in hospitality management. I was fortunate, however, to find Robert Cross' book which would provide the basic material to engage students in lively discussion and permit me to build upon the concepts in a way most suitable to instruct a primarily junior-level college course.

When I contacted the Providence campus of Johnson & Wales University to see what textbook or course pack they were using, I found out that they were in the same search process as I. Katie Davin, of our hospitality program in Providence, suggested that I try writing the text myself. After all, I had been an Assistant Vice President of Marketing when my employer at that time, Sage Hospitality Resources, began implementing manual revenue management techniques at our Aspen and Snowmass resort properties in the early 1990s. So I definitely understood the fundamentals of the revenue management process. I had also been actively placing revenue management professionals in corporate- and property-level positions for nearly a dozen years as the operator of my hospitality executive search firm, so I also understood what skills, knowledge, abilities, and training were required for success in this field. Teaching courses in strategic hospitality marketing and strategic hospitality management for the past five years also helped to round out the knowledge I needed to create a strategic revenue management process. So Katie put me in touch with Sheila Davitt, a Career Education Specialist with Pearson Education, and the textbook planning process begun.

I engaged the assistance of two top revenue professionals I knew in the Denver market. My association with Trevor Stuart-Hill, the Vice President of Accounts & Revenue Management at SynXis, goes back over a decade, that is, from the time that he originally accepted a revenue management position with Sage. During his tenure as Vice President of Revenue Services for Destination Hotels & Resorts, Trevor served as an extremely popular guest lecturer in my revenue management class at Johnson & Wales University since its first year of introduction. Recently, Trevor departed Destination Hotels & Resorts to accept the position of Vice President of Accounts & Revenue Management for SynXis, a wholly-owned subsidiary of Sabre-Holdings. We remain forever grateful to Destination Hotels & Resorts, and in particular Vice President of Marketing Maureen Callahan, for permitting our use of their beautiful portfolio of property photographs.

I became acquainted with Juston Parker through another former Sage associate, Renie Cavallari. I attended a seminar on revenue management being facilitated by Juston and asked him to also guest lecture to my revenue management class at Johnson & Wales University. I asked Trevor and Juston to join me as partners in developing this introductory textbook on revenue management.

Over the past 18 months, we have met to determine how to make our academic research and field experience applicable both to undergraduate-level college students and to hospitality revenue management professionals just entering the field. The concept and design of the RevMAP evolved through my attempts in trying to create a logical sequence of actions to follow in the development, implementation, and evaluation of a strategic revenue management process. Being the only academic of the three, I took on the role of writing the narrative at a collegiate level, while maintaining one consistent voice throughout the book. Trevor has been instrumental in providing me research, data, and real-world experience and applications throughout each stage in the writing process. He has been a true side-by-side partner in the creation of this textbook. My appreciation of his knowledge and my gratitude for his diligent efforts run deep. His invaluable insight in and authorship of Chapter 14 will prepare students for the future evolution of the discipline of revenue management and provide us the jumping-off point for our advanced textbook on the topic. And Trevor's founding leadership and continued active participation in the Hotel Internet Marketing Committee and Revenue Management Special Interest Group created within the auspices of Hospitality Sales and Marketing Association International (HSMAI) has enabled us to tap into the talents of the great team of revenue professionals assembled there.

Juston has contributed his knowledge of technique application at the consulting level. His vast world travels have enabled him to share his experiences regarding the attitude and application of revenue management principles and practices around the globe. And the photographs provided by Juston and his wife Lisa add an international dimension to the textbook as well.

An Introduction to Revenue Management: Principles and Practices for the Real World has been written in a sequential learning style, featuring self-contained chapters. However, the chapters are most effective when used in the order written as each lesson builds upon knowledge obtained from the previous chapters. Chapter 1 serves as an icebreaker and provokes initial thought on the subject matter. Chapter 2 serves as a brief history of the hospitality industry and begins to show the historical utilization of revenue management techniques over the centuries. Chapter 3 addresses the first step in the RevMAP, which is obtaining customer knowledge. Market segmentation and selection are contained in Chapter 4. Thus these two chapters take two fundamental elements of marketing and sharpen the focus to apply to revenue management. Chapter 5 turns the reader's attention to understanding the organizational self-assessment process and leads the reader into the competitive analysis process. Chapter 6 then addresses the economic principles underlying revenue management theory and helps readers understand the dynamics of creating a demand forecast. Next, Chapter 7 explains the workings of reservations and channels of distribution. Chapter 8 focuses upon the establishment of dynamic value-based pricing. Chapter 9 then returns to the topic of channels, this time addressing management of both channels and inventory. And the book addresses the human resource element in Chapter 10, which includes sample job descriptions and a list of applicable courses of study for those most interested in pursuing a career in this field. Chapter 11 brings the entire process together in the development of the RevMAP. The RevMAP reviews the eight fundamental elements as they now appear in the critical path to the four building blocks of the strategic revenue management process known as the IDEA. Chapter 12 provides tools and resources that may prove most helpful to young revenue management career professionals just starting out in the field. Chapter 13 addresses some of the legal and ethical issues present in the application of revenue management techniques and also delves into some possible problems that may be encountered along the journey. Chapter 14 contains the projected progression of this discipline in the years to come. The last four chapters on hospitality industry applications enable both students and readers to apply the lessons learned to concrete examples. Various hospitality industry sectors were covered to appeal to the broadest possible audience, enabling faculty to apply their lessons to a wide range of hospitality-related majors. Each chapter ends with several questions and exercises facilitating discussion and additional real-world application.

Although I started this project to fulfill a personal instructional need, I hope that this textbook fills the void for other academicians who are in search of an introductory-level textbook in revenue management as well. But it is also my hope that the contents of *An Introduction to Revenue Management: Principles and Practices for the Real World* extend beyond the classroom and into the field. I tried to develop a sequential narrative that could provide the historical basis and fundamental principles underpinning the actions being performed by today's revenue management professionals. It is my hope that *An Introduction to Revenue Management: Principles and Practices for the Real World* will therefore become a tool for all hospitality organizations seeking to enhance their revenues. And its applications actually extend beyond the hospitality field as these fundamental principles and practices may be equally applied to other fields of commerce . . . in the real world!

Kimberly A. Tranter, M.B.A., CHE
Assistant Professor and Lead Faculty Lodging
Johnson & Wales University, Denver
Email: ktranter@jwu.edu

Acknowledgements

I would like to thank my parents, Ron and Sandy, for instilling in me a love of learning and a passion for the written word. I wish to thank my employers in the hospitality industry, most particularly Sage Hospitality Resources, for providing me the opportunity and resources to drive top-line revenues. Thank you to all my executive search firm clients for sharing your needs and requirements for revenue management professionals in your own operations. And thank you to Peter Rainsford, formerly of Cornell University and the University of Denver, for getting me started in my career in academia. To my Chair, Stephen Pyle, and all of my colleagues at Johnson & Wales University in Denver, Providence, Charlotte, and Miami, I extend my deepest appreciation for your support. I would like to dedicate this textbook to all of my current and previous students at Johnson & Wales University. You provided me with the inspiration to write this textbook.

— Kimberly A. Tranter

My professional life has been influenced by a great many people and it is to those individuals who have shaped my experience that I dedicate this book. The lessons I have learned along the way, although not always easy, have all been good ones. I would also like to thank my family and, in particular, my wife Kathryn for her unwavering support.

I also would like to dedicate this book to you, the reader, as you embark on your journey, for it is you who will continue the revenue management story that starts here—within these pages.

— Trevor Stuart-Hill

I would like to acknowledge my partners Kim and Trevor for their hard work and dedication, for without them, this project would never have been completed. I would also like to thank people who have been mentors in my career, such as Bill Dougherty and Jay Furfaro. In this time, I would like to acknowledge my father and I am dedicating all of my royalties to the American Diabetes Association so that others may benefit like he did. Most importantly, I would like to recognize my wife Lisa. She has always been the light of my life and been there for me in good times and bad. Lisa, I love you!

— Juston Parker

We would like to thank the following reviewers: Massimo Bosco, Kendall College; Dan Creed, Normandale Community College; Catherine Davin, Johnson & Wales College; Miyoung Jeong, Iowa State University; and Amit Sharma, Penn State University.

Author Biographies

Kimberly A. Tranter, M.B.A., CHE, serves as Assistant Professor and Lead Faculty Lodging in The Hospitality College on the Denver Campus of Johnson & Wales University. Since joining Johnson & Wales in 2001, she has taught a wide variety of courses in hotel management and sports, entertainment, and event management and she rolled out the first course in Revenue Management on campus. She also occasionally teaches courses in the College of Business. *Ms. Tranter was the recipient of the 2005 Teacher of the Year Award for the Denver Campus.* She started her academic career as an adjunct instructor with the University of Denver, teaching hospitality courses in The School of Hotel, Restaurant, & Tourism Management and The Women's College. She possesses over a dozen years of hotel executive management experience, culminating in her position as Assistant Vice President of Marketing for Sage Hospitality Resources in Denver. As a member of an operations team, she directed the revenue generation efforts for a portfolio of hotels from New York to California. She left Sage to launch a very successful hotel executive search and marketing firm which she operated for over twelve years. She currently serves on the board of the Denver Chapter of Hospitality Sales & Marketing Association International (HSMAI) and is a two time recipient of the Outstanding Hospitality Ambassador Award. She also serves as Chair of the Scholarship Committee for the Front Range Chapter of Hospitality Financial and Technology Professionals (HFTP). She obtained her Certified Hospitality Educator (CHE) designation from The American Hotel & Lodging Association in 2006.

Trevor Stuart-Hill, CRME, currently serves as the Vice President of Accounts and Revenue Management for SynXis, the industry leader of distribution technology and services and a wholly-owned subsidiary of Sabre-Holdings. He previously held the position of Vice President of Revenue Services for Destination Hotels & Resorts, also based in Denver. At Destination Hotels & Resorts, he was responsible for the overall electronic distribution and revenue management functions of the second largest hospitality management firm in the nation with room revenues in excess of $550 million. Prior to joining Destination Hotels & Resorts, he served as the Corporate Director of Revenue Management for Sage Hospitality Resources, directing the efforts of a portfolio of 53 properties in 23 states. Trevor's experience covers a wide variety of hospitality industry segments having worked in management positions for Town and Country Tours in Phoenix, BTI/Atlas Travel Management in Vancouver, British Columbia, and Princess Cruises in Los Angeles. Trevor served as Chair of the Hotel Electronic Distribution Network Association (HEDNA) Collaborative Committee with Hospitality Sales and Marketing Association International (HSMAI), served as past Chair of the HEDNA Member Resources Committee, and was a founding advisory board member of the HSMAI Revenue Management Special Interest Group. He currently serves as an e-Commerce committee member of Travel Industry Association of

America and serves as a member of HSMAI's Hotel Internet Marketing Committee. Trevor became a Certified Revenue Management Executive (CRME) in 2006 and a Certified Professional Pricer in 2007.

Juston Parker began his hospitality career as a Reservations and Yield Manager for Outrigger Hotels and Resorts. He then accepted a similar position with the Kimpton Hotel Group, where he obtained experience in managing the unique inventory of boutique hotel properties. Juston also joined Destination Hotels & Resorts, where he served as Director of Revenue Management and Electronic Distribution for their mountain resorts. Today, Juston holds the position of President and CEO of Parker Hospitality Group, Inc. In this position, he has established premier revenue-improvement strategies for hospitality and travel e-commerce markets globally and has led the firm's expansion to six continents and over 14 languages. He has developed over 75 tested and licensed tools to improve revenue in multiple sectors, including hospitality, e-commerce, automotive, and financial verticals.

AN INTRODUCTION TO REVENUE MANAGEMENT FOR THE HOSPITALITY INDUSTRY

Fifteenth Hole at the Lodge at Ocean Hammock.

CHAPTER 1

An Introduction

Chapter Objectives

The objectives of this chapter are to:

- Initiate thought regarding restrictions placed upon the price and availability of hospitality products and services
- Define the concept of revenue management
- Generate discussion regarding the practice of revenue management techniques in the hospitality industry
- Review pertinent areas of study

The Music Men

Tristan and Tyler gripped the steaming hot cups of Starbucks coffee and stamped their feet in an effort to generate some warmth. Too tired to talk, their yawns created wisps of mist in the pre-dawn air. They had just spent the previous night huddled in their down sleeping bags atop hastily inflated air mattresses strewn along the sidewalk outside the concert hall. They were on a mission—a mission to purchase U2 concert tickets for their fraternity brothers. The venue limited the number of tickets sold per person to 10 at a time. After a quick survey of their fraternity brothers was conducted last night, it was determined that Tristan and Tyler should purchase the maximum allowable block of tickets. So they spent the night outside in the frigid air to ensure that they would be two of the first people in line to purchase tickets this morning.

Just as the students' caffeine was starting to kick in, two 30-something guys in leather jackets got out of a nearby BMW and headed toward the line. Tristan was wondering what they wanted, while Tyler was thinking, "Hey, no cuts!" The

---

two new arrivals started chatting with everyone waiting in line, beginning at the front of the line. Their curiosity now piqued, Tristan and Tyler strained to hear what the two guys were saying, but their voices were too low. Finally the two newcomers approached the two fraternity brothers and announced their purpose. The two older guys were offering $50 per ticket to anyone willing to sell them their tickets to the concert. Since $50 was higher than the price of a ticket being sold through the box office or online, anyone selling their ticket stood to make a profit.

So who were these guys? Were they ticket brokers? Scalpers? Was this legal? Was this ethical? Why were these guys making this offer? Would there be enough time for Tristan and Tyler to get their tickets, sell them for a profit on site, and then get back in line to buy more? Or could they try to purchase tickets online through Tyler's laptop while they waited in line to approach the ticket window? What was the limit on the number of tickets that they each could purchase online? Why would a venue allow this practice to occur on their premises? Was the venue in fact aware of the presence of these guys and others like them?

Pilgrim's Progress?

Kristen checked her voice mail and heard a message from her Mom. It was time for Kristen to book her flight home for the Thanksgiving holiday break from college. Her Mom had checked on some flights and had just emailed Kristen a list of the best flights available in terms of both cost and daylight arrival and departure times. Her mother worried about Kristen traveling at night, so they always tried to arrange flights that occurred during daylight hours. In her email, Kristen's Mom reminded Kristen to pick an itinerary that included seven nights and a Saturday night stay-over. And to save money, Kristen should not plan on flying the Tuesday or Wednesday before Thanksgiving nor the Sunday after the holiday.

Later that evening, Kristen went online and retrieved her Mom's email. She then went to the Web and started researching flights on her two favorite airlines' websites. She reviewed the itineraries sent by her Mom and reviewed the ticket prices. Just for comparison, she decided to check some of the travel websites utilized by her classmates when booking their own flights home. So she checked several sites including Travelocity, Orbitz, and Expedia. She was surprised to see similar flights home offered at much lower fares and with fewer restrictions than those flights researched by her Mom. And it did not appear to make a difference whether she stayed over on a Saturday night or flew seven days apart. However, fares did go up for flights scheduled for the two days before the holiday and the Sunday after the holiday, just as her Mom had admonished.

Curious, Kristen decided to ignore the usual length of stay and Saturday stay-over restrictions, and instead entered the dates that she really wished to travel, excluding Wednesday, Thursday, and Sunday of Thanksgiving week. To her surprise, she was able to obtain much lower fares without the restrictions than her Mom had found with the restrictions. Even more curious, Kristen went back to the airline websites to see if she would be able to obtain similar fares directly from the carriers as she was able to find on the third-party websites. What do you think she found?

The Magic Kingdom

Snow pellets tapped steadily against the windowpanes behind her as Professor Taylor gazed at the azure waters of the lagoon and pool displayed in the brochure spread open on her desk. "Only six more weeks to Spring break," she thought as she buttoned up her sweater. That reminded her that she needed an update from her student travel committee. She was planning on taking a group of a dozen students to Orlando over Spring break to attend an industry association trade show and conference. The students had formed a travel committee and were assigned various aspects of pricing and planning the itinerary.

Thus far, the students had all submitted their applications to attend the trade show and conference, accompanied by their registration fee of $250 each. Today, Professor Taylor had received their confirmations along with a complete convention packet. Included in the packet was information regarding hotel accommodations, airline discounts for registrants, car rental coupons, and a special incentive for booking tickets online for local area attractions including Disney World and Universal Studios.

Courtesy of Destination Hotels & Resorts.

Wailea Beach Villas.

Due to their anticipation and enthusiasm for attending this event, the student travel committee had been working overtime in conducting their research. They went online, visited the local travel agencies, contacted Orlando hotels directly, and visited their Student Activity and Alumni Offices to find special deals and discounts. And they were extremely successful in their efforts.

The student travel committee brought their findings to their meeting with Professor Taylor. They reviewed the convention packet received and were quite shocked to see that the prices in the packet were substantially higher than the prices that the committee had been able to obtain. They looked at each item individually. First, they reviewed hotel accommodations. By going online, the students had been able to find hotel room rates listed below the rates published in the packet that they just received. Why was this so? Why would the hotel offer prices that were higher for booking within the special group room block than attendees could find booking outside the block?

The airline fares found by the committee on the airlines' websites were lower than the discounted fares offered in the convention packet. Again, why was this so? And sometimes the students were able to find even lower airline fares for the same flights on travel websites such as Orbitz.

But the biggest surprise came when the students compared several of the package prices that were quoted by travel agents. These packages included airfare, hotel accommodations, car rental, and tickets to the major attractions. In some cases the package price was higher than if the items had been purchased separately, but in other cases the package price was lower than the sum of its parts. What was going on here? The students were confused as to how they should proceed in booking their trip. What advice would they receive from Professor Taylor? How should they proceed from this point? Would it make a difference if they booked inside or outside of the block of hotel rooms held by the conference organizers and to whom might this make a difference? Were there any restrictions for booking outside the block or any incentives for booking inside the block?

Sleigh Bells Ring

Every winter, the Bentleys spend the holiday season in Aspen. Like clockwork, the family arrives on the 20th of December and departs on the 3rd of January. For the past 10 years they have stayed at the Rustic Lodge at the base of the mountain. They always take advantage of the bounce-back coupon that they receive upon check-out to immediately reserve their suite for the next year.

This year however, the Rustic Lodge experienced some extensive hail damage from a late-fall storm. The roof must be replaced, which will require the Lodge to remain closed through mid-January. The Rustic Lodge notified all of

Courtesy of Lisa Marie Parker.

Vail Cascade in Winter.

their holiday guests holding reservations that they would have to seek alternative accommodations this year. The Lodge manager did provide a list of area hotels and inns with their telephone numbers and Web and email addresses.

As soon as the Bentleys received word of the Lodge's closing, Mrs. Bentley started calling the properties on the list provided by the Lodge manager. Her first preferences on the list were naturally already booked. However, she started finding some availability as she proceeded down the list. When she finally found one property that had availability for the entire length of her family's vacation, she was surprised at what she heard next. Yes, the inn had availability. The rate was double what they usually paid, but the reservationist explained that was due to how late in the season this was to be booking holiday rooms. In a rather snippy tone, the reservationist stated that Mrs. Bentley should consider herself lucky to be able to find availability at all at such a late date. Also, the inn required a full nonrefundable deposit due November 1st, which was just seven days away. They would accept a credit card number to hold the reservation until the full deposit arrived.

As Mrs. Bentley was reaching for her credit card, she told the reservationist that she would call her back in a few minutes. At double the rate, was this vacation still a good value? Would her family be crushed if they did not go to Aspen this year? Would they be better off booking a holiday cruise instead?

Courtesy of Professor Robert Lothrop.

Paris in Winter.

To the Four Corners of the World: Defining Revenue Management

So what do these four scenarios all have in common? They each focus on the purchase of varied hospitality products and services, including concert tickets, airline travel, trade show and conference registration, car rental, hotel accommodations, and tickets to major amusement attractions. Notice that in each case, both price and availability are major factors.

Incorporating an analysis of price and availability for hospitality products and services leads us to the topic of this textbook: the study of an emerging discipline known as Revenue Management.

What exactly is Revenue Management? To begin, let's examine each word carefully. According to Webster's, *revenue* may be defined as "an item or source of income."[1] And *management* refers to "the act, art, or manner of managing, or handling, controlling, directing."[1] But Webster's continues by also defining *management* as "skillful managing; careful, tactful treatment."[1] Thus, combining the two terms we derive the following definition: Revenue Management is the act of skillfully, carefully, and tactfully managing, controlling, and directing sources of income. But this definition is incomplete. Revenue is dependent upon three other elements which address price and availability: (1) capacity, (2) supply, and (3) demand. There are various definitions of **capacity**, but the one that applies here is "the amount of space that can be filled."[1] And we may add "during that particular time." For the airlines, space refers to seats on a particular flight. For a hotel, space may refer to guest rooms, meeting rooms, or restaurant seats available over a specified period of time. For a retail establishment, capacity refers to shelf space. And for a manufacturer, capacity may refer to either levels of production or inventory space. Economists define **supply** as the amount of a good or service that a seller is willing and able to sell for any given price at any given time. They define **demand** as the amount of a good or service that a purchaser is willing and able to buy for any given price at any given time. So adding the elements of capacity, supply, and demand, our definition becomes: *Revenue management is the act of skillfully, carefully, and tactfully managing, controlling, and directing capacity and sources of income, given the constraints of supply and demand.* The time element is implicit in the application of the principles of supply and demand.

The study of Revenue Management spans various other disciplines and major areas of student concentration. First, Revenue Management involves many of the basic concepts that comprise the field of Economics, such as markets, forecasts, cost, scarcity, and elasticity. For example, we will examine the opportunity costs involved with the purchase of the elements of leisure travel and the ramifications of decisions made on both an individual's budget and well-being.

A second discipline that is closely related to the study of Revenue Management is that of Marketing, in terms of both individual buying decisions and group purchasing dynamics. The **4Ps of marketing**—product, price, place, and promotion—are equally important elements in the development of Revenue Management techniques. We need to understand the needs, wants, desires, and expectations of individuals and groups.

Courtesy of Professor Robert Lothrop.

Singapore.

Third and closely related to the field of Marketing is that of Psychology. It is important to understand what motivates people to act upon their impulses. What makes them buy Brand X instead of Brand Y? And why during certain times of the year or at specific price points are they willing to switch and buy Brand Y instead of Brand X?

A fourth element helpful in the study of Revenue Management is an understanding of the world of finance. The future and current value of money, domestic monetary supply, and global monetary policies all have significant impact upon the field of Revenue Management.

And finally, an application of the study of Strategic Management is useful in developing goals and objectives in the creation of a strategic revenue management plan for the organization.

Current events, politics, and information technology all are important considerations for students delving into the study of Revenue Management. But even more important perhaps is the ability to study history, and from that study model intelligent forecasts for possible future events. For as we shall see, the best way to forecast the future is to understand the past. Thus, that is where we will begin. In the next chapter we will embark upon a journey to understand the historical development of the concept of Revenue Management.

SUMMARY

This chapter introduces the concept of revenue management and its roots in various fields of study. Its purpose is to provoke readers to consider their own experiences as consumers of hospitality products and services.

KEY TERMS AND CONCEPTS

The following key terms and concepts were presented in this chapter. Each term and concept is also contained in the Glossary of Terms located at the end of this book.

- capacity
- demand
- 4Ps of marketing
- revenue management
- supply

DISCUSSION QUESTIONS

1. Do you think changing prices to meet the current demand is ethical? Is it always legal?
2. Is scalping legal in this state?
3. Have you ever purchased tickets from a ticket broker? What was your experience?
4. The last time that you traveled to visit your family, did you purchase travel products and services online? If so, describe your experience.

INTERNET EXERCISES

1. Go to www.ticketmaster.com and check ticket availability for an upcoming concert at a local venue. Write a one-page narrative of your experience. Describe the prices and restrictions that you found on purchasing tickets for that artist at that venue. Critique the website and explain why you may or may not return to the website in the future.

2. Imagine that you are going to take a trip for 10 days over the winter holiday. Go online and separately find the cost of airfare to and from that destination, the cost of a hotel room for 10 nights in that destination, and the cost of renting a midsize car for 10 days over that time period. Add up the total price for these three elements. Now, go back online and using the same dates, see if you can find a cheaper price available for the same or similar three elements. Report your findings.

REFERENCE

1. *Webster's New World College Dictionary*, 4th ed.

Ship in San Francisco Bay.

CHAPTER 2

A History

Chapter Objectives

The objectives of this chapter are to:

- Illustrate the earliest applications of revenue management
- Review a history of the development of hospitality products and services
- Explain the evolution of yield management techniques developed by the airlines
- Describe the initial adoption and modification of yield management techniques by the hotel industry

While many hospitality students have learned about the evolution of hospitality-related products and services in their introductory courses, it is doubtful that they related that history to the emergence of revenue management practices and applications. This chapter takes us back to review the very earliest applications of revenue management techniques in the hospitality industry and witness their metamorphosis over the centuries.

Since the beginning of time, man has assigned value to items, particularly those in his possession. In the Stone Age, one fur pelt may command ten fish in trade. Or one fish would be worth two coconuts. Slowly, as villages developed, a standardized value was established for items of trade.

Barter was the first method of trade. One individual would exchange goods or services with another individual. The terms of the trade were established based upon an item's worth. Worth was typically determined either by an item's scarcity or by its perceived value in labor. If few salmon could be found in local waters, then the value of salmon would rise. If it took a craftsman two weeks to fashion a spear, its value would be reflected in the price of the item accepted in trade. The traded item had to be equivalent to the cost of the raw material and two weeks of labor.

The first markets sprung up in towns and villages to facilitate the exchange of goods and services. As merchants began to travel the globe in search of wares, new bazaars and markets appeared along major thoroughfares throughout Europe, Asia, and Africa. Items in the greatest demand could command the highest prices at these open-air affairs.

These first merchants practiced an early form of revenue management. The local butcher in a village held back his best meat for the king, and the butcher sold it to the king's cook for a premium price. Perhaps this is where the saying "fit for a king" originated. The baker sold day-old bread at a discount to the peasants. The dressmaker bought a variety of silks and tapestries from the traveling merchant. She then reserved the best-quality fabrics for her wealthiest customers. So from the start, prices have been set based upon availability, perceived value, and ability and willingness to pay. The laws of supply and demand dictated the wares bought and sold at these early marketplaces.

Travelers were not immune to this variation in pricing. Inns and hostelries were some of the very first establishments to set their nightly prices based upon availability. The more the inn filled up in the evening, the higher the price the innkeeper quoted to late-arriving guests. And the last available leg of lamb left on the spit in the inn's tavern would command a high price indeed!

All Aboard!

The earliest travelers moved about on foot with the help of pack animals such as donkeys and camels. Soon, they began to travel about on horseback and later in horse-drawn wagons and carriages. If they wanted to travel abroad, they ventured out onto the sea in sailing vessels and steamships. The first ocean liners brought travelers across the Atlantic from Europe in the first half of the nineteenth century. The initial voyages were not for the weak of heart or stomach, as the ocean crossings were long, arduous adventures. As more travelers ventured across the seas, the demand grew for more accommodating quarters onboard. And shipbuilders took heed. Most students are aware that the maiden voyage of the luxury liner the *Titanic* ended in tragedy in April of 1912 when it hit an iceberg. The *Titanic* was constructed to meet the demand of wealthy ocean travelers who desired a luxury experience apart from the seagoing masses. Thus the owners and operators of the *Titanic* were employing revenue management techniques in both the construction and operation of the famous ocean liner. The higher the perceived value of the ocean travel experience, the higher the price the cruise line company could charge per passenger on their luxury liners. Travelers wishing to cross the ocean on a budget fare could reserve a berth on one of the other numerous steamships that traversed the Atlantic at that time. Today, the cruise line industry offers a variety of vacation packages ranging from economy to opulence.

A more recent example of maximizing revenue in the luxury segment of the cruise line industry is the construction and launch of the *Queen Mary 2*. This magnificent vessel cost over $800 million to construct, requires a crew of over 1,200 to operate, and can take on over 2,600 passengers per voyage.[1] The average price of a transatlantic cruise aboard this luxury liner during its first year was £719 or about $1,375.[1]

Riding the Rails

It may be hard for some American students accustomed to watching Westerns to believe, but the railroads actually got their start in Europe. The first passenger rail service began when the Liverpool to Manchester Railway opened in England in 1830.[2] Transcontinental rail service in the United States was possible for the first time in 1869, when the Central Pacific and Union Pacific Railroads joined their tracks together at Promontory Summit, Utah.[3]

The railroads quickly caught on to the idea of maximizing revenue by charging higher prices for their more valuable seats on the most highly demanded routes. Luxury sleeper cars were created to house the upper class on cross-country journeys. The less fortunate travelers purchasing the lower priced seats were destined to spend the journey trying to sleep sitting up, a hardly restful mode of travel.

The railroads enabled travelers to now venture to new areas to visit friends and relatives or to explore new country. People began to use rail travel for leisure as well as for business. Wherever the railroad stopped, a town soon sprung up to service the weary travelers. The most popular destinations quickly began to charge the highest prices. Hotels and restaurants along the railway thrived during the end of the century and many small rail towns grew into larger and successful cities.

The railroads hit their peak in profitability around the turn of the century because, unfortunately, by the middle of the twentieth century, travel by automobile had greatly

Courtesy of Lisa Marie Parker.

Barcelona Train Station.

diminished the allure of the railroads. The advent of air travel by the masses continued the decline in the demand for railway travel. Today, travel by rail continues to be an alternative mode of transportation, with one major federally funded railroad, Amtrak, serving the passenger market. Ticket prices are competitive, but usually set slightly lower than most airline travel to the same destination. However, the cost differential is offset by the increased length of time that it takes to travel to the same destination via rail. For example, instead of flying from Denver to Chicago in two hours, the rail passenger would reach Chicago approximately 21 hours after departing Denver. For those travelers who wish to see the countryside or who are adverse to air travel, travel by rail remains a viable alternative.

See the U.S.A. in Your Chevrolet . . .

The first automobiles built in the United States actually operated on steam. It was not until the gasoline engine was perfected in the late 1880s by Gottlieb Daimler that automobile travel became a viable mode of transportation.[4] Henry Ford brought the automobile to the masses by utilizing an assembly line process which enabled the Ford Motor Company to mass produce automobiles at an affordable price in the early years of the twentieth century. As more and more people were able to purchase automobiles, they began to venture out first on day drives to the country and then on overnight excursions to visit friends and families. Soon, Americans were spending their entire vacations driving across the landscape to indeed see the U.S.A!

Along with the propensity to get out and see the nation came a need for motor travel-related products and services. First, motels sprung up along the major highways as convenient one-night stops for families traveling on vacation or businessmen traveling for commerce. Rest stops, also referred to as travel plazas or travel oases in the Midwest, were built along the toll roads and featured restaurants, filling stations, and general merchandise stores.

Americans became so comfortable and proud of their new automobiles that they quickly developed new pastimes that revolved around these new big amazing machines. A Friday night date soon began to consist of a trip to the drive-in movie theater for a sundown double feature, followed by a trip to the drive-in restaurant for a burger and a malted. Combined, the total evening would cost under $10, especially affordable with gasoline prices set at under 10 cents per gallon!

And Americans' fascination with the automobile has not diminished over the past century, but has rather continued to grow. Automobile manufacturers keep developing new models to satisfy the needs, wants, and desires of consumers at all price ranges. According to the Travel Industry Association, more domestic person-trips in the United States are taken by car, truck, camper/RV, or rental car.[5] In fact, vacation travel by automobile actually experienced a resurgence following the events of September 11, as Americans preferred to stay closer to home and to also avoid air travel. Even with gas prices pushing past the $3.00 per gallon mark in most areas of the country in the summer of 2006, Americans were reluctant to cut back on their driving. The American Automobile Association (AAA) estimated that 41 million Americans traveled via automobile over the 2006 Independence Day holiday.[6]

No Vacancy

The impact of the automobile on the hotel industry cannot be underestimated. Previously, hotels were primarily located in major cities or along railway stops across the country. Now, the automobile created the need for a clean place to stop, eat, and spend the night.

Kemmons Wilson, the founder of Holiday Inns, developed the moderately priced hotel chain directly as a result of one of his automobile trips with his wife and children. He had difficulty finding clean, consistent motels in which to stay with his family. He was appalled by the practice of charging additional dollars for young children to eat and stay at these overnight inns. So he created Holiday Inns in response. Travelers soon learned that they would experience a clean, comfortable, consistent stay at a Holiday Inn. In addition, their children would eat and stay for free.

Mr. Wilson also believed strongly in customer service and the advantages that could be gained from developing strong customer loyalty. He trained all of his front office personnel to inquire as to the travel plans of all departing guests. The front desk clerks were then trained to ask whether that guest would like the clerk to make a reservation at a Holiday Inn near the guest's destination that upcoming evening. This habit was a very nice personal touch that also increased revenue for the chain.

Courtesy of Destination Hotels & Resorts.

Restaurant in Richardson Hotel Dallas.

The hotel industry began to reach a level of maturation in the late 1970s that enabled it to review and revamp its methods of operation. In the 1980s, the hotel industry began to experiment with segmentation and developed products to fit new markets. Room rates reflected the features and benefits offered at properties at each level of service. Limited-service hotels soon sprung up in suburban areas and extended-stay properties entered the development pipeline nationwide. Hotels could charge lower rates for travelers staying for a week or longer at extended-stay properties as hotel labor and supply costs diminish with the increasing length of stay. For example, it takes less time for a housekeeper to clean a room of a continuing guest than it takes to strip the entire room for a new guest. The Marriott Corporation took the lead in both the research and the development of new hotel products designed to meet the needs of guests spanning from the upscale market to the budget traveler. Today, they operate properties ranging from upscale Ritz-Carlton Hotels and Resorts to Fairfield Inns, which were developed to meet the needs of the economy-minded business traveler.

Luck be a Lady Tonight

An outshoot of the hotel industry that has continued to reinvent itself is the gaming industry. Las Vegas celebrated its centennial year in 2005, and one of the festivities was the opening of the opulent new Wynn Las Vegas. Steve Wynn has long been credited with revitalizing Las Vegas by developing the theme concept of the mega resort properties like the Mirage and the Bellagio. His newest creation, simply called Wynn, features 2,716 rooms, an 18-hole championship golf course, 18 restaurants, 2 nightclubs, and nearly 30 retail boutiques.[7] Opening season rates ranged from $269 to $649 per night.[8]

Las Vegas understands the concept of maximizing revenue by looking at every single dollar available from each of the nearly 40 million visitors inbound annually. The cheap $2.99 buffet has given way to four and five star dining experiences. Show prices for headliners start at $100 per person. The stores dotting the promenades in the finest resorts along the strip feature names such as Gucci, Cartier, and Prada. And hotel room rates now rival the finest resorts in Scottsdale, Palm Springs, and Palm Beach.

In the late 1980s, Las Vegas tried to become a family destination with the development of such themed properties as Treasure Island and Excalibur. And while the city was able to capture increased market share in leisure travelers matching this demographic, it was not as great an increase as they had anticipated. So once again, Las Vegas is reinventing itself. The focus on the adult traveler seeking an upscale resort experience is clear in both the new properties being developed and in Las Vegas' new slogan intimating that what happens there should stay there. It appears that the themed park idea is best left to Mickey. Speaking of Mickey . . .

The House the Animated Mouse Built

The Disney organization entered a time of transition in 2005 with the stepping down of its chairman, Michael Eisner. The company has certainly come a long way since Walt Disney began his career at a cartoon studio in Hollywood in the 1920s. Disneyland opened its doors in Anaheim in 1955 and the Magic Kingdom sprung to life at Walt Disney World in 1971.[9] The company continued to expand and acquire new subsidiaries to make it the entertainment giant that it is today.

The Disney people understand two core concepts really well. First, they truly understand the value of the customer. Each cast member in the Disney organization is trained to appreciate and assist the customer. And in return, the customers truly value their Disney experience.

Second, Disney associates understand the value of merchandising. Every new creation, whether it is a movie or a ride in a theme park, is analyzed in terms of its future marketing and sales potential. Brainstorming takes place more than a year in advance of a new product launch and all possible revenue-generating opportunities are examined. Perhaps a new feature film is under development. A lead character is sure to be a huge hit with children. Disney toy designers begin the process by developing games and toys featuring the new character. Merchandising partnerships are reviewed. For example, could a small replica of the character be placed in perhaps Happy Meals to be sold at McDonald's? All forms of retail merchandise ranging from pajamas to backpacks are then created featuring the new character. Songs from the movie are packaged and sold. And the merchandising does not stop with the release of the movie. The movie next transitions into the movie rental market and eventually into the video retail market.

Today Disney is a diversified entertainment conglomerate, offering products and services to all segments of the market. Disney cruises feature learning programs in baking and pottery that are attractive to the middle-aged baby boomer. Television and movie products are developed to appeal to viewers ranging from age 5 to 50. Adult couples are being targeted by the theme parks as they are encouraged to fly away to Disney resorts for a great time without the children.

Up, Up, and Away . . .

One last mode of transportation needs to be addressed to complete our history and that is air travel. Commercial aviation began in earnest in the United States following the end of World War I. The first commercial flights in this country were commissioned by the U.S. Postal Service to deliver mail. The majority of the pilots were air force pilots returning home from the war. Occasionally, an independent pilot would offer to take a passenger along on one of his air mail flights.

It was not until Charles Lindbergh completed the first solo transatlantic flight in 1927 that investors sat up and took notice. These investors opened up their minds and their wallets as they envisioned the possibilities of air travel both domestically and internationally. Later that year, Pan American Airlines was established to deliver mail between the United States and Cuba.

However, it was nearly another decade before passenger planes were constructed and placed into service to carry the first regular passengers. It was not until 1958 that the first Boeing 707 jets were put into service. The jet age had officially begun.

Suddenly, it was possible to travel to the farthest corners of the world in a reasonable amount of time. The jet age led to the great interdependence between the airline industry and other travel-related products such as hotel rooms and car rentals. Airport hotels soon became some of the highest occupied properties and car rental companies opened fewer downtown agencies, switching their attention to expansion at the nation's major airports.

The airline industry was strictly regulated by the federal government in its early years. Severe restrictions existed regarding available routes and fares. The Airline

Hong Kong Airport.

Deregulation Act of 1978 changed the way the entire industry operated. Airlines were now free to compete for passengers, fares, and routes. The ensuing fare wars led to the development of a formalized method of managing and controlling revenues. This new process was called **yield management**.

Flying the Not-So-Friendly Skies . . .

Yield management was the precursor to what we now refer to as revenue management. The term **yield** refers to the amount of revenue received by the airline for each mile flown per passenger (also known as passenger mile). A second important term in yield management is *load factor*. **Load factor** refers to the percentage of seats sold. To calculate total passenger seat revenue per flight, first multiply the yield times the number of miles flown on that flight. Next multiply the number of seats on the plane times the load factor. Then multiply the results of the two calculations:

$$(\text{Yield} \times \text{Miles Flown}) \times (\text{Number of Seats} \times \text{Load Factor})$$

So for a 500-mile flight with a yield of 50 cents per mile and 80 percent of the 130 seats available sold, the calculation would be

$$(\$0.50 \times 500) \times (130 \times 80\%) = \$250 \times 104 = \$26,000$$

During the years that the airlines were regulated, the carriers were restricted to specific routes and were limited as to the fares they could charge passengers. Following deregulation, these restrictions were lifted and many lower-cost carriers began entering the market. They began to compete directly with the major carriers by flying the same routes within the same markets, but at lower fares. In addition, many established carriers began expanding their operations to include new routes as well. Soon, they were forced to compete directly by offering these new lower fares on those same routes.

And so began the furious pricing wars! Low fares, combined with the cost of operating additional routes and purchasing new planes, began to cripple the financial health of the major carriers. They needed a system of improving their revenues, and they needed it fast!

So they started manipulating the yield and load factors to try to develop an optimum mix per route. Airline pricing strategists would determine which fares to offer on which flights to which markets. Inventory managers would then determine how many seats to offer at each of the individual fare levels for each flight. First, the pricing strategists tried lowering the fares in an effort to both match the competition and increase sales. They believed that the lower the fare, the greater the number of passengers who would purchase at that fare price. Inventory managers determined the number of seats to offer at each fare level per flight. So they offered more discounted fares and more seats at the discounted level, and what happened? They also lowered their total revenue. Sure, they sold more seats, but at the lower fares, they actually lost money. Remember that yield is calculated by the amount of money received per passenger mile. As load increased and fares decreased, yield stayed flat or decreased. And there were costs involved with higher loads. Most carriers at that time offered meals or snacks to passengers on each of their flights. The more people on a flight, the higher the total cost of this meal/snack service rose. Ticketing and baggage handling costs also increased with increased volume.

So the next month, they would reverse the pattern by restricting the number of discounts and the number of seats offered at the discount. And what happened? They sold fewer seats, but at a higher yield per seat. Were they any better-off? Remember that there are fixed costs also involved with airline travel. The cost of a full load of jet fuel per plane remains the same whether it flies empty or full. So the pricing strategists continued to struggle with finding the right combination of yield and load to maximize revenues.

In the mid-1980s, American Airlines finally created a yield management system to resolve this yield/load dilemma. They had developed the Sabre reservation system in the mid-1960s and were now poised to turn the system into a more strategic weapon with which to fight the ever-increasing competition from lower-cost carriers. They were going to use the data stored in the reservation system to help them gain a competitive marketing advantage.

First, they analyzed the characteristics of each flight for each day of the week. Who was sitting in each seat—a business traveler or a leisure traveler? What fares were expected for these seats by these travelers? Business travelers expected to pay a higher fare for seats on weekday flights whereas leisure travelers were seeking discounted rates primarily on the weekend.

In the second step, the analysts assigned a value to each seat on each flight. Discounted seats were allotted per flight based upon the anticipated load factor and booking pace for that flight. The most highly valued seats were not discounted at all. In this way, the analysts were able to begin to manage the yield, or the revenue generated from each passenger mile.

Booking pace was a critical element in this analysis. **Booking pace** may be defined as the pattern and tempo of receipt and acceptance of advanced reservations. This term applies to airline seats, hotel rooms, dinner reservations, season tickets, and most other advanced purchases of goods and services. When did the majority of passengers book a particular flight? Leisure travelers typically book their reservations further in advance than business travelers. People usually book their flight arrangements as soon as they determine their vacation destination. On the other hand, business travelers book their flights as their needs arise, usually with much less advance notice than leisure travelers. The computer system was able to provide the historical booking pace for each flight. It was important for the inventory manager to understand this analysis, so as to not offer discounts prematurely. Last-minute travelers are often prepared to pay a premium to get to their destination, so deeply discounting unsold seats too early would result in filling up the flight with lower fares before the higher-paying passengers would normally book their reservations. The airlines were leaving money on the table, so to speak.

Third, fares were assigned to each level of seating per flight. It was possible for a flight to have several different fare levels, ranging from first-class (nondiscounted) to super-saver (highly discounted) fares. Restrictions were placed on the availability of the various fares. The goal was to maximize the revenue for the entire flight.

The final step was to analyze the results. How much did that same flight generate last week, last month, and last year before the computer aided in managing the yield? Did the system work? You bet it did! Robert L. Crandall, the then chairman of American Airlines, credits the yield management system for contributing $500 million annually to the airline.[10]

To understand this concept, it is best to provide a numerical example. So let's look at a single seat on United Airlines. Today, United operates more than 3,700 flights daily to over 210 domestic and international destinations.[11] Raising the fare on just one seat per flight per day by $10 would yield an extra $13.5 million annually! Reviewing the math,

$$3{,}700 \times \$10 = \$37{,}000 \text{ per day} \times 365 \text{ days} = \$13{,}505{,}000 \text{ a year!}$$

Could the system be enhanced even further? How could the airline continue to improve its revenue? Recently, several airlines started charging an additional $15 per seat for bulkhead seats, the first row of seats in the coach section. These seats offer more leg room for taller passengers. On an average domestic flight (nonwide body), there are usually six bulkhead seats. So using United as an example, the airline would generate an additional $121.5 million annually if they charged $15 extra per bulkhead seat and all seats were booked.

$$6 \text{ seats} \times \$15 = \$90$$
$$3{,}700 \times \$90 = \$333{,}000 \text{ per day} \times 365 \text{ days} = \$121{,}545{,}000$$

Now of course that is based on all bulkhead seats being full, which is not realistic. But assuming that just half of these bulkhead seats would be sold, the increase in revenue generated by this extra $15 per bulkhead seat would amount to over $60 million dollars a year!

Courtesy of Destination Hotels & Resorts.

Cinnamon Beach Guest Room.

Revenue Management Moves Inn . . .

Whatever you can do, I can do better . . . maybe. Hotels soon caught wind of this miraculous new revenue-maximizing system being used by the airlines and wanted to join in. Hoteliers had always been practicing a form of yield management by raising and lowering their rates based upon the season and offering discounts to their high-volume users. But they managed this manually, without the aid of a sophisticated computer system. How could the same elements being applied by the airlines be adapted to enhance room revenue? Airlines were all about butts in seats and hotels were focused on heads in beds. Same thing right? Not entirely.

The first problem revolved around technology. While the airlines were first-level adopters of new technology, hotels have been historically slow adopters of new technology. A **first-level adopter** is an organization which tries out new innovations first, before those innovations are mass produced or disseminated to the market. In other words, they would try out the beta version before the final version is ready. Since they have historically been such slow adopters, the immediate problem that the hotel sector faced was the lack of adequate technology on which to run and analyze the data.

Second, most hotels had not been capturing much data regarding their guests. They really did not know much about who was sleeping in their beds. The sales department had garnered some data regarding group bookings, but information on the individual traveler was sorely missing. Not only did the hotels not know *who* their guests were, in most cases they did not know *why* their guests were staying in the hotel's beds.

A significant gap arose when determining *when* their guests booked their rooms. Again, booking-pace data was available from the sales department on group-booking pace. And some individual booking-pace data was available through the central reservation system for corporate and franchised operations. Many hotels, however, did not analyze data on individual booking pace in any meaningful manner. They did not know whether there was a pattern as to when a particular type of customer booked his or her reservation.

Third, a key element differentiating hotel room revenue from airline seat revenue was length of stay. An airline seat was sold for a specified time period of one day. A hotel room could be booked for multiple-night stays. So the hotels had to determine how to optimize their room sales by managing inventory for individual and multiple nights. The hotel industry soon realized that developing a successful yield management system was not going to be easy.

Hotels had to combine the elements of price and duration to determine a method of maximizing their revenue per room. They began referring to this process of managing price and inventory as revenue management. Bill Marriott is often credited with being the pioneering force for championing revenue management initially in the hotel industry. The Marriott organization researched customer demand for their varied hotel products. Based upon their studies, they determined that customer behavior and demand could be forecasted. Price levels and inventory controls could then be established based upon the demand forecasted per day. In other words, they could decide which rooms would be offered at which price for each day based upon this forecast. Applying this technique to all hotels within their organization yielded Marriott an additional $100 million in revenue annually in the first few years of implementation.[10] Hoteliers began to seek new opportunities within their organizations for growing revenues. Soon they were looking at applying revenue management techniques to products and services other than rooms, such as spa services.

Like hotels, restaurants wished to improve their revenues. They soon started applying their own techniques to managing revenues. Car rental companies had already started implementing their own revenue management systems following the lead of their airline partners. Simultaneously, word of this new method of generating revenue was spreading to arenas, convention centers, concert halls, cruise lines, theme parks, and other sectors of the hospitality industry. Before we can examine the application of revenue management to these various hospitality sectors, we must first examine the fundamental elements that make it work.

SUMMARY

Revenue management techniques have been applied to hospitality products since the days of the very first markets. Merchants saved their best wares for their best customers. The last available room or meal available at the inn commanded a higher price than those served earlier in the evening. As the Industrial Revolution took hold, more and more people ventured further from their homes in search of commerce or relaxation. New modes of transportation developed to get travelers from here to there. And different prices began to be charged according to the manner in which these travelers experienced their journeys.

The Airline Deregulation Act of 1978 enabled the airlines to compete for fares, routes, and passengers for the very first time. Ferocious fare wars ensued and the airlines struggled to maximize their yields. American Airlines is credited with developing a system of managing yield through their computerized Sabre reservation system. This system soon generated an additional $500 million in revenue for American Airlines. All the other major carriers rushed to develop similar systems for maximizing revenues.

The hotel industry began to take notice and analyze how the application of similar techniques could increase room revenues just as it had increased seat revenues for the airlines. The Marriott Corporation applied these new techniques to their portfolio of properties and generated an additional $100 million in revenue annually. However, since the hotels did not utilize the term *yield* in their operations, they changed the name of the process of maximizing revenues to revenue management.

KEY TERMS AND CONCEPTS

The following key terms and concepts were presented in this chapter. Each term and concept is also contained in the Glossary of Terms located at the end of this book:

- booking pace
- first-level adopter
- load factor
- yield
- yield management

DISCUSSION QUESTIONS

1. What are some additional examples of early merchants using revenue management techniques?

2. Do you think that the airline system of pricing seats is fair? Please explain why you feel this way.

REFERENCES

1. *Queen Mary 2* luxury cruise ship facts accessed May 2, 2005, http://www.qm2-uk.com/id-10225/ship-facts.html

2. Liverpool to Manchester Railway's website accessed May 2, 2005, http://www.lmu.livjm.ac.uk/lhol/content.aspx?itemid=151

3. Central Pacific Railroad's website accessed May 2, 2005, http://www.cprr.org

4. European Automotive Hall of Fame's website accessed May 2, 2005, http://www.autonews.com/files/euroauto/inductees/daimler.htm

5. Travel Industry Association's website accessed May 2, 2005, www.tia.org/researchpub/eNewsline_february2_2004.html7

6. Automobile Association of America's website accessed June 28, 2006, http://www.AAA.com

7. Wynn Las Vegas' website accessed May 15, 2005, http://www.wynnlasvegas.com

8. *Wynn Las Vegas,* accessed May 15, 2005, http://www.whatahotel.com/Hotels/wynn.html

9. Disney Corporation's website accessed July 5, 2005, http://corporate.disney.go.com

10. Cross, Robert G., *Revenue Management: Hard Core Tactics for Market Domination*, New York: Broadway Books, 1997.

11. United Airlines' website accessed July 4, 2006, http://www.united.com

Lamb at L'Auberge Del Mar Resort and Spa.

CHAPTER 3

Customer Knowledge and Consumer Behavior

Chapter Objectives

The objectives of this chapter are to:

■ Describe today's more sophisticated "prosumer"

■ Explain what is meant by a customer-centric approach

■ Explore the price/value relationship and its impact upon consumer purchasing behavior

■ Examine the impact that the evolution of e-commerce has had on consumer purchasing behavior

■ Introduce the concepts of bundling, dynamic packaging, and branding

■ Define total customer value

■ Identify marketing intelligence resources available

WAITRESS: Hi! What can I get you?

HARRY: I'll have the number three.

SALLY: I would like the chef's salad please, with the oil and vinegar on the side. And the apple pie a la mode.

WAITRESS: Chef and apple on mode . . .

SALLY: But I'd like the pie heated and I don't want the ice cream on top, I want it on the side and I'd like strawberry instead of vanilla ice cream if you have it. If not, then no ice cream, just whipped cream, but only if it's real. If it's out of the can, then nothing.

WAITRESS: Not even the pie?

SALLY: No just the pie, but then not heated.[1]

Most of us chuckle when we see this scene in the movie *When Harry Met Sally*.[1] But how many of us also place our orders more like Sally than Harry? We are becoming a nation of very particular consumers, wanting *what* we want, *when*

27

we want it, and *the way* we want it. In other words, we would like our purchases to be customized.

Understanding consumer behavior is so fundamental to revenue management that we have dedicated this entire chapter to the topic. Organizations need to gain a deeper knowledge of their customers to enable their sales and marketing teams to develop products and services that will satisfy the wants, needs, and desires of their most valued customers.

Dell Computer was one of the very first organizations to take advantage of this new desire for mass market customization. Interested in purchasing a desktop or laptop computer, but don't need all the bells and whistles on the computers found in the big box computer store? Or interested in adding more bells and whistles to the computers found on those same shelves? In either case, Dell provides an answer. Enter Dell online and enter the world of the build-it-yourself customized computer. Dell immediately invites the virtual shopper to "customize it!" Once into this cyber superstore, it is just a series of clicks to arrive at the computer of one's dreams. And this personalized product is built and delivered to the customer's doorstop at a very reasonable price indeed. Dell's current advertising campaign revolves around "Purely You." They promote the fact that "we don't build for just anyone, we build for you."[2]

Best Buy stores have even adopted what they call a "customer-centricity operating model . . . The customer-centricity operating model enhances the ability of store employees to satisfy the unique needs of the people who shop in their store."[3] A **customer-centric approach** may be defined as any marketing or operational effort focused on the needs, wants, and desires of an organization's customers.

Now, customization of products and services is nothing new. Consumers of luxury items have long demanded personalized attention and service, from the chauffeurs of their vanity plated limousines to the monogrammed robes and individual butlers awaiting their arrival in penthouse hotel suites. But this hue and cry for personalized and customized products and services by the masses is a relatively new phenomenon. Americans went from "having it their way" at Burger King to personalizing their pet's bedding at the mega pet mart. Brides are able to create stamps bearing the picture of the happily engaged couple to place on the envelopes of their wedding invitations and then follow up after the honeymoon with personalized wedding photo stamps on their thank-you notes. Concierge medical clinics are springing up to personalize our health care and then personal trainers are hired in an effort to improve our original or our nip-and-tucked physiques. We can sip on one of the tens of thousands of possible drink combinations from Starbucks now while we grocery shop. And even our children can personally build their teddy bear of choice at the mall.

Today's Prosumers

The noted futurist Alvin Toffler first coined the phrase **prosumer** in his book *The Third Wave* in 1980. The term referred to what Toffler envisioned as the newly emerging consumer—a customer who was part producer and part consumer of the desired product or service.[4] The teddy bear–building customer clearly falls into this category. And many consumers of hospitality products and services may also be considered prosumers utilizing this vernacular. Consider any restaurant in which the diner becomes involved in the meal's production. From creating a salad at the salad bar to building a sky-high sundae at the dessert bar, the diner becomes an active participant in the development of his or her own dining pleasure. And travelers checking into a hotel with the new mattresses offering personalized numbered comfort can inflate or deflate their way to slumber.

A second meaning for the term *prosumer* has increasingly appeared in discussions of consumer behavior. This reference combines the word *professional* with the word *consumer* to arrive at the alternative definition of prosumer—that of a professional consumer. This is a buyer possessing considerable knowledge about the product or service being purchased. A serious hobbyist or regular viewer of the DIY Network may fall into this category. Or the term would also apply to the professional computer technologist who is searching online for technology products to purchase for home use.

Today's consumers fall into both categories of prosumers. They are more involved in the actual production of the products and services they purchase and they are more knowledgeable about their attributes. The Internet is facilitating this new form of consumption, or should we say prosumption? In some cases, the consumer merely sidesteps the brick and mortar store to order from the retailer directly online. In other cases, the consumer bypasses the retailer completely and buys directly from the manufacturer. An example of this second method would be buying a printer from the manufacturer directly, rather than through a retail computer or office-supply store.

All businesses, whether large or small, need to reach out to capture new customers and to entice current and previous customers to purchase the organization's products and services once again. This is typically accomplished through marketing. **Marketing** is often defined as the process of satisfying the wants, needs, and desires of customers. Marketing may take many forms, from electronic ads on websites to coupons mailed directly to the consumers' homes. In any form, marketing is aimed at capturing the customer's attention and inducing him or her to take action. That action may range from simply having the customer request additional information to ultimately, and desirably, having that customer make a purchase.

Marketers have always understood the importance of knowing the attributes and the behavior of consumers. They needed to know *who* they were, *what* they wanted, *where* they wished to make their purchase, *when* they made their purchase, and *why* they bought that good or service. This understanding is equally critical to the revenue manager. *Customer knowledge is the first fundamental element in the development of revenue management strategy.*

Consumers and the e-Commerce Evolution

To begin, we must analyze today's consumer. What are the general attributes of the average American consumer? First, he or she has become a much more educated consumer. Television viewers can turn to 500 possible satellite television channels to watch niche programming targeted specifically to their interests. **Niche** refers to a small, specialized market. Don't like to watch golf? Simply click from ESPN to the History Channel. Bored with history? Turn to a comedy on HBO. And who advertises on these niche channels? The answer is marketers trying to hone in on the specific needs, wants, and desires of the audience viewing that type of programming. Viewers are exposed to items ranging from the newest golf clubs to the most recent biography of a current world leader. The range of new television channels has enabled marketers to abandon their former shotgun approach of marketing, and to adopt a more-targeted rifle approach. In the past, they just shot out their message to the masses, hoping that their message would score some direct hits. Now, they can take direct aim at a concentrated and interested target market. Not only is this much more cost efficient, it also enables the marketers to continually refine the customization of their products and services to meet the specific needs of their customers.

A major source of information regarding products and services is the Internet. Retailers have noted a new trend practiced by their Internet-savvy customers. More and more consumers are going online to obtain information and comparison shop first before they venture out to the mall or superstore to make their purchase. A retailer's website is referred to as their **online store**, while the local building that houses their retail establishment is referred to as a **brick and mortar store**. Why is it that many shoppers will do their research online, but still travel to the brick and mortar stores to actually make their purchases? It depends both upon the nature of the purchase and the individual consumer. Some people want to use their senses during the purchase process. In other words, they want to touch, feel, smell, hear, or taste sample an item before they buy. Is it really that unusual to want to feel the weight of the fabric and see the color of a very expensive jacket before deciding whether to make the purchase? Absolutely not. There is also some correlation between the price of the product or service and the desire of the customer to physically view the item before purchase. The typical consumer now divides his or her purchases between bricks and clicks. Each year, online merchants are increasing their capture of the retail consumer. The importance of maintaining an easily navigable website continues to grow.

The coming together of buyers and sellers on the Internet is referred to as **e-commerce**. E-commerce is divided into three segments: business to business (**B2B**), business to consumer (**B2C**), and consumer to consumer (**C2C**). Business-to-business transactions still command the largest portion of online commerce. Business-to-consumer online transactions are increasing steadily. B2C transactions have become particularly prevalent in the hospitality industry with the advent of third-party travel websites such as Travelocity and Expedia. For some reason, consumers are more comfortable purchasing travel products online than they are purchasing many other products and services online. And consumer-to-consumer purchases occur primarily on major auction websites, such as eBay. Perhaps the largest global consumer market ever created, eBay has grown and prospered entirely in cyberspace. eBay facilitates the exchange of items between buyers and sellers who may never meet geographically in any form of traditional marketplace. The updated definition of the term **market** is simply any place, real or virtual, in which a buyer and seller may come together to exchange goods and services.

Buying products whether via bricks or clicks, today's consumers have also become much more discriminating and sophisticated in their purchasing behavior. Honestly, who would have guessed 10 years ago that sheet thread count would be a selling feature for hotels? Or customizable mattresses? And 20 years ago, how many people knew the brand names of their pans or other kitchenware? And could anyone have envisioned the day when the word *Bam* would immediately conjure up the image of a cook named "Emeril"? Or when college students would forego an evening out dancing at a club to compete in a home-version Iron Chef competition? Times, they are a-changing . . .

Bundling and Pressing Time

Time as well has become a valuable commodity in the life of the average consumer today. Our 24/7 society has made our day jam-packed with activity and communication. We are able to get more done, but the list of items that we need to accomplish each day also appears to be growing. We feel as if we are on constant call from the office, our friends, and our families. This has led us to seek out products and services enabling us to better manage our time. We pick up dinners at the drive-up windows of upscale restaurants in the same way that we used to pick up fast food. Grocery store delicatessens are filled with entrees and side dishes designed to aid in meal preparation. We can run our SUV through the car wash while having our pooch shampooed at the wag-n-wash operation next store. Even our dry cleaner offers two-hour express turnaround.

The practice of bundling has evolved from this new demand to save time. From early on, hospitality organizations have packaged together various travel components. A travel agent would prepare a travel package combining air fare, hotel accommodations, and rental car, and offer it to a leisure traveler for one set price. The traveler did not see the cost of each component, so the decision to purchase was based upon his or her overall perceived value of the package and the destination.

But today packaging has taken on a new dimension that is now referred to as **bundling**. Whereas packaging usually combined just the major key product components of a travel purchase, bundling combines both products and services. For example, a resort bundle may include air fare, hotel accommodations, car rental, dinner reservations, golf tee times, golf club and cart rental, spa services, an in-room massage, and coupons for shopping. Or a cruise bundle may include air fare, taxi transfers, cruise accommodations, all food and beverage purchases onboard, gambling chips, shopping vouchers, and activity and excursion fees. Organizations should investigate the appeal of a variety of differently bundled packages, again determining *what* their customers want, *when* they want it, and *how much* they are willing to pay to get it. This customer-centric approach to packaging is referred to as **dynamic packaging**. Hospitality providers may vary the products and services bundled in a package to suit the needs of the individual consumer. A consumer may review a menu of packages available and select the one that best suits his or her needs at that time. Vacation travelers really want to enjoy their leisure with the least amount of decision making required during their actual trip so they are most likely to purchase all inclusive packages at the time their reservations are made.

Business travelers are even more pressed for time. Most travelers simply leave the travel purchase decision making up to their corporate travel departments. The corporate travel planners negotiate for specially discounted rates for transportation and accommodations. Business travelers are also accustomed to staying within the parameters of the set per diem expenditures allowed per city. **Per diem** means per day. The General Services Administration of the U.S. federal government establishes a per diem rate listing for all markets both domestically and abroad. Some major metropolitan areas may include several different per diem rate structures for separate areas of the city. The per diem rates set are usually the maximum allowable expenditure on hotel rooms and each daily meal permitted for government travelers. Many businesses have also adopted this listing to serve as their guideline in establishing the maximum expenditures allowed by their personnel traveling to those markets. Even when the business traveler books his or her own travel components, there are often specific brands from which he or she may be required to purchase.

The Power of Branding

Branding is back and it is back in a big way. There was a brief moment around the turn of the millennium when prognosticators were predicting the demise of the brand. The new, younger purchaser was not loyal to brands in the same manner as his or her parents and grandparents. To the teenager and early-twenty-something purchaser, product features appeared to be more important than who manufactured the product. However, the end of branding has turned out to be a mere hiccup in the futurists' forecast.

Read the front page of any hospitality industry magazine today and the headlines simply scream of new branding initiatives. Hotels are adding brands, restaurants are developing more brands, and new airline brands are elbowing in alongside the major carriers lining up at the terminal gates. Just what is branding? **Branding** may be defined as placing an identifying mark or logo on a product produced by a specific organization or associating that brand with a service performed by that organization. A brand is unique to one specific organization. Marketing professionals often state that to the customer, perception is reality. A brand often equates expectations to perception. If a customer equates a brand to luxury, the customer will perceive that company's products and services to be of high quality and high price. Conversely, if a customer equates a brand with discounted economy, the customer will perceive that company's products and service to be of reduced quality and lower price. The company's use of a brand is an effective method of communicating or reinforcing a message. Therefore, it is critical that an organization properly positions its products and services to ensure that the expectations of its targeted customers match the reality of the price and quality of the organization's products and services.

The Price/Value Relationship

Value is a term used today in tandem with the idea of the more discriminating, yet time-anemic consumer. Consumers calculate value as their perceived value of a product or service, less the cost of obtaining that product or service. **Perceived value** may include material value and quality, benefits received from ownership or usage, and esteem associated with the product or service. **Total acquisition cost** may include intrinsic costs such as price and extrinsic costs such as the time it takes to make the purchase and the cost of gasoline it requires to get to and from the store. So the perceived product or service value must be equal to or exceed the total acquisition cost to produce total value to the consumer.

$$\text{Total Customer Value} = \text{Perceived Product or Service Value} - \text{Total Acquisition Cost}$$

Knowledge of this price/value relationship is critical to understanding consumer behavior and motivation. Customer satisfaction is dependent upon this meeting or exceeding of customer expectations. Customer dissatisfaction occurs when the product or service falls short of expectations.

Revenue managers must become astute observers of consumer behavior and also understand how various price/value relationships impact the purchase decisions made by their customers. All members of an organization should be involved in creating profiles of the company's current customers. The line-level employee who interacts daily with customers may have an entirely different perception of those customers than the manager setting selling strategy from a corporate office removed from the immediate premises.

There is another dimension of consumer behavior that needs to be addressed and that is the difference between individual and group purchasing behavior. The decision-making process becomes increasingly complex as the number of people involved increases. It will also vary based upon the purpose of a gathering. There will typically be more layers of people involved providing input and influencing decisions for an annual convention then there will be for a family reunion. It should be noted, however, that consensus within the family may be harder to achieve! Also, decision making often hinges upon whose money is being spent, the consumers' or their employers'.

Selling products and services to groups is exceedingly more complicated than selling to individuals. Instead of having to understand the wants, needs, and desires of just one customer, the salesperson now needs to understand the motives and perceptions of multiple customers in a group environment. And there are often multiple decisions makers involved in the purchasing decision. This takes more time, more resources, and

Courtesy of Destination Hotels & Resorts.

Royal Palms Tower.

also requires more finesse. This is why most organizations pass along group sales inquiries to members of their highly trained sales team, who have more time and resources available to cultivate the group customer.

The objective of revenue management has been described as ". . . selling the right product to the right customer at the right time for the right price."[5] So, as we stated previously, the first fundamental element in revenue management is learning about our customers. We need to find out *who* they are, *what* product or service they want, *what* price they are willing to pay, *where* they wish to purchase it, *when* they want it, and *why*? How do we accomplish this task?

Marketing Intelligence

In order to find out information regarding consumers, we must employ marketing intelligence. **Marketing intelligence** is the practice of conducting primary research and analyzing secondary research to understand the characteristics of a market. **Primary research** is research designed and conducted by an organization for its own purposes. An example would be the development of a survey to be disseminated to guests upon check-in at an airline, cruise ship, hotel, or car rental agency. Data is gathered, analyzed, and evaluated for its potential value to the organization. **Secondary research** is work conducted and published by other organizations. An example would be a statistical report generated by a travel association or professional research firm. Astute organizations today utilize a combination of primary and secondary research to grasp a better understanding of their individual markets.

The first place to begin market research is internally, with an organization's own gathered information and generated reports. The following list contains just a few areas from which an organization may glean basic information regarding its customers:

- Guest comment cards
- Guest registration cards
- Segmentation sales statistics
- Meal cover reports
- Beverage sales reports
- Season-ticket holder data
- Point-of-sale reports
- Automated sales systems
- Personal observation
- Mystery shoppers
- Listening to and speaking with the guests

The organization can also obtain information regarding consumer purchasing patterns by looking at:

- Booking patterns and pace reports
- Channel reports
- Cancellations and no-shows
- Reservation conversion percentages (the percentage of inquiries to reservations)
- Comparisons to historical sales
- Vendor reports

From these reports, an organization may determine *where*, *when*, and *how* customers are making their reservations. **Pace** here refers to a unit of time measurement. For example, pace may be the rate at which reservations are taken. It is common practice to measure the booking rate of reservations confirmed last year on this date to reservations confirmed today. This helps us determine whether demand is higher or lower than for the same period last year. A channel report tells the organization from which channel the reservation was generated. A **channel** refers to the source of the booking. The reservation may have been generated directly with the hotel, through the 1–800 telephone number, with a travel agent, or via an online travel site. Data may be obtained from the major credit card companies regarding the demographics and purchasing habits of the customers purchasing an organization's products and services.

Hospitality organizations are fortunate in the amount of data that they are able to capture regarding their guests. For example, a downtown hotel may be able to find out the following information regarding a business traveler from just one visit:

- Name
- Address
- Business/residence/cell phone numbers
- Email address(es)
- Employer and possible title
- Reservation channel
- Purpose of visit
- Room rate
- Room type preferred
- Food and beverage preferences and purchases
- Mode of transportation
- Method of payment
- Other ancillary purchases
- Any additional information captured by a frequent guest program

Compare this to a clothing store where a customer goes in and buys a shirt for cash. Very little customer information is captured in that retail transaction. Hospitality organizations are using powerful computer systems to further drill down to obtain additional highly specific information regarding their guests. The process of continually digging deeper into the data captured by a marketing intelligence system is referred to as **data mining**. Hospitality organizations may then utilize this data to create customized products, services, and packages for their guests.

However, it is also vital to understand customers in our market who may not be purchasing our products or services. These consumers are purchasing from other organizations within our market, some of whom may be our direct competitors. It is just as important to learn about the behavior and motivation of these potential consumers as it is to learn about our own current customers. This knowledge of potential customers may be obtained from a variety of sources, including:

- Convention and visitors' bureaus
- Chambers of commerce
- Resort associations

- Park services
- AAA motor club
- Ticket agencies
- Travel agencies and consortia
- Tourist organizations
- Tour operators and wholesalers
- Trade associations
- Trade publications
- Channel reports
- Vendor reports
- Retail sales reports
- Local colleges and universities

It is important to utilize information obtained from these resources to analyze visitor trends in terms of demographics, expenditures, length of stay, and purpose of visit. *Where* did these customers come from, *how* did they get here, and *why* did they come? While it is easy to see why this information is important to marketing personnel, it is equally important to managers of overall revenue. Revenue managers must understand the characteristics of customers in their markets to be able to develop the proper strategies to obtain and retain their customers. Now that we have gathered information and obtained knowledge about the consumers in our market, it is time to analyze their behavior by market segment to determine the optimal mix of customers for our organization. In the next chapter, we will delve into market segmentation and selection.

BOX 3-1

Revenue Management Professional Profile: Elizabeth Cambra[6]

HOW DID YOU FIRST ENTER THE REVENUE MANAGEMENT FIELD?

I believe the hospitality industry chose me. I was lucky enough to have a father in the industry. As a young child, my brother and I would inspect hotel rooms with my father on the weekends. We were tasked with looking for "dust bunnies" under the bed and counting the bathroom towels. Later, as an adult, I would reflect on this and laugh. Being an industry "brat," many people assume you don't have to work as hard and you just collect paychecks. Frankly, I found the opposite to be true. I worked twice as hard to prove myself that I was not getting a free ride and to

learn the business. Very early in my career I realized I found revenue management intriguing. What I didn't realize until a few years later was that the Revenue Management discipline is a balance of Operations, Sales, and Marketing, with a statistical/analytical approach. While I do believe the industry found me, I believe I have made my own mark and enjoy tremendously the path I have chosen.

WHAT ARE YOUR MAJOR RESPONSIBILITIES IN YOUR CURRENT POSITION?

Currently, I work with our hotels and condominiums, both owned and managed, within the Hawaiian Islands. I focus on weaving a revenue focus throughout our decisions at the corporate, business unit, and property level.

HOW DOES REVENUE MANAGEMENT FIT INTO YOUR ORGANIZATION?

Fortunately, Outrigger Enterprises Group has seen the value of this discipline for years. We are always sharpening our skills while at the same time, trying not to make things painfully difficult. We foster an open environment where communication is a priority for all. We need Sales and Marketing to know where we have "need dates," along with ensuring our Operational teams can meet the demands of our customers and deliver what Sales and Marketing has promised. No one department can be as successful without the other.

WHAT ARE SOME OF THE GREATEST ISSUES FACING REVENUE MANAGEMENT PROFESSIONALS TODAY?

One key issue facing the Revenue Management industry is the challenge of competitive pricing. It's important to know where in the "food chain" you belong, based upon your product, service, location, and amenities. This approach needs to be broken down by market segment as well. We do exactly that here at Outrigger. After all, what is important to the leisure customer may be different for a group or corporate customer. It is important that the entire hotel staff—from Sales and Marketing to the front-desk staff— participate in this exercise, as everyone has different opinions and perspectives. Once you have decided to change your prices, it's important to determine how long you will keep the new prices in place.

Also, it's important to remember you should not expect the competition to necessarily follow. Instead do it because it's the right effort for your property.

Another key issue is whether to use technology or not. I'm a firm believer in technology and am currently implementing a tool, but will be the first to admit that if the basic fundamentals or principles are not understood, the technology will not be utilized to its full capacity nor adopted into everyday life, which compromises the return on investment.

HOW DO YOU THINK THE REVENUE MANAGEMENT FIELD WILL EVOLVE OVER THE NEXT DECADE?

Knowledge is vital. Revenue Management must adapt as guest preferences/demographics, buying patterns, and technology evolve. Patterns change, although the basic revenue principles do not . . . we must learn to apply or use them in new ways. Change is constant, and we need to be prepared for that at all times.

WHICH COURSES OF STUDY (i.e., FINANCE, SALES & MARKETING, PSYCHOLOGY, etc.) WOULD BE MOST BENEFICIAL TO STUDENTS EAGER TO ENTER THE REVENUE MANAGEMENT FIELD?

If I had to choose one course of study for future Revenue Managers, I'd choose logical studies. The ability to reason through processes, numbers, and scenarios is a key component. Statistics or mathematical approaches give you the ability to reason. Independent thinking is also developed. In my opinion, this is not the only skill needed, but a key component. I truly believe this discipline is a balance of Operations, Sales, and Marketing with

(*continued*)

BOX 3-1 *Continued*

---

an analytical approach and feel all disciplines can lead you to this field.

WHAT ADVICE CAN YOU GIVE STUDENTS WISHING TO ENTER THIS FIELD OF ENDEAVOR?

First, I believe leaders of tomorrow's hospitality industry need to possess a drive to take care of others. No matter what discipline, the primary goal is to fill our rooms (of course, on the right dates, at the right rate, for the best length of stay needed) and ensure our customers are safe and comfortable. I had a General Manager who would walk around and ask every associate what their job was. When they replied "Restaurant Server" or some other position, he quickly replied, "No, you sell rooms." It didn't take long for that to sink in, and I've preached that same lesson over the years and quickly recognized this to be Outrigger founder Roy Kelley's same philosophy. Secondly, technical skills are also an important quality. Our systems and software allow us to check guests in quickly, to allow them to use their computer from anywhere in the building, and allow us to compile data for strong marketing campaigns. As much as technology is king, I encourage everyone coming up through the ranks to learn how to do things the "old fashioned way," which means doing it manually. Finally, tomorrow's leaders must have a willingness to work in an industry that constantly changes. Like most industries, what works today, may or may not work tomorrow. We must stay nimble and not get stuck in old patterns. We must use our knowledge of what has worked historically, but give ourselves permission to step outside the box and take a risk. I'm fortunate that my current employer, Outrigger Hotels & Resorts, understands this concept and allows me the flexibility to do just that.

WHAT IS YOUR NAME, COMPANY NAME, AND TITLE?

Elizabeth P. Cambra, Outrigger Enterprises Group, Corporate Director of Revenue Optimization

SUMMARY

Today's consumers are more sophisticated than ever before, partially due to the wealth of information available on the Internet. We have become a nation of prosumers[4], professional consumers who wish to both produce and consume our own unique blend of products and services. Organizations have developed a customer-centric approach to meet consumers' needs, wants, and desires in this new era of mass customization.

Marketing is defined as satisfying the needs, wants, and desires of customers. So marketers must continue to learn more and more about their customers in an effort to please them. Therefore, we have identified customer knowledge as the first fundamental element in the development of revenue management strategy. The e-commerce evolution is changing *where*, *when*, and *how* customers shop and purchase. The concept of a market has also changed. Today, anywhere that sellers and buyers may interact is considered to be a market. Possibly the largest market in the world, eBay, does not exist on the physical plain, but facilitates transactions only in cyberspace.

Hospitality organizations are bundling new products and services in response to changing consumer purchasing behavior. This has evolved into dynamic packaging, which enables hospitality providers to bundle products and services together to suit the needs of their customers. The power of branding is growing in strength as more and more organizations explore developing additional products and services under their brands.

One of the key equations presented in the revenue management process is the determination of total customer value. The perceived product or service value must be equal or exceed the total acquisition cost to produce total value to the consumer.

Hospitality organizations use marketing intelligence to obtain information on their current and potential customers. A variety of internal and external resources are available to enable organizations to obtain an abundance of data. Sophisticated computer systems then allow the organizations to mine the data to assist the organizations in developing customized products and services to meet the wants, needs, and desires of their customers.

KEY TERMS AND CONCEPTS

The following key terms and concepts were presented in this chapter. Each term and concept is also contained in the Glossary of Terms located at the end of this book:

- B2B
- B2C
- branding
- brick and mortar store
- bundling
- C2C
- channel
- customer-centric approach
- data mining
- dynamic packaging
- e-commerce
- market
- marketing
- marketing intelligence
- niche
- online store
- pace
- per diem
- perceived value
- primary research
- prosumer
- secondary research
- total acquisition cost
- total customer value

DISCUSSION QUESTIONS

1. What customized products or services have you purchased this year?
2. Are you a "prosumer"? In what sense?
3. Name a merchant from whom you purchase products or services both online and from a brick and mortar store. Which do you prefer, purchasing online or in person?
4. Have you ever purchased or sold anything on eBay? If so, what was your experience?
5. Which brands are your favorites? What factors might make you change brands?

INTERNET EXERCISES

1. Go to the General Service Administration's website at www.gsa.gov. Click on "Per Diem Rates." Then click on the state of your choice. Compare different cities and report your findings.
2. Consider a destination where you may wish to spend your Spring break. Which hospitality products and services would you like to see packaged together in a bundle for you to purchase? Go online and see if you can find a similar bundle. If not, see if you can find a bundle offering a few less products or services.

REFERENCES

1. *When Harry Met Sally*, Dir. Rob Reiner, Perf. Meg Ryan and Billy Crystal, Metro Goldwyn Mayer, 1989.
2. Dell Computer Corporation's website accessed July 5, 2006, http://www.dell.com
3. Best Buy's website accessed July 14, 2006, http://www.bestbuy.com
4. Toffler, Alvin. *The Third Wave*, New York: Bantam, 1980.
5. Cross, Robert G. *Revenue Management: Hard Core Tactics for Market Domination*, New York: Broadway Books, 1997.
6. Cambra, Elizabeth. Interview conducted via email, August 4, 2006.

Golf Shoes.

CHAPTER

4

Market Segmentation
and Selection

Chapter Objectives

The objectives of this chapter are to:

- Explain the concept of market segmentation
- Provide examples of market segments and subsegments
- Introduce the concept of environmental scanning
- Define total customer worth

FLIGHT ATTENDANT:	And what would you like?
SALLY:	Do you have any Bloody Mary mix?
FLIGHT ATTENDANT:	Yes.
SALLY:	No, wait. Here's what I want. Regular tomato juice filled up to about three-quarters and then add a splash of Bloody Mary mix, just a splash, and a little piece of lime, but on the side.[1]

Once again, we can chuckle about the peculiarities of Sally's method of ordering food and beverage as seen in the movie *When Harry Met Sally*,[1] but we also must recognize her desire to get exactly what she wants. Thus far we explored some of the dynamics impacting consumer behavior but now we would like to take a closer look. And that is most easily accomplished by dividing consumers into groups, which we will refer to as market segments and subsegments. Market segmentation is another fundamental element needed for the effective application of revenue management techniques. Revenue managers continue to refine their segmentation definitions, analysis, and selection to best enable them to optimize revenue opportunities.

Market Segments and Subsegments

Over the years, most organizations have broken down the analysis of their overall market into smaller, more manageable pieces known as segments. **Market segmentation** may be defined as the practice of dividing a market into smaller specific segments sharing similar characteristics. The simplest, least complex division of a travel market is to separate the market into two large segments based upon the reason for travel, being either business or leisure. While this simplistic division may be sufficient for a very tiny organization, it is far from adequate for the majority of hospitality organizations.

What are some of the other ways that a hospitality organization may segment its market? One common method is to break up the market into smaller segments based upon customer demographics. **Demography** is defined as the study of the characteristics of a population. Common characteristics considered include age, gender, marital status, education, occupation, income, race, religion, and nationality. Starting with the two broad segments of business and leisure, an organization is able to further subdivide each large segment into smaller segments based upon demographics. For example, it would be simple for an airline to compare the percentage of male business passengers to female business passengers. After gender though, the process of segmentation becomes a bit more complex. How would they determine age? Some people look much older than their physical age, while the reverse is true with other individuals. It would be difficult to correctly guess the age of every passenger on one plane, let alone a whole fleet of planes.

Now, most major carriers offer frequent flier program membership to their repeat passengers. Hotels offer similar frequent guest programs. Both of these **frequent traveler programs** are designed to reward loyal patronage and induce repeat business. The program membership application contains a lot of vital demographic information regarding the applicant, including his or her birth date, marital status, occupation, and nationality. The application may even ask more specific questions regarding income or educational level obtained. Frequently, there is a statement to the effect that answers to these questions are needed to best service the customer. And this is absolutely true! The more the hospitality organization understands its customers, the more able it is to design and offer products and services of value to those very same customers. But the organizations must also communicate their commitment to maintaining the privacy and security of the information being collected from the consumer.

Hospitality organizations usually break down the leisure and business segments first into individual and group subsegments. An individual traveling, dining, attending a game or performance, or staying alone is usually referred to as transient. **Transient** may be defined here as a temporary individual hospitality customer. This guest is alone and is purchasing a product or service to be used for a short period of time. Again, think of a single person purchasing an airline seat, a meal, a ticket, or a hotel room. **Group business** simply involves more than two individuals coming together for a common reason. A banquet, for example, is considered group business. A team flying together to a competition is also considered group business. Now, what about a group of individuals all traveling alone to attend a conference in a major destination? Is this group or transient business? This would be considered group business since the purpose of their travel involves a group activity.

It is also possible to further break down business and leisure travel into even smaller subsegments. What might be a reason for leisure travel? The first, and most obvious reason, would be vacation. But people travel for shorter periods on other leisure pursuits as well. The second and very significant subsegment of leisure travel is what is referred to as VFR. **VFR** stands for visiting friends and relatives. As college students, most of you have already booked your flights home for the holiday breaks to see your friends and families. There often exists a direct correlation between returning home for break and Dad paying your tuition bill too, isn't there? A third reason that people travel for leisure is to attend special events. A wedding, graduation, or the Super Bowl is each an example of a special occasion that usually involves travel.

People also travel on business for a variety of reasons. First, it may be one aspect of their job responsibilities. They travel to various sites to inspect the work being performed there. Second, they may be attending training or a seminar in a remote location. And third, they may be traveling with several coworkers to attend a meeting or conference. Business travelers are often further subsegmented by industry sectors such as corporate, government, and association. And remember that restaurants and stadiums are also interested in booking groups, both for business and leisure. Corporate luncheons and holiday parties may be major revenue generators to a downtown restaurant. The sticker price for the annual group use of a corporate sky box at most major stadiums ranges from the tens of thousands to the hundreds of thousands of dollars. Many stadiums and arenas have also created internal event departments to book meetings, trade shows, and parties. Team building takes on a whole new meaning when it occurs on the 50-yard line of a national football team's field.

Returning to our previous example of Best Buy in Chapter 3, the retailer has identified five segments on which to focus in its new customer-centric operating model. "Each of the converted stores are expected to include elements designed to appeal to one or two of the company's five key customer segments, including affluent professional males, young entertainment enthusiasts who appreciate a digital lifestyle, upscale suburban moms, families who are practical technology adopters and small businesses with fewer than 20 employees."[2] The initial top-line results have proven this new model to be a success. According to Brad Anderson, vice chairman and CEO of Best Buy,

> We believe this new operating model offers our customers a richer in-store experience, including better shopping assistance as well as more of the products and services they want . . . Customer centricity empowers employees to recognize unique sets of customers and to build offerings and experiences to meet their needs. Our employees also like this model because it gives them more power to make decisions about how to satisfy their customers. Over time, we believe that our customer centricity work will help us attract new customer segments to our stores, which leverages our existing assets. In addition, it gives us an engine for continuing to innovate and respond to changing customer needs.[2]

Each hospitality sector and each individual organization will define its market segments and subsegments differently. The following is just one way to consider dividing up a larger travel market.

Business (or Corporate) Transient Segment

This segment pertains to individual business travelers, including:

- Business individuals paying full rate. This is also referred to as the **rack rate**. In earlier days, many hotels had a key rack behind the front desk. Perched above the rack was a sign stating the night's room rate. Walk-in guests would be offered that rate upon check-in. Thus the term *rack rate*.
- Corporate negotiated rate business, often referred to as LNR—**locally negotiated rates**. Usually large-volume producers are given their own subsegments for tracking purposes. Negotiated corporate business may be included either in this segment or in the contract segment listed below.
- Frequent customer club members
- Participants in other individual business clubs sponsored by the franchise.

Leisure Transient Segment

This segment pertains to individuals, couples, or families purchasing products and services for non–business-related reasons, including:

- Leisure individuals paying full rate (also known as rack rate)
- AAA members
- AARP (American Association of Retired Persons) members
- Discount Club members (Encore, Entertainment, etc.)
- Purchasers of weekend or other packages
- Purchasers of leisure programs promoted through the franchise
- Individual ticket purchasers.

Government/Military Transient Segment

This segment pertains to individuals from all state and federal agencies and divisions of the government/military possessing valid government identification, including:

- All government employees paying per diem
- Government employees working on joint government/corporate contracts, for example, Lockheed Martin working in conjunction with NASA.
- Government/military leisure-related travelers booking through Morale and Welfare Offices, SATO, I.T.T., and so on.

Contracts

This segment includes all business generated through the negotiation of a contract. For example, travelers who are required to purchase airline seats or hotel rooms from brands stipulated as part of a contractual agreement. A **contract** is defined here as a binding agreement that specifies rates, terms, anticipated volume, minimum usage, and effective dates. Contract business may include, but is not limited to, the following:

- Corporate contracts, also known as locally negotiated rates (LNR). See under section "Business (or Corporate) Transient Segment."
- Airline and train crews
- Airline-distressed passengers

- Training accounts
- Timeshares and fractional ownership
- Season ticket holders.

Association Transient Segment

This segment is highly location specific. Depending upon an organization's location, it may or may not receive individual association travelers. For example, businesses located in New York, Washington, D.C., and Chicago, where the major national associations are headquartered, usually maintain a separate segment for association business. If the only association business received by an organization is group business, then this individual association segment is not needed. Association business, whether individual or group, may be further subsegmented into national, regional, state, or local.

Tour and Travel Segment

This segment pertains to consumers buying an inclusive travel package, such as:

- **FIT** (foreign or free independent traveler) programs
- Domestic and international wholesalers
- Airline wholesale programs
- Tour operators/group tour series
- Voucher programs
- Fly/drive programs
- Motorcoach tour operators
- Franchise related tour programs
- Internet wholesale programs

This segment includes both blocks and free sell space agreements. The meaning of this statement will be explained shortly.

Group Segment

Group bookings are determined by a signed contract committing to a specified number of units sold to one group for a specified period of time. Each organization will establish the parameters of what constitutes a group booking. Group business is often classified into the following categories:

- Corporate group
- Leisure group
- Government group
- Association group
- **SMERFE**
  - Social (weddings, bar mitzvahs)
  - Military (reunions)
  - Educational (college sporting teams)
  - Religious (youth groups or gatherings)
  - Fraternal (Elks convention)
  - Entertainment (rock bands)

Today, organizations are further segmenting their customers into new and growing segments, including adventure travelers, and growing subsegments based on lifestyle preferences. Other organizations are starting to track segments by channel—Where is the reservation generated? However, a problem is also developing regarding the blurring of the lines between segments. For example, under which segment would you track a passenger who booked a flight on Travelocity to attend a Monday through Wednesday conference, but who stayed over Thursday and Friday to ski? While segmentation is becoming more complex, it is also becoming more critical to understanding customers.

Wholesale Terminology

Before we proceed, there was a sentence under the tour and travel segment stating that it included both blocks and free sell space. What does this mean? Let's consider a hotel example here. A **wholesaler** is a person who purchases individual travel components at a discount based upon volume, and repackages the components and sells them to a consumer on a retail basis, either directly through the wholesale organization or via a travel agent or tour operator. For example, a wholesaler may contract with a ski resort for four rooms every Saturday night during season at a discounted rate. That same wholesaler may purchase four seats on an inbound flight to that same ski resort every Saturday night. And that wholesaler also purchases a block of ski passes at a substantial discount. The wholesaler then creates a package including airfare, room, and ski pass with a price set higher than the sum of the component prices paid by the wholesaler, thereby ensuring a profit.

So the ski resort holds four rooms every Saturday night during ski season. Those four rooms are reserved, in other words blocked, for the wholesaler until some set cut-off date stipulated in the wholesale agreement. Cut-off dates can and do vary, but they normally range from 7 to 14 days in advance of the scheduled date of arrival. If the cut-off date goes by and the room block is not filled, the rooms are released to be sold to other customers. Once the block is released, it will be up to the hotel as to whether to continue to honor the discounted rate for any late reservations made by the wholesaler for that night. If the block is sold out and the wholesaler has additional room needs for that night, it will also be at the discretion of the resort as to whether or not to sell additional rooms to the wholesaler at the same discounted rate. Anytime rooms are needed by the wholesaler outside of those originally blocked, those rooms are considered to be sold based upon free space, in other words **free sell**. A wholesaler may also enter into a free sell agreement with a hotel that states that any time rooms are available, and the hotel is interested in taking a reservation at the wholesale rate, the reservation will be accepted. In this case, no rooms are specifically reserved, or blocked, for the wholesaler. They are simply purchased freely, based upon availability.

This is a good time to introduce another concept here known as a wash factor. A **wash factor** may be defined as a predetermined percentage of usage based upon historical data and experience. Returning to the above example of our wholesaler, let's say that the wholesaler has been booking with the same ski resort for a period of five years. During that time, a pattern has emerged. With the exception of the week directly preceding or following a major holiday, the wholesaler only fills three of the four rooms blocked on Saturday nights. Therefore, the hotel may apply a wash factor of 75 percent to all rooms booked by the wholesaler for weeks other than those directly preceding or following a major holiday. In other words, the hotel will only hold three rather than four rooms on those nights. The contract states that four rooms will be blocked, but the hotel only blocks three. Is this ethical? Should the hotel be required to sell a fourth room if needed by the wholesaler? What happens if the hotel holds four rooms but the wholesaler only sells three? Should the wholesaler be required to pay for the unsold room? This is a great topic for discussion and one to which we will return later.

For the moment, let's return to our topic of market segmentation. Each segment possesses unique purchasing characteristics. The answers to the questions *what, where, when,* and *why* they buy are different for each and every segment. The purchasing behavior of groups is vastly different from the purchasing behavior of individuals. And, leisure travelers make their purchase decisions quite differently from seasoned corporate road warriors. An organization should continue to narrow and refine its analysis of

Courtesy of Destination Hotels & Resorts.

Teton Mountain Lodge Lobby.

customer behavior as it drills down further into each of its subsegments. While it is vital to understand current customer behavior, it is also just as critical to project potential future behavior as well. This is best accomplished through environmental scanning and trend analysis.

Environmental Scanning

External environmental factors have a significant impact upon a consumer's propensity to purchase. These external factors may include the economy, social and cultural trends, the political climate, the natural environment, and technological advances. Constantly monitoring and assessing the environment to spot changes and emerging trends is referred to as **environmental scanning**. Economic issues such as inflation, the cost of living, gasoline prices, and stock market performance all play a key role in the daily buying behavior of the public. The high cost of gas has been impacting sales at the discount retailers. Why is this so? Consumers who frequently purchase at the big discount stores often possess lower income levels and have less disposable income. As gasoline prices rise, the amount spent on gas consumes a greater percentage of their disposable income. As gasoline prices continue to rise and impact all modes of travel from the auto to the airline, we can expect to see even more changes in consumers' behavior and propensity to purchase.

Campaigning politicians may be proposing a cut in taxes or conversely an increase in government spending. The latter may result in increased services to the consumer but may also lead to increased taxes. And some consumer purchases have become both politically and socially unpopular, such as the purchasing of fur or some seafood items cultivated from endangered species.

Students are quite aware of the frequent advances in technology and the resulting impact upon their wallets. How many students in this room own a laptop? An iPod? A cell phone able to capture digital pictures or short videos? And what new items are on your wish list to be purchased as soon as you have some spare money in your pocket?

Trend Analysis and Generational Targeting

Tracking what is on the wish list of students is just one small aspect of looking at trends. Trend analysis has become a widely accepted practice in nearly every field of endeavor. Every business forecasts future sales, and future sales are dependent upon the behavior of customers. Many futurists and forecasters break trends down by generation. For example, one trend often mentioned is the **graying of America**, which refers to the fact that Americans are living longer and a significant portion of the population is now pushing past the age of 40. Generational analysis is just another way of segmenting a larger population. Since buying behavior is vastly different based upon the age of the purchaser, analyzing trends by generation is also helpful. The commonly defined American generational subsegments are:

- Silver-haired seniors aka (also known as) the silent generation
- Baby boomers
- Baby busters, aka Generation X
- Baby boomlets, aka Generation Y or echo boomers
- The millennials

The oldest generation, the **silver-haired seniors**, is comprised of all individuals born prior to 1946. Most of them survived the Great Depression and also one or both world wars. They have personally experienced economic hardship, so as a group they are very avid savers. They do not broadcast their purchasing intentions. They are also not agents of change. They buy with purpose and expect value for their dollar. Due to their saving and astute buying habits, they have accumulated great wealth. The growth of the stock market has also had a huge impact on a portion of these savings. The Dow Jones Industrial Average is one of the most widely quoted stock market indices. It is the average of 30 stocks of the largest and most widely held public companies in the United States. Over the past 110 years, the Dow Jones Industrial Average has risen from its opening level of 40.94 to its current level of approximately 11,000. As a whole, this generation has a great deal of discretionary income to spend on hospitality products and services. However, with their frugal nature, many of this generation's members will also resist the opportunity to spend and instead leave great streams of wealth to their heirs.

The **baby boomers** are these fortunate heirs. Born between the years of 1946 and 1964, the baby boomers are not only the largest generational segment at nearly 78 million members, they are also the most powerful in terms of both wealth and propensity to spend. They have inherited from their grandparents and as a group they are about to inherit huge accumulations of wealth from their parents. They are anxious and ready to spend. It is estimated that the largest transfer of wealth ever recorded is about to occur, as the silver-haired seniors leave their baby boomer children and Generation X grandchildren in excess of $45 trillion between 1998 and 2052.[3] Yes, that's trillion, with a "t"! This is perhaps the greatest economic ship to ever sail. Don't be one of the few who choose not to board this lucrative boat by failing to appreciate the continually growing purchasing power of the baby boomers. Students often equate the words "baby boomer" with "about to retire," which is simply not the case. The oldest boomer just turned 60 in 2006 and the youngest is merely 43, just now entering his or her peak earning years. The "graying of America" is still touching up its roots. As a group, the baby boomers possess the highest medium income of any generation. And many of them have absolutely no plans to retire. They are choosing instead to leave their high powered, stressful jobs to pursue less demanding and yet more fulfilling careers. This will also provide them with additional free time to fill with their leisure pursuits, including travel, recreation, and tourism. The hospitality industry must develop new products and services to meet the changing demands of the baby boomer consumers. They are still a force to be reckoned with and one not to be taken lightly. They shaped more trends than any generation in history, with no signs of slowing in their power and enthusiasm to bring about change.

As previously stated, Generation X will also be a recipient of this huge generational wealth transfer. **Generation X** is defined as those people born between 1965 and 1976. They are sometimes referred to as the baby busters, since as a group they only number 45 million, a huge slowdown from the birth rates generated by their grandparents. This is partially attributed to the fact that following World War II, women were for the first time able to seek and obtain fulfilling careers outside the home. Establishing their careers took time, so many couples forestalled starting a family later than had previous generations. Members of Generation X are very individualistic. While some social critics have labeled this group as skeptical and cynical, others have found them to be environmentally and socially conscious, actually becoming more community-focused individuals. They are technologically savvy, well educated, and sophisticated consumers of customized products. They are most likely to use the Internet to comparison shop and purchase products and services. They are extremely value conscious, seeking out products and services offering the best price/value relationship. Hospitality organizations need to develop niche products and services to reach and attract this generational segment.

Following the baby busters is the group called the echo boomers, also known as the baby boomlets or **Generation Y**. This population is defined as those nearly 72 million people born between 1977 and 1994. They are the children of the younger population of baby boomers. As a group, the echo boomers are almost as large in population as the baby boomers. As they age, their power and influence will shape the future development of products and services. They are the most technologically competent generation in history, and they are extremely comfortable with technology in any form. Echo boomers appear to also echo some of the purchasing characteristics of their boomer parents. They are inquisitive, upbeat, future focused, and excited and embracing of change. They are more happy-go-lightly than their Generation X friends and colleagues. They are also extremely brand conscious but not as blindly brand loyal as their parents. This is the generation to watch, as their buying habits change with age and their purchasing power increases with income.

Now some sources actually extend the range of the population defined as Generation Y to include all people born through the year 2002 or 2003, which increases the population of this generation. And yet others refer to children born after 1994 as **millennials**, children born at the turn of the century, this time the turn of a new millennium. There is ongoing debate as to when Generation Y ends and the millennial generation begins. Marketers usually stick with the traditional definition, while some Human Resource professionals now refer to anyone born after 1977 as a millennial. Even as this debate continues, the millennial generation will become more narrowly defined as they age and grow.

Hospitality organizations need to understand which generations buy which of their products and services. They then need to examine the purchasing traits and future buying potential of each generation. New trends must be researched and analyzed. Here is just a sample of some headlines pulled from trendwatching.com's free monthly *Trend Briefing*:

Jan/Feb 2005: READY-TO-KNOW: Demanding consumers are in a constant 'Ready to Go, READY-TO-KNOW' state of mind, expecting any information deemed relevant to be available instantly, at their own terms. Think of it as the Google effect (demanding and getting instant answers) permeating all aspects of daily life.

March 2005: NOUVEAU NICHE: The new riches will come from servicing the new niches. From hyper-individualization to millions of new niche producers to full transparency to no-cost inventory, mass will soon make way for niche. Neglect at own risk.

April 2005: TRYVERTISING: Much has already been said about search-based advertising and initiating word of mouth as new and more relevant ways to replace mass advertising, but trendwatching.com has spotted a third alternative: TRYVERTISING, which is all about consumers becoming familiar with new products by actually trying them out.

June/July 2005: TWINSUMER: Word of mouth may be big, but consumers looking for the best of the best, the first of the first increasingly don't connect to 'just any other consumer' anymore, they are hooking up with (and listening to) their taste 'twins'; fellow consumers somewhere in the world who think, react, enjoy, and consume the way they do.

November, 2005: ÜBER-PREMIUM: Status-craving consumers are hunting down the next wave in über-exclusive goods, services, and experiences that are truly out of reach for the masses, now that MASSCLUSIVITY has commoditized all but the most luxurious products on earth.

January 2006: INSPERIENCES: In a consumer society dominated by experiences in the (semi) public domain—often branded, designed, themed, and curated to the nines, INSPERIENCES represent consumers' desire to bring top-level, professional-grade experiences into their domestic domain.

April 2006: INFOLUST: Experienced consumers are lusting after detailed information on where to get the best of the best, the cheapest of the cheapest, the first of the first, the healthiest of the healthiest, the coolest of the coolest, or on how to become the smartest of the smartest of the smartest. Instant gratification is upon us.

May/June 2006: CUSTOMER-MADE Update: The phenomenon of corporations creating goods, services, and experiences in close cooperation with experienced and creative consumers, tapping into their intellectual capital, and in exchange giving them a direct say in (and rewarding them for) what actually gets produced, manufactured, developed, designed, serviced, or processed.

July 2006: YOUNIVERSAL BRANDING: As a business professional, you can have the ride of a lifetime with YOUNIVERSAL BRANDING. There are interactive billboards to be placed, virtual product placement strategies to be executed, scripts to be written, friends to be made, avatars to be dressed, fed, and equipped, and virtual stores to be opened.[4]

Based upon market segment and trend analysis, organizations will be able to develop new products and services to attract and retain their desired mix of customers.

And that is what customer knowledge and market segmentation is all about. Offering products and services designed to meet the wants, needs, and desires of customers. Who are the organization's customers? What percentage do they obtain from each market segment and subsegment? Which segments do they desire to attract and capture? By understanding their markets and their customers, organizations are able to determine their optimal mix of business. Are they content with their current mix of business? Or should they consider replacing lower rated business for higher rated business, in other words, changing their market mix?

Displacement Analysis and Total Customer Worth

Replacing one customer for another is also referred to as **displacement**. Many organizations now conduct a **displacement analysis** when determining the optimal mix of business. They assess the worth of one customer versus another. **Worth** is defined as the sum value of the customer to the organization. Value in this sense relates to the sum of current monetary expenditures in both the primary purchase and ancillary purchases made by a customer. A **primary purchase** is defined as the main purchase made during a single or series of transactions. An **ancillary purchase** is defined as a supplementary or additional purchase made in a series of transactions. For an airline passenger, the primary purchase would be the airline ticket. Parking and food and beverage purchases within the terminal would be considered ancillary purchases. In equation form, this would be:

$$\text{Total Customer Worth} = \Sigma \text{ Primary} + \text{Ancillary Revenue}$$

But this equation is incomplete as it overlooks the cost of attaining that customer. Costs are incurred in the acquisition of each customer, ranging from the costs of marketing, to the costs of taking reservations, to the costs of actually serving the guest. So our amended equation should be:

$$\frac{\text{Total Customer}}{\text{Worth}} = \frac{\text{Primary}}{\text{Revenue}} + \frac{\text{Ancillary}}{\text{Revenue}} - \frac{\textbf{Acquisition}}{\textbf{Cost}}$$

However, one must also factor in each customer's future propensity to purchase from the organization once again. Assigning a number and value to this propensity for future expenditures is a bit trickier and will vary among organizations. For now, let's just state future propensity to purchase as **Propensity Y**. Now, our equation becomes:

$$\frac{\textbf{Total Customer}}{\textbf{Worth}} = \left(\frac{\text{Primary}}{\text{Revenue}} + \frac{\text{Ancillary}}{\text{Revenue}} - \frac{\text{Acquisition}}{\text{Cost}} \right) \times \text{Propensity Y}$$

Let's use a hotel traveler for an extremely simplified numerical example. A business traveler visits Denver 10 times per year and stays one night each time. His company has a locally negotiated rate at the Brown Palace Hotel at a rate of $250 per night. The traveler always eats dinner in the restaurant the evening of his arrival at an average cost of $35. And in the morning, he grabs a quick breakfast from room service at a cost of $15. For ease of analysis, let's say that due to the volume of his company's business, the acquisition cost to the hotel of obtaining this individual business traveler is $1 per visit.

We are now able to calculate his worth to the hotel:

1. The primary revenue received is $250 per night for the hotel room.
2. Ancillary revenue received by the hotel is $35 for dinner plus $15 for morning room service. So ancillary revenue received totals $50 per visit.
3. Acquisition cost is $1 per visit.
4. Propensity Y is equal to 10 nights per year.
5. Thus the total customer worth of this single business traveler equals:
   ($250 + $50 − $1) × 10 = $299 × 10 = $2,990.

There is one last element that could be built into the equation. The operative word here is *could*, as assigning a value to this element blurs the line over into acquisition cost. And this element is the cost it takes to maintain a customer to ensure future business. In other words, once we get them, how do we keep them? Remember that today's consumers want *what* they want, *when* they want it, and *where* they want it. Customization and personalized service are key factors in their overall satisfaction. Let's return to the movie *When Harry Met Sally* for an illustration:

HARRY: Ooh, Ingrid Bergman, now she's low maintenance.
SALLY: Low maintenance?

HARRY: There are two kinds of women, high maintenance and low
maintenance.

SALLY: And Ingrid Bergman is low maintenance?

HARRY: An LM definitely.

SALLY: Which one am I?

HARRY: "You're the worst kind. You're high maintenance but you think you're
low maintenance."

SALLY: I don't see that.

HARRY: You don't see that? "Waiter, I'll begin with the house salad,
but I don't want the regular dressing. I'll have balsamic
vinegar and oil, but on the side, and then the salmon
with the mustard sauce, but I want the mustard sauce
on the side." On the side is a very big thing for you."

SALLY: Well, I just want it the way I want it.

HARRY: I know. High maintenance.

Total Customer Worth and Total Customer Value

An important distinction needs to be highlighted here. Whenever we speak of customer value in this textbook, we are referring to the value that the customer imparts upon a good or service. In other words, customer value is from the perception of the consumer. Conversely, customer worth refers to value an organization places upon a customer. Customer worth is from the perception of the producing organization.

Courtesy of Destination Hotels & Resorts.

Golf Course at Skamania.

Selection of the Optimal Mix of Business

It is important for an organization to assign worth to each customer when analyzing its business mix. In order to visualize the concepts of optimal business mix and displacement, think of packing a piece of luggage. Let's consider three possible scenarios. A traveler places all the clothes and shoes needed for two weeks of travel on a bed. If, in the first scenario, the traveler grabs the pile of clothes and shoes and just throws them into the suitcase, there is a good likelihood that the suitcase will be difficult, if not impossible, to close. Not to mention that the clothes would be a wrinkled mess when the suitcase was reopened at the traveler's destination. We can compare this to taking reservations as they are received, with no thought given as to how they fit into the organization's mix of business.

In the second scenario, the traveler carefully folds all of the clothes. However, remember that there are enough shoes and clothes for a two-week stay. So if the traveler just loads the suitcase without much planning, it might once again be difficult to close. This is like taking reservations in the order received, but applying a few restrictions.

In the final scenario, the traveler diligently plans the loading of the suitcase, placing the shoes on the bottom, layering the clothes carefully on top, and then placing smaller items like socks along the side. This same type of careful planning should be done when determining the optimal mix of business. The organization should start by placing the heaviest items as the foundation. These may be their biggest revenue generators. Each successive layer should be based upon total customer worth in filling up the remaining revenue gaps and opportunities. These various sources of business should be evaluated individually to assess their total revenue potential.

Selection of the optimal mix of business takes a lot of research and planning, as well as continual monitoring to remain effective. And the optimal mix continually changes based upon the day, week, and month of the year. Market segments targeted must be large enough to generate sufficient revenues to cover the cost of customer acquisition. The organization must also possess the resources to attract these new customers. There is no sense in pursuing a customer if an organization's products and services fall short of that customer's expectations of value. And segmentation strategies must be in alignment with the overall goals and objectives of the organization. *Market segmentation and selection is the second fundamental element in the development of revenue management strategy.*

Once an organization determines the customers it wishes to keep and pursue, it must develop a plan to attract and retain them. **Customer relationship management (CRM)** is the term used to describe strategies and tactics developed to acquire and retain customers. This will involve all aspects of the organization's operation, from reservations to final payment. CRM is a key element in the development of marketing plans, strategic management plans, and budgets. Developing a service model to meet or exceed the expectations of an organization's desired guests is an ongoing process. The organization must continually assess its internal operations, while also continuing to scan the external environment. For one of the greatest threats to the organization's acquisition and maintenance of its customers is its competitors just beyond its doors. So at this point, let's open those doors to take a look at the competition.

BOX 4-1

Revenue Management Professional Profile: Kristi White[5]

HOW DID YOU FIRST ENTER THE REVENUE MANAGEMENT FIELD?

I accepted a position with Servico in their newly created Yield Management department. I was responsible for six hotels across the southwest. I was two years out of college and in my second management position.

WHAT ARE YOUR MAJOR RESPONSIBILITIES IN YOUR CURRENT POSITION?

Currently, I work as a consultant so my responsibilities change based upon the overall needs of the client. But, primarily, I work directly with customers to analyze their revenue strategies in all areas of the hotel and contrast those against best practices. Then I work with them to close those gaps and create strong revenue practices throughout the hotel and the organization. While on an immediate basis our goal is to help customers increase revenues, the long-term goal of our service is to help owners increase asset value.

HOW DOES REVENUE MANAGEMENT FIT INTO YOUR ORGANIZATION?

In my current organization, revenue management fits in many ways and at many different levels. We have people in Service Delivery positions that help customers optimize revenues through the electronic channels. Then there are the people in my position that work with hotels on a more holistic basis to increase revenues at all levels of the hotel. But, regardless of the level, the goal is to educate customers on how this process can help them be more successful.

WHAT ARE SOME OF THE GREATEST ISSUES FACING REVENUE MANAGEMENT PROFESSIONALS TODAY?

Owners and managers that don't fully understand what Revenue Management is. As a result, they don't always respect what it can ultimately do for a hotel or a company. Because of this lack of understanding, Revenue Management can sometimes be ignored or neglected in favor of other areas of the hotel. This often results in the erosion of overall profitability at hotels. When ownership and management commits to a revenue management culture at all levels of the hotel the results lead to increased revenues and profits.

HOW DO YOU THINK THE REVENUE MANAGEMENT FIELD WILL EVOLVE OVER THE NEXT DECADE?

As owners become more invested in the field of Revenue Management, the need for qualified Revenue Managers will increase. As a result, the strategies and tactics applied at the transient and hopefully group level will begin to be applied at all revenue outlets at hotels. This will require Revenue Managers to expand their knowledge base in order to effectively manage the different revenue centers at hotels.

(continued)

BOX 4-1 *Continued*

WHICH COURSES OF STUDY (i.e., FINANCE, SALES & MARKETING, PSYCHOLOGY, etc.) WOULD BE MOST BENEFICIAL TO STUDENTS EAGER TO ENTER THE REVENUE MANAGEMENT FIELD?

All of these areas are crucial to Revenue Managers as they are all integral parts of the position. Being able to utilize different areas of knowledge to develop strategies that increase the profitability of a hotel is what the job is about. Overall, the best candidate is well rounded in the operations of a hotel, in their educational base and understands how those pieces blend together to create the most optimal mix.

WHAT ADVICE CAN YOU GIVE STUDENTS WISHING TO ENTER THIS FIELD OF ENDEAVOR?

Never stop learning, develop strong relationships and embrace change; this is a field that is constantly changing. By constantly looking for ways to grow your knowledge, leveraging the relationships that you develop over the years and accepting that change is inevitable and learning to be the catalyst of that change, you will ensure that you remain at the forefront of any field of endeavor.

WHAT IS YOUR NAME, COMPANY NAME, AND TITLE?

Kristi White, TravelCLICK, Manager of Client Revenue Strategy

SUMMARY

To help better understand their customers, organizations have broken down their customers into smaller, more manageable pieces known as segments. Segments may be broad, dividing up a market into just two segments such as business and leisure, or they may be narrow, breaking the market up into numerous subsegments. Most organizations today divide up their markets into both segments and subsegments to enable them to best service the consumers in each.

It is important to continually monitor the external environment for changes in consumer behavior. This is referred to as environmental scanning. Organizations should be alert to emerging and receding trends and analyze their potential impact upon consumer purchasing behavior. Marketers may also wish to target different generations with specific products and services most suited to their interests.

Organizations must determine the total customer worth of each market segment and subsegment to enable the organization to target the optimal mix of business. Displacement analysis is a useful tool in determining total customer worth. *Market segmentation and selection is the second fundamental element in the development of revenue management strategy.*

KEY TERMS AND CONCEPTS

The following key terms and concepts were presented in this chapter. Each term and concept is also contained in the Glossary of Terms located at the back of this book:

- acquisition cost
- ancillary purchase
- baby boomers
- contract
- customer relationship management (CRM)
- demography
- displacement
- displacement analysis
- environmental scanning
- FIT
- free sell

- frequent traveler program
- Generation X
- Generation Y
- graying of America
- group business
- locally negotiated rate
- market segmentation

- millennials
- primary purchase
- propensity Y
- rack rate
- silver-haired seniors
- SMERFE
- total customer worth

- transient
- VFR
- wash factor
- wholesaler
- worth

DISCUSSION QUESTIONS

1. Are you a member of any frequent traveler programs? If so, what prompted you to join?
2. What products do you think appeal most to the different generational market segments?
3. How can you find out what appeals to different market segments?

4. What are some current trends that are hot? What are some trends that are becoming not so hot?
5. Calculate the total customer worth of a student to your college or university.

INTERNET EXERCISE

Go to trendwatching.com's website. Review the current and recent headlines. Select two trends that you have personally witnessed and write a one-page narrative about your experience.

EXPERIENTIAL EXERCISE

Visit a local Best Buy store to personally experience their customer-centric approach to sales. Write a two-page narrative on your experience.

REFERENCES

1. *When Harry Met Sally*, Dir. Rob Reiner, Perf. Meg Ryan and Billy Crystal, Metro Goldwyn Mayer, 1989.
2. Best Buy's website, accessed July 14, 2006, http://www.bestbuy.com
3. Levenson, Eugenia. "How Much Will You Inherit?" *Fortune*, June 26, 2006, 68.
4. Trendwatching.com's website accessed July 5, 2006, http://www.trendwatching.com
5. White, Kristi. Interview conducted via email, July 27, 2006.

Courtesy of Destination Hotels & Resorts.

Ocean Hammock Resort Entertainment Room.

Internal Assessment and Competitive Analysis

The objectives of this chapter are to:

- Present the concept of competitive set
- Explain the meaning and components of competitive intelligence
- Describe the process of internal assessment
- Identify the elements in a SWOT analysis
- Learn how to develop strategies based upon the SWOT analysis

Coke versus Pepsi . . . Microsoft versus Apple . . . Ford versus General Motors . . . Reebok versus Nike . . . McDonald's versus Burger King . . . the Avalanche versus the Red Wings . . . the Broncos versus the Raiders . . . Ali versus Frazier . . . Ohio State versus Michigan . . . Harvard versus Yale . . . and brother versus sister . . . Rivalries have evolved alongside the history of humankind. Since the Roman gladiators battled it out in the first Coliseum, man has continually sought out opportunities to engage in competition. Over the centuries, this desire to obtain superiority over one's foe has crept from the sporting arena into the boardroom. From their very conception, companies keep one eye over their shoulder focused on the competition. And as these companies grow and change, so do their rivals. This continually changing competitive landscape now commands the attention of all organizations, big and small alike.

Any CEO will tell you that competition today is fierce. Many liken it to a battlefield, with skirmishes to be fought and wars to be won. And the competitive landscape has entirely changed in the last decade due to rapidly changing technology. Whereas 40 years ago, a company competed with another company located just down the street, today that company is competing with an organization from another continent. The

Internet has forever changed the marketplace, with any company or any consumer merely a click away.

To survive and compete in this new global marketplace, organizations must understand both their customers and their competitors. We discussed the importance of an organization knowing its customers in the last chapter, so now we turn to the importance of an organization knowing and understanding its competitors as well as itself. *Internal assessment is the third fundamental element and competitive analysis is the fourth fundamental element in the development of revenue management strategy.* To begin any competitive analysis, the first step is to determine and identify the competition.

Identifying the Competition

A **competitor** is defined as a rival with whom one competes. A business may have several competitors locally, nationally, or today even globally. An organization must first make a list of all of its potential competitors. This list should contain competitors with whom it competes both directly and indirectly. For example, the greatest competitor to the Coca-Cola Company is Pepsi. Now some loyal patrons of Coke and some of Pepsi will claim that these two products are simply not interchangeable. But when ordering a beverage at a restaurant, the majority of consumers will simply accept the substitution of one of these two cola products for the other. But Coke and Pepsi also compete with other sodas, like Dr. Pepper and 7-Up. Don't forget about Schweppes Ginger Ale, A&W Root Beer, RC Cola, and Squirt. And what about Coke's and Pepsi's own products, including Diet Coke, Diet Pepsi, Coke Zero, Pepsi One, and Mountain Dew? What if the customer prefers something else to drink? The soda giants also compete against a variety of other beverages, including Evian, Perrier, Propel, Gatorade, Snapple, Country Time Lemonade, Red Bull, Ocean Spray Cranberry Juice, and even Starbucks Frappuccino. It is easy to see that the soft-drink makers have a lot of competition for the consumer's beverage dollar.

Let's look at another example, that of McDonald's. Who are McDonald's competitors? Considering just hamburgers, the competitors would include Burger King, Wendy's, Good Times, In-N-Out, Carl's Jr., and White Castle. But say it is lunch time and none of the above franchises are nearby. What about Arby's, Dairy Queen, Nathan's, Sonic, or Subway? Hungry for something other than a sandwich? How about stopping at KFC for some chicken? Perhaps Taco Bell or Chipotle for a south-of-the-border treat. Or grab a slice at Pizza Hut. Prefer something lighter? Consider popping into the neighborhood grocery store deli to build a nice cold refreshing salad. Again, it is easy to see how many organizations compete for the consumer's food dollar.

One method of determining a company's competitors is to research the organization on the Internet. Go to any of the financial websites, such as Yahoo! Finance, and type in the name of the company. If the company is publicly traded, in other words, if it sells shares of its stocks to investors on an open market such as the stock market, its ticker symbol will appear. Click on the ticker symbol and you will be redirected to a page containing the most recent financial information regarding the organization. A series of topics is usually listed on the side of the page. Just click on competitors and up pops information on that firm's major competitors, with links to each. Often, both privately held and publicly held firms will be listed here as competitors. Another method of looking for competitive information is to read the company's annual report, usually found on its website under the category entitled "Investor Relations."

However, when analyzing more than one company in the same sector, make sure to review the financial pages for each company individually. The following lodging example illustrates this point. Pull up the financial page for Hilton, and the three major competitors listed are Choice Hotels, Intercontinental Hotel Group, and Marriott. Pull up Intercontinental Hotel Group, and the three competitors listed are Accor, Cendant, and Marriott. Pull up Marriott, and the three top competitors are Accor, Hilton, and Intercontinental Hotel Group. The list of competitors all depends upon from whose perspective one is looking. Each of these lodging chains operates a variety of products across various segments, ranging from luxury to budget. Each product competes differently both internally and externally. And the competition also changes by market. That is why each unit needs to determine whom it considers to be competitors for its own customers. Brand alone is usually not enough of a differentiating factor.

In the hospitality industry, most organizations determine their list of direct competitors based upon a variety of factors, including price, location, facilities, features, amenities, and level of customer service. Those organizations against which they compete directly are joined together into a group called the competitive set. The **competitive set** is defined as an organization's primary direct competitors. If your facility is sold out, a direct competitor would be the facility that your customer would select next. It is with whom an organization competes directly for the customer's dollar. It is important to be honest when selecting your competitive set. Don't compare yourself with whom you *wish* you could compete against or those whom you can easily beat because they are really not your competitors. Compare yourself with whom you actually compete against. In other words, compare apples to apples, and not apples to oranges.

Secondary competitors are not listed in an organization's competitive set, but they must remain visible on the organization's radar. These are organizations that also compete with a firm for a portion of that firm's customers, but they may do so indirectly. For example, a hotel may also compete against a campground, a timeshare, a bed and breakfast inn, or a friend's or relative's sofa when trying to capture a guest for the night. And in our previous example, the fast food chains offering alternatives to burgers would be considered to be secondary competitors to a hamburger franchise.

Right now many of you are probably feeling so confused as to how to properly define and categorize the competition. You needn't be worried. Determining an organization's direct and indirect competitors, and selecting a competitive set, is usually accomplished through a team effort. Long-time employees know from experience who the existing competitors are and they can usually tell from a combination of instinct and experience what, if any, threat is posed by new competitive supply entering the market. In addition to listening to employee opinion, it is just as important to gather competitive intelligence when determining and identifying the competition.

Competitive Intelligence

What is **competitive intelligence**? No, it is not illegal espionage. It is the practice of conducting primary research and analyzing secondary research to understand the characteristics of the competition. There is a national association, named the Society of Competitive Intelligence Professionals (SCIP), dedicated to enhancing the rapidly growing field of competitive intelligence. SCIP describes competitive intelligence as "the legal and ethical collection and analysis of information regarding the capabilities, vulnerabilities, and intentions of business competitors."[1] Most major organizations today employ staffers whose sole responsibility it is to conduct research and continually monitor the competitive environment. It is almost certain that all competing organizations are keeping a very watchful eye on each other today.

Remember that primary research is designed and conducted by an organization for its own purposes. Data is gathered, analyzed, and evaluated for its potential value to the organization. One of the most common methods of researching a competitor in the hospitality industry is to perform a site visit. Actually go into the premises of a competitor and experience its products or services for yourself. Or if you are analyzing competitive modes of transportation, ride the rails or book a flight to personally experience the journey. Does it meet, exceed, or fall short of your expectations? Utilize all of your senses when performing the site visit or experiencing the ride and then record your impressions. Was the facility clean? Did it smell fresh? Were you greeted promptly and politely? Did it look warm and inviting or cold and intimidating? Was it too noisy? Who were their customers? Did their customers appear satisfied? Primary research data may also be obtained through the use of the following methods:

- Visit and read competitors' daily event or reader boards for group business
- Observe the parking lot—look for company vans, out of state license plates, and rental car stickers
- Ask your customers which other competitors they utilize
- Employ mystery shoppers
- Ask your vendors
- Perform nightly call-arounds to assess availability
- Listen to and speak to competitors' employees
- Stand in line and listen to other guests

In addition to conducting primary research on the competition, an organization should be continually monitoring external sources of secondary research and information available on its competitors. The following resources are just a few areas in which to look for competitive information:

- Financial websites
- Company annual reports
- Brochures
- Press releases
- News articles
- Business journals

- Trade publications
- Trade associations
- Marketing material
- Online databases
- Sector performance reports
- Convention and visitors bureaus
- Chambers of commerce
- Resort associations
- Park services
- Ticket agencies
- Travel agencies and consortia
- Tour operators and wholesalers
- Channel reports
- Vendor reports
- Local colleges and universities
- Guest reviews and comments posted on websites

As you can see, many of the sources of competitive intelligence are also the sources of market intelligence on consumer behavior listed in the previous chapter. So when analyzing any secondary source of data, make sure to scan the material for pertinent material on both an organization's customers and its competitors. Important information to obtain on each competitor includes:

- Company historical background
- Physical and online presence
- Ownership and management entities
- Analysis of key financial ratios when available
- Products and services, available and pending
- Facility demand, capacity, and condition
- Corporate and location-specific marketing initiatives
- Pricing strategies
- Distribution strategies
- Key personnel and cultural environment
- Forward-looking plans for acquisition, disposition, repositioning, expansion, or contraction

Perhaps one of the best methods used to continually obtain the most current information on an organization's competitors is to develop a team of **competitive intelligence specialists**. Each specialist is assigned one primary competitor. That individual is then responsible for maintaining the most current data on that competitor. This may include regularly visiting the competitor's premises, occasionally sampling the competitor's products and services, and monitoring all media sources and publications for any news on the competitor. In addition to being assigned one competitor to watch, a competitive intelligence specialist may also be assigned to monitor one specific trade publication for news on any direct, indirect, or potentially new competitors. All information obtained by the competitive intelligence specialists should be regularly submitted and disseminated to enable an organization to maintain its competitive edge.

Competitive Advantage

Today the term *competitive advantage* is commonly used to describe a competitive edge. But how does an organization develop a competitive advantage over its competition? **Competitive advantage** is defined as that component of an organization's operation in which it excels or maintains an advantage over its competitors. It is not only important to attain a competitive advantage over one's competitors, it is equally important to sustain that advantage. When determining an organization's competitive advantage, we must first examine the organization's core competencies. **Core competencies** are the central activities that an organization performs well and that differentiate it from other firms. This is its essence. The core competency of FedEx is the on-time delivery of overnight packages. The core competency of any airline is to get passengers from point A to point B in a timely fashion. The core competency of a concert hall is to provide the highest quality musical entertainment. And the core competency of an upscale restaurant is to provide a superior dining experience.

A competency that an organization performs exceedingly well may be described as a distinctive competency. A **distinctive competency** may be defined as an operational element which an organization performs so well or possesses so uniquely that it distinguishes the organization from its competitors. It should not be easily matched or duplicated by that organization's competitors. In other words, it is distinct to that organization. Think of organizations that provide one-of-a kind products or services. A distinctive competency often develops into a competitive advantage.

The SWOT Analysis

To determine whether an organization possesses any competitive advantage, it must first perform an honest self-assessment. This self-analysis is often referred to as an *internal assessment* and this is the second step in conducting the competitive analysis. Traditionally, most organizations begin this internal assessment process with the development of a **SWOT analysis**. The letters in the acronym SWOT stand for **s**trengths, **w**eaknesses, **o**pportunities, and **t**hreats. In performing a competitive analysis, these elements must be assessed relative to the competition. Strengths and weaknesses are internal to the organization, while opportunities and threats may be either internal or external. An internal opportunity would be the pending acquisition of new land, labor, or capital or perhaps a change in reporting structure. An internal threat would be the potential tightening of the budget in an effort to reduce expenditures or also a change in reporting structure. Every manager has experienced the ease or difficulty of implementing strategies based upon the support or lack of support from management or ownership. So an impending change in operational leadership may represent either an internal opportunity or a threat. Usually strengths and weaknesses are current attributes, while opportunities and threats are more future oriented. For example, one strength may be the organization's beautiful brand new facility. That is a current internal element in the organization's operation. A weakness may be lack of free parking at the facility. Again, this is a current internal factor of the operation. Conversely, an opportunity may be the chance to partner with the new golf course being built adjacent to the building. The golf course is an external element that is about to be added in the near future. A threat may be a new building that is being considered for construction that may obscure a portion of the facility's view. Again, this is external to the organization and will also take place in the future.

In assessing its strengths, an organization should first ask itself the questions, "What do we do well and what are our best features and characteristics?" A list of all of the organization's strengths should be developed. The following are some common strengths found in hospitality organizations:

- Location
- Destinations serviced
- Facilities
- Amenities
- Excellent price/value perception
- Brand/image
- Reputation
- Product positioning
- Human resources
- Financial resources
- Technological resources
- Customer loyalty/repeat business

Next, an organization should examine its weaknesses. This time, the organization should ask itself, "In which areas could we improve and what are our worst or weakest features and characteristics?" Common weaknesses found in hospitality organizations include:

- Location
- Destinations serviced
- Facilities
- Amenities
- Poor price/value perception
- Poor brand/image
- Poor reputation
- Poor or incorrect positioning
- Weak or lacking human resource talent
- Low financial resources
- Inadequate or dated technological resources
- Little repeat business

Are you starting to see a pattern emerge here? Most items are common to both lists, only modified by different adjectives. The majority of items on this list appear within all hospitality organizations. The manner in which they are practiced or maintained may be the differentiating feature. The goal of any organization is to maximize and capitalize on its strengths and minimize or eliminate its weaknesses.

Next, the organization should examine its opportunities. This is not so straightforward and requires a bit of legwork. The organization needs to look outward to see its opportunities. Environmental scanning of the external environment usually produces the greatest number of opportunities. Some common opportunities presented to a hospitality organization may include:

- New demand generators entering the market
- Current demand generators expanding their operations within the market
- An upswing in the economy
- New technological advances
- Increased consumer propensity to spend
- Customizable bundling of hospitality products
- New channels and more effective channels of distribution
- New opportunities for segmentation
- Increased demand for newer products and greater services

A **demand generator** is defined as an organization or event that drives customers into a marketplace. A demand generator may be a new theme park, a new manufacturing plant, a new university, or a major sporting event, such as the Olympics. It is the task of the organization to seek out and capitalize on the greatest number of opportunities given its current resources.

Courtesy of Destination Hotels & Resorts.

Teton Mountain Lodge Restaurant.

And finally, an organization must assess its threats. As with opportunities, threats must be determined through continual environmental scanning. Some common threats to hospitality industry organizations include:

- Terrorism
- Fear of travel
- Cost of fuel
- Weather
- A downturn in the economy
- Political upheaval
- The devaluation of currency (country specific)
- Changing consumer behavior
- Changing demographics
- Changing tastes and trends (what is hot and what is not)
- Changing cultural values and mores
- Other goods and services competing for disposable income
- Bird flu pandemic

It is the responsibility of an organization to first, identify potential threats; second, assess their probability; and third, develop action plans to diminish or avoid them entirely.

Competitive SWOT Analyses

Once the SWOT analysis is complete for the organization, it should then try to develop an individual SWOT analysis for its top three to five competitors. In most cases, it is appropriate to develop a SWOT analysis for each member of an organization's competitive set. Be aware that conducting a SWOT analysis for each competitor is going to be more time consuming than completing a self-analysis, as it will take more time to gather and assess the data from both internal and external sources. It may require personal visits to the competitors' facilities or it may require contacting the competitors directly to determine their future plans. Fortunately, a vast amount of competitive intelligence on hospitality organizations broken down by market is published annually. So with a little time and effort, a great deal of information may be obtained from these published sources. It may also lead an organization to redefine its competitive set based on new information obtained in its research. Thus, the development of the competitive SWOT analyses is time and effort well spent as merely completing the process will bring about new insights into the actions and directions of each of the competitors.

Then once all of the competitors' SWOT analyses are complete, an overall analysis of the market must be undertaken. In reviewing the internal and competitive SWOT analyses, certain key elements and trends will begin to emerge. It will become easier to determine which organizations possess one or more competitive advantages and which organizations may be at a disadvantage. Both opportunities and threats will begin to become more apparent. The organization must again return to evaluate and revise its internal SWOT analysis based upon this more complete picture of the marketplace. Does it possess any competitive or distinctive advantages? Or does a competitor currently possess a competitive advantage that we could meet with spending some capital on facilities and training? Perhaps the recent action of a competitor has created new opportunities. For example, a competitor decides to cease operations in the organization's market. This would present an opportunity for the organization to increase its market share by capturing all or some of the departing firm's customers. **Market share** is defined as that percentage share of an overall market captured by an individual organization.

Or, new threats could also be presented. Perhaps a direct competitor has been purchased by a larger organization with greater resources. Not only is that organization about to embark upon a major renovation and upgrade of its facilities, but it is also prepared to launch a significant marketing campaign to attract and capture new customers. This would pose a substantial threat to its existing competitors. Or new competitors are scheduled to enter the market. This new supply could delete the market share of the current competitors.

So, now that additional information has been obtained from preparing the SWOT analyses of the competition, an organization may need to revise its opportunities and threats lists as follows:

Opportunities:

- New demand generators entering the market
- Current demand generators expanding their operations within the market
- An upswing in the economy
- New technological advances
- Increased consumer propensity to spend
- Customizable bundling of hospitality products
- New channels and more effective channels of distribution
- New opportunities for segmentation
- Increased demand for newer products and greater services
- Current supply leaving the market
- Contraction of current supply
- No scheduled renovations or expansions of existing competitive supply scheduled
- Change in ownership or operational direction of top competitor

Threats:

- Terrorism
- Fear of travel
- Cost of fuel
- Weather
- A downturn in the economy
- Political upheaval
- The devaluation of currency (country specific)
- Changing consumer behavior
- Changing demographics
- Changing tastes and trends (what was hot is now not)
- Changing cultural values and mores
- Other items competing for disposable income

- Bird flu pandemic
- New supply entering the market
- Expansion of current market supply
- Planned renovation or expansion of existing competitive supply
- Change in ownership or operational direction of top competitor

Positioning

One other element must be discussed here and that is the concept of positioning. **Positioning** is defined as the physical and mental perceptual placement of a product or service in a customer's mind. For example, when you think of the word *skybox*, you probably equate it with luxury. The opposite is true when you hear the term *discount ticket*. This will probably conjure up an image of being seated in the nose-bleed seats too far away to really see any of the action. The easiest way to envision the concept of positioning is to develop a perceptual map. The following is an example of a positioning map of service-level versus price.

In this example, service is plotted on the horizontal axis and price is plotted on the vertical axis. Each competitor may then be plotted as a point on the graph based upon the combination of its price and its level of service. A word of caution must be expressed here. Remember that perception is reality in the minds of the consumers. So when developing a perceptual map of the competitors in a marketplace take into consideration both the organization's and the customer's perceptions of each competing organization.

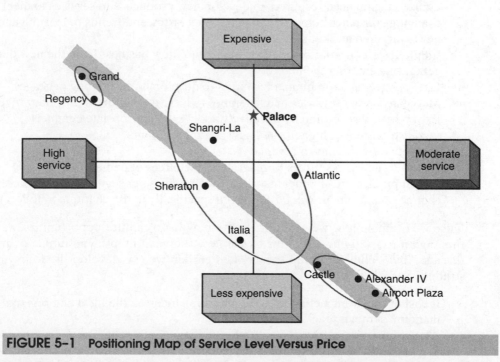

FIGURE 5-1 Positioning Map of Service Level Versus Price

Source: Christopher Lovelock. *Services Marketing*, Upper Saddle River, NJ: Prentice Hall, 1996, p. 178.

Once the perceptual positioning map is complete, an organization may wish to once again return to its SWOT analysis to make further adjustments. Perhaps the perceptual map illustrated the fact that the organization's positioning places it above one of its competitors. But perhaps that competitor is charging and getting higher rates. The organization should analyze and possibly reevaluate its pricing strategies. Or conversely, if the organization is being perceived lower than where it believes it should be positioned based upon the price/value of its facilities and services, the organization may need to launch sales and marketing campaigns to educate and change the perceptions of the customer.

Developing Strategies Based upon the SWOT Analysis

To enhance the probability that an organization makes the most of its opportunities and avoids the greatest number of threats, strategies must be developed based upon the SWOT analysis. To do this, we first pair strengths with opportunities (SO) and then strengths against threats (ST). For example, from the previously noted lists of strengths and opportunities, we could develop the following SO strategies:

- Pursue a new demand generator due to our location and proximity to their premises
- Induce trial of a new demand generator with special offers
- Based upon the upswing in the economy, utilize our financial resources to expand our operations
- Pursue the clients of an organization closing or departing the market
- Utilize our financial resources to develop new products and services to meet changing consumer behavior, demographics, tastes, and trends of existing and newly targeted market segments
- Capitalize on our brand and image to capture new business from the new demand generators entering the market
- Use creative talent in human resources to develop more exciting packages
- Merchandise our facilities and amenities to increase capture of ancillary revenue
- Expand our distribution by selectively adding the appropriate channels
- Increase capture of higher-rated new market segments
- Seek out new streams of revenue
- Utilize franchise resources to generate new sources of demand
- Adjust pricing and channel management strategies per segment (pricing and channel management will be addressed specifically in the chapters to follow)

Once we examine how we can utilize our strengths to capture opportunities, we must then again look to our strengths to see how they can help us minimize or reduce threats. Again, combining the lists created earlier, we can develop the following ST strategies:

- If cost of fuel is impacting inbound air travel, focus on the local and regional drive markets
- Also overcome the fear of travel by appealing largely to the local drive market
- Sell price/value to overcome rate objections during economic downturns

- Build in added value to compensate for the devalued currency
- Utilize service to overcome rate resistance
- Develop new products and services to meet changing consumer behavior, demographics, tastes, and trends of existing and newly targeted market segments
- Match existing products and services to changing cultural values
- Increase marketing efforts or create new events to capture a larger share of the customers' disposable income
- In cases of political upheaval, divert business to another safer division or location to keep revenues within the organization
- Seek out new streams of revenue
- Utilize franchise resources to generate new sources of demand
- Adjust pricing and channel management strategies per segment

Following this pairing of strengths with opportunities and threats, we now turn to pairing weaknesses with opportunities and threats. So turning next to creating strategies to turn our weaknesses into opportunities (WO), we may develop the following WO strategies:

- Lower price to attract cost-sensitive consumers
- Add new destinations to be serviced
- Renovate facilities
- Add or change amenities
- Change the brand or enhance image
- Utilize new public relations opportunities to overcome past poor reputation
- Reposition the facility or service
- Dismiss poorly performing personnel and hire new talent
- Increase or improve customer service training
- Seek new avenues to increase revenue or obtain capital
- Upgrade technology
- Develop new products and services to meet changing consumer behavior, demographics, tastes, and trends of existing and newly targeted market segments
- Match existing products and services to changing cultural values
- Develop new customer loyalty programs to generate additional repeat business
- Seek out new streams of revenue
- Utilize franchise resources to generate new sources of demand
- Adjust pricing and channel management strategies per segment

Continually seek out opportunities to minimize or overcome weaknesses.

And finally, we must face the combination of our weaknesses with potential threats (WT). Developing WT strategies is not a pleasant task. However, as events in 2001 so clearly illustrated, creating a contingency plan is necessary in today's environment. Some possible WT strategies that may be developed include:

- Utilize older facilities to attract lower-rated business emerging in the marketplace due to local economic downturn
- Contract operations by closing a portion of the facility in the off-season

- Reduce prices during seasons of projected inclement weather
- Seek out new markets
- Increase focus on local drive markets
- Develop products and services to satisfy changing customer behavior and demand
- Hire a more aggressive sales and marketing team
- Increase expenditures on facilities and features
- Develop new products and services to meet changing consumer behavior, demographics, tastes, and trends of existing and newly targeted market segments.
- Implement training programs to improve customer service
- Dismiss poorly performing personnel and hire new talent
- Seek out new streams of revenue
- Utilize franchise resources to generate new sources of demand
- Adjust pricing and channel management strategies per segment

Again, it is evident that many strategies may be used to address both opportunities and threats presented by an organization's strengths and weaknesses. To recap, the organization should pair the individual elements in the SWOT analysis to develop the following strategies:

- Strengths and Opportunities (SO) strategies
- Strengths and Threats (ST) strategies
- Weaknesses and Opportunities (WO) strategies
- Weaknesses and Threats (WT) strategies

Once an organization completes its internal assessment and prepares its competitive analysis, it possesses a better understanding of the competitive forces impacting its operation. By this point in the process, the organization has obtained a better understanding of its customers, its markets, its competitors, and itself. Now it is time to take a look at what this will all mean to the organization's profitability going forward. So now it is time to take a look at another external environment factor, and that is focused on the economy.

BOX 5-1

Revenue Management Professional Profile: Courtney Granger[2]

HOW DID YOU FIRST ENTER THE REVENUE MANAGEMENT FIELD?

Transitioned from Reservations Manager to Revenue Manager back when the title first surfaced.

WHAT ARE YOUR MAJOR RESPONSIBILITIES IN YOUR CURRENT POSITION?

I am responsible to ensure all hotels in "The Americas" are maximizing every possible revenue opportunity through our brands. I also manage a team of four Revenue Managers as well as manage our Call Center relationships.

HOW DOES REVENUE MANAGEMENT FIT INTO YOUR ORGANIZATION?

Reservation transaction fees are almost 50 percent of our company's revenues, so the Revenue Account Manager role is highly regarded in our organization.

WHAT ARE SOME OF THE GREATEST ISSUES FACING REVENUE MANAGEMENT PROFESSIONALS TODAY?

I still think there are hotels and/or individuals that do not recognize the importance of RM to a hotel's success. If there is not 100 percent support from the top down, a Revenue Manager will struggle.

HOW DO YOU THINK THE REVENUE MANAGEMENT FIELD WILL EVOLVE OVER THE NEXT DECADE?

Looking back over the past 10 years, RM has been one of the fastest evolving fields in our industry and has become one of the most respected positions. That said, I believe RM will continue to grow and will become an executive-level position in most properties.

WHICH COURSES OF STUDY (i.e. FINANCE, SALES & MARKETING, PSYCHOLOGY, etc.) WOULD BE MOST BENEFICIAL TO STUDENTS EAGER TO ENTER THE REVENUE MANAGEMENT FIELD?

A wide range of courses is required to be a successful Revenue Manager. You must understand all aspects of how a hotel operates, not only to perform well, but to gain the respect and trust of others. Front Office Operations, Sales & Marketing, Selling Techniques, Finance/Accounting, Economics, Psychology, Effective Persuasion, Effective Communications, Basic Writing—all of these are beneficial.

WHAT ADVICE CAN YOU GIVE STUDENTS WISHING TO ENTER THIS FIELD OF ENDEAVOR?

If you have strong analytical skills, are willing to consider different points of view, will stand behind your decisions and enjoy success, Revenue Management is the perfect field for you.

WHAT IS YOUR NAME, COMPANY NAME, AND TITLE?

Courtney Granger, Director of Revenue Account Management—Americas, Preferred Hotel Group

SUMMARY

Once an organization understands its customers, it needs to understand its competitors. The first step in performing a competitive analysis is to identify the competitors. The competitors with whom an organization most directly competes are included in its competitive set. Organizations use competitive intelligence to conduct primary research and gather secondary research regarding their competitors. There are a variety of methods and resources available for gathering this data.

The organization next compares itself to its competitors by completing an internal assessment. The easiest way to conduct this assessment in through the use of a SWOT analysis. In a SWOT analysis, an organization assesses its strengths, weaknesses, opportunities, and threats relative to its competition. After completing its self-assessment and SWOT analysis, the organization should prepare a SWOT analysis for each of the competitors in its competitive set. Then it should analyze its SWOT against those of its competitors.

Once the SWOT analyses are complete, the organization should use the information contained to develop a set of strategies. First, it should pair its strengths with opportunities and its strengths against threats. It should do the same pairing of its weaknesses with opportunities and against threats. *Internal assessment is the third fundamental element and competitive analysis is the fourth fundamental element in the development of revenue management strategy.*

Firms today seek to obtain a competitive edge or advantage over their competitors. A competitive advantage is some component of its operation in which it excels or maintains a competitive advantage over its competitors. Organizations also use their core and distinctive competencies to obtain and maintain these competitive advantages.

KEY TERMS AND CONCEPTS

The following key terms and concepts were presented in this chapter. Each term and concept is also contained in the Glossary of Terms located at the end of this book:

- competitive advantage
- competitive intelligence
- competitive intelligence specialists
- competitive set
- competitor
- core competencies
- demand generator
- distinctive competencies
- market share
- positioning
- secondary competitors
- SWOT analysis

DISCUSSION QUESTIONS

1. Identify your school's competitive set. Why did you select those competitors?
2. What are your school's strengths, weaknesses, opportunities, and threats?
3. Does your school possess a competitive advantage? How so? What are its core competencies? Does it have any distinctive competencies?
4. How could your school develop a strategy to use its strengths to take advantage of an opportunity?
5. How could your school develop a strategy to use its strengths to reduce or eliminate a threat?

EXPERIENTIAL EXERCISE

Visit the site of any hospitality organization. It may be a hotel, a restaurant, an airport, a stadium, a golf course, or a concert hall. Make a note of all the competitive intelligence data that you obtained during your visit. Make sure to observe the parking lot and look at license plates, see what products and services they sell, look to see what vendors they use, assess the volume of business, carefully observe the physical facilities for cleanliness, inventory, and product availability, and listen to the employees and other patrons. Write a report detailing all of the competitive intelligence that you were able to gather in this one visit.

INTERNET EXERCISE

Review and critique two of the following financial websites:
www.bloomberg.com
www.finance.yahoo.com
www.money.cnn.com

www.wsj.com
www.today.reuters.com
www.cnbc.com
www.moneycentral.msn.com

REFERENCES

1. Society of Competitive Intelligence Professionals' website accessed July 18, 2006 http://www.scrip.org

2. Granger, Courtney. Interview conducted via email, August 5, 2006.

Golf Course at Skamania.

CHAPTER

Economic Principles and Demand Forecasting

Chapter Objectives

The objectives of this chapter are to:

- Explore the concepts of scarcity and opportunity costs
- Illustrate the dynamics of supply and demand and explain how the market reaches equilibrium
- Consider the effect of price on substitutes, complements, and inferior goods
- Provide the formulas used to calculate the price elasticity of a product or service to determine its price sensitivity
- Investigate the impact of price elasticity on consumer spending and revenue
- Examine alternative methods for managing demand
- Explain the components present in demand forecasting

Economics. The mere mention of that field of study is able to send shivers up the spines of many college students. It means statistics, graphs, curves, and all that math. It is all about theories and concepts, with absolutely no relationship to real life. Ah, but that is where student perception is wrong. Economics has specific and direct practical applications to our study of revenue management. The dynamics of supply and demand and price in a market economy are key components to optimizing revenue. This chapter will focus on those aspects of economic theory that relate most directly to the principles and practices of revenue management in the real word.

Opportunity Costs

Every human being has needs, wants, and desires for products and services. But unless that person is on the financial level of Bill Gates, his or her resources are limited and choices must be made in the pursuit of these products and services. It is not possible to satisfy every single need, want, and desire. Resources are scarce and some resources are **finite**, meaning that once the last unit of the item is utilized, that item will cease to be available in the future. Due to this scarcity of resources, people are continually forced to make choices. A family must make choices regarding which food and beverage items to purchase from the grocer based on the weekly grocery budget. A manufacturing firm must decide how best to use its resources in land, labor, and capital given the constraints of the marketplace to produce the most profitable mix of products. An amusement park must decide which rides to construct based upon the availability of land within the park. A restaurant must decide which menu items to offer and which meals to serve based upon the availability of ingredients and the strength of market demand. And a hotel developer must decide upon the best mix of guest rooms and common areas when constructing a new property.

One of the key principles of Economics is the concept of opportunity cost. The **opportunity cost** of taking any action is the loss of opportunity of taking any alternative action given the same time and resources. A simple everyday example of an opportunity cost is the choice that a student makes at the food court at lunch time. Two luncheon specials are available for the price of $4.75. The first is a chef's salad with a cup of chicken soup and the second one is a bacon cheeseburger with fries. An athlete enters and selects the soup and salad special. The opportunity cost of that decision is the cost of missing out on eating a bacon cheeseburger with fries. Some people will feel that the decision is good and the opportunity cost of selecting the soup and salad is the avoidance of fat and cholesterol. Others will feel that the opportunity cost of selecting the soup and salad is missing out on the comfort of devouring the burger and fries. So opportunity costs may be both objective and subjective.

An opportunity cost is present in every decision that we make from the mundane to major choices affecting society. For example, Americans have faced greater airport delays since the events of 9/11. We, as a society, have chosen safety over convenience. The opportunity cost we are willing to pay is in time and inconvenience, as we must wait longer in line and remove our shoes before walking through the screening devices leading to the gates. That hassle factor is the price that we are willing to pay for safer air travel.

Government also faces decisions that involve opportunity costs. Given a state's limited resources, decisions must be made each year regarding the funding of goods and services needed by the state's residents. There are never enough resources to implement all of the programs needed or wanted by every constituent. So we elect government leaders to represent our district with the hope that their needs, wants, and desires will mirror our own. And our leaders are faced with having to make increasingly hard decisions when allocating resources to schools, roads, and various human services.

Opportunity cost is also a key concept in the study of revenue management. Consumers must decide which product or service is worthy of their time and money. Our choices are constrained, or limited, by our available resources, including time. A business traveler from Los Angeles who needs to be in Chicago tomorrow for a last-minute meeting will forego money in terms of a higher fare due to his or her last-minute booking. A road warrior just passing through town may forego the luxurious accommodations and higher rate of a downtown hotel for the lower rate and convenience of a roadside hotel near the highway. A worker may select a fast food chain for lunch, foregoing a more relaxed fine-dining experience in order to save time as her end of the month report is due that afternoon. Therefore, it is critical for a business to learn what motivates its customers to purchase its products and services at different times.

The concept of choice plays a significant role in both the study of Economics and the study of consumer behavior. This 'either-or' thought process enables consumers to arrive at a final decision. In weighing their choices, consumers have to determine the opportunity cost of selecting choice A over choice B. Organizations use sales and marketing techniques to help educate customers and persuade them to buy the organization's products and services. Most consumers possess more decision-making power in their leisure travel purchases than in travel purchases prescribed by their employers. And remember that there are ramifications attached to each decision. For example, the consumer who chooses a budget hotel in order to vacation in an upscale resort area trades off comfort and possibly safety for the enjoyment of the higher priced destination. Or the person who purchases a discounted air fare may forego the time and convenience of a direct flight for cost savings. That same person may then utilize those savings for purchases, such as gifts or meals, which possess a greater value in his or her mind than a higher-priced direct flight. Once again, we return to the concept of value and the fact that value to one person is different than value to another.

Therefore, a business must understand the costs involved with pricing and supply decisions made internally and their possible impact upon each market segment. What will be the opportunity cost of raising the price? Will the cost be a loss of some customers, a loss of overall revenue, or both? Or will the cost be the loss of some customers, but the gain of new customers at the higher price, corresponding to an increase of revenue overall? These are just a few of the questions that each organization must pose internally and attempt to answer before embarking on any revenue management program.

All Things Being Equal . . .

Whenever we discuss economic concepts, one concept must always be considered as a constant in our examination of ideas. And that is the concept of **ceteris paribus**, which simply means all things being equal. So when we refer to a principle or concept, we do so considering that all other variables remain constant. For example, if we discuss the cost of hamburgers today, we do so without taking into consideration what would happen if the price of beef suddenly shot up or down. We are looking at one variable and assuming all other variables remain the same. Also, the term *products and services* will be interchangeable with the term *goods and services* for purposes of our discussion in this chapter.

Supply and Demand

Another fundamental concept in Economics is that of supply and demand. *Supply* may be described as the amount of a good or service that a seller is willing and able to sell for any given price at any given time. *Demand* may be described as the amount of a good or service that a purchaser is willing and able to buy for any given price at any given time. This is best illustrated through the use of a few graphs.

Courtesy of Lisa Marie Parker.

Pike Place Market, Seattle.

First let's look at supply. A typical supply curve will go up. Why is that? Well, isn't nearly every seller willing to sell more of any item as the price goes up? In our example, we are going to look at the supply of hamburgers. Most college students are used to paying between $1.50 and $4.00 for a burger, depending on whether it comes with

Quantity of Hamburgers for Sale	Price per Hamburger ($)
20	10
20	9
18	8
16	7
14	6
12	5
9	4
6	3
3	2
0	1

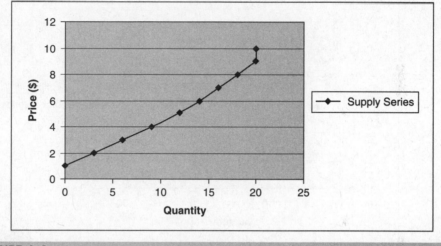

FIGURE 6-1 Supply Curve for Hamburgers

bacon, cheese, pickles, onions, special sauce, lettuce, and/or assorted condiments. Carl's Jr. launched "The Six Dollar Burger" loaded to the hilt on a sesame-seed bun.[1] And for the true gourmands, the record for the most expensive burger is still held by Chef Daniel Boulud at his Manhattan restaurant DB Bistro Moderne. This ground sirloin and black truffle delight called the DB Burger Royale was added to the menu in 2003 at a price of $50.[2]

Since the DB Bistro's prices seem a little high for most college students (and the majority of burger buyers in general for that matter), we will limit the price range on our graph from $1 to $10 per burger.

As we can see in Figure 6–1, the higher the price increases the more burgers that our sellers are willing to sell. **The law of supply** states that as price rises, the quantity supplied increases and as the price falls, the quantity supplied decreases.

Now, let's consider the demand for burgers by college students. Again, we will limit our consideration to burgers ranging in price from $1 to $10.

Notice that the graph in Figure 6–2 has a downward sloping curve. This shows that the lower the price, the more students will be willing to purchase more burgers. This just makes common sense. **The law of demand** states that the quantity of a good or service demanded by buyers tends to increase as the price of that good or service

Quantity of Hamburgers Demanded	Price per Hamburger ($)
2	10
2	9
2	8
2	7
3	6
4	5
5	4
6	3
10	2
20	1

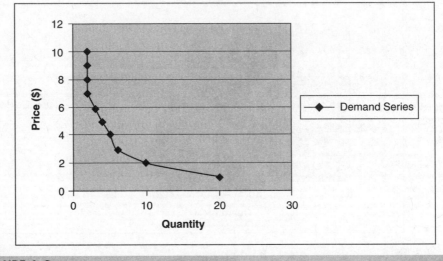

FIGURE 6–2 Demand Curve for Hamburgers

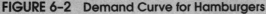

decreases, and tends to decrease as the price increases, all other things being equal. This represents an inverse relationship between price and the quantity demanded.

Now let's combine the supply and demand curves on the same graph (Figure 6–3). The point at which the two curves intersect is called market equilibrium. In this case, the equilibrium price is $3.

Market equilibrium occurs when the quantity supplied is exactly equal to the quantity demanded at that point in time. The equilibrium quantity in this example is six hamburgers. Equilibrium is a fleeting condition due to the constantly fluctuating environment of the marketplace.

A **surplus** occurs when the quantity supplied exceeds the quantity demanded. There is greater supply of the good or service than may be sold at this price at this point in time. This may be seen on the graph in Figure 6–4 as the area above the point of equilibrium. A surplus places pressure on the suppliers as a group to lower their prices. This naturally occurring downward pressure on prices is even stronger when the product being sold is perishable. **Perishable** means that if the product is not sold within a given time period (a day, a night, a week) that product cannot later be sold. An example is an airline seat. Once the plane takes off, the seat cannot be stored for later sale.

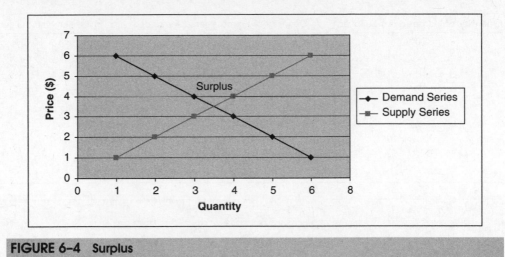

FIGURE 6-4 Surplus

a corresponding decline in the demand for printer paper may occur. When the increase in the price of one good causes a decrease in the quantity demanded of another good, all things being equal, the goods are considered to be **complements** of one another. The general rule for complementary goods or services is that the price of one good or service and the demand for the other good or service will move in the opposite directions.

Some goods and services are impacted by changes in income. As consumers' incomes rise, they will purchase the same or more of normal goods. But the opposite impact will occur in regard to inferior goods. With **inferior goods**, the more a consumer's income rises, the less that person will purchase of the inferior good. For example, once a college student graduates and lands a well-paying job, he or she may purchase more expensive designer clothes and less off-the-rack items. Another student may purchase more steak and fewer hot dogs with his or her corresponding increase in income. And yet another graduate may trade in his or her bus pass for a Vespa or a small car.

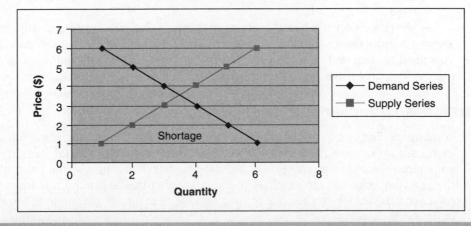

FIGURE 6-5 Shortage

Quantity of Hamburgers Supplied	Quantity of Hamburgers Demanded	Price per Hamburgers ($)
20	2	10
20	2	9
18	2	8
16	2	7
14	3	6
12	4	5
9	5	4
6	6	3
3	10	2
0	20	1

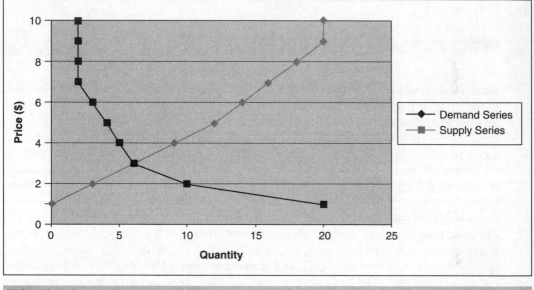

FIGURE 6–3 Equilibrium for Hamburgers

A **shortage** occurs when the quantity demanded exceeds the quantity supplied. There are more buyers than there are goods or services at this price at this point in time. This may be seen on the graph in Figure 6–5 as the area beneath the point of equilibrium. A shortage places pressure on suppliers as a group to increase their prices.

Substitutes, Complements, and Inferior Goods

Sometimes the price of one item may affect the demand for another. If the price of one item goes up causing the increase in the demand for another similar item, those two items are referred to as **substitutes** for one another. For example, the price of coffee rises, causing customers to purchase (demand) more tea. The general rule for substitute goods or services is that the price for one and the demand for the other will both move in the same direction.

Conversely, sometimes an increase in the cost of one item will cause a decrease in the demand for another item. For example, if the price of printer toner quadrupled,

Price Elasticity

Knowing the extent to which quantities supplied or demanded change when a price changes is critical to most organizations. This enables the organization to determine the price sensitivity of their product or service. The more price sensitive an item, the greater effect the price will have on the quantity demanded. Several formulas have been developed to measure these changes in quantities supplied and demanded in response to changes in price. These are referred to as measures of elasticity.

The first measurement is the **price elasticity of supply**, which is calculated by taking the absolute value of the percentage change in quantity of a good supplied and dividing that by the percentage change in the price of that good. The brackets denote absolute value and the symbol Δ represents change.

$$\frac{\% \Delta Q^s}{\% \Delta P} = \text{Price Elasticity of Supply}$$

For example, if a 10 percent increase in the price of coffee created a 20 percent increase in the quantity of coffee supplied, we would calculate the elasticity for the supply of coffee to be 2.0.

$$20/10 = 2.0$$

The second measurement is the **price elasticity of demand**, which is calculated by taking the absolute value of the percentage change in the quantity of a good demanded and dividing that by the percentage change in the price of that good.

$$\frac{\% \Delta Q^D}{\% \Delta P} = \text{Price Elasticity of Demand}$$

For example, if a 10 percent increase in the price of milk results in a 5 percent decrease in the quantity of milk demanded, we would calculate the elasticity of demand for milk to be 0.5.

$$-5/10 = 0.5 \text{ (taking the absolute value)}$$

The greater the price sensitivity of a good or service, the greater will be its price elasticity of demand.

Whenever a 1 percent change in price causes more than a 1 percent change in quantity supplied or demanded, the elasticity calculation will result in a number greater than 1. When this occurs, we say that the supply or demand is **elastic**. In this case, the quantity demanded or supplied is very sensitive to price.

In the very rare case in which the supply or demand of a good would change without a change in price, the supply or demand of that good would be considered to be **perfectly elastic**. Since you cannot divide a number by zero, which is what would occur if there was no change in price, this example cannot be represented numerically. However, it would be graphically represented by a horizontal supply or demand curve (Figure 6–6).

Whenever a 1 percent change in price causes less than a 1 percent change in the quantity supplied or demanded, the elasticity calculation will result in a number less than 1. When this occurs, we say that the supply or demand is **inelastic**. In this case, the quantity supplied or demanded is not very sensitive to price.

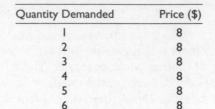

Quantity Demanded	Price ($)
1	8
2	8
3	8
4	8
5	8
6	8

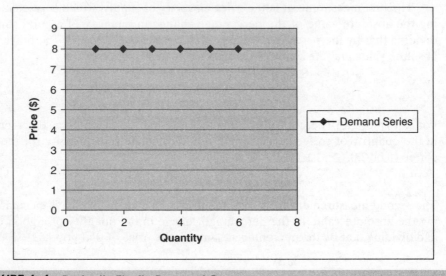

FIGURE 6-6 Perfectly Elastic Demand Curve

In the other rare case in which the quantity supplied or demanded does not change at all in response to a change in price, the supply or demand of that good is considered to be **perfectly inelastic**. Numerically, this would be equal to zero (zero divided by the change in price). Graphically, this would be represented by a vertical supply or demand curve (Figure 6–7). No matter the price, the quantity supplied or demanded remains the same. An example of this would be a medicine with no substitute available.

There is one last measurement of elasticity which is referred to as **unit elasticity**. This occurs when a 1 percent change in price results in exactly a 1 percent change in the quantity supplied or demanded. This measure of elasticity numerically equals 1.

Why do we take the absolute value of these numbers? Let's go back to our milk example where the price increased by 10 percent. So we know that our denominator will be 10. And we also know that our numerator will be *minus* 5 since a rise in the price of milk will cause the quantity demanded to fall. This calculation would result in a negative number. When we take the absolute value of any number, we ignore the minus sign. It has simply become the practice in Economics to always take the absolute value when calculating elasticity.

Calculating the percentage changes

There is an important distinction that must be made before determining the percentage change in price or quantity when calculating elasticity. A simple example will illustrate

Quantity Demanded	Price ($)
7	1
7	2
7	3
7	4
7	5
7	6

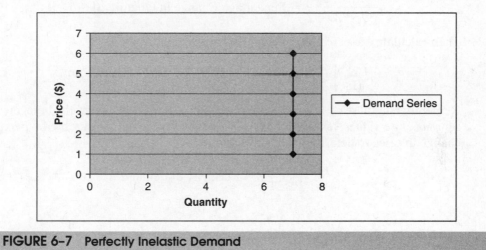

FIGURE 6-7   Perfectly Inelastic Demand

the reason why. Let's say the cost of a pen increased from 75 cents to $1.00. That represents a 33 percent increase in price. However, if the price of a pen goes down from $1.00 to 75 cents, the price change represents a 25 percent decrease in price. Thus, our percentage change in the price of the pen would differ depending upon the direction of the price change.

Therefore, we use the average of the two prices to calculate the change. P_1 represents the price before the change and P_2 represents the price after the change. So to determine the change in price, we use the following calculation:

$$\frac{P_1 - P_2}{(P_1 + P_2)/2}$$

Continuing with our pen example from above, the change in the price of the pen would be 28.57 percent regardless of whether the price rose or fell. We can do the same calculations to determine the percentage change in quantity supplied:

$$\frac{Q_1 - Q_2}{(Q_1 + Q_2)/2}$$

Revised formula for calculating elasticity

Just as before, we use P_1 to represent the price before the change and P_2 to represent the price after the change. We also use Q_1 to represent the quantity before the change and Q_2 to represent the quantity after the change. Thus, our revised formula is:

$$\frac{(Q_1 - Q_2)/(Q_1 + Q_2)}{(P_1 - P_2)/(P_1 + P_2)} = \text{Elasticity}$$

Or if it is more comfortable, first calculate the percentage change in quantity:

$$\frac{Q_1 - Q_2}{(Q_1 + Q_2)/2} = \text{Percentage Change in Quantity} ([\%\Delta Q])$$

Then calculate the percentage change in price:

$$\frac{P_1 - P_2}{(P_1 + P_2)/2} = \text{Percentage Change in Price} ([\%\Delta P])$$

Remember, in these equations, the symbol Δ represents change and the brackets represent absolute value. Next, divide the percentage change in quantity by the percentage change in price to determine the elasticity:

$$\frac{[\%\Delta Q]}{[\%\Delta P]} = \text{Elasticity of demand}$$

Factors Impacting the Elasticity of Demand

What are some of the factors that impact the elasticity of demand? The first factor is whether the product or service is considered to be a luxury or a necessity. An example of a necessity that is often insensitive to price, in other words inelastic, is medical care. This may be one of the reasons that medical costs continue to skyrocket. If an item is considered a luxury, a change in price will typically cause a decrease in demand, which would be an example of elastic demand.

A second factor affecting the elasticity of demand is the availability of substitutes and complements. Whenever a close substitute for a product or service is available, demand for that product or service tends to be elastic. In analyzing complements, however, determining elasticity tends to be more difficult. The less important the complement is to the main product or service, the more inelastic the demand for that complement tends to be.

A third factor affecting the elasticity of demand is the time factor. The longer the time period, the more elastic will be the demand. For example, the demand for air conditioning will tend to be inelastic in July, when temperatures hit 100°. In January, air-conditioning prices tend to be more elastic as people do not feel the need to rush their purchase.

A final factor affecting the elasticity of demand is the price relative to a consumer's budget. Items costing a few cents that are bought regularly to maintain the household are often price inelastic as a small change in price is usually too insignificant to notice. The recent major increase in the cost of gasoline, however, illustrates that the price of gasoline is more elastic. While most people cannot give up driving entirely in response to this hike in gas prices, they are modifying their driving habits to drive fewer miles for both business and pleasure.

The Impact of Price Elasticity on Consumer Spending

Remember that the law of demand states that the quantity of a good or service demanded by buyers tends to increase as the price of that good or service decreases, and tends to decrease as the price increases, all things being equal. So when the price increases, consumers may buy less of a product but still end up spending more money in total due to the increased price per unit.

So what happens to consumer spending as prices change? First, let's examine the case of elastic demand. In this case, the percentage change in quantity demanded is greater than the percentage change in price. Thus an increase in price will cause the consumer to decrease his or her spending on this item, while a decrease in price will result in increased expenditures on this item.

In the case of inelastic demand, the percentage change in the quantity demanded is less than the percentage change in price. In this case, an increase in price will increase expenditure since it will cost more per unit. A decrease in price will likewise decrease overall expenditure on this item since it will cost the consumer less per unit.

The Impact of Price Elasticity on Revenue

A simple example will help to illustrate how the elasticity of demand affects total revenue in response to changes in price. Your city needs to increase revenues to fund the expansion of the existing convention center so they are considering changing the cost of riding the new light rail system. Should the price be increased or decreased? Will a decrease in price attract more passengers? Will this increase in the number of passengers offset the decrease in price to maintain or increase total revenue? Or will an increase in price result in fewer passengers? Will the increase in price offset the decline in the number of passengers to maintain or increase total revenue? If light rail demand is elastic, a price cut should increase revenues. However, a price increase will only increase revenues if light rail demand is inelastic.

So why should you care about price elasticity at all? Price elasticity of a product or service plays a huge role in determining future customer behavior. If a product's demand is elastic and an organization raises prices too high, it may in practice eliminate a substantial portion of the demand for its product. Remember that when demand for a product is elastic, consumers are very sensitive to its price. Conversely, if the demand for a product is inelastic, an organization may be able to increase price without impacting customer demand, as customers are less sensitive to changes in price. An organization should monitor the price elasticity of its products and services following changes that it makes in price. How do increases or decreases in price determine the quantity demanded? Do customers react the same way to increases or decreases in price regardless of the time of year? How can we utilize this information obtained by our research to strategically determine what quantities we are able to sell at which prices for the upcoming year? Since we can manage price, can we also manage demand?

Managing Demand

Once again, let's review our definition of demand. Demand is the amount of product or service that a purchaser is willing and able to buy at any given price at any given time. So demand is based upon consumer behavior. However, what a consumer wishes to purchase and what he or she is able to purchase may be two entirely different matters.

To make this analysis easier, let's just refer to the consumer's **propensity to purchase** as their probability of purchasing an organization's products and services in the future. And let's define **managing demand** as the act of controlling, directing, influencing, and creating consumer purchasing propensity for a specific point in time.

So, again, let's ask the question, Can we manage demand? Absolutely! How can we do it? First, we can control demand through the use of a reservation process. A restaurant has only a set number of seats available. It uses reservations to control the flow of customers in an effort to maximize the number of people seated over a meal period. Other sectors of the hospitality industry such as airlines, hotels, cruise ships, and car rental agencies commonly use the reservation process to control demand.

An organization is also able to direct demand. The restaurant could offer early-bird specials to direct demand to a slower period of the day, or offer two-for-one coupons for dining during slower periods of the week. In this manner, the restaurant helps to direct, or shift, demand from a high volume period to a slower period in the week. Box 6-1 contains a real-world example of shifting demand for guest rooms from The Gant in Aspen.

BOX 6-1

Case Study:
The Gant Summer Group Pattern Strategy, 2004–2007

Early in 2004 we mutually decided that something needed to be done with two long-time return medical groups. After the slump of 2002–2003, the groups had the upper hand due to the fact that they had worked themselves into the last week of July and the first week of August. These are our two busiest weeks of the summer; however, the groups do provide a significant amount of summer conference revenue.

Assuming that one of the groups' dates were always set to follow another annual Aspen summer conference, staff members did not initially think we could convince a change of dates. The decision was made to offer one of the groups their 2004 rates for the next three years if they would move to an earlier week in July. The second group was offered the same rate for 2005 and then a lower rate for 2006 if they agreed to move to the week after the 4th of July holiday (typically lower

demand). Involved in the decision and negotiation process were the Director of Sales & Marketing (DOSM), General Manager (GM), Director of Revenue Management (DORM), Conference Services Director, and Sales Manager.

After making this deal we had to wait one summer (2005), with the groups taking the prime weeks. Now we are set up for next summer with an ideal group base from July 9 to 19, 2006, and we have also used rate to influence another group into July 5–8, 2006, preceding these two groups.

This pattern has set us up for potentially one of our best Julys ever and gives us the opportunity to book higher rated group and individual business during peak periods. This could not happen at a better time with inventory at The St. Regis (a major meeting hotel in Aspen) reduced because of a fractional ownership conversion and the four-star Hotel Jerome undergoing a full renovation next summer.

Source: Courtesy of Lex Tarumianz, The Gant, Aspen, Colorado.

Influencing consumer demand is one of the key tasks of an organization's marketing department. Advertising is the most obvious method that organizations utilize to create customer demand for their products and services. Public relations activities, such as obtaining good reviews from the local food critic, also impact customer demand. When analyzing consumer behavior, always remember the adage that trends are our friends. If we understand what is currently hot in the marketplace, we can create products and services to capitalize on the current craze.

Organizations are also able to create demand through the use of special promotions and events. Many resort destinations create special festivals or events to attract visitors in their soft or off-seasons. A soft season is often referred to as a shoulder season. A **shoulder season** is merely a time of year immediately before or after a peak or weak season. A **peak season** may be defined as a season with the highest demand while a **weak season**, also referred to as a **valley season**, is a season facing the lowest demand. Some hospitality sectors may also refer to the weak season as the **off-season**.

Now, price impacts all methods of managing demand. An organization uses price to control demand, direct demand, influence demand, and create demand. But before an organization can decide how it wishes to use price to impact demand, it must first understand the demand for its products and services in the marketplace. The process of determining this demand is called forecasting.

Courtesy of Destination Hotels & Resorts.

Estrella Room at the Royal Palms.

Demand Forecasting

Forecasting is the act of estimating, calculating, or predicting conditions in the future. So **demand forecasting** may be defined as the act of estimating, calculating, and predicting consumers' demand for products and services in the future. The first step in forecasting demand is to determine overall demand for the market. The best place to begin is to examine the existing demand generators within that market. A demand generator is an activity or entity that produces demand. A hospitality demand generator would be a reason why an individual would travel to a specific location. Some typical demand generators are corporate offices, convention centers, sporting arenas, meeting venues, resorts and recreational activities, government and military installations, shopping centers, and special events. All are reasons why a person would visit a particular location. The demand forecasting process begins with the creation of a list of area demand generators.

Once that list is complete, the organization should look at date-specific demand generators on the horizon for the upcoming year. The easiest method for compiling the list of special-event demand generators is to create a 365-day calendar. All special events for an area should be listed on the calendar. What if the event is happening downtown and the organization is located in the technological center just outside of the city? Should the organization still list the event? The answer is yes, and the reason is called compression. Compression occurs whenever an activity or event forces demand to be pressed outward to the surrounding areas. For example, a city-wide convention is scheduled for the first week of September. It is anticipated that the convention will book nearly all of the downtown hotel rooms. Therefore, all other travelers will need to seek accommodations outside of the downtown area. So the high demand for downtown hotel rooms will squeeze, or compress, the demand out into the suburbs. **Compression** is defined here as pressure placed on a market as a result of demand.

It is also important to realize that not all events are demand generators. Some events are actually demand drainers. A **demand drainer** may be defined as an activity or event that causes demand to decrease. The most typical demand drainers for business travel are the holidays. Businesses are usually closed on the major holidays and therefore corporate travel declines. Leisure travel may increase or decrease on holidays based upon an individual's proximity to friends and relatives. Inclement weather is also a common demand drainer.

So now that an organization has prepared this forward-looking calendar, it must pause and look back to the past. How did last year's forecast compare to actual production? How did demand look for this time last year? Historical performance should then be also noted on the calendar. How many sales were made on this date last year? Actual performance for the previous year should be noted on each date on the calendar.

Another key historical factor needed in analyzing demand is *booking pace*. Remember that booking pace refers to the pattern and rate at which reservations were requested and accepted. Booking pace also needs to be added to our calendar. Now, booking pace continually changes over time, so a specific point in time must be set when adding booking pace to the calendar. For example, an organization may use booking pace as of this date last year.

Additional historical reports to review and incorporate into our demand calendar include those regarding:

- Denials and regrets
- Lost business
- Cancellations
- No-shows
- Walk-ins
- Group arrival/departure and stay patterns
- Transient arrival/departure and stay patterns

A **denial** occurs when a facility is not able to accommodate a guest due to unavailability of product or service at that price. For example, a cruise ship may be sold out, or a hotel only has high-priced penthouses available for the night and the customer requested a standard room. A **regret** occurs when the facility has the product or service available, but the customer chooses not to buy based upon price or some other factor. For example, a standard room is available but the price is higher than the customer wishes to pay. Or a patron calls a restaurant to find out about the evening specials and then chooses not to make a reservation. Denial and regret reports are important both in forecasting and in setting pricing strategies.

Most organizations maintain a lost business file. Usually lost business refers to group business, although some organizations are now attempting to track lost business for individuals as well. **Lost business** is business that had considered an organization's products or services, but in the end decided to purchase from another organization. Why is this important information to obtain? Lost business reports are valuable for several reasons. First, they may help to highlight physical deficiencies in an organization, helping management to justify needed capital expenditures. Second, they may point out problems with customer service, helping an organization see gaps in customer satisfaction and institute additional training. Third, they often open the organization's eyes to other competitors outside of its competitive set. And fourth, it may help to evaluate the appropriateness of the organization's pricing policies and strategies.

The organization should also determine last year's daily percentage of cancellations and no-shows and add these to the calendar. Walk-in business also greatly impacts forecasting, so last year's daily percentage of walk-in business should be added to the calendar as well.

Group and transient arrival/departure and stay patterns help a facility determine peak and weak periods. On which day or days of the week do most business travelers arrive? On which day or days do most of them depart? What about leisure travelers' arrival and departure days? A **stay** is defined as the number of nights a guest occupies a specific product, whether it is a hotel room, a cruise berth, or a campground space. A **stay pattern** may be defined as a pattern in the arrival day, number of nights stayed, and departure day for a guest. Groups and individuals behave differently in their stay patterns, so it is important to analyze each type of business separately. These may highlight opportunities for future capture of additional business and should also be illustrated on the calendar.

Whenever an organization is creating a demand-forecasting calendar, it should try to list as many of the above items by market segment as possible. Once again, this highlights the importance of obtaining and maintaining as much guest information as possible. The better the guest information is captured, the more it will be useful in forecasting future demand. The best predictor of the future is often past performance. Technology has made capturing this data and modeling sophisticated forecasts possible today. However, small mom-and-pop organizations may also utilize these same methods using just a simple Excel spreadsheet to begin.

Once an organization examines how its previous customers behaved and reviewed the area demand generators for the upcoming year, it needs to stop and take a look at the local supply, in other words, its competition. For demand for the products and services of one individual organization does not occur in a vacuum. The actions and plans of competing organizations will have a major effect on the demand for an individual organization's products and services. Competition impacts both the supply and demand for products and services at all levels of the marketplace.

First, the organization should review its most recent competitive intelligence on the competitive set. Are any of the competitors renovating or expanding in the upcoming year? Are any competitors leaving the market or shifting their operations to attract new demand? Perhaps a hotel is changing its operation to become an assisted living facility. Does the organization have data on the performance of the competitors last year? Most sectors of the hospitality industry generate competitive performance reports monthly. These reports contain extremely valuable information and should be analyzed in depth. For it is so very important that an organization understand its share and competitive positioning within its market before even beginning to develop any forecasts or strategies for the future.

There is one last concept to address when discussing demand forecasting. And that is the difference between constrained and unconstrained demand. **Constrained demand** may be defined as demand that is held back or confined by rules, restrictions, and availability. An example of constrained demand would be trying to book a flight using your frequent flier mileage. Rules and restrictions exist regarding when these tickets may be redeemed. There are blackout dates and expiration dates all acting to restrict usage, in other words constrain demand. Another example would be attempting to reserve the 201st camping spot for a holiday weekend after the only available 200 spots have already been taken. **Unconstrained demand** may then be defined as naturally occurring demand that occurs in the absence of restraints and restrictions. It is important to create an organization's forecast initially based upon unconstrained demand. This will enable the organization to determine its pricing and inventory management strategies. Once these strategies have been determined, however, it is important for the organization to return and revise the forecast based upon the resulting constrained demand. This final step is critical in avoiding overstating the total revenue potential for the period. We will return to this aspect of demand forecasting when we look at applications by industry sector.

For now, it is important to add demand forecasting as our fifth fundamental element in the development of revenue management strategy. Better forecasts lead to better decision making, which leads to higher revenues. Demand forecasting is part perspiration and part intuition. No matter how much data is collected or fed into a computer, it usually requires the experience and analysis of a human being to apply that information in the creation of a reliable prediction of the future. Consumer behavior possesses that human element that often eludes the capabilities of technology. Once we are able to project *when* consumers will buy our products and services, we need to address *where* they will make their purchases. So the next topic that we need to address is distribution.

SUMMARY

Consumers have a long mental list of their needs, wants, and desires. Unfortunately, most consumers have limited resources with which to satisfy the items on their list. So they have to decide which purchases to transact. This involves the concept of opportunity cost. They trade off the opportunity to purchase one item for another.

Supply is described as the amount of a good or service that a seller is willing and able to sell for any given price at any given time. Demand may be described as the amount of a good or service that a purchaser is willing and able to buy at any given price at any given time. Market equilibrium occurs when the quantity supplied matches the quantity demanded at a specific point in time. Whenever more goods or services are available than there exist buyers, there will be a surplus in supply. Whenever less goods and services are available than there are buyers, there will be a shortage in supply.

The availability of substitute products or services enables a purchaser to shift his or her demand for a product or service if the price becomes too high or the supply becomes unavailable. Or products and services may be complementary, meaning that the demand and price for one may impact the demand and price for another. An example may be coffee and cream. If the price of coffee goes too high, the demand for both coffee and cream may decrease. The availability of substitutes and complements impacts the price elasticity of demand.

Organizations should determine the price elasticity of their products and services. This will enable them to project their customers' possible reactions to changes in price. Price elasticity refers to the consumers' sensitivity to a change in price. The greater the price sensitivity of a good or service, the greater will be its price elasticity of demand. One of the major factors impacting the elasticity of demand is whether the product is a necessity or a luxury. Some necessities, such as healthcare, are relatively inelastic, meaning that the demand will remain moderately stable with changes in price. The price elasticity of a product or service plays a major role in determining future consumer purchasing behavior.

Organizations try to manage demand by controlling, directing, influencing, and creating consumer purchasing propensity for a product or service at a specific point in time. The better an organization is able to manage demand, the better able it will be to manage its corresponding revenues.

Demand forecasting is the act of estimating, calculating, and predicting consumers' demand for products and services in the future. *Thus, we add demand forecasting as our fifth fundamental element in the development of revenue management strategy*. Better forecasts lead to better decision making, which leads to higher revenues. But always remember that demand forecasting is part perspiration and part intuition, and that every organization is susceptible to the vagaries of the marketplace.

KEY TERMS AND CONCEPTS

The following key terms and concepts were presented in this chapter. Each term and concept is also contained in the Glossary of Terms located at the end of this book:

- ceteris paribus
- complements
- compression
- constrained demand
- demand drainer
- demand forecasting
- denial
- elastic
- finite

- forecasting
- inelastic
- inferior goods
- law of demand
- law of supply
- lost business
- managing demand
- market equilibrium
- off-season

- opportunity cost
- peak season
- perfectly elastic
- perfectly inelastic
- perishable
- price elasticity of demand
- price elasticity of supply
- propensity to purchase
- regret

- shortage
- shoulder season
- stay
- stay pattern

- substitutes
- surplus
- unconstrained demand
- unit elasticity

- valley season
- weak season

DISCUSSION QUESTIONS

1. You have been given $100 by your grandmother to spend any way you wish this weekend. What are some of the possible options you may consider? Select one option and explain the opportunity costs involved in your decision.

2. In addition to price, what may cause changes in the quantity demanded for a product or service? Provide specific examples.

3. In addition to price, what may cause changes in the quantity supplied of a product or service? Provide specific examples.

4. Think about the concepts of substitutes, complements, and inferior goods. Provide a list of three possible substitutes and complements and then list three items that may become inferior goods in your eyes the first year after you have graduated. Be prepared to discuss your rational for each.

5. Which products and services do you currently purchase that you would continue to purchase regardless of changes in price? Which products and services do you currently purchase that you would cease to purchase if the price increased past your price/value perception. Is there an available substitute for this product or service?

INTERNET EXERCISES

1. Access the Travel Industry Association's travel forecast center by the URL http://www.tia.org/Travel/travelforecast.asp. Review the forecasts and then select a destination and explain how you believe this forecast may impact providers of hospitality products and services in this destination.

2. Select two products and then go online and see if you can find out the price elasticity for each of the products. Report your findings. If you are unsuccessful finding the information online, check with your librarian to see if a reference book is available containing charts of price elasticity for various products. Utilize available reference material to obtain the price elasticity for your two products and report your findings.

REFERENCES

1. Carl's Jr. website accessed July 16, 2005, http://www.carlsjr.com/home.

2. Guinness Book of World Records website accessed July 16, 2005, http://www.guinnessworldrecords.com.

Estrancia La Jolla Hotel & Spa Meeting Room.

CHAPTER

Reservations and Channels of Distribution

Reservations and Channels of Distribution

Reservation Evolution

In the early days, if a person wanted to buy a piece of fruit in the marketplace, he or she brought an item of exchange with which to barter. With the advent of currency, these exchanges became easier and more frequent. Buyers could come to the market with their purse in their hands without having to preplan a barter exchange for each item. At the end of an arduous day, travelers hoped to find an inn that offered food and rest from their weary journey. They stopped where they dropped and hoped to find a roof over their heads and some small respite for the evening.

As travelers and modes of transportation became more sophisticated, hospitality merchants began to take advance requests for their goods and services. An ocean traveler would venture down to the shipping office to purchase passage in advance to ensure a berth on the next voyage. During those early days, reservations were not accepted without prepayment. A **reservation** is defined as an arrangement between a buyer and a seller to hold a product or service in advance of purchase on a promised intention of future purchase made by the buyer. Hotel guests would either write a letter of inquiry or send a telegram requesting specific dates of stay at an inn. Some hotels still required payment along with the request, while others began to accept these advance booking requests on faith. Soon railroad passengers began having the telegraph office send word ahead to request a room at a hotel located at the next stop. The hotels would usually accept these reservations without prepayment since the passengers were obviously on their way.

Travel agents have been in existence since Thomas Cook began selling group excursions in Europe in the mid-1800s. Exotic posters displayed in agency storefronts lured passersbys inside. Once inside, they were given brochures and presented with sales pitches to entice them to book passage on the next available voyage. Travel agents made their income on commissions paid by the hospitality providers. When these providers needed more business during the off-season, they often increased the commissions they were willing to pay in an effort to entice the travel agents to push more business their way. **Retail travel agents** sold directly to the public, and **wholesale tour operators** created travel packages to be sold to travelers directly or through travel agencies at a discount.

Tour operators also began to spring up to serve as intermediaries between the traveler and the destination. The tour operator would create a tour and then either purchase the individual travel components directly from the providers in advance at a discount or the tour operator would receive a commission for each component following the eventual sale of the tour. The tour operator would bundle these components and set a price for the entire package and sell that package either directly to the end consumer or market it creatively through travel agencies. And sometimes tour operators bought packages from travel agents, added a few additional components, and repackaged the bundle for resale to groups or individual consumers. Reservations for these tours were usually accepted with a small deposit.

The telephone enabled the mass prepurchase of hospitality goods and services to be transacted with relative ease. Toll-free numbers were established by the airlines and hotels to encourage customers to call directly for reservations. Advertising space was purchased on the major television networks and in the newspapers of most metropolitan areas to promote these 1–800 numbers to the traveling public. The toll-free numbers enabled consumers to book directly, saving the airline or hotel the commission that it otherwise paid to a travel agent. Savvy travelers understood these commission savings and quickly began to negotiate for better rates when calling the hotel direct. They would also ask the airline for its lowest available fare. The telex and fax facilitated international purchases of hospitality products and services at any time of day and night.

In the beginning, whenever a reservation was received via letter, telegram, telephone, or advanced purchase, the reservation was entered into a manual booking system. The space, whether it was a seat, a room, or a meal, was preblocked and written into a reservation log for that specific date. Sometimes a chart or diagram was created with the names written above each available space. In other cases, strips of colorful tape containing the name and reservation number of the customers were pasted on the chart. A visual glance at the chart revealed any remaining availability. It was a cumbersome process and frequently marred by human error.

As technology advanced, these manual systems were replaced by automated reservation systems. With the increase in volume, more hospitality organizations began requesting credit card numbers to hold a reservation. Customers were notified that they would be billed for the purchase if they did not cancel by a specified date in time. This was an attempt to reduce the number of customers who failed to show up or cancelled at the last minute. It was also a method of helping organizations to better forecast demand.

The new technology enabled organizations to obtain more information regarding their customers prior to their actual arrival. Soon, the marketing department envisioned opportunities to capitalize on the reservation process. First, they began training reservation agents to upsell products and services to customers who called in to make reservations. The reservation agent was provided with a script of leading questions designed to encourage the customer to purchase additional or upgraded products and services. A variety of shopping services emerged to test call the reservation departments to determine how well they performed in this task. Next, the marketers replaced the music that used to play when a calling customer was placed on hold with prerecorded messages regaling the features and benefits of a variety of products and services that the customer could purchase when the reservation agent came back on the line. And finally, the marketers used the guest information captured by the reservation agent to send the customer promotional material to peruse prior to arrival.

The evolution of the World Wide Web and the increasing Internet literacy of the general public are factors that are continually changing the way hospitality products and services are purchased. Today, customers may shop a variety of online sources to view a multitude of products and services and their available prices. They may book an airline seat, a rental car, a hotel room, dinner reservations, and a ticket to a Broadway play in a single transaction on the Internet. And they are able to pick up their e-tickets along the way or print them out at home or work before their departure. Each year brings about exciting new technological innovations and applications for the hospitality industry.

The Early Channels

The first computerized reservation systems were created by the airlines in the 1960s and the systems were referred to as **ARS**s, which stood for **airline reservation systems**. The previously mentioned Sabre system operated by American Airlines is one example of this early airline reservation system. At first the airlines only trained internal personnel to input reservations. Both travel agents and individual passengers had to telephone the airline reservation line directly to personally speak with a reservation agent located in the airline's reservation center. The reservation agent would then check flight and seat availability in the computerized reservation system. If a seat was available, the agent obtained the needed information from the caller to book the reservation directly into the computer.

As airline traffic grew, the airlines decided to enable travel agents to book directly into the ARS. So the airlines offered extensive travel agent training and installed systems in the travel agencies generating the highest volume of tickets. The airlines benefited from the labor cost savings of having external travel agents take reservations rather than their own internal airline reservations agents. So they quickly installed systems in additional agencies. The computer programs utilized cryptic codes only understood by travel agents, ensuring continued dependence of consumers upon travel agents.

The ARSs became more sophisticated due to the combination of advances in technology and the growing demands of travel agents and their clients. Originally, travel agents could only view one airline's inventory on its proprietary ARS. **Proprietary** here is defined as being owned and operated by that entity. Airline passengers wanted their travel agents to be able to review price and availability of numerous flights of the various carriers at the same time. So travel agents began installing terminals from each of the major carriers in their offices and their personnel were trained to become adept in entering reservations in each of the systems. The next logical step was to complete the transportation purchase loop by enabling travel agents to offer car rentals to their clients traveling by air. The airlines and car rental agencies developed partnerships to package these fly/drive opportunities.

Going hand-in-hand with the increase in airline traffic was the increased demand for hotel rooms. Once again advances in technology and the demands of travel agents and their clients led to the growth of another computerized reservation system, this one for hotels. Hotel companies created **central reservation offices (CROs)** to take reservations for all properties within their organization. For example, CROs were established for Hilton, Marriott, Sheraton, Holiday Inn, and other franchises to accept reservations for any hotels within the chain. The travel agent simply had to dial a 1–800 telephone number to reach the CRO. The reservation agent could check availability and book reservations at any property in the world that maintained inventory, in this case available guest rooms, in the system. **Inventory** is defined as products or services made available for sale through various channels of distribution. We will discuss channels in a moment.

In addition to containing inventory, the CROs maintained basic information regarding the hotel's facilities, amenities, and location relative to nearby businesses and attractions. The agent would be able to assist a caller in selecting the most appropriate hotel based upon the purpose of that traveler's upcoming visit. Once a room was booked, the agent would send the information regarding the reservation directly to the hotel via telex or other internal computerized communication system. The hotel was ultimately responsible for maintaining and controlling its own inventory at the local level. Again, this was usually done manually in a dated reservation log book. And although each property established its own room rates, limited technology made frequent changing of rates to match fluctuating demand difficult at best and was discouraged by the CROs at worst.

Due to the numerous variables involved in booking a hotel room, the transaction took more time and effort than booking an airline seat. The reservation agent had to ask how many people were arriving, how many beds were preferred, what types of beds (kings, doubles) were desired, which location was preferred (mountain view or poolside), whether the guest preferred a smoking or nonsmoking room, the date of arrival, anticipated length of stay, method of payment for reserving the room, and all the contact information for the guest. The reservation agent also had to strive to obtain the best rate and then wait for the transaction to be entered before providing the caller with a confirmation number. So in the beginning, the airlines maintained and expanded their ARSs while hotels maintained and controlled their own CROs. Eventually technology advanced to enable the two systems to merge and a travel agent could book an airline seat, a rental car, and a hotel room on one computerized reservation system now referred to as a **CRS** or **central reservation system**.

It was the deregulation of the airlines in 1978 that fostered the next major growth spurt for the CRSs. Initially, each CRS was a proprietary entity of the corresponding airline that owned and operated the system just as Sabre was for American Airlines. The CRSs were able to restructure following deregulation, which enabled them to configure systems offering the inventory of multiple carriers and various suppliers of hospitality products and services. They rapidly expanded the capabilities of the CRS to incorporate hotel accommodations as well. The term *CRS* soon gave way to the term **GDS, global distribution system**, as the technology enabled the sale of products and services around the globe.

Today, there exists a global marketplace in which buyers and sellers of hospitality products and services converge to complete transactions. When students hear the term *travel buyer*, they immediately think of the traditional leisure traveler. They conjure up the image of a vacation shopper venturing onto the Internet to research flights, hotel accommodations, and recreation packages available at luxurious destinations. In reality, the majority of the world's travelers are on the road for business rather than pleasure. In fact, the majority of the hotel rooms in the United States are occupied by business travelers, although the market mix has shifted a bit since the change in travel behavior following the events of September 11.

There are a multitude of sellers of hospitality products and services today. Sellers include transportation companies (airline, train, cruise line, motorcoach, and car rental), accommodations (hotels, motels, inns, bed and breakfasts, condominium hotels, vacation rentals, timeshares, and fractional ownership resorts), recreation products and services (ski, golf, rafting, surfing, fishing, hiking, biking, etc.), entertainment (gaming, sports, music, theme parks, etc.), and personal health and relaxation (spas).

To facilitate the purchase of these varied hospitality products and services, numerous avenues have developed to bring the buyer and seller together. These are referred to as **channels of distribution**. These channels act as distribution outlets through which the sellers offer their products and services for sale to their customers. Channels may be electronic or nonelectronic. Whereas the source of a reservation used to be referred to as the source of business, today all sources of business may be tracked via both market segment and the channel that generated the business. Some customers still prefer to make their purchases in person and will therefore venture to a brick and mortar outlet of the seller. For example, they will go to the airport or stadium to personally purchase their tickets in advance. Others still prefer paper transactions, such as sending a fax. And many others will let their fingers do the walking and call the seller directly. These examples showcase the fact that customers prefer to use different channels for booking their reservations. Different strokes for different folks. As customers become more adept at using the computer and also become more comfortable with electronic modes of distribution, more and more reservations will be made electronically.

Global Distribution Systems (GDS)

Today, the two common modes of electronic distribution are through a (1) global distribution system (GDS), and (2) through the Internet distribution system (IDS). **Electronic distribution** is defined as the selling of hospitality products and services via the computer. Think of these basically as electronic warehouses in which a person may conduct one-stop shopping for a variety of hospitality products and services. A GDS may be defined as a computerized reservation system facilitating the sale of hospitality products and services primarily to organizational buyers, such as travel agents. The four major global distribution systems (GDSs) today are Sabre, Amadeus, Galileo, and Worldspan. They are still responsible for a substantial volume of reservation activity generated by travel agents. Now travel agents are able to book a variety of products and services from a variety of different providers through each GDS.

The larger hospitality providers, such as the chain hotels, cruise lines, car rental agencies, and gaming operations, are connected directly to each GDS through an expensive link or interface. The travel agent booking via the GDS may then access the providers' inventory directly. Smaller providers, who may not be able to afford such a large expense, connect to the GDS through a switch. A **switch** is defined as a single electronic connection through which a hospitality provider must pass first before being connected to the GDS. There are just two switches operating today that connect the entire hospitality industry, Pegasus (originally known as THISCO—the hotel industry switch company) and Wizcom, which was originally developed to connect select car rental companies to the GDSs. Think of going through a switch as an extra internal click in the electronic booking process. The extra click is imperceptible to the travel agent. The cost of this switch is less than the cost of connecting directly to the four

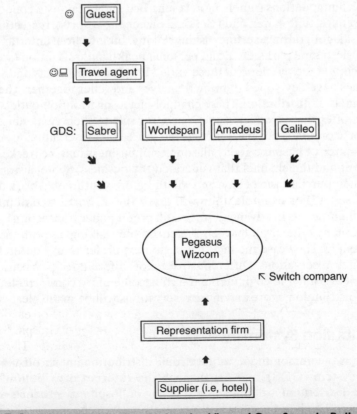

FIGURE 7-1 Global Distribution Network—View of One Sample Path

GDSs for some suppliers. So either directly or through a switch, the products and services of connected hospitality providers are available for sale to travel agents and others through the GDS. Figure 7–1 illustrates one possible transaction path from consumer to provider through the global distribution system.

Internet Distribution Systems (IDS)

Most people conjure up the image of an online travel site such as Expedia, Orbitz, or Travelocity when they think of booking any travel components over the Internet. In fact, Travelocity was actually spun off from Sabre to serve the consumer market. These online travel sites are referred to as **third-party websites**. They serve as an intermediary, in other words a third party, between the consumer and the hospitality product or service providers who comprise the other two parties. The electronic system that facilitates purchases of hospitality products and services by consumers is referred to as the **Internet Distribution System or IDS**. The Internet Distribution System (IDS) is actually comprised of a variety of components each falling into one of the following eight categories:

1. Proprietary site (individual unit and/or CRS)
2. Merchant model
3. Retail operation
4. Opaque site
5. Auction site
6. Referral service
7. Special interest or niche site
8. General Web portal

The first and most important component in the IDS is the organization's own proprietary website. Many brands maintain websites for their central reservation systems (CRSs), with links to their individual unit websites. Central reservation systems may serve related or unrelated properties. For example, Hilton's CRS manages reservations for all properties in the Hilton family of products. Other CRSs handle reservations for a variety of smaller brands or independent hotels. Consumers frequently visit proprietary websites and central reservation systems first to obtain needed information on a product, service, or destination. The development and maintenance of websites and CRS connectivity is extremely important to independent organizations that lack connectivity to a major brand.

The second component of the IDS is the familiar online travel site, the third-party website, which is often referred to as a **merchant model**. To help understand these models, pull up the websites www.travelocity.com, www.orbitz.com, and www.expedia.com. Take a moment to review the hospitality products and services available on each site.

The travel site obtains inventory at a wholesale rate from a hospitality provider and then acts as a merchant, selling it to the consumer at a retail rate. The **wholesale rate**, also referred to as the **net rate**, is often 20 to 30 percent or more off the retail rate. For example, Travelocity obtains 50 rooms from Hotel X for $100. Travelocity then offers these 50 rooms for sale on its site for $125. The $25 difference is their mark-up on the inventory. The explosion of the online travel sites occurred as a result of the downturn in travel after the terrorism attacks of 2001. Airlines, hotels, car rental agencies, and other hospitality providers jumped to unload inventory that they couldn't sell, which they referred to as **distressed inventory**. Due to the lack of demand, they were prepared to accept deep discounts rather than let the rooms sit vacant. Issues soon arose regarding control of the inventory. As demand started to return, some websites began selling inventory above the rack rates set by the hotels. Customer dissatisfaction occurred when the customer learned that the rate was higher than others received by calling the hotels directly or booking through other websites. The carefully crafted pricing strategies developed by hotels to meet customers' perceptions of value were being eroded by this lack of price control on the Internet travel sites. Once demand began to return, some hotel company providers threatened to cease selling their inventory to these sites. But, unfortunately, the genie had been left out of the bottle and was not about to be put back in. Consumers had rapidly become accustomed to using the Internet both to book online and to obtain a better deal than through more traditional channels. Today, the operators of merchant models and their hospitality providers are working in partnership to ensure the best possible solutions for all parties involved.

Retail operators sell products and services of various hospitality providers at the prices set by the providers. They may maintain both an online presence and brick and mortar stores. An example of a retailer would be a travel agency that promotes both its physical location and its website. Or it could just exist in cyberspace, like Quikbook. The retailer receives a commission, often 10 percent, on all sales generated at its physical or online site.

In both merchant models and retail operations, the customer knows the product or service he or she is purchasing prior to the transaction taking place. In an **opaque channel**, either the price or the product is hidden to the customer. Examples of opaque sites are Hotwire and Travelocity Packages. For example, a customer may be seeking a four-star hotel property in Scottsdale or alternately he or she may just be looking for a hotel with a rate of less than $200 per night. And the price is determined by the winning bid on **auction sites** such as Priceline and Luxury Link. Consumers purchasing through the opaque and auction sites are typically very price sensitive. Inventory is usually sold to these sites at net rates.

Referral sites are also called **meta search engines**. They scour other sites for the best price or deal. Examples of meta search engines are TravelZoo, TravelAxe, Sidestep, Kayak, and Mobissimo. Referral sites are also paid on a commission per customer booking basis, typically at 10 percent. Take a moment to pull up the websites www.travelaxe.com, www.kayak.com, and www.mobissimo.com and review the order in which these sites list hospitality products and services.

Consumers may also enter the Web through alternative means and yet ultimately end up making online purchases of hospitality products and services during their surfing of favorite or **special interest websites**. For example, an individual venturing to an online poker site may end up booking a trip to Las Vegas. Or a tennis player looking for a new racquet may see an exhibition of favorite tennis stars coming to a nearby city, and decide to purchase a ticket to the event. Or yet another consumer looking to purchase new skis sees an online advertisement offering a substantial discount for the early purchase of a season ski pass and decides to make the purchase that day instead of later. Substantial traffic passes through these special interest websites, leading to potentially new streams of revenue for the hospitality provider. These sites are also referred to as **niche sites** as they target small specific subsegments of the market.

And the elements making up the last component of the IDS are the various mainstream websites and information portals, such as Yahoo, MSN, and Google. A **portal** is defined as a website gateway designed to provide access to other websites and services. These sites are accessible from the home page of almost every Internet service

Courtesy of Destination Hotels & Resorts.

Bath with Rose Petals at the Royal Palms.

provider, with stories and advertisements encouraging the reader to click on to read more. Many hospitality transactions occur as a result of links to these sites.

Throughout our analysis, we have been referring to the individual traveler. However, it must be noted that more and more small groups are making their reservations through the GDS and IDS. And remember that group purchasing decisions involve more data, more interaction, and more personnel than individual consumer purchasing decisions. So elements conducive to booking group business also need to be incorporated into electronic booking channels. As electronic purchasing becomes more complex, hospitality organizations must invest in more advanced technology.

Property Management Systems

One last system needs to be addressed here and that is the property management system, also referred to as the **PMS**. A **property management system** is a computerized system used to manage the inventory of products and services available at a single location. In the case of hotels, all customer data is entered into the PMS, regardless of its original source, when a guest checks in. So the PMS is the natural first choice for obtaining captured guest information. The PMS is usually linked to all point-of-sale terminals within a property. Therefore, guest information is obtained regarding not only primary purchase, but all ancillary purchases on site as well. It also captures stay pattern information. Note, an exception often occurs for products and services purchased for cash as the point of salespeople may not capture any guest information during these cash transactions. The PMS may also serve as a channel production mechanism as it records source of business for all transactions.

Distribution Cost

About this time, students may be thinking that an organization should utilize all of these channels to obtain the most business. And the organization should just allocate its inventory in order of the greatest production, right? Not so fast. There are various distribution costs involved with Internet transactions. The cost of getting a product or service to market is referred to as a **distribution cost**. First of all, there is the discount, or net rate, at which the provider sells its product or service. The difference between the net rate and the organization's retail rate may represent a substantial reduction in total revenue received by the producer of that product or service. Again, students may argue here that a net rate is better than no rate, which is true when an entity is trying to sell highly distressed inventory. But in determining the costs and revenues involved with normal everyday transactions, we need to know the actual distribution cost involved in selling each unit of inventory. Distribution cost is also spread over the entire length of stay, so longer stays are more cost efficient.

The second possible cost is a **commission**, sometimes also referred to as a **load**. That is the percentage or flat fee above the selling price that goes to an intermediary that must also be added to a product's or service's cost of distribution. And third, there is frequently a transaction fee involved with actually selling the product or service via the GDS or IDS. Therefore, it is important that an organization conduct a thorough analysis of its costs of distribution per channel. To illustrate, turn to Figure 7–2, which is a comparison of distribution costs per channel for a hotel room.

Assumption: $179 selling rate for 2.5-night average length of stay (ALOS)
$179 × 2.5 = $447.50

Proprietary website

Sell Rate	Net Rate	Commission /Load	Transaction Fee	ALOS	Cost	Revenue	Efficiency
179.00	N/A	0.00	5.00	2.5	**$5.00**	**$442.50**	**99%**

After-hours reservation service

Sell Rate	Net Rate	Commission /Load	Transaction Fee	ALOS	Cost	Revenue	
179.00	N/A	0.00	25.00	2.5	**$25.00**	**$422.50**	94%

GDS

Sell Rate	Net Rate	Commission /Load	Transaction Fee	ALOS	Cost	Revenue	
179.00	N/A	44.75	13.00	2.5	**$57.75**	**$389.75**	87%

Online Internet site at 20% margin

Sell Rate	Net Rate	Commission /Load	Transaction Fee	ALOS	Cost	Revenue	
179.00	143.20	89.50	5.50	2.5	**$95.00**	**$352.50**	79%

Online Internet site at 25% margin

Sell Rate	Net Rate	Commission /Load	Transaction Fee	ALOS	Cost	Revenue	
179.00	134.00	112.00	0.00	2.5	**$112.00**	**$335.50**	75%

FIGURE 7-2 Distribution Cost Comparison by Channel

As evident in this comparison, the hotel would receive revenue ranging from $335.50 to $422.50 depending upon which channel generated the booking. This represents a revenue spread of $87.00. The number of transactions generated by channel is referred to as its **channel production**, while the revenue generated from a single transaction is considered to be its **channel contribution**. Average channel contribution may be determined by dividing the total revenue generated by the channel by the total number of transactions it completed:

$$\textbf{Average Channel Contributions} = \frac{\text{Total Revenue Generated}}{\text{Total Number of Transactions}}$$

For example, let's say a channel produced 1,000 room nights for a hotel over the course of a year, which generated total revenues of $200,000. A **room night** is calculated by multiplying one room times one night. A guest booking one room for three nights would be said to generate three room nights. A guest booking two rooms for three nights would generate six room nights. So to calculate the average contribution of this channel, divide the total revenue the channel produced by the number of transactions it completed:

$$\text{Average Channel Contribution} = \frac{\$200,000}{\$1,000} = \$200 \text{ per room}$$

It may also be helpful to calculate the channel's contribution percentage by dividing the channel's total revenue by the total revenue produced by all channels. The equation for calculating channel contribution percentage is:

$$\frac{\textbf{Channel Contribution}}{\textbf{Percentage}} = \frac{\text{Total Channel Revenue}}{\text{Total Revenue Generated by All Channels}}$$

Keeping with the same example, let's say that all channels combined generated annual revenue of $2 million last year. Since the channel under consideration contributed $200,000, that would represent 10 percent of the total revenue generated by all channels combined:

$$\text{Channel Contribution Percentage} = \frac{\$200,000}{\$2,000,000} = 10\%$$

Returning to our distribution cost analysis, students may be thinking that the hotel should simply sell its entire inventory on its proprietary website to maximize revenues. Unfortunately, it would be extremely rare for a hotel to sell out by keeping all of its inventory to itself. Maybe the highest producing channel in terms of volume is the GDS, which falls in about the middle of the distribution cost comparison. Each channel provides an organization with a monthly production report showing the revenue generated each month by that channel. How much inventory should the hotel provide to the GDS? Obviously, an organization cannot determine where to place its inventory based upon either volume or cost alone. What other factors may be involved with channel selection?

Channel Selection

The first step in channel selection is to look at the numbers. An organization should conduct production, contribution, and cost analyses for each channel of distribution under consideration. This includes both electronic and nonelectronic channels. Just a few of the distribution costs to consider in nonelectronic channels would be print and media advertising, special promotions (coupons, discounts), direct mail, personal sales efforts, ticketing, and other technology costs. Some of these costs may also apply to electronic channels as well. The previous example highlighted some of the standard electronic costs of distribution. Once an organization understands the level of production that it receives per channel and knows the costs of distribution per channel, it needs to turn to the most important element in channel selection, and that is the customer. Where are customers buying?

The organization needs to determine the worth of the customers being delivered via each channel of distribution. Remember our equation for determining total customer worth?

$$\text{Total Customer Worth} = \left(\frac{\text{Primary}}{\text{Revenue}} + \frac{\text{Ancillary}}{\text{Revenue}} - \frac{\text{Acquisition}}{\text{Cost}} \right) \times \text{Propensity Y}$$

Breaking this down, the primary revenue is the revenue generated by the major product or service being purchased, such as an airline seat or a hotel room. Ancillary revenue is the additional money that customer spends on products and services other than the primary product or service. This may be food and beverage purchased in the terminal by an airline passenger, or a spa service purchased by a hotel guest. Acquisition cost is the cost incurred to capture that guest. Acquisition cost includes sales and marketing costs, labor costs to transact the sale, accounting costs to process the sale, and distribution costs to actually produce the sale. And finally, what is the probability of that customer purchasing products and services from the organization again in the future, the variable that we refer to as Propensity Y? Determining customer worth takes time and effort, but it will pay off with increased revenues in the end. Assessing primary and ancillary revenue potential may be extrapolated from guest history reports, and should be assessed per market segment and per channel. And each hospitality organization needs to determine the elements and value that go into its calculation of acquisition costs. It may be beyond the capability of an organization, based upon its existing data, to determine the customer's propensity to buy once again in the future. If so, it may just be appropriate for the organization to assign a value of 1 on all business that it perceives to be one-time purchases only, and assign a value of 2 for all other business that possesses the possibility of being repeated. It may be easiest to determine the average worth of a customer by market segment and then determine which market segments book through which channels.

Once these calculations are complete for every channel through which the organization currently distributes its inventory and other channels under consideration, the organization should select the channels that generate the greatest total customer worth to the organization. *Channel analysis and selection is the sixth fundamental element in the development of revenue management strategy*. It is important to understand that not all channels will produce in the same manner over each date in the course of a year. So the organization must determine which channels will optimize revenues for each specific date of the year and then assign the appropriate levels of inventory to each channel on each date. Remember that the goal is to select those channels that deliver the greatest total customer worth. Managing channels and the inventory loaded in each are the topics of our next chapter.

BOX 7-1

Revenue Management Professional Profile: Shawn McAteer[1]

HOW DID YOU FIRST ENTER THE REVENUE MANAGEMENT FIELD?

I came up through Front Office in the 90's and in those days before we had dedicated Directors of Revenue Management (DRM's) at our hotels, I used to handle this discipline as a Director of Front Office. When our company moved to dedicated DRMs in our hotels it was a natural move for me. I really enjoyed the discipline and was ready to move out of operations.

(continued)

BOX 7-1 *Continued*

WHAT ARE YOUR MAJOR RESPONSIBILITIES IN YOUR CURRENT POSITION?

In the last year I have moved out of Revenue Management and into Brand Performance Support. But when I was the Senior Director of Revenue Management for my brand, my major responsibilities were driving brand-wide strategies and developing the discipline at the property level through my regional team.

HOW DOES REVENUE MANAGEMENT FIT INTO YOUR ORGANIZATION?

It is a big part today and has grown tremendously over the last three years. We have an eight-person corporate team just for our brand, all of our hotels have full-time revenue managers and we have successfully developed several "consolidated" offices across our brand. The discipline in our hotels is one of their top priorities today.

WHAT ARE SOME OF THE GREATEST ISSUES FACING REVENUE MANAGEMENT PROFESSIONALS TODAY?

To me, getting General Managers to understand it, believe in it, and ensure their hotels are executing properly on the discipline.

HOW DO YOU THINK THE REVENUE MANAGEMENT FIELD WILL EVOLVE OVER THE NEXT DECADE?

I think it will continue to grow in its importance. I mainly see the continuation of consolidation of the discipline. It will also gain more prominence in the area of group and catering revenue management.

WHICH COURSES OF STUDY (i.e. FINANCE, SALES & MARKETING, PSYCHOLOGY, etc.) WOULD BE MOST BENEFICIAL TO STUDENTS EAGER TO ENTER THE REVENUE MANAGEMENT FIELD?

Sales and Marketing

WHAT ADVICE CAN YOU GIVE STUDENTS WISHING TO ENTER THIS FIELD OF ENDEAVOR?

I think today this is pretty easy as a student, you just have to understand its importance and raise your hand as someone who is interested.

WHAT IS YOUR NAME, COMPANY NAME, AND TITLE?

Shawn McAteer, Embassy Suites Hotels, Hilton Hotels Corporation, Senior Director of Hotel Performance Support

SUMMARY

Since early days, travelers have called ahead to reserve their room and board for the night. The earliest reservation systems were manual systems. Automated systems were developed that made the reservation process faster and more efficient. The first computerized reservation systems were developed by the airlines. Soon travel agents began requesting the ability to make computerized hotel and car rental reservations as well. Thus was born the first central reservation system. The term *central reservation system* soon gave way to the term *global distribution system* as more and more products and services became available through this channel of distribution.

Today, in addition to the global distribution system, the Internet distribution system exists to serve the needs of individual consumers. These are basically electronic warehouses where a person may conduct one-stop shopping for a variety of hospitality products and services.

There are costs, referred to as distribution costs, involved with selling products and services through these various channels. An organization must assess a channel's production and its distribution cost when determining which channels to provide its inventory. The organization needs to review the total customer worth of guests booking through that channel. And then it should select those channels that generate the greatest total customer worth. *Channel analysis and selection is the sixth fundamental element in the development of revenue management strategy.*

KEY TERMS AND CONCEPTS

The following key terms and concepts were presented in this chapter. Each term and concept is also contained in the Glossary of Terms located at the end of this book:

- airline reservation system (ARS)
- auction site
- average channel contribution
- central reservation office (CRO)
- central reservation system (CRS)
- channel contribution
- channel contribution percentage
- channel production
- channels of distribution
- commission
- distressed inventory
- distribution cost
- electronic distribution
- global distribution system (GDS)
- Internet distribution system (IDS)
- inventory
- load
- merchant model
- meta search engine
- net rate
- niche site
- opaque channel
- portal
- property management system (PMS)
- proprietary
- referral site
- reservation
- retail operator
- retail travel agent
- room night
- special interest website
- switch
- third-party website
- wholesale rate
- wholesale tour operator

DISCUSSION QUESTIONS

1. Which channel do you usually use to make your travel reservations?
2. Have you ever purchased a hospitality product or service on an opaque site or an auction site? If so, describe your experience.
3. What do you foresee for the future of travel agents? Will they disappear or grow stronger in both knowledge and in market share?
4. How do you think the Internet distribution system will evolve in the future?
5. From the school's standpoint, how would you assess your total customer worth as a student?

INTERNET EXERCISES

1. Go to www.quikbook.com and critique the website.
2. Review the websites for TravelAxe, www.travelaxe.com, and Kayak, www.kayak.com.

Critique the sites and state which one you prefer and explain why.

REFERENCE

1. McAteer, Shawn. Interview conducted via email, August 3, 2006.

Royal Palms Presidential Suite.

CHAPTER

Dynamic Value-Based Pricing

Chapter Objectives

The objectives of this chapter are to:

- Examine the components of a value-based approach to pricing
- Understand the impact of the product or service life cycle on price
- Define price transparency, price parity, rate integrity, and price fencing
- Explore the impact of demand on price
- Discuss channel pricing strategies
- Identify issues involved with discounting
- Introduce the secret pricing formula

Special inventory reduction sale . . . Only $19.99 . . . Act now . . . Two-for-one . . . 30% off . . . Buy one, get one free . . . Clearance . . . Half price sale . . . Everyday low prices . . . Double points for booking today . . . Step right up! Everyone is familiar with pitchmen hawking these special deals across radio and television channels. Similar captions are blazoned across the daily newspaper. And now, pop-up ads even invade our channel surfing on the Web.

So why all of this focus on price? Price is one of the four foundations of marketing, known as the *4Ps:* product, price, place, and promotion. **Product** refers to the goods and services presented for sale. **Place** is where a product or service is sold and relates to channels of distribution. And **promotion** means the methods used to market the products or services. Price is the cornerstone that is most often equated with revenue generation. But what exactly is meant by the term *price?* Price is frequently defined as the amount of currency needed to acquire a product or service. However, that definition is missing one key element and that is the concept of value. Remember that marketing seeks to satisfy consumers' needs, wants, and desires and consumers assign value to all products and services that they purchase. Consumers calculate value as their perceived value of a product or service, less the cost of obtaining that product or service. Thus, our definition may be revised to state that **price** is the value that consumers exchange during the acquisition of products and services.

Price/Value Recap

Once again, let's review the concept of price/value that we touched on briefly in Chapter 3. We had stated that perceived value may include material value and quality, benefits received from ownership or usage, and esteem associated with the product or service. Costs to the consumer may include intrinsic costs such as price, and extrinsic costs such as the time it takes to make the purchase and the cost of gasoline it requires to get to and from the store. So the perceived product or service value must be equal to or exceed the total acquisition cost to produce total value to the consumer.

$$\text{Total Customer Value} = \text{Perceived Product or Service Value} - \text{Total Acquisition Cost}$$

Total customer value is a major determinant in the establishment of pricing strategies. An organization needs to understand its customers and their motivation for making purchasing decisions. It should analyze customer purchasing behavior by market segment and determine the discriminating elements of price that are unique to each segment. For example, are their leisure transient customers sensitive to price? First, the organization could look at its broad base of leisure customers. Perhaps the organization is an upscale golf resort. In this case, there is a high probability that their leisure transient guests are less sensitive to price than customers of a midscale resort. However, some subsegments of their leisure transient market, such as senior citizens, may be a bit more price sensitive than the general population of their overall leisure transient market segment. This once again underscores the importance of organizations being able to drill down to understand each layer of each market segment. They must learn how their customers perceive and react to price. The more an organization understands its current and potential customers, the better it will be able to develop products and services matching its customers' price/value perceptions.

Visualize the price/value relationship as a teeter-totter as depicted in Figure 8–1. As price increases, value goes down. As price decreases, value goes up. This is what occurs for the average product or service. Naturally, there are some exceptions to this example. For example, with luxury items, a reduction in price is sometimes equated by the consumer with a reduction in quality and thus value actually decreases with price. Upscale organizations often practice a technique referred to as **prestige pricing**. The goal of a prestige pricing strategy is to use high price to elevate the positioning of an organization's products and services and increase the perceived value to the consumer. However, in most other cases, the price/value relationship acts like a teeter-totter, with its corresponding impact upon demand.

A Value-Based Approach to Pricing

The organization should develop a customer-centric approach to pricing. In other words, it should establish pricing strategies that are centered upon the perceptions and buying behaviors of its customers rather than focused solely upon the attributes of its

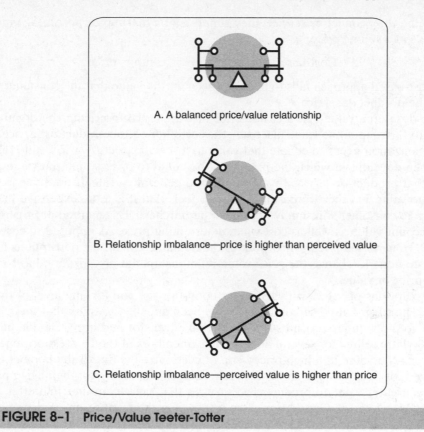

A. A balanced price/value relationship

B. Relationship imbalance—price is higher than perceived value

C. Relationship imbalance—perceived value is higher than price

FIGURE 8–1   Price/Value Teeter-Totter

products and services. Traditionally, many firms utilized a cost-based, or cost-plus, approach to setting price. This meant that they first determined the cost of resources that went into creating a product or service, such as materials, land, labor, and capital. Some costs were fixed, such as rent (the amount paid will remain the same regardless of the quantity of products or services sold), while other costs were variable, such as wages. **Total cost** is calculated by adding together fixed and variable costs:

$$\text{Fixed Costs} + \text{Variable Costs} = \text{Total Cost or FC} + \text{VC} = \text{TC}$$

On a daily basis, hospitality managers focus more on variable costs than on fixed costs. Variable costs fluctuate greatly with the volume of demand. Managers must understand demand and continually improve their forecasts to better control their variable costs. Anticipated volume will play a significant role in determining purchasing and labor levels for the organization. For example, the number of wait staff needed at the golf resort clubhouse varies based upon the season, day of the week, and time of the day. The number of entrees ordered is a variable cost in producing a banquet. The number of guests is a variable cost in planning a wedding. Every event planned at the clubhouse will involve both fixed and variable costs. Under the **cost-based method of pricing**, once the organization has calculated the overall cost of producing the product or service, they simply add a markup or percentage increase to arrive at a selling price.

$$\text{Cost-based pricing: Cost} + \text{markup} = \text{price}$$

This cost-based approach fails to take into account the value that the consumer places upon the product or service.

To develop a value-based customer-centric approach to pricing, the organization needs to focus upon the value placed by the customer on the product or service. Next, the organization needs to equate that value to a specific price. A price/value relationship then develops in which the price must be equal to or less than the value placed upon that product or service by a consumer to generate a sale. If the price is higher than the value, in other words, the consumer feels that it is more expensive than it is worth, the consumer will simply not make the purchase. This method of pricing takes into account value as well as cost when determining price. As opposed to cost-based pricing, **value-based pricing** incorporates the human element, the perceptions held by the customers. To change the price/value relationship, the organization has to adjust either price or value.

Perceptions of value will vary based upon the age and income level of the consumer. The silver-haired seniors would have been appalled to think that their 10 cent cup of coffee with cream and sugar would have transformed into a double hazelnut espresso latte selling for several dollars. Many members of the Depression generation fail to see the value in a high-priced cup of customized coffee. Baby boomers, being squeezed for time between caring for their children and caring for their aging parents, assign a greater value to products and services that save them time and offer convenience. Members of Generation X may place greater value on environmentally friendly products and services. The echo boomers place value on the latest, greatest innovation in technology. And the youngest millennials place value on products and services in demand by their friends. Consumers within each generational market often place value on products and services based on value assessments attributed to others, including their friends and family.

Income also plays a significant role in determining value. The value an individual places on a product or service will change with income. As income level rises, the percentage cost spent on the basic necessities also changes. For example, a recent college graduate may spend $250 a month on food, which equates to $3,000 per year. If his or her starting salary following graduation is $30,000, food purchases represent 10 percent of his or her annual income. As annual income increases, the *percentage* spent on food will actually decrease in most cases. For example, at an annual salary of $60,000, those same annual food expenditures would only represent 5 percent of the individual's annual salary.

It is common practice for hospitality organizations to build in special amenities to add value to their products and services in an effort to command higher prices. For example, the golf resort may include one free round of golf with every seven-night stay at the hotel. The hospitality provider needs to focus on the consumer's perception of value rather than focusing primarily on price. Remember that one element in the determination of value is the benefit that the consumer believes he or she will receive from making the purchase. Salespeople become quite skilled in selling benefits along with features. A benefit of golf club membership may be the use of the clubhouse. And the golf resort may also emphasize the benefit of having banquet and meeting space available to both groups and individuals. Each organization must very carefully analyze the elements that add up to value for each product and service it offers. Frequently a value analysis will highlight the fact that certain components of an organization's products or services only add to cost and do not add value to the consumer. For example, if no one uses one of the bathroom amenities offered in a hotel room, perhaps the hotel should consider eliminating that item or changing its mix of amenities.

The increasing demand for customized products and services is a direct offshoot of consumers' need to obtain value in their purchases. They want *what* they want, *when* they want it, and *where* they want it, and they are willing to pay for the privilege of obtaining it their way. One method of providing value to customers is in the creation of special packages, which we previously referred to as bundling. Bundling of products and services enables an organization to combine various elements to increase the overall value of the purchase. For example, an afternoon golf foursome package could be developed, including greens fees, golf cart, club rental, and one round of beverages at the clubhouse. It would be offered at an attractive price as the intent of the package is to shift demand from the busier mornings to the slower afternoons. Since the final bundle is sold for one set price, the individual component prices are opaque to the consumer. However, it is important that the total price approximately equates to the value the consumer places upon the bundle. Priced too high, the package won't sell. Priced too low, the organization is leaving money on the table.

In addition to continually seeking new ways to bundle components to create new packages, organizations must continually scan the external environment to be alert to emerging consumer trends. Consumers' perception of value is continually shifting. Early trend spotting by an organization may often bring it a competitive advantage if it capitalizes on the trend by creating new products and services. And it also pays to be observant of the decline of trends and to discount items slipping out of demand before they totally lose their value. So setting prices is a dynamic process, continually in motion. As factors impacting demand shift and change, prices must also be adjusted to meet the changing demands of consumers. *Thus dynamic value-based pricing becomes our seventh fundamental element in the development of revenue management strategy.*

Product or Service Life Cycle

Another element in establishing price rests upon the product's or service's life cycle. The first phase in the cycle is referred to as the **introductory stage**. This is when the product or service is brand new and only the most adventurous consumers are poised to purchase. An example of this would be the first brave souls who hit the slopes to try snowboarding. Consumers who strive to be the first to try any new product or service are referred to as **early adopters**. They want the newest, fastest, coolest product on the market. And they are willing to pay a higher price to be the first person on their block to buy one. Often products and services are priced artificially high during their introduction to capture these early adopters. Conversely, many hospitality products and services are not innovative new products but are rather new facilities in new locations. Often these new facilities will open with a special reduced rate to induce trial. The term **induce trial** means to entice customers to try out new products or services.

Two pricing strategies often used in the introductory stage are **market penetration** and **market skimming**. Most organizations leap into their new markets with a market penetration approach. They desire to steal existing business from their competitors. In this case, the organization sets its price lower than its competitors in an effort to create a better price/value perception in the minds of consumers and lure the consumers away from the competition. These lower prices are only temporary. Once the organization has captured a healthy market share, it will adjust price to displace lower rated business with higher paying customers. These lower introductory prices also have the effect of dissuading other potential entrants into the market. The second pricing strategy often used in the introductory phase is one of market skimming. An organization using a market skimming approach would set prices high to create the perception of value and position the product or service higher in the minds of consumers. They would use this high price/value perception to capture, or skim, the top-paying customers from their competitors.

Following the introductory phase, the product or service enters a period of growth. During the **growth stage**, volume sold increases, which in turn generates economies of scale in production. **Economies of scale** is an economic concept that means the more of a product or service that is produced, the lower its per unit cost of production. So as costs fall, so do prices. An example is the cost of cell phones. As sales increased, prices came down. When college students were in high school, cell phones were more expensive and contained less features than they do today.

In the product or service life cycle, the **mature stage** follows the growth stage. This is the time when nearly every consumer has purchased the product or service and it is no longer considered to be a hot item. Telephone voice mail is an example of a service that has entered the mature stage. Skiing is a mature recreational activity. Once a product reaches the mature stage, producers either need to lower the price or add more features to generate additional sales or stimulate interest from new market segments. For certain generations, cell phones have entered the mature stage. Cell phone manufacturers added new features such as digital cameras and Internet connectivity in an effort to generate new and additional demand.

The final stage in the product or service life cycle is decline. In the **decline stage**, sales of the product or service are flat or falling. Both volume and prices continue to fall. Newer products or services are competing directly for customers. Unchecked decline will ultimately lead to the death of a product or service. The producer or provider needs to either innovate or evaporate. An example of this is the drive-in movie theater. Drive-ins have fallen in popularity and number over the past three decades. However, due to innovative marketing, repackaging, and repositioning of the concept, drive-in movies are experiencing a bit of resurgence in some areas of the country.

Customer Loyalty and Brand Equity

There are several other elements to address when considering adopting a customer-centric approach to pricing. The first to consider is customer loyalty and repeat business. Frequent customer programs are popular in all facets of the hospitality industry. Pricing is a key factor in attracting membership. **Loyalty program** members are rewarded either by receiving reduced rates or increased value, such as added amenities. Some programs provide both reduced rates and added amenities. In addition, most programs contain a point reward system for each purchase. Guests are eligible for prizes or free travel components after accumulating a certain number of points. It is important to consider the impact of these loyalty programs when developing pricing strategies. For there are costs involved and lost revenue to consider. Some airlines and hotels disallow the receiving of points for travel booked through the merchant models. This is an attempt to entice the frequent flier or guest to book directly with the airline or hotel, thus saving the cost of commissions. Organizations need to continually monitor and assess the total worth of these frequent customer segments.

Another element to consider is the value of a brand in establishing price. **Brand equity** is the value generated by a brand. The hospitality industry is comprised of both branded and unbranded products and services. The value of the brand is a key component in price and product positioning. Consumers often equate expectations to brand-named products or services they have purchased or experienced. If price is set above expectation, the value of the purchase to the consumer will fall. If the price is set below expectation, one of two scenarios may occur. In the first, the consumer feels that he or she is getting a deal and will make the purchase. In the second, the price signals an alert that the quality of the product or service may not be up to normal expectations for the brand. In this scenario, the customer will either hesitate or decline to make the purchase at all. Brand loyalty has long been a major determinant in an organization's

Courtesy of Destination Hotels & Resorts.

Ocean Hammock Resort Guest Room.

marketing and pricing strategies. Consumers who are loyal to a brand are often less sensitive to small changes in price. Branded organizations should try to capitalize on brand equity whenever possible.

Internal Price/Value Assessment

Now in tandem with understanding its customers' value perception of its products and services, an organization should also perform an internal assessment of price/value. What value does the organization place on each of its products and services? Returning to our resort example, how would the organization value its golf course, its hotel rooms, and its food and beverage service? Members of the organization must ask themselves how much they would be willing to pay for these products and services. Sometimes they cannot answer this question as they have not experienced the product or service personally. How can an organization expect its members to sell and service the unknown? Every manager should sample every product and service from spending a night in the room, to eating in the restaurant, to getting a massage. Value should then be assessed to each experience. Having members of the organization determine price/value levels for each product and service serves as a sort of baseline, or barometer, in determining value.

Keep in mind that it is the customer's perception of value that should be considered when making final pricing decisions. What may appear outrageously expensive to an employee of a resort may actually be perceived as having tremendous value by the guest. Experiencing the products and services of the establishment will also be of tremendous help in creating employee pride in the property. This sense of pride will carry through in their actions and attitudes, which will also positively impact the guest's perception of value.

The organization should return to objectively assess where each of its current market segments values its products and services. Guests who purchase regardless of price, may value the products and services of the organization higher than the organization's own members. Conversely, guests who only purchase when offered substantial cost savings in the form of discounts or incentives may value the products and services of the organization beneath the value set by its members. Understanding the customer assessment of value placed above or below the baseline will assist the organization in determining price strategies per segment.

The organization should return to its internal SWOT analysis. What are its strengths? If our golf resort is rated number one in the region, is this reflected in our greens fees? Conversely, if the golf carts lack global positioning systems (GPS), are rates set more moderately than neighboring courses that do provide carts containing GPS equipment? The organization should also consider its core competencies and ask whether it is maximizing all opportunities to sell its best products and services. Does the organization possess a competitive advantage or distinctive advantage? If so, have all opportunities for developing products and services capitalizing on these advantages been taken? And have prices for these products and services been set accordingly?

Once the organization reviews pricing opportunities and challenges presented by its internal SWOT analysis, it should return to review the SWOT analyses of its competitive set. What are their strengths and weaknesses? How does the organization's prices compare with those of its competitors? Do we appear to be too high in some cases, and too low in others? How do we know?

Price Transparency

Price transparency is defined as the ability to observe prices. The Internet has made price transparency a feature of all products and services offered online. The availability and transparency of prices across numerous channels has enabled hospitality organizations to obtain a better overall picture of the pricing strategies of their competitors. Continually monitoring the prices of competitors and watching for trends and patterns will assist an organization become more adept in setting its own pricing policies and strategies as well. Numerous tools and reports are available to assist organizations in capturing competitive rate information.

However, price transparency has also enabled the customer to assess an organization's prices across various channels and against its competitors. Consumers dislike being charged different prices for the same products or services depending on how they arrived at their purchase, in other words which channel they used. They resent the need to have to shop around to find the best price. Consumers usually understand setting different prices based upon the level of demand. But they do not understand obtaining different prices from one website over the other. The fact that there are different costs associated with each channel is simply not their concern. They do not assess value to the distribution costs. This realization has led hospitality organizations to the implementation of price parity. **Price parity** is defined as the practice of maintaining consistent prices across all channels of distribution. This reduces customer dissatisfaction. Customer dissatisfaction usually translates into an erosion of market share as consumers switch their purchases to other competitors. In addition to price parity, many organizations have adopted a **best-rate guarantee program**. If a consumer can find a better price than the one posted on the organization's website, the organization will match that price. This is the variation on the familiar refrain often heard from car dealers, "if you can find a better price anywhere, we will meet or beat that deal."

A related concept is that of rate integrity. The term *honest price* often applies here. **Rate integrity** may be defined as the maintenance of consistent prices for similar purchase conditions. A customer calling in for a single ocean-view room for Friday night would receive the same price quote whether he or she called the hotel or the central reservation system. One of the greatest complaints of airline passengers used to be the change in price from one moment to the next when telephoning for reservations via the call center. In the 1980s, it was possible to obtain five different fare quotes from five different agents in a single business day. Maintaining rate integrity seeks to avoid this form of customer dissatisfaction.

Price Positioning

Thinking about its competitors next leads the organization into assessing its current price positioning. Where does the organization's prices for each product and service fall in comparison to its competitors? Returning to our resort example, the resort may wish to determine where its prices should be set on products and services that are superior or inferior to its competition. An example would be membership in the clubhouse. If the golf course is truly the best in the region, services available in the clubhouse should be of matching quality. If that is the case, the resort may want to consider being the price leader in the region for their services. A **price leader** is defined as an organization that leads the market in price. **Price leadership** applies to the organization setting the highest rates, while **discount price leadership** applies to an organization setting the lowest rates. Price leadership alone is not always the goal. The organization should try to capitalize on its greatest strengths by ensuring the appropriate price/value is perceived by the customer. If the services in the clubhouse are not of the same level as the course, they should either be improved or their price should be adjusted to more closely match the price/value perception set by club members.

Visualizing how customers perceive an organization as compared to its competitors is best done through the use of a **perceptual positioning map**. We have developed the following map in Figure 8–2 to illustrate the position of the Peachwood Hotel & Marina.

This positioning map illustrates the price/value relationship of several properties within the competitive set defined by the Peachwood Hotel & Marina. The revenue manager should place calls to shop the local competitors, solicit the assistance of a travel agent, check online channels, or subscribe to third-party competitive intelligence reports to determine the pricing strategy that each competitor is deploying over a certain set of dates. Price is then plotted on the vertical or Y axis. We know that guests value products and services differently. The revenue manager should determine where different segments of guests value each competitor's products and services. So one positioning map could be developed for business travelers and another one developed for leisure travelers. The value (or perceived quality) rating,

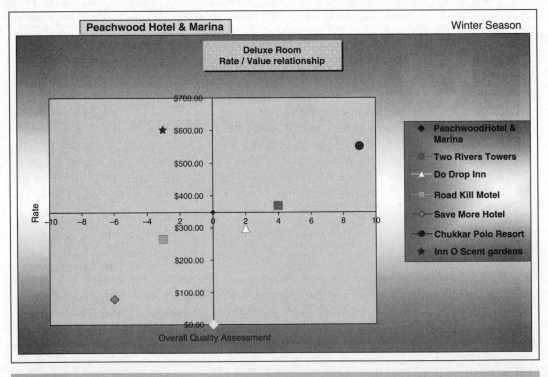

FIGURE 8–2 Perceptual Positioning Map for the Peachwood Hotel & Marina

relative to the Peachwood Hotel & Marina, of each competitor is then plotted on the horizontal or X axis. In Figure 8–2, the Peachwood Hotel & Marina is plotted in the intersection of the two axes. The Chukkar Polo Resort is deemed to be of higher quality by this market segment than the Peachwood and is also more expensive, while the Save More Hotel is considered to possess less desirable attributes and is priced under the Peachwood property.

Thus each property is properly positioned based upon perceived price and quality relative to the other competitors on the map. The Inn O Scent Gardens is deemed to be of lesser quality but is priced higher in relation to the Peachwood. This may mean that either the Inn O Scent Gardens is priced too high or the Peachwood Hotel & Marina is priced too low. It could also mean that the market segment in question values the Inn O Scent Gardens higher than it is perceived by the Peachwood. Or the Inn O Scent is nearly sold out over the time period and wishes to fill its last remaining rooms with higher-rated business. What could you assume about the positioning of the other properties?

Development of a perceptual positioning map will help an organization to visualize where it stands in the mind of the consumer. That position may or may not jive with the internal perceptions of the organization. When customer and internal perceptions diverge, the organization must either change the physical product or service to match the consumers' need, adjust price, or reposition the product or service. The map may highlight opportunities to capture higher rates or the need to reposition. **Repositioning** of price or product may also be needed to target and attract new consumers.

Competition also helps to regulate the marketplace. If one supplier raises the price of his or her products or service, a buyer may choose to purchase from a lower-priced supplier. Many businesses today require a minimum of three price bids, one each from three separate vendors, before entering into a purchase agreement. So price may be the major determinant for purchasing. Competition serves as a gauge, and businesses must continually monitor the temperature of both the consumers and their other competitors when establishing price.

The organization must also understand how other organizations react to competitive changes in price. Historically, airlines often engaged in fare wars to retain current customers while attempting to capture additional market share. One airline would issue a statement announcing major reductions in fares, and two days later the other carriers would follow suit. The customer appears to be the victor in the fare war, but that victory is fleeting. Soon afterward, the airlines will raise prices, often higher than the levels established before the fare war began. Many equate this response to dieting. Each time, a person loses weight on a diet for a while. However, when the diet ends, more weight creeps back on than the amount that the person carried before the diet. Continually entering into price wars may have a similar inflationary effect upon market prices.

Some competitors will refuse to play along in a price war, resulting in the erosion of previously friendly competitive relationships. It is critical for the organization to understand the impact that changing price will have on both its customers and its competitors. Will an increase in price drive away business? Will an increase in price be matched by the competition? Or will the competition use an increase in price to emphasize price/value comparisons in an effort to capture the organization's customers.

What happens when the organization lowers prices? Will customers' price/value perception change? Will consumers reduce the value they place on the product or service, making it difficult or impossible to raise price at a point in the future? Or will the reduction in price lead them to increase the volume of their purchases? In other words, does value lead to volume? Will the competitors also reduce price? Will these matching discounts lead to a general devaluation of the overall market?

How does the organization react to competitors' changes in price? Does it immediately react to match the increase or decrease in price? Do knee-jerk reactions occur due to the fear of the loss of market share? All too often, organizations feel pressured to keep step with their competitors when it comes to establishing price. This is a mistake. First, this follow-the-leader mentality assigns too much credit to the competition. Is their strategic pricing plan so much better than ours? Are they really that much smarter than us? Also, it assumes that customers are as obsessed with competitive pricing as are the competitors. Do customers really know when a competitor changes its prices? Do consumers perform price comparisons every day, every week, or every month? Or do consumers only comparison shop just before they are planning on making a purchase? These are all factors to consider when assessing competitive pricing. If an organization has developed and implemented a well-conceived strategic pricing plan, it should have little to fear from the minor pricing fluctuations of its competitors.

So now that an organization understands the value of its own products and services, the prices and value of the products and services of its competitors, the motivations and value perceptions of its different customer segments, it is able to establish its pricing strategy, right? Not yet. First the organization needs to take a look at

Courtesy of Destination Hotels & Resorts.

Family on Beach.

demand. The organization needs to carefully analyze its demand forecast. Which dates are hot, and which are not? How is the booking pace? Ahead or behind last year at this time? What special events and demand generators will impact demand?

The Impact of Demand on Price

Demand is a function of price and price is sometimes a determinant of demand. An organization uses price to control demand, direct demand, influence demand, and create demand. An important distinction needs to be made here and that is that price does not create demand for the market, but it may create demand for one organization's products and services over another at a specific point in time. We will return to this concept in more detail when we discuss discounting. Once an organization understands the demand for its products and services in the marketplace, it is able to decide how to use price to capture that demand.

First let's examine how some of the intelligence gathered to create the demand forecast may be useful in the establishment of price. To some hospitality providers, denial and regret reports are important in setting pricing strategies. Denials occur when a consumer tries to purchase a product or service but none is available. Denial reports show us how much more business we could have captured if we had additional capacity or inventory. Since there was more demand than supply, we need to assess whether our rates were too low for that time period. Regret reports may highlight when and where our prices are set too high. Remember that a regret occurs when a customer inquires about a product or service but fails to make a purchase. Regrets often indicate an imbalance in the price/value relationship. In most cases, the consumer considers the price to be too high. However, in other cases the guest is calling the reservation line for other reasons. For example, he or she may have called just to get an idea of the property's rate range for future vacation planning. So when rate resistance is obvious, it should be recorded to aid in forecasting and to refine tactical revenue management decisions.

Lost business reports help an organization evaluate the appropriateness of its pricing strategies. Lost business reports can also highlight opportunities for capturing more business by adjusting rates. If a large portion of the business is lost due to facilities rather than price, then the organization needs to reassess its positioning and customer perception of price/value. This may prompt the organization to improve its products or services rather than adjusting price. Or, it may lead the organization to adjust prices to better meet customer price/value perception.

Pricing strategies revolving around date-specific demand variations, including major events and holidays, usually take a lot of coordination both internally and externally. Organizations often employ promotional pricing strategies to generate demand. **Promotional pricing** may be defined as a pricing strategy established to increase capture of date-specific demand. Some events generate excess demand, in which case organizations increase their prices to capture the increased revenue potential. However, there is a fine line between pricing for demand and **price gouging**. Some hotels in the south substantially raised their rates during the days immediately following Hurricane Katrina. This was considered to be price gouging, which is illegal. So remember that there are limits and ethical consequences to taking advantage of rate opportunities. The opportunity and appropriateness for potential revenue generation must be assessed for each individual event. Also displacement analyses may be needed to determine the cost of displacing other group and transient business interested in those same dates. It is critical to examine the price positioning of the competitors for those dates too. Have they increased their rates? Applied restrictions? What impact will the competitors' rates have on the organization during that time period?

Next, the organization needs to take a closer look at booking pace and what it represents regarding demand. Are we ahead of pace, meaning that we have booked more business for a select future period than this time last year? Or are we behind pace, meaning the demand for our products and services was greater at this time last year? Booking pace is a critical element in establishing and adjusting price. As booking pace increases, restrictions may need to be placed on prices and inventory. Continual monitoring of booking pace is crucial to maximizing revenue opportunities.

Group and transient arrival and departure patterns help highlight the dates of peak transaction volume. An organization should consider adding a premium to transactions occurring on peak dates. Stay patterns will also highlight pricing opportunities. If Wednesdays typically sell out, then discounting business on Wednesdays early well in advance of arrival represents unnecessary loss of revenue. Price may be used to help change the stay pattern by increasing or decreasing the length of stay. Now that an organization understands its own products and services, the products and services of its competitors, the motivations and value perceptions of its different customer segments, and its forecasted demand, it is able to establish its pricing strategy, right? Once again, the answer is not yet.

The organization must also look at the price elasticity of demand. It needs to determine the price elasticity of each product and service it sells by market segment and subsegment. In general, business travelers are considered to be less sensitive to changes in price than are leisure travelers. Generally people are more sensitive to price when they must pay for a product or service out of their own pocket. If a business traveler is given a $75 limit on meal per diem, does a dollar or two difference on the price of a dinner really have any impact on this traveler's decision to eat in the restaurant? Business travelers sometimes opt for a fast-food lunch in order to save time or money. They may also receive a continental breakfast complimentarily from the hotel. So often, business travelers have a substantial dollar allotment to spend on dinner. There is a sort of "use it or lose it" mentality. As long as a dinner's price is in alignment with a traveler's value perception and also remains within his or her per diem allowance, that traveler will give little additional thought to the actual price of the dinner. Therefore a slight increase in price will have no impact upon its purchase. Price and value must converge. They must also move in concert with each other. If a gap occurs between price and perceived value, sales will soon begin to suffer.

Convenience and time pressure also impact sensitivity to price. A traveler arriving after midnight due to a delayed flight will be more concerned with the availability of a hotel room than its price. However, a salesperson traveling by automobile arriving in town at midday may shop for alternatives if the hotel's price seems too high.

Remember that the availability of substitutes also has an impact upon the elasticity of demand. A variety of substitutes are available, for example, in the fast food industry. If Wendy's line is too long, a consumer may simply drive over to McDonald's. However, the availability of substitutes changes based upon the spatial elements of time and location. A skier arriving at the slope has no choice but to purchase a lift ticket at the going price if he or she wishes to ski the mountain that day at that destination. There is no other substitute available at that location at that moment. However, when planning for a ski vacation, the skier is more price sensitive and may shop alternative lift prices at competing resorts. This again addresses the importance of knowing the booking pace per segment. Last-minute purchases are typically less price sensitive than advanced purchases. However, there is a growing population of opportunistic travelers who prefer to wait until the last minute to make arrangements for leisure travel. They may not have a destination in mind and are flexible in their travel times. They are therefore able to take advantage of special deals offered by those travel providers willing to discount rather than leave perishable inventory go unsold. These special deals often contain restrictions and steep penalties for changes or cancellation. By placing severe restrictions on these offers, travel suppliers create a barrier, or fence, around these uniquely flexible travelers. In most cases, their regular travelers will not attempt to jump this fence, but will rather adhere to their normal booking habits. This reduces the chance of revenue loss to the provider. The concept of a customer leaving a higher-rated market segment to jump over a fence and gobble up lower-priced products or services offered by the same provider to other lower-rated market segments is referred to as **cannibalization**.

Another factor to consider is the price relative to total purchase expenditures. In our ski example, the lift ticket may represent 75 percent of the total expenditure to a day skier. The other 25 percent may be made up of equipment rental, food and beverage purchases, and fuel consumption to reach the resort. However, lift tickets may represent the opposite percentage of total expenditure on a week-long ski vacation. The ski passes may represent just 25 percent of the total expenditure. The remaining 75 percent would be made up of airfare, hotel accommodations, food and beverage purchases, shopping, and other transportation costs such as shuttle service. In this case, the price of the ski passes alone would not determine purchase. At the conclusion of each transaction, a consumer evaluates the value of the overall experience.

One other element impacts the price elasticity of demand. And that is the notion of fairness. The hospitality industry once believed that consumers were not sensitive to the price that they paid for long-distance telephone service. After all, everyone called home once they reached their destination right? Boy, was the industry ever wrong! They quickly found out that consumers were indeed sensitive to the price that they paid to phone home. Many hotels had established a policy of charging a surcharge to connect the guest to the long-distance carrier. The hotel also assessed per-minute charges on all long-distance calls. Some hotels even charged a small flat rate, perhaps 50 cents, for all local calls. Immediately guests began to complain and complain loudly. For it was not so much that they were being charged a fee to phone home, it was that they considered the fees charged to be outrageous. The price/value teeter-totter had hit bottom! The price so greatly exceeded the guests' perception of value that they resisted. Business and leisure travelers alike began to choke the check-out desks at 6 A.M., demanding adjustments be made to their bills. Rather than being a revenue generator, these new telephone charges became expense generators in terms of the labor cost incurred at the front desk and in accounting for adjusting these charges off guests' folios. But the greatest potential expense was standing right there in front of the clerks and that was the threatened future loss of business. Since telephone surcharges so quickly became a customer dissatisfier, most hotels adjusted or eliminated these charges. Today's hotel guest often eliminates the possibility of even incurring any long-distance call or access charges entirely by utilizing his or her cell phone to call home or the office.

Channel Pricing Strategies

Remember that *where* a consumer buys is often as important as *what* they buy. An organization needs to determine the channels through which its existing and targeted customers purchase its products and services. Pricing strategies must be determined for each customer/channel combination, as well in a customer-centric approach. For example, perhaps an organization receives 10 percent of its leisure business through one of the merchant models such as Travelocity. Seven percent of this business is represented by families, while the remaining 3 percent is generated by couples and individual travelers. The organization will need to determine how it will set different prices for families and couples booking through this same channel. As previously mentioned, setting up rules and restrictions regarding the eligibility of an individual to purchase products and services at a specific price is known as **price fencing**. **Price fences** are constructed to prohibit customers from leaping from one segment to another in an attempt to receive a lower rate. Examples of price fences include requiring advance reservations or requiring nonrefundable advanced deposits. In contrast to our previous example, this precludes the last-minute booker from receiving the same low rate as someone who books in advance. Reduction in rate is one of the primary motivators of early-booking customers. They may also want to insure availability by booking in advance. If the price fence were torn down, the rate-reduction incentive would be eliminated and some guests would cease booking in advance. Others who wished to ensure the availability of the product would continually check availability and only book when it was apparent that inventory would soon run out. Both actions would have a detrimental impact on the organization's ability to accurately forecast demand.

Pricing strategies also have an impact upon an organization's travel partners. Rising airfares are decreasing the affordability of remote locations or those requiring multiple travel segments to reach. So the higher cost to fly to these destinations is having a direct impact on hotels, restaurants, meeting facilities, and transportation providers located there. Hospitality providers must also consider the implications that their pricing decisions may have on their suppliers. Again, the higher cost to fly to remote destinations will add to food cost and will result in higher menu prices. The hospitality industry is one of the most interdependent of all industries, as segments rely upon each other for business. For example, a business traveler may take a cab to the airport, jump on a airplane, grab a shuttle to the hotel, check into the hotel, go for a walk and do some shopping, get a bite to eat, and catch a movie. If the flight is cancelled, all other providers may lose their revenue opportunities from that traveler for the day.

There also exists a condition known as the **multiplier effect**. For every dollar that a traveler spends in direct costs to reach a destination, some multiple of that amount will be spent on total products and services during that traveler's visit. For example, a business traveler may spend $500 on transportation to reach his or her destination. Once there, he or she spends an additional $800 on hotel accommodations, $400 on food and beverage purchases, $100 on ground transportation costs, $100 on entertainment, and $100 on gifts and souvenirs. These additional expenditures add up to $1,500. The total cost for the trip to the traveler is $2,000. Convention and visitors bureaus and resort associations use the multiplier effect to calculate the total value of tourism to a destination.

The multiplier effect may also be applied to a single organization. The organization should determine how much ancillary revenue a customer generates per dollar of primary revenue. Next, it should determine opportunities for increasing the amount of ancillary revenue spent per customer. Some organizations use the term **total spend** to define the amount of primary and ancillary revenue that is spent per customer. The customers representing the highest total spend are the most desirable.

To increase the amount of total spend, organizations need to create new and additional opportunities for the guest to make a purchase. Gift shops, room service, and spa services are all great examples of services added to generate ancillary revenues. The organizations need to determine how they will sell these services to their guests. **Merchandising** is the strategic selling and packaging of products and services. Merchandising is a key element in an organization's overall marketing plan. For example, Disney began developing merchandising strategies for its *Pirates of the Caribbean* sequel prior to the movie going into production. A "pirates" attraction was constructed in Walt Disney World. The actors attended a grand opening celebration before the actual movie premiere. "Pirates" toys, clothing, costumes, and other merchandise went into production. Once the movie ended its first run in theatres, it was broadcast on pay-per-view. After that, it appeared on network television and cable stations. And eventually, it was released in VHS and DVD format. And since the movie broke all ticket sales records at the box office, Disney was assured of capturing a significant stream of ancillary revenue from their merchandising efforts as well. The movie series was becoming so successful that a 'three-quel' was quickly ordered for development.

Additional revenue streams may also be developed by partnering with other hospitality providers. For example, hotels capture additional revenue by selling discounted tickets to local theme parks to their guests. The hotels buy the tickets at wholesale rates and resell them at higher retail rates to their in-house guests. The retail ticket price at the hotel is set less than the price of admission at the gate, so the customer perceives a good price value.

Discounting

This leads us to the subject of discounting. When people first heard the terms *yield* and *revenue management*, their first thoughts went to the subject of discounted rates. They mistakenly thought that yield or revenue management was just about learning when to offer discounted rates. At this point in your study, it is obvious that offering discounts is just one element in establishing pricing strategies. For our purposes, we define **discounting** as the practice of offering special reductions in price. Learning when and how to apply discounts is a key principle in optimizing revenues.

The primary reasons that hospitality organizations offer discounted prices are usually based on time and volume. Destinations offer substantial discounts to attract business in the off-season. Restaurants offer early-bird discounts to senior citizens in an attempt to shift demand to a slower time. Hotels offer volume discounts to corporations based upon the number of rooms contracted. While discounts can help shift demand, discounting alone does not create demand within a market. Demand for the market already exists. Discounting usually only shifts demand from one competitor to another. Discount offers are quickly copied by competitors. It becomes a battle for the cheapest business. Each organization should establish its discount policies based on demand per segment, per date, and per product or service. No blanket policy should be implemented, simply discounting across the board. While this may be the easiest road to take, particularly when faced with little to no demand in weak periods, it is not the right road to take as it fails to optimize revenues.

Organizations with more sophisticated revenue management systems are aware of the pitfalls of discounting. One of the major mistakes made by hospitality providers is that they enter into volume agreements with no allowances made for demand forecasting. For example, a hotel agrees to provide 1000 rooms to Company B over the course of the year at a reduced rate of $100. In the off-season, the hotel's best available rate to corporate travelers is $110, so the Company B traveler pays $100 and saves $10 on the rate. The cost to operate a room is $40. So the hotel is making $60 profit on the rooms booked by Company B and $70 on the rooms of the other transient guests. Now, in the peak season, the hotel's corporate rate is $225. So the hotel is making a profit of $185 on a room booked by a corporate traveler. However, Company B is only paying $100. So the profit on the rooms booked by Company B is still just $60. The hotel is actually losing $125 per night in potential profit during peak season on each room booked by Company B. Yes, but remember that Company B is guaranteeing the hotel 1,000 room nights over the course of the year. That must be worth something, right? Yes, but how much is it worth? And is it worth continuing this practice of offering discounts regardless of demand?

Best Available Rates

This dilemma is being addressed by more and more hotels as the recovery from the slow-down of 2001 puts additional pressure on demand. A few of the major hotel operators believe that they have arrived at a solution, which they refer to as best available rates. A **best available rate** may be defined as the lowest available rate per room available to the general public on a given night. In a best available rate agreement, the hotel agrees to provide Company B with a set percentage discount off the best available rate that it can offer per night based on demand. In return, Company B agrees to contract with the hotel for 1,000 rooms in annual production. The rate for each of these rooms will depend entirely upon the demand for rooms each evening. How would best available rates apply to our previous example? Company B would probably receive a rate in the $100 range in the off-season if the hotel offered preferred corporate clients a 10 percent discount off of their best available transient corporate rates. But in the peak season, Company B would most likely be receiving a rate of $202.50, which would be 10 percent off the best available corporate transient rate (in the example $225). This is a simplified example based only upon seasonality. In reality, the rate would vary each day for each type of available room. Using best available rates ensures that the hotel captures the optimal amount of revenue and that the preferred corporate client receives the best rate available.

When negotiating contracts, hotel providers also need to take into consideration which inventory is available at the best available rate. Does Company B receive 'run of house' based upon its agreement. **Run of house** simply means that the best available rates will be available for all room types. Another element of a contractual hotel room arrangement is the concept of **last available room**. If a contract states availability is based upon 'last available room' that means if a traveler from Company B shows up at the last minute wanting to purchase the last remaining room in inventory, he or she would be able to occupy that room at the established negotiated rate. Without this clause in the contract, an organization may decide to permit only the sales of the then current, and normally higher, best available rate as inventory nears depletion.

A related concept here is holding the best products for the organization's best customers. Sometimes this means saving the best for last. Booking pace is a key element in determining when to continue to hold and when to sell better products at a lower rate. For example, hotels traditionally hold their best suites for their highest paying customers. Last-minute travelers are typically less price sensitive and are willing to pay higher rates than early booking travelers. If the best inventory is available at the highest rate, they will usually accept the situation. They often assess a high price/value to the experience too as the inventory was upgraded along with price. In the past, hospitality organizations often offered discounts for those people who booked out the furthest in advance. For example, super-saver fares on airlines were deeply discounted for booking 21 days in advance. These travelers are usually very sensitive to price and were always looking for deals. Fares would remain fairly steady until departure date neared. The inventory managers would start to panic over unsold inventory and start slashing fares. However, it often happened that the very last seats available were taken by the least price-sensitive travelers, those business travelers pressed for time. In reality, the last remaining seats could have been sold at the highest rate of all the fares had they not been discounted precipitously. This once again highlights the importance of an organization understanding its customers and their purchasing behavior.

The proper construction and placement of price fences becomes particularly critical when a firm discounts. There must be restrictions that prohibit consumers who are already receiving one form of discount, from adding another in a further attempt to reduce price. An example would be a business traveler receiving a preferred corporate rate trying to also receive the AAA discount on top of the first discount. Too often, hospitality organizations enable members of frequent guest programs to cross the fences. These members are already receiving a discounted rate and/or special points for their loyalty. Enabling them to reduce their price even further simply erodes the organization's revenue potential unnecessarily. In most instances, discounts should clearly state that they cannot be combined with frequent guest rates and points. Then, if a frequent guest prefers the publicly offered discount, he or she may obtain the rate, but will not receive any loyalty points. When business was down in 2002, many organizations permitted double dipping by their guests. Guests could combine discounts with their loyalty program benefits to obtain the lowest possible rate. Now that the recovery is in full swing, this practice is being reevaluated by most firms.

Secret Pricing Formula Revealed!

Now that students understand the factors involved in establishing a pricing strategy, it is time to provide a pricing tool to use when they are conducting a displacement analysis. And while this formula is not a secret to seasoned revenue management professionals, it may be a revelation for new participants in the field. There are four components in developing this formula, defined as follows:

1. **Fixed costs**: Costs that do not change with a change in the activity level of a business. Rent is a fixed cost.
2. **Variable costs**: Costs that change in direct proportion to a change in the activity level of a business. Fuel is a variable cost.
3. **Gross margin**: Revenue minus cost of goods sold (COGS)

4. **Gross margin percentage**: (Revenue − COGS)/Revenue × 100
5. **Cost of goods sold**: Direct expenses in producing a good for sale. This includes variable costs but does not include indirect fixed costs such as rent, advertising, or office equipment.

To begin, let's assume that we have a hotel with a corporate client who produced 500 room nights per year. The client's current rate for these rooms is $129 per room per night. The hotel is proposing a rate increase to $149. The hotel's variable cost per room is $35. Naturally the client is not happy about this proposed rate increase and may select another hotel. If this occurs, the hotel may need to replace that customer. Using the above data, how many room nights could the hotel afford to lose and still make the same profit?

First, the current contract generates a total of $64,500. This is calculated by multiplying the number of room nights by the current rate:

$$500 \times \$129 = \$64,500$$

Next, divide that revenue by the proposed new rate to determine how many rooms would be needed at the new rate to generate the same revenue:

$$\$64,500/\$149 = 433 \text{ rooms}$$

And then calculate the difference by subtracting the original room nights needed by the proposed room nights needed to generate the same rate:

$$500 - 433 = 67 \text{ rooms}$$

What if the hotel wanted to take this a step further and determine how many rooms would be needed to generate the same *profit* rather than the same *revenue?* The secret pricing formula revealed here is:

$$\frac{\text{Gross Margin\%}}{(\text{Gross\%} +/- \text{\%Change in Price})} \times 100$$

The result is multiplied by 100 to express it as a percentage. First, gross margin is calculated by taking revenue and subtracting the cost of goods sold. At the current rate, the gross margin is:

$$\$129 - \$35 = \$94$$

Second, the gross margin percentage is calculated by dividing the gross margin by revenue and multiplying that by 100:

$$(\$129 - \$35)/\$129 \times 100 \text{ or}$$
$$\$94/\$129 \times 100 = 0.7286 \times 100 = 72.9\% \text{ rounded up}$$

Next, the percentage change in rate is calculated as follows

$$\frac{(\text{Proposed Rate} - \text{Current Rate})}{\text{Current Rate}} \times 100 \text{ or}$$
$$\frac{(\$149 - \$129)}{\$129} \times 100 \text{ or}$$
$$20/129 \times 100 = 0.1550 \times 100 = 15.50\%$$

So now applying the secret pricing formula, we arrive at the following:

$$\frac{\text{Gross Margin}\%}{\text{Gross Margin}\% + \%\text{Change in Price}} \times 100$$

$$\frac{72.9\%}{(72.9\% + 15.50\%)} \times 100 \text{ or}$$

$$\frac{72.9\%}{(88.4\%)} \times 100 = 82.46\%$$

So multiplying that percentage times the total number of originally booked rooms equals:

$$500 \times 82.46\% = 412.3 \text{ rooms}$$
$$500 - 412.3 = 87.7 \text{ rooms}$$

So in this case, the hotel could actually afford to lose approximately 88 rooms rather than 67 rooms to generate the same amount of profit. This formula may be used regardless of the type of inventory under consideration.

Pricing Alphabet Soup

While the recipe for developing dynamic pricing strategies changes by organization and industry segment, the basic ingredients remain the same.

A   *Adjust* to meet changing internal and external environmental factors.
B   *Booking pace and pattern* should be analyzed to spot demand trends.
C   *Create* value per market segment and subsegment.
D   *Demand forecasting* calendar serves as a guide for establishing price.
E   *Elasticity* of demand is a major determinant of price.
F   *Fences* must be established to coral customers to prevent cannibalization.
G   *Group* and transient displacement analysis should be performed.
H   *Hold* the best for last pricing strategies developed.
I   *Inventory* allocation must be aligned with optimal business mix.
J   *Justify* prices and fences to customers when needed.
K   *Knowledge* of the impact that price will play on demand.
L   *Leadership* objective may be price or market share.
M   *Merchandise* products and services to increase ancillary revenues.
N   *Negotiate* contracts based on best available rates.
O   *Opportunities* should be assessed for capturing new revenue streams.
P   *Packaging* and bundling of products and services should be customized
Q   *Quality* should be built into products and services.
R   *Reservation* conversion must be improved to increase capture.
S   *Seasonality* is a factor in demand.
T   *Time* and duration of stay or visit are key considerations.
U   *Upselling* opportunities must continually be sought.
V   *Value*-based pricing requires a customer-centric approach.

W   *Worth* of total customer spend must be calculated.
X   *X factor* is the unknown, so develop contingency strategies.
Y   *Yield* the optimal amount of total revenue.
Z   *Zoom* in on emerging pricing opportunities quickly.

It is easy to see that our pricing strategy mix contains a multitude of different ingredients or variables. To be competitive today, organizations should strategically price their products and services to optimize revenue and increase profitability and value to the stakeholders. A **stakeholder** is defined as anyone with an interest in an activity, entity, or event. The organization needs to take a proactive rather than reactive approach to pricing policy. They should eradicate any remaining cookie-cutter attitudes to establishing prices. In today's competitive global economy, one size, or in this case one price, does not fit all. And pricing strategies must remain fluid as factors in the internal and external environments continually shift and change. Price must be as dynamic as demand. Price plays a role in the management of channels and inventory, as we shall see in our next chapter.

SUMMARY

We once again looked at the importance of determining the perceived price/value relationship for hospitality products and services. Organizations must strive to develop a dynamic value-based approach to pricing. *This dynamic value-based pricing is our seventh fundamental element in the development of revenue management strategy.*

Each product or service goes through a life cycle, starting with introduction, passing through growth and maturity, and eventually ending up in decline. The position of a product or service in its life cycle has a significant impact upon the price established for it.

Customer loyalty and brand equity are two very closely related concepts. A loyal customer will conduct repeat business with a favored organization and is less sensitive to small to moderate changes in price. Brand equity is the value generated by a brand. Consumers equate value with price. As long as price and value are in balance, consumer satisfaction will remain high. However, if price increases over value, then consumer preference for a product or service may begin to wane. Conversely if value increases while price decreases, consumers may perceive a good value for the product or service.

It is important that an organization conduct an internal price/value analysis to assess its perceived value of its products and services. It is important to remember, however, that it is the price/value perception of the consumer that matters when setting price and establishing value.

Price transparency is a consequence of commerce being conducted across the online channels of distribution today. So many organizations now try to achieve price parity across channels, while retaining rate integrity.

An organization may also develop a series of perceptual positioning maps to determine how it is positioned in various market segments against the competition. It is critical that an organization understands how its customers and its competitors react to a change in price. Also how does the organization respond to changes in the prices of its competitors?

Demand plays a key role in establishing price. An organization should gather all of its competitive and marketing intelligence together when trying to develop a pricing strategy. It should also look at denials, regrets, lost business reports, upcoming events and promotional activities, booking pace, and stay patterns. It should then assess the price elasticity of demand to determine the price sensitivity of its customers. The availability of substitutes and complements, and who is paying the tab are also factors in establishing prices. And it is important to price products and services appropriately by channel.

Discounting should be used judiciously and appropriately. Particular care should be exercised whenever the organization is entering into agreements based on time and volume. Rather than offer the same rate to a client for any date throughout the year, a contract may be entered into offering best available rates. A best available rate is the lowest available rate per room that evening. An organization should also understand when it should save its best products and services for its best customers. Often the organization will need to build price fences to keep customers from one market segment from trying to access the discounted rates of another market segment.

And finally the secret pricing formula was revealed. There are many ingredients in our pricing strategy alphabet soup. They may be mixed differently or varied entirely depending upon the needs of the organization.

KEY TERMS AND CONCEPTS

The following key terms and concepts were presented in this chapter. Each term and concept is also contained in the Glossary of Terms located at the end of this book:

- best available rate
- best rate guarantee program
- brand equity
- cannibalization
- cost-based method of pricing
- cost of goods sold
- decline stage
- discount price leadership
- discounting
- early adopters
- economies of scale
- fixed costs
- gross margin
- gross margin percentage
- growth stage

- induce trial
- introductory stage
- last available room
- loyalty program
- market penetration
- market skimming
- mature stage
- merchandising
- multiplier effect
- perceptual positioning map
- place
- prestige pricing
- price
- price fences
- price fencing
- price gouging

- price leader
- price leadership
- price parity
- price transparency
- product
- promotion
- promotional pricing
- rate integrity
- repositioning
- run of house
- stakeholder
- total cost
- total spend
- value-based pricing
- variable costs

DISCUSSION QUESTIONS

1. Identify one item that is priced according to the cost-based pricing method and one item that is priced according to the value-based approach to pricing.
2. Name a product or service that you feel is currently in the decline stage and identify what modifications you would make to that product or service to induce additional sales from current markets or to attract new markets.
3. Prepare a list of your school's competitors. Think about where you would position your school and its competitors on a perceptual positioning map. Be prepared to defend your decisions.
4. When you are considering a major purchase, how many different channels do you access to review available products, services, and prices? Do you always purchase from the lowest priced channel? Why or why not?
5. Which products or services do you purchase only when a discount is offered?

INTERNET EXERCISES

1. Select a date- and location-specific hospitality product or service. For example, a ski vacation in Vail over the Thanksgiving holiday weekend. Then go online and find three channels (other than the company's proprietary site) in which this product or service is available during those times for that location. Did you find price parity across channels? Next check the company website and see if the rate was higher, lower, or equal to the other prices. Report your findings.
2. Select a date-specific hospitality product or service. For example, a New Year's Eve package at a hotel. Go online and assess the application of price fencing on this product or service. Prepare an analysis.

The Driscoll Conference and Banquets.

Channel and Inventory Management

- Explain the concept of matching capacity to demand
- Present the hospitality inventory warehouse as a visual image for understanding channel and inventory management
- Discuss electronic and nonelectronic channel management
- Explore the topics of price parity, cross-channel behavior, and customer ownership
- Highlight the opportunities for conducting competitive analyses of price and inventory
- Describe the inventory management process per channel
- Provide an example of stay control application

Now that we have examined the reservation process, channels of distribution, and dynamic value-based pricing, we next turn to the management of the inventory to be sold through those channels. How do we sell as much inventory as possible at the optimal price? The best place to start is in understanding the concept of capacity.

Matching capacity with demand is a challenge faced by most organizations. **Capacity** is defined as the amount of space available to be filled. In manufacturing products, capacity may also refer to the maximum number of units an organization may produce or store as inventory. The maximum capacity for a restaurant is measured in total number of seats, for a hotel it is the total number of rooms, and for a venue it would be the total number of tickets since both seats and standing room space are frequently sold. Organizations often try to change their capacity to meet demand. They may add more seats, add more rooms, or build a larger venue. Most of these solutions to meeting excess demand usually require significant capital expenditures and are long-term solutions to matching capacity with demand.

However, there are short-term solutions that organizations may also implement to best capture excess demand. One solution is to rent additional facilities, such as a tent or adjoining property. Another is to reconfigure existing space to maximize potential capacity. Restaurants often reconfigure their seating arrangements from four tops to two tops at various times to optimize capacity. Managing capacity in the short term is of the utmost importance to hospitality providers as their products and services are perishable. **Perishable inventory** is defined as products or services that possess the possibility of spoilage or loss. Food is a perishable commodity. A hotel room and an airline seat are also perishable products. An empty airline seat on a flight cannot be stored for another flight. Once the airplane takes off, the revenue for an empty seat is lost forever. The same analogy applies to a hotel room that remains vacant for the evening.

In addition to modifying the physical elements of an establishment, an organization may also adjust elements in its service delivery to meet excess demand. For example, hotel restaurants often utilize breakfast buffets to increase the speed of service and get both their business and leisure travelers on their way to enjoy their day. A restaurant may extend its hours of operation to service a greater number of guests. An organization may also hire additional employees, contract temporary labor, and cross-train existing employees in an effort to service more customers in the same amount of time. Each additional customer served represents incremental revenue to the organization.

And technologically, an organization is able to manage capacity through reservations, price controls, and implementing rules and restrictions for purchase. Many hospitality organizations replace the term *capacity* with *inventory* when speaking of the process of managing the sale of their products and services. **Inventory management** is the process of controlling the number of units and availability of products and services across various channels of distribution. Both long-term and short-term strategies for managing capacity and inventory are required for optimizing revenue.

Hospitality Inventory Warehouse

Let's expand our previous warehouse example to now include both electronic and traditional channels of distribution. Visualize this distribution network as a warehouse with rows and rows of shelves filled with inventory comprised of products and services. An organization's entire inventory is stored on these shelves by date. Each date section contains a series of smaller bins labeled by channel. For example, there is one bin labeled "Travelocity," one bin labeled "Expedia," one bin labeled "travel agent," one bin labeled "wholesaler," one bin labeled "locally negotiated rates," one bin labeled "group sales," one bin labeled "packages," one bin labeled "AAA," one bin labeled "point of sale," and another bin is labeled "promotions," and so on. The organization decides how much inventory to place in each bin and these amounts will vary by date. Inventory may be airline seats, hotel rooms, cruise berths, tickets, or automobiles for rental. Restaurants may have fewer bins labeled "social events (weddings)," "group events (corporate banquets)," "individual diners," "couples," "families," "senior citizens," "frequent diner club members," etc.

Whenever a reservation is called in, a box of inventory is removed from that channel's bin on that day's shelf and placed in a holding container for that date. The holding containers are lined up by date on the floor in a big section across from the inventory shelves. Imagine that a reservation comes in for one hotel room on September 19, 2008, from Travelocity. One small box is removed from the Travelocity bin for September 19, 2008, and placed in the holding container for September 19, 2008. A day's worth of inventory occupies the same amount of space on one shelf as a day's worth of holding container's inventory occupies on the floor. Imagine workers scurrying between the shelves and containers throughout the day, moving inventory about as it is sold. Once a shelf is empty, no more inventory is available for sale for that date. Likewise, once a holding container is filled for a date, no more reservations should be taken and the inventory bins for that date should be empty.

Now, often the inventory from one bin sells out first. And yet, reservations calls are still coming in requesting to buy inventory from that bin. The organization must decide whether to pull inventory from another bin on that same date to help restock the empty bin. For example, the 10 boxes allocated to Travelocity sell out first. There are still six boxes of inventory in the promotions bin. Reservation requests for the Travelocity bin will be turned away if it is not restocked. So the organization may decide to shift a few boxes from the promotions bin into the Travelocity bin. When an organization performs this type of inventory reallocation, it usually pulls from similarly priced bins. If the organization decides not to restock that bin, then no additional inventory may be sold from that bin for that date. That bin is sold out. This is also referred to as **closed out**.

Sometimes bins are closed out without ever receiving a single box of inventory in the first place. This would occur for discounted bins on high demand dates. For example, all discounted inventory bins are ordered closed out for graduation. Envision yellow tape being placed across the bins for these dates to discourage anyone from placing any boxes inside.

When a holding container is filled to capacity, the workers are supposed to refuse any additional reservations for that date container. However, the workers know that sometimes boxes fall out of the bins, or someone decides not to pick up a box he or she reserved. A few boxes are usually left lying in the bottom of the holding container on sold-out dates. Since the workers know this and they develop a feeling for how many boxes may be left over, they will accept a few more boxes than the bin is supposed to hold. They set these boxes gingerly on top, hoping not to disturb the boxes beneath. They know this is a gamble, because if the people reserving those last boxes on top arrive first, and no boxes fall out or fail to get picked up, then people coming to retrieve the last boxes will find the holding containers empty, containing no inventory at all. They will be mad, maybe even furious, as they may have been the very first people to request a reservation the moment that inventory first became available. The organization may risk losing business from these customers forever due to this lack of available inventory held back for them. This is what often occurs when an organization overbooks its inventory.

To begin stocking the warehouse, an organization needs to determine how many bins it wants for that date and what channel labels to place on the bins. The organization first looks at its demand forecast for that date. The forecast shows the organization how many customers from each market segment and subsegment are expected for that date. The organization must decide which customers that it really wants to attract and capture for that date. Next, the organization determines through which channels it anticipates these desired customers will make their reservations and purchases. It labels one bin for each of these channels on that date. The organization then needs to decide how much inventory to allocate to each channel, in other words, how much inventory to place in each bin. Oh, and price range is noted on each box in each bin.

There may be more than one price range available in each bin. The organization must make this allocation determination for each date in the future for which it is accepting reservations.

As reservations come in and inventory gets removed from the bins on the shelves and placed into the holding containers, an inventory manager continually roams up and down the rows looking for opportunities to reallocate inventory. The goal of the inventory manager is to optimize revenue for each date. Sometimes he or she will see a shelf selling out very quickly. So the decision may be made to pull all inventory from the lower-rated bins for that date and shift it to that date's higher-rated bins. At other times, the inventory manager will see a date rapidly approaching on whose shelves still rest a lot of bins full of boxes. In this case, the inventory manager may decide to reduce the prices on some of the higher-priced inventory and move it from the higher-priced bins to the lower priced bins to help sell more inventory. It is obvious that this constant scurrying about of the workers and inventory manager is challenging and exhausting and they may miss a few opportunities along the way. An automated system would save the inventory manager a lot of racing through the rows, but he or she would still have to make the same decisions regarding allocation and reallocation of inventory as reservations are received.

Therefore channel and inventory management are best achieved through a combination of computerized systems and human judgment and decision making. ***Channel and inventory management become our eighth fundamental element in the development of revenue management strategy.*** The process is date specific and begins with a determination of the organization's targeted customers by market segment and subsegment. The demand forecast is reviewed for each available date up to a certain point in the future. The organization determines its optimal mix of business and then assesses which channels would most likely produce this optimal combination. Channel selection must address both production and cost of distribution. A price must be established for each unit of inventory. The appropriate levels of inventory are then allocated to each of these channels by date. The organization needs to determine total customer worth and then select the channels that deliver the greatest amount of worth and, therefore, total revenue.

As reservations are received and booking pace determined, these levels of inventories are reallocated in a continual effort to optimize revenues for each and every date. This is a daunting challenge as most predictions of the future are based upon historical actions of the past. These historical results may or may not be repeated in the future. As we have seen, numerous internal and external environmental factors impact demand. As new scenarios present themselves with no historical model for the computer to assess, human judgment is needed to make the required inventory reallocations. Managing inventory across multiple channels based upon projected consumer behavior and channel production is extremely complex. For example, an organization must determine its onward distribution strategy. **Onward distribution** is defined as the conveyance of rates, inventory, and content to various channels through the GDS or through the Internet via switching mechanisms. New tools are continually being developed to assist inventory managers with this onward distribution process. As time progresses and more data is entered into more sophisticated computer forecasting models, the better these automated systems will become in accurately reallocating inventory to meet demand without such intensive human intervention.

Courtesy of Destination Hotels & Resorts.

The Driscoll Historic Guest Room.

Nonelectronic Channel Management

Inventory needs to be available to customers who prefer to purchase hospitality products and services through traditional, or nonelectronic, methods. The first traditional method of making a reservation is via the telephone. A consumer may call an airline, a hotel, a restaurant, or a ticket office directly to purchase a product or service. The employee accepting the call may be located either on the property or in a call center. In either case, the employee must be able to easily access a list of available inventory and prices to effectuate a sale. An airline or hotel employee would access a computer screen, while a restaurant employee frequently looks at the manual reservation log. Inventory appearing on the screen or in the log must be available at the price noted. It is vitally important that inventory levels are continually updated to maintain inventory on a real-time basis.

A consumer may also wish to make a reservation via fax, mailed-in request form, or via email contact. Even though email may be considered an electronic communication tool, for our purposes here we are going to equate an email reservation request with a more traditional method of reservation. A process must be in place to accept and record these reservations as soon as they are received, again to approximate real-time levels of inventory.

And finally, employees at physical purchase locations such as ticket counters of airlines, car rental agencies, and venues must be able to access and sell inventory available directly to consumers walking up to the counter. Sometimes the employee will delay a purchase due to lack of inventory available, as in the case of a restaurant employee informing potential walk-in diners of their anticipated wait time before being seated. We have all experienced a time when we called to make a reservation and were asked to call back as the computers were down. Every instance in which a customer is turned away is a potential loss of revenue to an organization. Therefore managing real-time inventory availability in the traditional reservation channels is as important as it is in the electronic channels.

Group bookings are usually handled through the sales and marketing department. Often, an organization will also have a group coordinator position on the reservations staff. Group reservations must be entered into the system as soon as the business has been confirmed to ensure efficient on-time maintenance of inventory and management of associated prices.

Electronic Channel Management

The first place an organization should begin in developing its electronic channel management plan is with its proprietary website. It should review and critically assess its website from the booking customer's point of view. Questions that the organization needs to ask include:

- Does the website load quickly regardless of whether the consumer is using traditional dial-up or high-speed Internet access? Remember that often both business and leisure travelers surf for travel components at home at their convenience.
- Is the website easily navigable?
- Does the website enable visitors to reach the reservation page in one or two clicks?
- Is making a reservation easy on the website?
- Can the visitor email a question while trying to make a reservation and be able to obtain an immediate response?
- Can groups also make reservations on this website?
- Does the website contain all of the primary information that either a business or leisure consumer would need to induce them to make a purchase?
- Are the graphics and copy contained on the website related to substance or are they just flash?
- Does the website come up easily when inquiries are made via the major search engines?
- Are other websites linked to this website visited by its targeted customers?
- Is the website marketed on all of the organization's collateral?
- How many clicks does the site receive per month?
- What is the conversion rate from clicks to bookings?
- What is the average amount of time that a visitor spends on the site?
- Are best available rates always listed on this site?

This type of assessment will highlight deficiencies and opportunities for the organization to capture more business. Many hospitality websites are notoriously loaded with exotic photographs and swaying graphics. However, the "wow" factor has gone out of a lot of these bells and whistles now as consumers are more interested in clicking through to the information they need rather than being just dazzled by color and movement.

The organization must also develop a plan for managing inventory through its central reservation system and capturing customer information through its property management system. The two are critical elements in the organization's revenue management strategy.

Next, the organization should assess its management of the inventory it provides to the online, or merchant model, sites. A mutually beneficial relationship needs to be developed with each of the online travel merchants. For this really is a partnership in the true sense of the word. The online sites would not exist without inventory being provided by the hospitality organizations. So the balance of power is now shifting back to the providers of hospitality products and services. They need to allocate inventory to these online merchants on the organization's terms. For example, following the terrorism attacks in 2001, hotels were anxious to sell their distressed inventory. They would sell perhaps up to 50 percent of their inventory to these online merchants at steeply reduced rates. The online merchants would then increase the rate to sell this inventory to the public. The difference between the rate the online merchant paid to the hotel and the rate received from a consumer represented profit before expenses to the online merchant. They quickly took advantage of this situation, acquiring great volumes of inventory at reduced rates and substantially increasing the rates at which that inventory was sold to the consumer. The hotels quickly began to lose control of their inventory and their pricing strategies were falling apart. Problems immediately arose. Rates were being increased above the price/value appropriate for specific hotel inventory. Guests would arrive and be disappointed that the price they paid did not match the physical level of the property. They often found out before or during check-in that their rate was much higher than another guest who booked through the hotel directly. Other guests who booked through their travel agents would sometimes end up paying more than their neighbor who booked online just that day. Hey, what was going on? The guests started feeling that they were being taken advantage of and that this system was a method of unfair pricing. The hotels became upset and took out their frustrations on the merchants, who bristled because they had just helped fill up the hotel after all. This situation became highly contentious and some major hotel brands decided to restrict the amount of inventory that they provided to these online merchants. Cooler heads have since prevailed and the relationship between the hospitality providers and the online merchants continues to improve with each passing day. They need each other to provide the best customer experience in this new electronic age.

The organization should also build strong relationships with the referral sites, such as Kayak, Mobissimo, or SideStep. Commissions or pay per click fees are paid on business generated through the referral sites. A **pay per click fee** is a small fee assessed for each time a consumer clicks to access a specific site. The organization is able to quickly see which sites produce revenue and which do not. They may want to find out why a site is not producing revenue. Are their rates set too high? Are they popping up too far down the list of booking possibilities? They may also wish to increase the inventory available to top producing sites.

Nearly every destination today operates a proprietary website. There may be several of these websites in operation per destination. For example, a meeting planner wishing to book a conference in Denver may check the sites of the Denver Metro Convention and Visitors Bureau (www.denver.org), Denver International Airport (www.flydenver.com), the Denver Metro Chamber of Commerce (www.denverchamber.org), the Colorado Tourism Office (www.colorado.com), and the Colorado Hotel & Lodging Association (www.coloradolodging.com) for just a sampling of the wide variety of products and services available for planning an event. A provider of hospitality products and services in Denver will want to ensure a presence, either via advertising, Web address linkage, or both, with these destination-based websites.

Some students may be wondering how in the world an organization finds out about special interest sites that may be visited by targeted customers. First, the organization should use all of its internal data on the customer to mine for information. *Data mining* is the process of digging through layers of data and filtering out applicable information. So guest history may reflect the fact that the guest used the spa or golf course on his or her last visit. Or the guest was a skier who booked more than one visit last season. Second, volumes of guest information are available from consumer purchases made. The major credit card companies also sell data on their customers, particularly in regard to their purchasing preferences. All of this information will enable the organization to look into marketing or linking with the special interest sites that may be most visited by its targeted guests.

The organization also wants to make sure that its name comes up whenever a search is conducted for similar product and service offerings on general Web portals such as Yahoo!, MSN, and Google. It may also analyze the cost of advertising on these sites.

Two new channels to be managed are television and wireless connections. Interactive and Web TV enables viewers to link to purchases over a telephone line connected to their cable or satellite provider. And of course, the various home shopping networks encourage viewers to call in and place their orders with employees manning the phones at a call center. Many business travelers are also booking their reservations through wireless devices such as cell phones, laptops, and handheld PDAs (personal digital assistants). Organizations must include these channels in their strategic plans as well.

No matter the channel, an organization must continually monitor and update its price, availability, and content. Strategies must be developed for managing these three elements on a daily basis. As booking volume and pace constantly fluctuate, the flow of information to the channels must be continually adjusted. This includes prices and inventory available, plus general information of interest to guests considering booking during that time period. Resources and tools have been developed to assist revenue managers in updating price, availability, and content across channels. And as systems become more fully integrated, managing this process will become less complex.

Organizations should also seek out new opportunities to market their products and services via these channels of distribution. The proper placement of key words on search engines, one-day advertisements strategically placed with the GDSs, linkages available on travel agent screens, and enhanced features present on Internet travel websites may all have an impact on the number of reservations sold through each channel. Thus, all aspects of channel management must be assessed by an organization when constructing both the annual marketing plan and the strategic plan for the revenue management team.

Price Parity, Cross-Channel Behavior, and Customer Ownership

Three other issues need to be addressed here. The first one is price parity. As a result of the problems that arose with disparate prices being offered by different channels of distribution, many organizations today have adopted a policy of price parity across channels. This policy tries to maintain the same price for the same type of inventory across various channels.

The second issue to address is **cross-channel behavior**. This occurs when a customer accesses more than one channel when making a purchase. For example, many travelers will check the hotel or airline site first to check availability and then venture to an online merchant to shop for the best available rate. It is crucial for an organization to understand the methods used by consumers when making a purchase and the results of their cross-channel behavior.

The third issue is customer ownership. Let's refer back to our hotel example. When a hotel sells inventory to an online merchant and then the merchant sells a room to a consumer, is that consumer considered the hotel's or the merchant's customer? Many people think that this becomes a shared ownership relationship. The online merchant "owns" the customer prior to his or her actual arrival at the hotel. If any problems arise prior to check-in, the customer contacts the merchant for resolution. However, once the customer checks into the hotel, he or she becomes the hotel's guest and ownership of the consumer shifts to the hotel. If problems arise, the guest will usually look to hotel management for resolution. Now in extreme cases of dissatisfaction, the customer may contact the online merchant to complain about the product or service and request action.

So again, who "owns" the customer, especially when considering repeat bookings? The real answer is both! The online merchant hopes that the consumer will revisit the website when booking all future travel. This may or may not be to the same destination. The hotel will also pursue repeat business from this traveler, hoping he or she returns to the hotel's destination. But the hotel will encourage the traveler to book directly with the property next time. This eliminates the cost of distribution that the hotel incurred by the guest booking through the online merchant. So the merchant may lose a future sale of a hotel room if that guest books directly with the property next time. However, a happy guest makes a happy customer of both entities. If the guest was happy with the hotel booked through the online merchant, he or she will most likely return to that online merchant when booking a hotel in another destination or purchasing additional travel services. So a happy guest will actually become a happy repeat customer of both the hotel and the online merchant.

Competitive Analysis of Price and Inventory

Electronic distribution systems also enable an organization to keep a closer eye on the actions of its competitors than ever before possible. The organization simply needs to Google in the competing organization's name or enter its website to find out basic information about that organization. Then the organization may click on a series of merchant sites, opaque and auction sites, or referral services to see how each of its

Courtesy of Destination Hotels & Resorts.

The Pool at Ocean Hammock.

competitors is positioning its pricing per date. A wealth of competitive intelligence is now available with just a few key strokes. This online data should be combined with the data obtained by the competitive intelligence specialists on their personal visits to develop a fuller picture of each competitor. This pricing information may help an organization position itself in the marketplace. It may also help the organization set rates and allocate inventory in periods of peak or weak demand.

Inventory Management Process Per Channel

Once an organization selects the channels it wishes to use for distributing its inventory, it needs to actually manage the daily inventory loaded into each channel. The key elements to consider in this process are:

1. Pricing
2. Unit availability
3. Purchasing rules and restrictions

Managing these three elements effectively will lead to optimal revenues. Taking the first letter of each of these three key elements spells out the word *pup*. Students may want to equate this acronym with an animal pup. If the pup is properly taken care of it will become a loving companion. If neglected, it will turn around and bite you. Inventory that is appropriately managed will generate the optimal revenue, while inventory that is not actively managed will fail to produce the optimal revenue for the organization.

So to begin, each item in inventory must be assigned a price for the date. Prices are usually grouped into categories for ease of management, for example, standard queen rooms, first-class airline seats, and luxury sedans. Prices per category fluctuate per channel. Then the appropriate amount of this priced inventory must be loaded into each day's bin based upon the organization's desired optimal mix of business for that date. Each box of inventory will be priced based upon its customer worth. Then rules and restrictions will be placed on each box of inventory.

Rules and restrictions may be based upon price, duration, or volume. Remember that price fencing is the establishment of rules and regulations regarding the eligibility of an individual to purchase products or services at a specific price. Price fences are constructed to prohibit customers from one segment from trying to purchase lower priced inventory held for customers of another segment. For example, a price fence is set up to prevent a walk-in customer from receiving the discounted rate paid by a customer who booked well in advance. Rules and restrictions may also apply to duration. For example, rates are usually based on the number of days a product or service is needed. Organizations often discount the rate for multiple-day purchases. They look at the total customer worth over the entire length of stay. Duration rules and restrictions may apply to arrival dates, departure dates, and minimum length of stay. These are referred to as **stay controls**. And rules and restrictions based on volume would restrict one-time or occasional purchasers from receiving the same pricing discounts as volume users. For example, a single business traveler would not be able to receive the same rate as a traveler from a firm possessing a locally negotiated rate agreement. Nor could an individual game-day ticket holder receive the same seat price as a season-ticket holder.

There are several different stay controls that may be placed on inventory with the objective of optimizing the revenue potential of future sales. When no restrictions are in place, the inventory is said to be **open for sale**. When inventory is **closed**, it means that all inventory has been reserved and no more reservations are being taken. The closed inventory restriction is the most severe of all controls since no additional guests can stay through or check in on the night that has been closed out. Therefore, they cannot arrive prior to the closed date and continue to stay through that closed date.

Between these two extremes, and well before the organization needs to put any closed restrictions in place, there are several other controls that may be applied to effectively manage remaining inventory. The most common inventory controls are:

- Closed to arrival
- Minimum length of stay
- Maximum length of stay
- Must stay
- Full pattern length of stay

Closed to arrival means that the customer cannot arrive on that date no matter their intended length of stay. It does allow a guest who checks in the day before to remain in house over the night that has a closed to arrival restriction in place, so it is a little less restrictive than a closed control. A **minimum length of stay** restriction dictates how many nights a person checking in on the night that has this restriction must stay. Naturally, an organization cannot prevent a guest from physically checking out and leaving its premises, but it can charge the guest for leaving early based upon the reservation restriction. With a **maximum length of stay** restriction, a guest may only stay a certain number of nights. A maximum length of stay restriction may apply to packaging, special discounted pricing, or the dates leading up to a big event where a group has reserved exclusive use of the facilities. A **must-stay restriction** is very similar in nature to a minimum-stay restriction in that it requires a guest to stay a minimum number of nights; however, the biggest difference relates to when a guest intends to arrive. A minimum-stay restriction only applies to those reservations that arrive on the night on which the restriction is placed, whereas a must-stay restriction applies to all reservations that stay over on the night on which this restriction is placed, including those guests arriving on that night. Finally, a **full-pattern length of stay** restriction (also arrival based) may allow a guest to stay for one, two, four, or seven nights but not for three, five, or six nights, for example.

Sounds confusing? Here is an example of how a hotel may place restrictions on incoming reservations for a busy week. The hotel has 100 rooms available for sale each night. Here are the reservations on the books the week before arrival:

Sunday	Monday	Tuesday	Wednesday	Thursday
60	85	90	80	55

The first restriction the inventory manager could choose to apply is to close out Tuesday night. Would this be a smart decision? Keep in mind that the hotel has 100 rooms and only 90 are currently sold. The closed restriction would prevent any guests from either arriving or staying over Tuesday night, so this is probably not the best choice. What if the manager placed a closed to arrival restriction on Tuesday night? That would protect the remaining 10 rooms on Tuesday for use by guests arriving on Sunday and Monday night who wish to stay over Tuesday night. This would be a good choice if historical demand data indicated this scenario has a strong probability of occurring. What else could the inventory manager do? He or she could place a three-night minimum length of stay restriction on Tuesday night. This would mean that any arrivals on Tuesday would need to stay at least three nights. In this case, would a guest be permitted to check in on Monday and stay just two nights? Yes, as the length of stay restriction is arrival date dependent and this guest is not arriving on Tuesday. The hotel could also choose to place a three-night must-stay restriction on Tuesday night, meaning that the above guest arriving on Monday must stay or pay through Wednesday night. If the hotel anticipated a lot of last-minute demand for arrival on Tuesday and these Tuesday-arriving guests typically stay for a longer period of time at high rates, the inventory manager could place a maximum stay of two nights for Sunday arrivals and a maximum stay of one night for Monday arrivals. The inventory manager would then be protecting the remaining 10 nights for those highly valuable Tuesday arrivals. Of course, if this was the case, they may also wish to place a minimum-stay restriction on Tuesday night to prevent anyone from arriving on Tuesday and staying just one night.

Care must be used in applying stay controls. Applied too early, they may restrict sales to a point of diminishing total revenue. Consumers often get discouraged from booking when too many rules and regulations apply. Many frequent fliers have simply given up trying to redeem their free tickets over the holidays, for example. Combined stay controls must be carefully assessed so that dates are not closed out inadvertently. In the above example, what would happen to Sunday night if the property placed a must-stay three-night restriction on Monday night and a must-stay four-night restriction on Tuesday night? This would be the same as placing a full pattern length of stay restriction on Sunday night. Stays would be accepted for one or four nights but not for two or three nights. As you can see, properly placing stay controls requires careful thought and a very good understanding of your guests' arrival and departure patterns. Properly placing stay controls is also very time consuming. Stay controls are almost always applied in periods of high demand to turn away business that impedes the hotel's ability to maximize revenues over that time period. Stay controls should only be applied when they possess the capability of capturing increased revenue.

The above example is a very simplistic view of applying stay controls. Similar restrictions may also be placed on specific inventory such as room types or rate plans. Before applying any controls, the organization must analyze its demand forecast and booking pace for each date. And it must also understand how each control works in every channel of distribution. In some electronic channels, a stay control may actually close out inventory rather than merely restrict it, so understanding system capabilities and limitations is also an important consideration.

Once the initially priced inventory is loaded, the inventory manager must continually monitor individual channel inventory by date and booking pace. As demand changes, rates may need to be changed on the boxes in the bins, boxes must be reallocated to different channels, or new restrictions may need to be placed on remaining inventory. The more sophisticated computerized inventory management systems allow rates to be automatically adjusted across numerous channels when a change is needed. In other cases, the inventory manager must manually adjust the rates and levels of inventory available in each channel.

One last topic to discuss here is the human element in channel and inventory control. First, all individuals involved in accepting reservations must be properly trained in the desired method of selling inventory via that channel. Proper reservation training is key to capturing the highest revenue-generating sales. All organizations, ranging from the hospitality provider to the online merchant, must strive to increase their **reservation conversion percentage**. That is, the percentage of reservations that progress from inquiry level to final sale. Second, we have been speaking of the inventory manager here to help students visualize the process. While some larger organizations may have individuals whose only task is to manage inventory, in most hospitality organizations this task is performed by the revenue manager. We will delve into the topic of human resource management in our next chapter.

SUMMARY

Numerous components go into managing inventory across all channels of distribution. Envision a warehouse maintaining and distributing inventory to both electronic and traditional channels. As products and services are demanded by the consumer, inventory is transferred from the available bin to the sold bin. And as this process continues, the inventory manager reallocates inventory and adjusts prices. *Channel and inventory management become our eighth and final fundamental element in the development of revenue management strategy.*

One of the key elements of electronic channel management is proprietary website design and maintenance as this usually represents the least expensive channel of distribution. An organization must also learn how to best manage its relationship with the other electronic channels to ensure the optimal guest purchasing experience. Maintaining price parity and understanding cross-channel behavior are also important components in any channel and inventory management plan. In addition, organizations should take advantage of the competitive intelligence available to continually monitor the rates and inventory of their competitors. And organizations should seek out new opportunities to market their products and services via the various channels of distribution.

The three key elements that an inventory manager must consider in managing daily inventory are pricing, unit availability, and purchasing rules and restrictions. These restrictions are referred to as stay controls. An example was provided to aid students in understanding the proper application of these restrictions.

And finally, the human element involved with managing channels and inventory was addressed. All individuals taking reservations must be properly trained to obtain the optimal revenue from each channel.

KEY TERMS AND CONCEPTS

The following key terms and concepts were presented in this chapter. Each term and concept is also contained in the Glossary of Terms located at the end of this book:

- capacity
- closed
- closed out
- closed to arrival
- cross-channel behavior
- full pattern length of stay
- inventory management
- maximum length of stay
- minimum length of stay
- must stay restriction
- onward distribution
- open for sale
- pay per click fee
- perishable inventory
- reservation conversion percentage
- stay controls

DISCUSSION QUESTIONS

1. Discuss some ways in which your school physically manages capacity on campus.
2. What do you like or dislike about websites used to sell hospitality products and services?

What would cause you to use that site more and what would cause you to use that site less?

3. What channels of distribution are used by your school to market products and services?

4. What are some date-specific events scheduled for your community upon which a local hospitality provider could place stay restrictions?

5. Whom do you believe 'owns' the customer? How could an organization strengthen its ownership?

INTERNET EXERCISES

1. Consider your school's website and answer the questions posed in the chapter regarding how it operates. Should the website be redesigned? How?

2. Select a date-specific event that is upcoming in your community. Go online and review how one local provider of hospitality products or services is managing inventory for that date through various electronic channels.

The Royal Palms Pool.

CHAPTER

10

The Revenue Management Team

Chapter Objectives

The objectives of this chapter are to:

- Present a variety of organizational charts containing members of the revenue management team
- Examine the professional characteristics needed to be successful in the revenue management field
- Review prior job experience and topics of study useful to a revenue management professional
- Explore compensation levels and issues surrounding incentive plans
- Describe a revenue management professional's roles and responsibilities articulated in a variety of included job descriptions
- Provide a typical revenue management team routine and schedule

We have placed the final step in our critical pathway leading to the strategic revenue management process. The eight steps have been carefully laid down one by one. Before us lies the construction of goals, objectives, strategies, and tactics. Some of the specialists on the team constructing the steps will remain on the team to work on the four building blocks in the strategic revenue management process. Some people will now depart the construction team and others will come on board. We are going to refer to those individuals who participate in the strategic revenue management process as members of the **revenue management team** or RMT. Some RMT members will just provide marketing or competitive intelligence along the path, while others will be instrumental in developing, executing, and evaluating strategies and tactics for the upcoming year.

The old adage that "everybody sells" may now be restated to become "everyone should assist in optimizing revenue." Personnel involved most actively in the strategic revenue management process are usually the General Manager, the Director of Sales and Marketing, the Director of Sales, the Controller, the Director of Revenue Management, the Revenue Manager, the Reservations Sales Manager, Reservations Sales Agents, the Front Office Manager, and possibly the Rooms Division Director. The composition of the RMT will vary in each individual hospitality organization. The following are several organizational charts showing the possible placement and reporting structure for members of the team. The first chart (Figure 10–1) shows one possible structure occurring at a specific hotel location.

In this hierarchical structure, the Director of Revenue Management resides on the same level as the other members of the Executive Committee. The Executive Committee is comprised of the top Director or Manager in each department and will vary greatly in size and composition depending upon the size of the operation. In this first scenario, the Director of Revenue Management reports directly to the General Manager. Students will note that in our organizational charts, the Director of Catering reports directly to the Director of Sales and Marketing. In some organizations, the Director of Catering reports directly to the Director of Food and Beverage instead. In addition, sometimes a Rooms Division Director is present in the organization. This

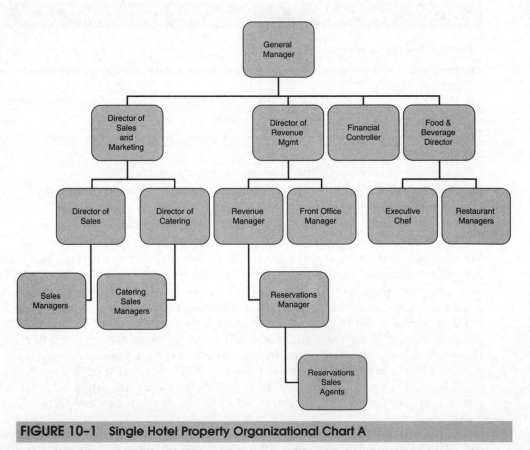

FIGURE 10-1 **Single Hotel Property Organizational Chart A**

Scenario #1: Director of Revenue Management Reports Directly to the General Manager person would also be an Executive Committee member and would shift the Front Office position and possibly some beneath it from reporting to the Director of Revenue Management to reporting to the Rooms Division Director. Each organization structures its reporting hierarchy differently and it would be impractical to re-create them all here. Instead, we maintained consistent reporting structure in the other disciplines to focus only upon changes made in the reporting structures surrounding Revenue Director or Manager.

In the second scenario, the Director of Revenue Management reports directly to the General Manager and is positioned on a separate level from the Executive Committee (Figure 10–2).

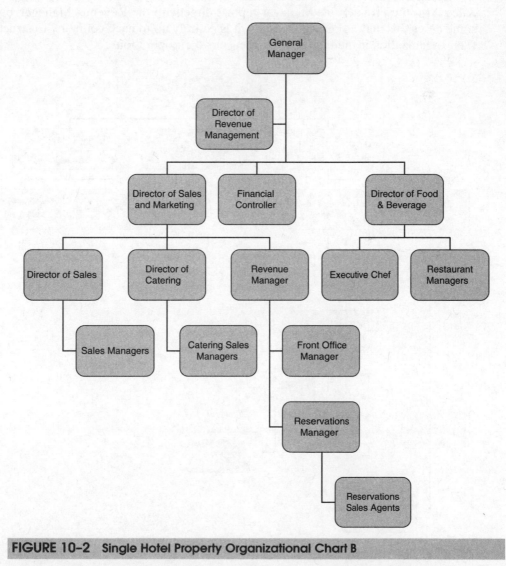

FIGURE 10–2 Single Hotel Property Organizational Chart B

Scenario #2: Director of Revenue Management Reports Directly to the General Manager

The Director of Revenue Management neither reports to nor directs the efforts of the Executive Committee members. Instead, the Director of Revenue Management serves in more of an independent agent function, overseeing and making recommendations on revenue strategies and tactics to be executed in all departments. His or her goal is to optimize revenues generated from all avenues within the organization.

The first two scenarios represent larger organizations as both a Director of Revenue Management and a Revenue Manager are present in the organizational charts. In smaller properties, these are usually rolled into one position (Figure 10–3). We will use the term *Revenue Manager* in our sample charts, but the position may sometimes be titled *Revenue Director* as well.

In this reporting format, the Revenue Manager reports directly to the Director of Sales. Also the Front Office Manager reports directly to the Revenue Manager, but in some cases this may be reversed. Again, it is entirely up to each company to structure their organization in the manner that best suits their operation.

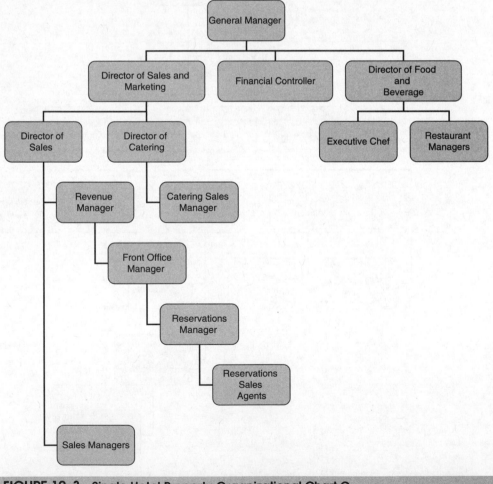

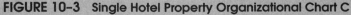

FIGURE 10–3 Single Hotel Property Organizational Chart C

Scenario #3: Smaller Property with Revenue Manager Only

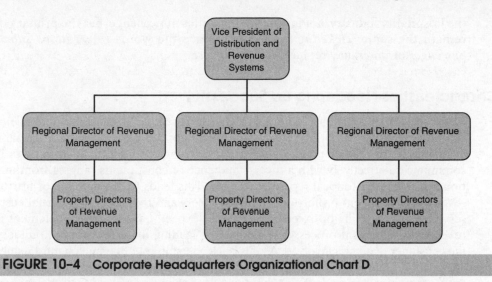

FIGURE 10-4   Corporate Headquarters Organizational Chart D

Scenario #4: Vice President of Distribution and Revenue Systems, with Regional Directors of Revenue Management Reporting Directly

Our next example shows the organizational chart at the headquarters of a corporation (Figure 10–4). In this structure, each property-level Director of Revenue Management reports directly to his or her corresponding Regional Director of Revenue Management. The Regional Directors then all report to the Vice President of Distribution and Revenue Systems. The Vice President's title may also be Vice President of Revenue Management. Again, it just all depends upon the organization.

And our final organizational chart represents the corporate headquarters of a smaller organization (Figure 10–5). In this scenario, the property-level Directors of Revenue Management report directly to the Vice President of Distribution and Revenue Systems. These corporate reporting structures are similar for all sectors of

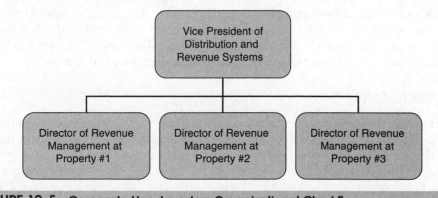

FIGURE 10-5   Corporate Headquarters Organizational Chart E

Scenario #5: Vice President of Distribution and Revenue Systems, with Property Directors of Revenue Management Reporting Directly

the hospitality industry, not just hotels. The titles may change, but the primary duties remain the same. *Ticketing sales* may replace the words *reservations sales*, and *passenger* or *diner* may replace the word *guest*.

Characteristics Needed to Be Successful

Regardless of whether an individual's title is *Director of Revenue Management* or *Revenue Manager*, the primary duties of this important position remain the same. To begin, this person should possess outstanding interpersonal skills to enable him or her to communicate effectively with a diverse audience of constituents ranging from international wholesalers to local repeat customers. This leads to the next major attribute a revenue management professional should possess and that is an exceptional customer service focus. Meeting or exceeding customer expectations is a crucial element in the revenue management process, and the person leading the effort needs to understand the consumer dynamics involved. As this is a leadership role, that person must exhibit the ability to select, train, and develop subordinate personnel. The best leaders are those able to teach, mentor, and guide their subordinates to achieve a level of knowledge and expertise equal to their own. This should never be perceived to be a threat, as the best leaders surround themselves with the greatest talent. A highly skilled team and a well-oiled operation always reflect positively on the person at the top. Besides, a leader cannot be promoted until he or she has groomed someone to fill his own shoes or her own pumps.

Previous sales experience is also an asset. The ability to negotiate with customers, peers, and superiors is vital whenever the element of trade is present. Reaching a satisfactory conclusion for all parties involved is the goal. Members of the RMT must be able to present, persuade, and influence other associates who may be reluctant or resistant to accepting differing opinions. Salespeople in particular become very territorial about their clients, so the RMT often has to present an objective analysis to overcome any objections raised by the sales team. However, extreme care needs to be exercised to spare any ill will or hurt feelings. For while good debate is always healthy, creating an adversarial environment is detrimental and may eventually start to destroy an organization's culture.

And finally, a person pursuing a career in revenue management should demonstrate outstanding financial and analytic aptitude. This is a numbers game. Now, the individual does not need to know complex theorems or have completed advanced calculus, but a basic comfort in and aptitude for analyzing numbers is extremely important in a revenue management position. Understanding basic financial terms and concepts will prove to be most useful in making real-world decisions regarding price and demand.

Courses to Take

Students often ask which courses they should take if they are interested in the revenue management field. A broad-based knowledge is the best approach. First, they should take a course in microeconomics to grasp a greater knowledge of the dynamics of supply and demand and understand the underpinnings of a market economy. A course in macroeconomics will provide insight into how factors in the external economic environment, such as interest rates, taxes, and the employment rate, will impact an organization's operations. Finance and accounting courses will also prove to be most useful as alluded to previously. Sales and marketing courses will provide the student with a good foundation in promotion and channel management. Basic information technology courses will enable students to more fully understand the basic technological features of conducting commerce online. They already have a wonderful familiarity with the Internet from the consumer side. Courses in sociology and psychology will aid them in acquiring knowledge surrounding the motivation of individual and group behavior and some insight into the elements of perception and reaction to stimuli. A course in customer service is de rigueur for any student entering the hospitality field. For that is the primary reason for any hospitality organization's existence—to serve the guest.

Useful Experience

What are some of the prior positions that may prove beneficial to an individual aspiring to a career in revenue management? Reservations Sales is a wonderful area in which to start. In a Reservations Sales Agent position, an individual learns about the organization's inventory, observes booking pace and patterns, and understands the impact of prices and restrictions on sales. The agent also grasps an understanding of the needs, wants, and desires of the organization's customers and may be able to spot emerging consumer purchasing behavior trends. Connectivity to the GDS and IDS also becomes evident as the reservations sales agents learn about the channels of distribution. As the Reservations Department is on the front line of customer contact, they understand the process of converting a customer from inquiry to sale. And they become adept in the process of upselling inventory.

Many Reservations Sales Agents are promoted to supervisory positions at the Front Desk. Here they obtain an understanding of the total guest experience as they post and review transactions previously posted to a guest's folio. A **folio** is simply a record of in-house charges made by the guest since arrival. They start to grasp the idea of primary and ancillary products, services, and revenues. They see the potential in upselling more than just rooms. The Front Desk is the hub of activity in various organizations. This is where customers make purchases, ask questions, obtain information, and generally turn to first to determine how and where to fulfill their needs, wants, and desires. Front-desk personnel also grasp an understanding of the impact and reality of forecasts. And they get first-hand experience with both the problems and opportunities presented by overbooking actions as they are the ones who must deal with the customer reactions.

Individuals working at the Front Desk are highly visible to the other departments. So it is not unusual for the Director of Sales to spot talent working at the desk and hire that person (whom we will now refer to as the associate) away to work in the Sales Department. The associate learns more about the process of soliciting and capturing group and contracted business. Or the Director of Catering sees the associate first and hires the associate as a catering sales manager. In this case, the associate broadens his or her base of knowledge and experience from rooms only to include food and beverage operations. The concept of displacement now begins to become abundantly clear as the associate gains a better focus on the concept of total customer worth.

Often larger organizations have a position referred to as **food and beverage cost controller**. This person audits the price and inventory on all food and beverage purchases and makes recommendations for cost savings whenever available. An associate coming from this position into a revenue management position will be able to apply financial and analytic skills gained from the food and beverage position to the overall operation.

Royal Palms Lobby View.

The Accounting Department may also be an excellent stop for a person interested in pursuing a revenue management career path. Learning the impact of sales and expenses on daily operations is of vital importance in managing revenues. Accounting personnel often oversee the night audit function, which generates a series of important statistical reports on the operation's daily transactions. They start to obtain a feel for the pace and rhythm of inflow and outgo of revenues and expenses. They analyze the variances between expected results and actual results. And they understand the implications of an accurate versus a poorly constructed forecast.

Compensation: Salaries and Bonuses

The ideal candidate for a revenue management career would be part salesperson and part financial analyst. This is a unique dichotomy, which makes those individuals most suited to a career in revenue management hot commodities indeed. The following nationwide comparative salary information demonstrates the fact that Directors of Revenue Management are in high demand:

Director of Revenue Management Base Salary	
Minimum	$33,357.67
25th Percentile	$50,832.40
50th Percentile	$70,176.96
75th Percentile	$82,143.33
Maximum	$114,317.73

Source: HVS Executive Search, Mineola, New York.

A percentile is a descriptive statistic used to assign value to a range of data. So the 25th percentile would contain the 25 percent of the range that makes $50,832.40 or less. At the 50th percentile, half of the people make more than $70,176.96 and half make less than that amount. This is the median or middle range of salaries for this position. And the salary levels and demand for revenue management professionals continue to grow at a rapid pace as more and more companies seek to perfect the revenue management techniques used within their own organizations. They frequently look outside the organization when seeking to fill a Director of Revenue Management position as they believe that candidate may bring a new perspective and insight to the organization.

However, the rapid acceptance of the revenue management process in some sectors of the hospitality industry has led to a shortage of trained personnel in some markets. Therefore, many organizations have chosen to groom current internal personnel to move into newly developing revenue management roles and positions. But since this is such a new discipline, tools and resources are still being developed and new technological innovations are continually advancing the learning curve forward. Without a clear understanding of the entire process and obtaining a grasp of the big picture, some individuals will find the revenue management experience just to be an exhausting experiment in report generation. We will explore this topic further when we discuss potential roadblocks to success.

One other issue needs to be addressed here and that is the issue of bonuses and incentives. Traditionally, hospitality organizations have paid their salespeople on a salary plus bonus plan. For example, a salesperson may make $50,000 per year plus bonus. An average bonus may range from 25 percent to 40 percent of annual base salary[1]. So this salesperson has the potential to make an additional $12,500 to $20,000 annually in bonuses. This is a substantial portion of that salesperson's total annual compensation.

We will use hotel sales for an example. At first, hotel salespeople's bonuses were paid based upon production. And production used to be based upon occupancy figures. **Occupancy** refers to the percentage of the hotel's rooms sold last night. Occupancy may also refer to other segments of the hospitality industry, such as cruise lines, but for our purposes here we will focus specifically on hotels. An **occupancy percentage** is calculated by dividing the total number of rooms occupied by the total number of rooms available. If a 100-room hotel sold 80 of its rooms last night, it would be 80 percent occupied. So it would be said that the occupancy was 80 percent.

Originally, hotel salespeople were given set production goals based upon the total number of rooms they needed to sell. If they met their goal, they received a bonus. Total bonus money was based on how far they exceeded their booking goals.

Then in the late 1980s and early 1990s, hotels started shifting their focus away from occupancy and toward a measurement known as RevPAR. **RevPAR** stands for revenue per available room and is calculated by dividing the actual room revenue by the number of rooms available. Another important statistic here is ADR, which stands for **average daily rate**. ADR is calculated by dividing room revenue by the number of rooms sold. For example, if the hotel generated $8,000 in room revenue last night and it sold 80 rooms, this means that the average rate per room was $100. The easiest way to calculate RevPAR is to multiply the average daily rate times the occupancy as follows:

$$\text{RevPAR} = \text{ADR} \times \text{Occupancy}$$
$$\$100 \times 80\% = \$80$$

So the revenue per available room is $80. Let's walk through another example. In this case our hotel has 280 rooms, and it sold 196 rooms last night, generating $24,500 in room revenue. To begin, we will calculate the occupancy percentage:

$$\text{Occupancy Percentage} = \frac{\text{\# Rooms Occupied}}{\text{\# Rooms Available}}$$
$$196/280 = 0.70 = 70\%$$

Next, we calculate the average daily rate:

$$\text{ADR} = \frac{\text{Room Revenue}}{\text{\# Rooms Sold}}$$

$$\frac{\$24,500}{196} = \$125$$

Now to calculate the RevPAR, we simply multiply the two results:

$$\text{RevPAR} = \text{ADR} \times \text{Occupancy}$$

$$\$125 \times 70\% = \$87.50$$

So the revenue per available room last night was $87.50. Remember that while the average rate was $125, we only sold 70 percent of the rooms. Anytime that we sell less than 100 percent of the rooms, the RevPAR will be lower than the average daily rate (again based on room revenue only).

Note that occupancy is always expressed as a percentage and average daily rate is always expressed in monetary amounts, in this case, dollars. RevPAR is also expressed in monetary terms. Please notice that the results of any calculations based on rates or revenue will be expressed in dollar (or other unit of currency) terms.

As often occurred when bonuses were based on occupancy, salespeople would reduce rates to increase their volume sold. Thus began the rate versus occupancy debate. If owners wanted higher rates, they often sacrificed occupancy. Conversely, raising occupancy often required lowing rates. If an owner stressed increasing rates, salespeople complained that they could not then reach their occupancy numbers and their bonuses were therefore unattainable. If the owner returned to focus on occupancy, salespeople were given higher bonuses, but rates were decreased. So around 1990, many hotels began to shift their sales team's bonus basis to production based upon RevPAR. Using RevPAR as the yardstick enabled salespeople to negotiate to obtain the best mix of average daily rate and occupancy.

Today, the focus has been refined even further to focus on total customer worth. Remember that total customer worth is calculated by adding primary revenue and ancillary revenue and subtracting acquisition cost. This is a much truer evaluation of what a customer is really worth to an organization. The most progressive organizations are moving from paying bonuses based on RevPAR to now paying bonuses based upon total customer worth.

A similar situation arose regarding incentives being paid to Front Office and Reservations Sales personnel. Traditionally clerks and agents were enticed with **incentive pay** paid for upselling products and services. For example, every time that a Front Office Agent would convince an arriving guest to upgrade from a standard room to a suite, the agent would receive $5. Agents soon looked for opportunities to upsell at every turn to boost their incomes. However, this system of incentive pay also needs to be revamped. Agents would focus on the immediate sale before them without looking at the total customer worth. So getting an arriving guest to upgrade became more important than, say, assisting a guest who was already booked in a standard room for three nights. But in the scheme of things, the guest staying three nights was most likely worth more revenue to the hotel. Again, total customer worth was not being considered in these incentive programs. How could an organization revamp these programs to ensure that the agents are optimizing revenue when interacting with the guests? This is a good question to ponder while we examine the daily activities of several members of the RMT.

Roles and Responsibilities

It may appear daunting at first to consider all of the tasks that a Revenue Manager or Director needs to perform. However, once we break down those duties on a daily, a weekly, a monthly, and an annual basis, it very quickly becomes achievable.

The first task that a revenue professional will usually perform in the morning is a quick analysis of the previous day's results. Many organizations produce a report, sometimes referred to as a **flash report**, to briefly recap the previous day's transactions. The Revenue Director should immediately address any major deviations from expectations that occurred and find out their cause. Any deviation between forecast and actual production is recorded on a **variance report**. Once the variance report is written, adjustments need to be made to ensure that these issues do not impact upcoming demand. Then the Revenue Manager must prepare the **short-term 3 to 5-day forecast** by utilizing the most currently received data. Next, he or she should adjust the **90-day forecast** based upon the most current data. All selling strategies in place for the next 90 days should be reviewed to ensure their continued application. Any needed changes to selling strategies should be made in the appropriate channels.

The Director of Revenue should review these changes with the Reservations Manager and ask for his or her input. Remember that the person closest to the customer often possesses the best insight into behavior and trends. And together, the two of them should review the **reservation call statistics** from the previous day. This will include the number of calls received, number of calls answered, and the number of calls converted from inquiry to sale. As previously defined, the number of calls converted from inquiry to sale is referred to as the **conversion rate**. This value is usually expressed as a ratio by dividing the number of reservations booked by the number of reservation calls received as expressed in the following equation:

$$\text{Conversion Ratio:} \quad \frac{\text{Reservations Booked}}{\text{Reservation Calls Received}}$$

For example if 100 reservation calls came in the previous day and 58 reservations were booked, the conversion ratio would be 58 percent:

$$\text{Conversion Ratio} = 58/100 = 58\%$$

An analysis of customers who did not convert should be conducted after reviewing the statistics from the previous day's denial report, regret report, and lost business report.

On a weekly basis, the Revenue Director will review and assess a series of reports. First, he or she must review the pickup activity by day for the 90-day forecast period. Pickup refers to the number of rooms sold. If 10 rooms were reserved yesterday for September 1, and this morning there are 16 rooms reserved for September 1, then the daily pick-up for that date was six rooms. There were six additional rooms sold for September 1 in the past 24 hours. Next, cut-off dates and group block pickup are reviewed to determine the action to be taken. Again, a **cut-off date** is the date that all unconfirmed reservations will be released to general inventory for resale. **Pickup** here means how many units have been confirmed as sold within that block. For example, often a bride will reserve 10 rooms for family members arriving for a wedding. Each family member is responsible for making all of his or her own arrangements to purchase a room in that block. Since the bride does not wish to be responsible for paying for any unsold rooms, she will release the block on the cut-off date. Family members may still call in, but they may not receive the previously negotiated rate that had been extended to the block. In some cases, a reminder call may be placed to the bride before the cut-off so that she is able to contact and remind her family members before the block is released. In other cases, when only a few calls have come in, the Reservations Manager may call the bride to see if she anticipates any more reservations being made. If the answer is no, then the Reservations Manager may ask her if it is okay to release some rooms or the entire block prior to the cut-off date. This would allow more time to move, or sell, this newly available inventory.

Next, the Revenue Director would prepare a **midterm forecast** generally covering 10–14 days and review the accuracy of the previous week's forecast. Then a check must be made on peak and weak periods occurring in the next 6 to 12 months. All selling strategies for those dates should be reviewed and adjusted as needed.

Attention must then be focused upon market segments and the competition. The Revenue Director should review all third-party vendor reports to assess how the organization fared over the previous week in market and competitive set performance. **Tracking reports** should be analyzed to determine where the organization's business is emanating from to seize any potential opportunities arising from the appearance of new customers and new segments. Production should be assessed per channel. And the effectiveness of pricing strategies should also be determined.

Most organizations set anticipated production figures of business expected from their key and target accounts. Each week the Director of Revenue should compare these figures to actual production. Should discrepancies appear, strategies and tactics may need to be reevaluated.

Upon completion of the weekly reviews, the Revenue Director should reforecast demand based on a rolling 12-month basis. All selling strategies should be adjusted as needed to fit the newly projected demand. Now, based upon the size of the revenue management team, the size of the organization, and the amount of resources available, many of these weekly tasks will also be performed on a monthly basis.

To further review what the roles and responsibilities of different members of the RMT may look like, we have included three job descriptions. These job descriptions go into further detail regarding the tasks required for each position. The first one is a sample job description for a Director of Revenue Management, as seen in Figure 10–6.

A job description serves as a legal document outlining the duties and responsibilities required in a position. Each individual in an organization should understand and sign his or her job description upon position acceptance.

The second job description displayed in Figure 10–7 applies to the position of Revenue Manager. While the two formats vary a bit, it is evident that many of the duties included in the Director of Revenue Management job description are also present in the list of duties required from a Revenue Manager.

The final job description presented here in Figure 10–8 applies to the position of Reservations Manager. It is important for students to understand that the duties performed by the Reservations Manager are so much more involved than simply managing the Reservation Agents. The Reservations Manager plays a key position on any organization's revenue management team.

POSITION TITLE: Director of Revenue Management
DEPARTMENT: Sales & Marketing
REPORTS TO: Director of Sales and Marketing

POSITION PURPOSE:
Maximize overall hotel revenue through development and implementation of effective transient/group inventory and pricing strategies based on future demand forecasts. Oversee Reservation Department.

ESSENTIAL FUNCTIONS:
- Formulate and deploy transient/group inventory restrictions and pricing strategies to maximize revenue from a rate and occupancy perspective.
- Manage hotel inventory control, including stay controls, open/close status.
- Achieve and maintain rate integrity within all distribution channels. Minimize rate issues with group contracts.
- Grow market share.
- Grow ADR over budget with the Corporate and Leisure discount market segments through promotions with our e-commerce partners.
- Secure relocation rooms in the event of a relocation.
- Provide "walk day" support for the front office team.
- Train and mentor Reservation Manager. Train and mentor Reservation Manager to maintain and exceed current service levels in the Reservation Department. (Use Unifocus to assist in evaluation of service.)
- Ownership of rate integrity throughout the distribution system.
- Compile revenue and occupancy pace and forecast reports; market segment (group and transient) pace, transient sub-market segment pace, daily revenue pace report, daily inventory pick up, 10-day and 4-day forecast via Reservation Manager.
- Compile 90-day forecast report in accordance with the scheduled deadline.
- Consult with Sales Managers on rate/inventory suitability of all potential group business that exceed group ceiling.
- Conduct displacement analysis utilizing profit calculation.
- Analyze End of Month Reports and compile Revenue Management Recap.
- Manage group block activity. Through Reservation Manager, responsible for management of group cutoff dates, securing and reviewing all rooming lists, monitoring group block activity (i.e., pickup, wash). When necessary or appropriate, communicate with group contacts and/or housing bureaus.
- Participate in Daily Business Review and weekly Marketing Meeting in accordance with company standards.
- Manage/monitor Central Reservations System and Global Distribution Systems to maintain consistency with property-level inventory strategies and align with company's Best Available Rate (BAR) pricing philosophy.
- Prepare weekly and monthly occupancy and revenue forecasts. Assist in preparation of annual budget and Strategic Business Plan.
- Prepare Quarterly Action Plans.
- Prepare Monthly Summary Report.
- Mentor, coach, and supervise Reservations Manager relating to the daily operation of the Reservations Department. Oversee recruiting, hiring, and training within the department.
- Oversee divisional matters as they relate to federal, state, and local employment civil rights law.
- Adhere to Sales and Marketing expense budget.

FIGURE 10–6 Job Description for Director of Revenue Management

SUPPORTIVE FUNCTIONS:

In addition to performance of the essential functions, this position may be required to perform a combination of the following supportive functions:

- Professionally represent the hotel by participating in and/or conducting client and industry functions (pre-convention meetings, guest receptions, industry events, etc.)
- Develop working relationships with managers in the Group and Catering Sales Offices, providing consultation on strategies for booking optimal group and catering business.
- Continually monitor actions of competitive hotels (product quality improvements, supply changes, pricing strategies, service offerings, etc.)

MEETINGS TO ATTEND:

- Daily business review
- Weekly yield meeting
- Weekly pickup meeting
- Weekly one-on-one with Reservations Manager
- Monthly sales and marketing meeting
- Weekly marketing meeting
- Weekly staff meeting (on rotation—once a month)

This document does not create an employment contract, implied or otherwise, other than an "at-will" employment relationship.

I have read and understand all information in this job description and agree with its content.

_____   _____
Date   Signature

FIGURE 10-6   Continued

Source: Courtesy of Destination Hotels & Resorts

POSITION TITLE: Revenue Manager
DEPARTMENT: Sales & Marketing

JOB OVERVIEW:

To manage internal and external programs, processes, systems, inventory, and information for the Reservations/Sales/Accounting Departments, including rate and inventory management in all internal and external global distribution systems (GDS), alternative distribution systems (ADOS), website, and other distribution partners. This includes all pricing for all products, packages, room inventory, and amenities sold in and through reservations. This position is to provide analysis, reports, information, and data that allows the property management and staff to optimize and maximize its room inventory sales, revenue, and services, which includes Group and FIT travel sales, wholesale, and other markets.

REPORTS TO:

Direct: Controller, Director of Sales and Marketing for Revenue Management

STANDARD SPECIFICATIONS:

Requirements are representative of minimum levels of knowledge, skills, and/or abilities. To perform this job successfully, the associate will possess the abilities to perform each duty proficiently.

FIGURE 10-7   Job Description for Revenue Manager

QUALIFICATIONS:

Essential:

1. Experience with hotel Resort PMS systems preferably Springer Miller
2. Strong verbal communication and sales skills. Must be able to communicate and receive information clearly. Must be able to read and write in English.
3. Strong computer skills
4. Strong analysis and financial accounting aptitude
5. Ability to provide strong leadership, guidance and coaching, counseling
6. Interpersonal skills
7. Ability to work within and as part of a larger team
8. Previous telephone sales skills and experience
9. Strong desire to deliver high quality customer service
10. Detail oriented and organized as it pertains to accuracy and efficiency.
11. Personnel management skills
12. Sales experience
13. Customer service
14. Computer skills: Excel spreadsheet, WordPerfect, and PMS Operating systems, Microsoft Office 95, Windows experience

ESSENTIAL JOB FUNCTIONS:

- Develop and maintain a record and reporting system which provides current and historical data for analysis on sales, inventory of all room types, rates, revenue, length of stay patterns, source of business.
- Manage all rates, inventories, and information necessary to represent and sell the property in all distribution channels including but not limited to the GDS, Internet—Expedia, Orbitz, HRN, Travelocity, Site 59, and other alternative and Internet distribution channels.
- Provide information and reports to the management company as required.
- Review all group billing procedures and group blocks for accuracy and consistency.
- Maintain an excellent working relationship and information flow process with accounting, reservations, and sales.
- Maintain all contracts, billing procedures, and account reconciliation with wholesalers both domestic and international.
- Find new avenues to produce incremental revenue during soft time periods.
- Participate in and execute some marketing and sales strategies directed to the FIT and Group and wholesale market segments of the property, including but not limited to direct mail, packages, web specials, past-guest mailings, and newsletters, communication with domestic wholesalers and travel agents.
- Assist in the development and marketing of FIT travel through input on packaging, pricing, and promotion.
- Maximize homeowner revenue monthly, including identifying "distressed" properties and using rotation. Responsible for yield management of properties.
- Manage/input homeowner stays via direct calls and owner response forms.
- Manage all reservations changes that occur as a result of properties being added or removed to the rental inventory.
- Manage complimentary and special rate business.
- Develop and maintain correspondence in SMS (short message service).
- Develop and build rate package plans for all reservations.

FIGURE 10–7 Continued

- Attend weekly departmental, staff, revenue meetings.
- Produce a weekly, monthly, and 90-day forecast and distribute to staff. Produce monthly statistics report, including source code, travel agent, and top states report.
- Have a comprehensive understanding of the property and community activities, recreation, cultural, and dining opportunities.
- Maintain a professional appearance and attitude at all times in dealing with clients or potential clients.
- Provide any other reports or information as may be requested.
- Can interface with homeowners, vendors, wholesalers, group contacts, and industry-related contacts professionally and with the ability to handle their needs.

NOTE: This description has excluded the marginal functions of the position that are incidental to the performance of fundamental job duties. All duties and requirements are essential job functions.

This job description in no way states or implies that these are the only duties to be performed by the associate occupying this position. Associates will be required to perform any other job-related duties assigned by their supervisor.

This document does not create an employment contract, implied or otherwise, other than an "at will" employment relationship.

I have read and understand all information in this job description and agree with its content.

_____   _____

Date   Signature

FIGURE 10–7   Continued

Source: Courtesy of Destination Hotels & Resorts

POSITION TITLE: Reservations Manager
DEPARTMENT: Sales & Marketing

JOB OVERVIEW:
To manage all reservation sales and staff, internal and external programs, processes, systems, inventory and information for the Reservations/Sales Department, including rate and inventory management. This includes participation in development of pricing for all products, packages, room inventory, and amenities sold in and through reservations. This position is instrumental in Reservations cross training of all Front Office Associates and the maintenance of the property's commitment to exceptional customer service.

REPORTS TO:
Direct: Director of Sales & Marketing

STANDARD SPECIFICATIONS:
Requirements are representative of minimum levels of knowledge, skills, and/or abilities. To perform this job successfully, the associate will possess the abilities to perform each duty proficiently.

FIGURE 10-8   Job Description for Reservations Manager

QUALIFICATIONS:

Essential:

1. Experience with hotel Resort PMS systems preferably Springer Miller
2. Strong verbal communication and sales skills. Must be able to communicate and receive information clearly. Must be able to read and write in English.
3. Strong computer skills
4. Strong analysis and financial accounting aptitude
5. Ability to provide strong leadership, guidance and coaching, counseling
6. Interpersonal skills
7. Ability to work within and as part of a larger team
8. Previous telephone sales skills and experience
9. Strong desire to deliver high quality customer service
10. Detail oriented and organized as it pertains to accuracy and proficiency
11. Personnel management skills
12. Sales experience
13. Customer service
14. Computer skills: Excel spreadsheet, WordPerfect, and PMS operating systems, Microsoft Office 95, Windows experience

ESSENTIAL JOB FUNCTIONS

- Hire and train all Reservations Sales Agents in Springer Miller software, properties, booking procedures, the Tariff Book, and other elements of their job description.
- Develop and implement comprehensive Sales Training with the use of various training resources.
- Manage block space from wholesalers.
- Develop and maintain a comprehensive resource and training manual that provides information on the property, its services, amenities, packages, products, and programs.
- Provide information and reports to the management company as required.
- Establish goals and objectives for sales staff consistent with the overall goals of the sales office.
- Establish and maintain all group billing procedures and process all necessary paperwork as outlined and required.
- Maintain an excellent working relationship and information flow process with accounting and revenue manager.
- Establish and maintain strong relationships with all wholesalers, both domestic and international.
- Find new avenues to produce incremental revenue during soft time periods.
- Travel if necessary (e.g. to ski shows, product training for wholesalers, travel conferences) to promote and sell the property.
- Participate in and execute some marketing and sales strategies directed to the FIT, Group, and wholesale market segments of the property, including but not limited to direct mail, packages, web specials, past guest mailings and newsletters, and communication with wholesalers and travel agents.
- Develop, implement, and oversee the daily routine for the effective operation of the Sales Department, which includes processing of leads, follow-up, contracting, and group maintenance.
- Assist in the development and marketing of FIT travel through input on packaging, pricing, and promotion.
- Responsible for moving reservations as deemed necessary by General Manager, Homeowner Relations, Maintenance, and Front Desk.

FIGURE 10-8 Continued

- Develop, manage, and execute incentive programs for all personnel in the Reservations Department.
- Coordinate/communicate with Group Sales Manager as it related to room blocks and group reservations.
- Attend weekly departmental and staff meetings.
- Develop and manage reservations agents' conversion ratios. Track phone volume.
- Have a comprehensive understanding of the property and the community activities, recreation, cultural, and dining opportunities.
- Maintain a professional appearance and attitude at all times in dealing with clients and potential clients.
- Provide any other reports or information as may be requested.

Can interface with homeowners, vendors, wholesalers, group contracts, and industry-related contacts professionally and with the ability to handle their needs.

NOTE: This description has excluded the marginal functions of the position that are incidental to the performance of fundamental job duties. All duties and requirements are essential job functions.

This job description in no way states or implies that these are the only duties to be performed by the associate occupying this position. Associates will be required to perform any other job-related duties assigned by their supervisor.

This document does not create an employment contract, implied or otherwise, other than an "at will" employment relationship.

I have read and understand all information in this job description and agree with its content.

_____   _____
Date   Signature

FIGURE 10–8   Continued

Source: Courtesy of Destination Hotels & Resorts

Revenue Management Meetings

One essential duty on the job descriptions that we have not yet addressed is the subject of meetings. Meetings are a daily event in nearly every large organization, and occur with varying frequencies in smaller ones. We have stated all along that revenue management is a team process. So the team coming together to assess information and then review and adjust strategies and tactics is critical to obtaining optimal revenue management success.

Many hospitality organizations have a daily meeting to assess the previous day's activity and prepare for the upcoming day. Depending upon the size of the organization and the efficiency of the RMT, this meeting will range from 15 minutes to 2 hours each day. In addition to its immediate needs, the team reviews changing forecast information and suggests possible adjustments to rates and inventory in the various channels. **Displacement analyses** are conducted on any group business pending decision. During group displacement analysis, the organization needs to determine the total customer worth of two or more competing pieces of business and select the business which will generate the highest total customer worth. It should be noted that displacement analyses may also apply to individual transient business. It is important that an organization calculate the total customer worth of its various market segments and subsegments to facilitate future displacement analyses. We have included a case study from the Adam's Mark Hotel in Denver in Box 10-1 that illustrates the importance of conducting a displacement analysis.

BOX 10-1

Case Study: The Adam's Mark Hotel, Denver[2]

BACKGROUND/HISTORY

Located in downtown Denver within walking distance to all major attractions is the Adam's Mark Denver Hotel. This property consists of 1,225 sleeping rooms, inclusive of 92 suites, and is the largest hotel in Denver.

There is a large citywide convention in downtown Denver that is filling most of the properties. The Adam's Mark Hotel is 92 percent full for the coming weekend and the mix of business is 75 percent group and 25 percent transient guests. Within the 8 percent of rooms left to sell, are 30 Executive Suites. The Director of Sales wants to give the group the 30 suites at the discounted group rate. The group will occupy the rooms for three nights. However, Reservations believe they can sell at least half of those rooms at rack rate for that weekend with an average length of stay of two nights.

Question: Should the Revenue Manager allot the 30 rooms to the group, if not, why? If so, how many?

The group rate is $69.00; the selling rack rate for the suites is $199.00. The group attendees cannot pay more than $69.00 per night.

DECISION-MAKING PROCESS

- How much revenue will be generated from the group as opposed to the leisure guest?

- What additional cost if any will need to be allocated if the group takes all of the rooms?
- How does length of stay influence this decision?
- Will compression in the city drive leisure demand?

ACTUALIZED

The Adam's Mark compromised and gave the group 15 rooms and sold 12 rooms on the leisure market. The hotel maintained a positive relationship with the group contact and maximized revenue.

30 group rooms × $69.00 group rate
× 3 nights = $6,210.00 + tax

15 transient rooms × $199 rack rate
× 2 nights = $5,970.00 + tax

15 group rooms × $69.00 group rate
× 3 nights = $3,105.00 + tax

12 transient rooms × $199.00
× 2 nights = $4,776.00 + tax

Total Room Revenue would be $7,881.00, which was more overall revenue with this mix of business.

Source: Courtesy of Maureen Schilling and Desirée Sandoval

On a weekly basis, the team reconvenes to assess the previous week's performance. To begin, forecast to actual production will be assessed and reasons for variances will need to be determined. What occurred to change the forecast? Was the team just too optimistic last week, or did events occur that impacted the organization's demand? This is the time for serious self-assessment but it is not a time for finger pointing. Remedies should be applied wherever possible, and adjustments made to future forecasts. These changes in forecast may lead to further adjustments in rate and inventory. This is sometimes referred to as the weekly yield meeting as the analysis of revenue produced versus revenue anticipated is the major thrust of this meeting.

Another weekly meeting that either may be combined with the above meeting or held separately is the weekly group business review meeting. In this meeting, each tentative group is evaluated to see if it is picking up as anticipated. Low reservation volume may indicate a need for the salesperson to place a telephone call to the client. Exceedingly high reservation volume may alert the team to the need for additional capacity or alternative space in neighboring facilities. In this case, an assessment of total customer worth must once again be conducted in conjunction with a transient displacement analysis to determine whether the organization should increase the size of the block being held. The team should also analyze the potential worth of any other major prospective group business being pursued by the sales team.

On a monthly basis, the RMT should meet to review demand and adjust the forecast for the upcoming month. They should also review performance from the previous month. Once again, a report should be generated explaining any variance between the forecast and actual production. Strategies and tactics of both the revenue management strategic plan and the marketing plan should be evaluated very closely and carefully at this meeting. Some strategies may need to be abandoned if they are not working. Or more resources may need to be applied to enable some of the tactics to actually work. Other strategies may be working so well that they should be expanded. Once again, the importance of obtaining team opinion and buy-in cannot be overemphasized here. We have included Figure 10–9 as one example of a revenue management team routine and schedule. Again, this will vary greatly by organization.

And finally, we complete the circle. We are nearing the end of a calendar year, so now it is the time to prepare for and schedule the next meeting or retreat to create the strategic revenue management plan. The very first step in the process will be an evaluation of this year's performance. How did the team perform? What successes did the team experience? What challenges did it face? Which strategies and tactics do we want to change or eliminate for the upcoming year and which ones do we wish continue? Short-term and long-term goals and objectives then need to be identified and strategies and tactics need to be developed for the next 12-month period. This is an ongoing process which will be continually refined by the team in its overriding quest for revenue optimization.

DAILY ACTIVITIES:
- Review daily activity from previous day
- Prepare short-term (3 to 5 day) forecast
- Review previous day booking report
- Review availability for next 90 days in all systems
- Evaluate strategies for next 90 days
- Implement changes to selling strategies in all systems
- Meet with Reservations Manager to reaffirm selling strategies
- Review and track reservation call statistics from prior day, including:
  - Number of calls to reservations office
  - Number of calls answered in reservation office
  - Number of calls converted to bookings (conversion ratio)
  - Lost business reports, denial and regret reports
- Review group block and pickup for the next 30 days
- Meet with Front Office Manager to discuss that day's selling strategies
- Review competitors' rate strategies
- Attend the daily business review meeting

WEEKLY AND MONTHLY:
- Review rooms picked up by day for the next 90 days since prior review
- Review group cut-off dates
- Review group blocks and pickup for the next 90 days
- Analyze the variance from forecast to actual production from last week or last month
- Prepare mid-term (10 to 14 day) or monthly forecast
- Evaluate peak and weak demand periods for the next 6 to 12 months adjust selling strategies and tactics as needed.
- Review channel reports to evaluate market and competitive performance
- Track and review source of business coming from the following:
  - Geographic location
  - Mode of transportation
  - Channel or booking method
  - Reason for travel
  - Rate plans booked
- Evaluate key account production and compare to established target
- Meeting with other property departments to discuss additional revenue opportunities
- Evaluate 1–800 number logs
- Reforecast for a rolling 12-month period and adjust selling strategies and tactics as indicated
- Attend weekly yield meeting and weekly group business review meeting
- Attend monthly forecast meeting and marketing plan update meeting

ANNUALLY:
Attend all strategic revenue management planning meetings assigned.

FIGURE 10–9 Revenue Management Team Routine and Schedule

SUMMARY

Our critical pathway to strategic revenue management is complete and it is important to consider the roles and responsibilities of the people that will travel that path. A variety of possible property-level and corporate-level organizational charts were presented. To be successful in a revenue management position, a person should possess a wide variety of skills, including outstanding interpersonal skills, an exceptional customer service focus, leadership skills, the ability to select, train, and develop subordinate personnel, previous sales experience, and outstanding financial and analytic aptitude. Prior experience in reservations, the front desk, sales and catering, or accounting will prove most useful as well.

Revenue management personnel are in high demand as evidenced by high levels of compensation. Incentive plans will need to be restructured throughout an organization to get all personnel focused upon optimizing revenue. Today many hotel sales teams focus on attaining goals based upon RevPAR objectives rather than either rate or occupancy alone. Additional refinement of incentive plans is necessary to ensure that all departments are focused on total revenue and not just individual sales.

The roles and responsibilities of a revenue management professional are extensive as evident in the job descriptions presented. Included in these responsibilities is the need to attend various daily, weekly, and monthly meetings to continually monitor the organization's performance. The sample revenue management team routine and schedule will provide students with a better picture of the life of a revenue management professional.

KEY TERMS AND CONCEPTS

The following key terms and concepts were presented in this chapter. Each term and concept is also contained in the Glossary of Terms located at the end of this book:

- 90-day forecast
- average daily rate
- conversion rate
- cut-off date
- displacement analyses
- flash report
- folio
- food and beverage cost controller
- incentive pay
- midterm forecast
- occupancy
- occupancy percentage
- pickup
- reservations call statistics
- revenue management team
- RevPAR
- Short-term 3 to 5-day forecast
- tracking reports
- variance report

DISCUSSION QUESTIONS

1. Do you feel that you would make a good revenue management professional? Why or why not?
2. How do you believe that organizational charts and reporting structures may change for revenue management teams in different sectors of the hospitality industry?
3. Think about the many possible employees in a hospitality organization who could be eligible for incentive pay. What types of incentive programs would you design for these various positions to induce personnel to focus on optimizing revenue?
4. Which revenue management roles and responsibilities would you enjoy and which ones would you dislike? Would you consider pursuing a revenue management career?
5. What do you feel the future will hold for the revenue management profession?

INTERNET EXERCISES

1. Go online to www.careerbuilder.com and search for positions under Revenue Manager, Director of Revenue Management, and Vice President of Revenue Management. Repeat this process again for www.hcareers.com and www.monster.com. Report your findings.

2. Go online and search for an organizational chart containing a Revenue Manager or Director of Revenue Management position. How does it differ from the charts included in the text?

REFERENCES

1. Tranter Resources Hospitality Executive Search, Monument, Colorado.

2. Schilling, Maureen and Desiree Sandoval, Adam's Mark Hotel, Denver, Colorado, February 2006.

Seventeenth Hole at the Lodge at Ocean Hammock.

Strategic Management and Following the RevMAP

Chapter Objectives

The objectives of this chapter are to:

- Explain the four building blocks supporting the strategic management process
- Review the eight fundamental elements that now create our critical path
- Combine the eight steps with the four building blocks to create the strategic revenue management process

Most of us have experience in attending a planning meeting, whether it was for a team competition, a family event, or a school project. We may have helped to formulate the plan, implement the plan, or both. With team competitions, the results of the plan are immediately clear—either we won or we lost. And the evaluation process takes place right after the game in the locker room. Team members are either celebrating or getting chewed out by the coach.

Outside of team events, we rarely take the time to go back and assess the success of the plans we make. We may discuss whether an event or project was a success or failure, but we never really analyze what happened to enable us to apply the lessons learned to future planning sessions. As far as we are concerned, the event and any associated planning are over when the fat lady sings—or at least when the bride leaves the reception hall! So the next time we have to plan an event or project, we simply do what we have always done.

In business, the formal process of strategic planning is now referred to as strategic management. **Strategic management** may be defined as the process of developing, implementing, and evaluating strategies that enable an organization to achieve its objectives. The importance of this process is once again gaining prominence after a decade of decline. In the 1990s, the speed of technological innovation, the significant ascent of the stock market, and the aberration of the dot-com success bubble made many businesses think that the strategic planning process was obsolete, a dinosaur from the past. However, the burst of the dot-com bubble and the arrest and decline of the stock market following the terrorist attacks of 9/11 left many businesses reeling. With no plan in place, and no contingency plans to turn to, they were adrift in a sea of panic with no captain or map.

So strategic management is back and it is back with a vengeance in a more sophisticated form. Strategists are in high demand and most business schools are filled with courses articulating the evolution of this discipline for the new millennium. And the structure has changed. While the plans are increasingly strategic, they are also formulated to be much more fluid and adaptable in this environment of rapid and continual change. Organizations must be prepared to operate competitively in today's 24/7 global environment.

Previously, strategic planning was an annual event marked on the corporate calendar. The call would go out to each leader of a division or a department to make plans to attend the annual retreat to prepare the strategic plan. These annual meetings took place at both the corporate level and the individual business unit level. Each attendee would come to the meeting with an agenda of items to obtain for his or her own realm and a rational for his or her area's needs. For the strategic management process is all about the allocation of resources—time, materials, financial, technological, and human. The person who made the best arguments in terms of needs often garnered the commitment for the best or most resources. So it was critical to come to the retreat armed with reports, statistics, forecasts, and wish lists to be used in this master arm wrestling for next year's resources.

In most cases today, the revenue management department falls under the umbrella of another, larger department or division. That leader has to look at all disciplines within his or her area of influence and determine which areas need which resources for the upcoming year. The leader also has to consider the long-term needs of his or her realm of control. This involves anticipating larger divisional needs such as capital expenditures, technological innovations, personnel recruitment, succession planning, revised sales and marketing efforts, process engineering, operational requirements, financial management, and research and development.

To obtain visible consideration in this short-term and long-term strategic management process, the revenue management team has to develop and present a cohesive, realistic, and achievable plan of action. And in order to develop this plan, the revenue management team should meet to create its own strategic revenue management plan well in advance of the corporate- or business-unit–level retreat. So let's first examine the steps involved in the strategic management process and then, second, determine how this process may be adapted specifically for revenue management.

The Process

The strategic management process may be broken down into four primary activities, which we will refer to as the **IDEA**:

I = *Identification of goals and objectives*

D = *Development of strategies and tactics*

E = *Execution of selected strategies and tactics*

A = *Analysis, evaluation, and adjustment of strategies and tactics*

The process is **circular**, meaning that once the process is complete, it simply begins once again. We will refer to these four primary activities as our **four building blocks** to strategic management.

Identify the Goals and Objectives

Before an organization is able to identify next year's goals and objectives it must analyze its current position. For new organizations, the strategic management process begins with the development of the organization's mission, vision, and values. For existing organizations, the process begins with a review and possible revision of the current mission, vision, and values. These are usually expressed in the form of statements. The **mission statement** reflects what the business currently is and the **vision statement** reflects what the business desires to become. For example, a mission may state that a firm is an upscale provider of hospitality services, whereas the vision may state that the firm's goal is to become the preeminent provider of those specific hospitality services. The **values** are simply the principles by which the organization operates. Values include being responsible corporate citizens or active protectors of the environment. Often the mission statement will reflect the organization's distinctive competencies and any competitive advantages that it maintains.

The External Environmental Assessment

Next, the organization must conduct a series of analyses. This begins with an external environmental assessment. We previously identified the process of environmental scanning as continually assessing and monitoring changes in the external environment. In this section, we expand the scope of this topic a bit more. An organization needs to know which elements in the environment effected the operation in the past year and which elements are projected to affect it going forward. External environmental factors include:

- Customer and market demographics
- Social and cultural trends
- Market supply and demand
- The state of the economy
- The competition
- Channels of distribution
- Suppliers
- Creditors and investors
- The labor force and unions
- Technological innovation
- Governmental and regulatory actions
- Political forces
- The natural environment

Each factor should be assessed individually as to its overall impact upon the organization in the previous year and its anticipated potential impact in the upcoming year.

Customer and market demographics are important elements in forecasting demand in every department. Each level of the organization should understand the needs, wants, and desires of the organization's customers in an effort to best allocate resources to meet or exceed their customers' expectations. Social and cultural trends are important in the development of new products and services, as well as in the reallocation of resources.

Market supply and demand are also key elements in determining the allocation of resources. If demand is rising, additional resources may be required to fulfill the growing needs of the business. If supply is increasing in the market, demand for the organization's products or services may be diluted, resulting in a reduction in revenue. Organizations need to be constantly vigilant to changes in the market's supply and demand, which may have substantial impact upon their operations.

We are all aware of the impact that the economy has on business. Some economic variables that an organization should continually monitor include interest rates, inflation, unemployment, and the fluctuation of the stock market. All of these variables will impact an organization's internal resources, external resources, and its customers. And the economy can turn in an instant. We just need to reflect back to 2001 to see how one day in the history of the United States dramatically altered the landscape of industry, hitting the hospitality industry particularly hard. One of the significant consequences of the downturn in the American economy was the recognition that organizations need to prepare contingency plans to face the uncertainties of the future in this new global economy.

We previously addressed the need to know our competitors and understand our suppliers. In the external environmental analysis, organizations not only need to assess their current competitors, but they also need to remain alert to new competitors entering the marketplace from both expected and unexpected quarters. And they need to continually seek out new and varied means of distributing their products and services through new and existing channels.

Suppliers to hospitality organizations are those firms that supply the organization with the products and services needed for operation. Suppliers of furniture, fixtures, equipment, energy, utilities, amenities, and consumable goods all play a key role in an organization's success. They are also excellent sources of competitive intelligence.

"What have you done for me lately?" may be the question heard most often from the lips of today's investors. Following the accounting scandals of WorldCom and Enron, investors are cynical at best and suspicious at worst. The high-paid CEOs of organizations are expected to perform, and if they cannot perform, they should expect to be replaced. Complacency has been replaced with diligence and firmly set expectations. Stung by the dot-com demise, creditors want to assess the financial fundamentals supporting an organization before considering it as a potential investment opportunity. Responsibility, accountability, and performance are the bywords of the investment community today.

The changing labor force is a major issue currently on the minds of many executives. The graying of America is impacting the workforce. As more and more baby boomers retire, more and more upper-level management positions will need to be filled. But at the same time, new jobs are also being created. These two factors, combined with the relatively smaller size of the generations immediately following the boomers, are projected to create an extended labor shortage. The impending labor shortage will force organizations to strategically compete for available talent. The increasingly diverse workforce is requiring organizations to revise not only their recruitment, selection, and training plans, but to also implement changes in the way they conduct business. Immigration will continue to be an explosive issue and pose a serious dilemma to those organizations employing manual and entry-level labor.

Unions—the mere word has strong connotations in the minds of both managers and workers. In American society overall, unions have been diminished in power and influence. However, in several sectors of the economy, unions still play a major role. There are several sectors of the hospitality industry which are still greatly influenced by the actions of the unions. One need only observe the airline industry to see the impact of the unions supporting pilots, flight attendants, and mechanics. Wage freezes and wage demands each affect the allocation of resources within an organization. And the potential, real or perceived, of a strike is a significant factor in the development of both annual strategies and contingency plans.

Today, technology is changing at speeds never before even considered. Just when employees master a software application, a newer, faster, better version appears. While it is increasingly difficult for individuals to remain on top of each new advance in technology, the expanding capabilities of technology are allowing businesses to perform at the highest level and achieve quantum leaps in productive capacity. The sheer volume of knowledge available today is staggering. And we now have the computing capacity to make the most use of this information. For example, hotels may pull up a guest history profile and use the information recorded there to stock the incoming guest's mini-bar with his or her favorite selections of food and beverage. They may also have the guest's favorite radio station playing softly in the background.

These rapid technological advances are fueling the new global economy. Individuals around the world may now access the same exact data at the same exact moment. Purchases are made in real time and inventory is updated instantaneously. Resources may be obtained from around the globe and delivered overnight. Physical borders and barriers to commerce are being eliminated through the use of all manner of electronic networks.

Governmental regulations can quickly change the operating dynamics of an organization. Witness the chaos originally caused by the deregulation of the airline industry, with new carriers coming and going and fare wars exploding all over the country. Regulatory issues have arisen regarding commerce being conducted over the Internet. Who should receive the sales taxes from virtual organizations existing only in cyberspace? Taxes charged on energy products continue to climb alongside the price. This increase in tax is being passed along to the consumer. And recent retail sales figures reflect a decline in sales at the big box discount stores in response to the high price of gasoline. Consumers are cutting back on their purchases to accommodate the increased slice of their disposable income now consumed at the pump. Will consumer buying power continue to erode as energy prices continue to rise? How will this impact an organization's mix of available products and services in the future?

Political forces may impact an organization at the local, state, regional, or national level. Having a majority of no-growth proponents on a city council may block construction of new facilities. Local water restrictions may have an impact on a developer's decision as to whether or not to build a new recreational facility. Tax revenues may have to be reallocated from funding community festivals and events to building a new hospital.

And water supply issues play a dual role in protecting the natural environment and enabling the continued operation and expansion of businesses and communities. More and more organizations are seeking new environmentally friendly solutions and strategies. Being identified as an environmentally conscious and responsible corporate citizen is not only good for business; it is also the right path to take in our global community.

The Internal Assessment

Now that the organization understands the external environmental factors surrounding its operation, it is time to do some honest self-reflection. This requires an internal assessment, beginning with the development of a SWOT analysis. Remember that the letters in SWOT stand for strengths, weaknesses, opportunities, and threats. We previously created a SWOT analysis when conducting our internal analysis and when analyzing the competition. In the strategy development process, we develop a more comprehensive SWOT to incorporate all areas of the organization. The analysis will be used in developing strategies to capitalize on opportunities and reduce or eliminate threats.

Goals and Objectives

Once the external and internal assessments have been completed, the organization needs to develop its long-term and short-term goals and objectives. **Long term** is usually defined as more than one year. **Short-term goals and objectives** are targets for the upcoming year. Goals and objectives are complementary. A **goal** is an end to strive for while an **objective** is a target at which to aim. Think of a goal as the end zone and the objective as moving the ball toward the end zone. An organization must establish goals and objectives to help it grow and prosper. These are the big-picture elements, the overall guiding course for the next five to ten years. Designed correctly, these goals and objectives will move the organization toward its vision.

The strategic management team should brainstorm to create a list of all possible goals and objectives desired by the organization. This is often done on the first day of a strategic management retreat. The morning would be spent reviewing the previous year's performance reports and the recently gathered marketing and competitive intelligence reports. Next, traditionally after lunch, goals and objectives would be written on flip charts that would be hung up around the room. The various lists would then be whittled down to the top 10 or 20 goals and objectives for the next perhaps five years. Everyone would agree on the list and then they would break for the day.

On day two, the participants would return to work on developing the strategies and tactics needed to achieve the goals and objectives established the previous day. A **strategy** is defined as *how* the organization plans to achieve a goal or objective. **Tactics** are defined as skillful methods used to achieve desired results. So the strategic management team would brainstorm and develop a list of strategies to consider in leading the organization to achieve both its long-term and its short-term goals and objectives. Usually, **long-term strategies** are broad and far reaching, while **short-term strategies** are plans of action to be achieved in the upcoming year.

Now, no organization could possibly afford to attempt all of the strategies developed by the strategic management team. For each strategy represents expenditure in terms of time, materials, capital, technology, labor, and other resources, and there is a limit to any organization's resources. So once again, the team breaks for lunch, and comes back to review its list. It pares the list down to possibly 10 or 20 possible achievable strategies to implement for the upcoming year. It must select the strategies that have the best opportunity for success. And the selected strategies must be **SMART**:

S = *Specific*

M = *Measurable*

A = *Achievable*

R = *Realistic*

T = *Trackable*

Let's look at each of these points separately. First, the strategy must be specific, in other words it should not be ambiguous or vague. For example, an airline may state that it wishes to increase business in the Denver market. There is no specificity in this strategy. This strategy should be clarified by stating that the airline wishes to increase business in the Denver market by 1 percent per year for a period of five years. Second, a strategy should be measurable, which is true in the airline example as changes in market share may be measured. Third, the strategy must be achievable. Depending upon its resources, and the strength of its competitors, this 1 percent increase in the airline's market share is probably achievable. And the strategy must be realistic. If the airline had stated that it wanted to increase its market share by 50 percent over the next year that would be totally unrealistic. And finally, increases and decreases in market share are usually able to be tracked to the efforts that generated them. Strategies must be trackable to ensure accountability for their achievement. Many times salespeople are given goals that are set too high for the resources with which they have to work. These are often referred to as being unrealistic and unachievable. It is important to differentiate between the terms *realistic* and *achievable*, for while they appear similar they are really quite disparate. A goal may be realistic, in other words, it should be entirely possible to attain based upon the organization's core competencies. However, that goal may be unachievable due to a lack of resources provided to reach it. So a goal may be realistic, but not achievable. Conversely, an organization may provide an abundance of resources, but the goal may be neither realistic nor achievable. An example of a goal that would be unrealistic and unachievable would be striving to make all Coke drinkers switch to Pepsi or vice versa.

Once the strategies have been determined, the tactics needed to achieve each strategy must be developed. Again, allocation of resources comes into this analysis. The strategic management team must consider the best possible combination and use of resources needed for achieving its goals and objectives. Once the tactics have been determined, they are usually mapped out in action plan form. An **action plan** is a calendar used for planning and assigning tasks to be completed over the course of a year. Many organizations develop a monthly action plan, with specific duties, tasks, and due dates assigned by individual. Performance is evaluated each month, and achievement pace is adjusted as needed.

The strategic management team assigns and allocates the resources needed to achieve these strategies and tactics. This may require a reallocation of resources, especially in labor and finances. Other resources such as materials and technology may also have to be reassigned to best implement these strategies. Once this portion of the planning is complete, the team members return to their offices to implement the strategies and tactics developed during the retreat.

Now, those strategies not selected should not simply be discarded. Instead they should be retained for possible use should some of the other selected strategies fail. They may also be valuable for next year's strategic management process. And some of them should be used to develop a contingency plan. One of the major lessons learned by the hospitality industry following the events of 9/11 was the need for contingency plans. Nearly every U.S. hospitality organization can honestly state that it was entirely unprepared for the outcome and fallout of the terrorist attacks. Americans had become complacent. We had never been attacked on our shores before, at least not since our American Revolution. Pearl Harbor was a distant memory and an ocean away. So the events of 2001 caught us all by surprise, and with our pants down. No one knew what to do next. There simply had been no plans made to deal with a tragedy of this magnitude. And we were not the only people stunned; our world travel partners did not know how to react either. We felt blindly through those first few years, just trying to stay alive.

Airline bankruptcies, hotel foreclosures, restaurant failures, and the ripple effect across our industry have taught us to prepare for all possible events going forward. Threats may not only come in human form as we have seen from the Indonesian tsunami and the devastation wrought by Hurricane Katrina. So organizations today must make **contingency planning** a part of their annual strategic management process.

A concrete example of the importance of contingency planning occurred on August 10, 2006, when authorities in London thwarted a terrorist plot to blow up several U.S.-bound airplanes simultaneously over the Atlantic Ocean. Airports were immediately sent into gridlock as governments across the globe tightened security restrictions. All forms of liquid were prohibited as were all carry-on pieces of luggage, even purses. The impact was quickly felt as officials began advising travelers to arrive at the terminal three to five hours ahead of domestic flights and a minimum of four hours before any international flight. Airline and hotel stocks immediately fell on projections that a fearful public would revise or cancel their travel plans, although many U.S. stocks rebounded by day's end as travelers patiently dealt with the delays. And the prices of crude oil and jet fuel also fell based on these same fears of decreased travel. One of the authors of this textbook, Trevor Stuart-Hill, issued the following email message to all Destination Hotels & Resorts properties:

BOX 11-1

Email message sent following aversion of London terrorist plot

LADIES AND GENTLEMAN

You have undoubtedly heard of the events/arrests that have occurred in the U.K. last evening. It is difficult to predict what sort of impact the increased security measures at our nation's airports may have on our business, so we will need your help over the next several weeks to help us understand what is happening at your specific location.

Please take extra care in noting:

1. Call volumes
2. Conversion percentages
3. Reservation lead times
4. Cancellations
5. No-shows
6. Unexpected departures (early outs)
7. Walk-ins

If you identify any anomalies to your typical business patterns or booking activity for this time of year, please quantify this and let me know by return email. It would also be helpful for you to note anything of significance on your weekly pick-up report so that everyone reading this report can gain a bit more understanding of your business dynamics. Thank you!

Source: Courtesy of Trevor Stuart-Hill, Destination Hotels & Resorts

---

Therefore, revenue management personnel across the globe were placed on alert to carefully monitor any fluctuations in demand occurring at their specific location or locations. In addition to monitoring the demand, how could hotels and other hospitality providers apply their customer-centric approach to assisting their guests in this situation?

First, hotels could lift any cancellation penalties for travelers who decided to cancel their plans or who missed flights due to the extended airport delays. Now some may argue that could cost hotels millions in lost revenue, which is true. But a hotel company may also risk losing millions in future revenue from these same travelers by charging them cancellation fees for events beyond the guests' realm of influence or control. Imagine charging guests fearful for their lives a penalty for not wanting to risk their lives. The airlines also waived any charges to travelers who wished to change their flight arrangements that day.

Next, hotels could try to reduce the hassle factor for their guests who did arrive that evening. A cool beverage would be most welcome upon arrival since even bottled water had been banned on the planes. So bottled water could be provided to weary guests as they boarded shuttles or arrived at their hotels. And since the airlines banned their passengers from bringing any liquids, the hotels could provide some essential toiletries to their guests. They should send some associates to a local store to stock up on the most needed supplies. For example, they could provide small, complimentary tubes of toothpaste. Or they could provide contact lens solution at cost. And many hotels already provide shampoo, crème rinse, hand lotion, and mouthwash in their room amenities baskets.

Conference centers and meeting facilities could offer groups facing substantially diminished demand a change in dates or waive any penalties for falling short of group food and beverage guarantees. Or they could also move the group to smaller meeting rooms and adjust the rate accordingly.

Now some businesses would actually benefit from this situation. For example, private charter air companies were expected to see an immediate increase in demand for their services. Many domestic hospitality providers such as casinos, theme parks, and entertainment venues actually experienced an increase in their stocks as Americans were expected to return to their practice of cocooning that developed following the 2001 terrorist attacks. Consumers would then spend their money closer to home rather than return to air travel until they once again felt the skies were safe. Most prognosticators predict that fear of terrorist attacks is now a permanent element of our psyches. Since human beings are amazingly resilient and adaptable, most of us will resume our normal patterns while maintaining a higher level of alert.

Execution of Strategies and Tactics

This step really encompasses two concepts: implementation and execution. The first place that an organization needs to begin when implementing strategies is to obtain **organizational buy-in**. In other words, it needs to convince its managers and employees of the need for taking this action. An organization should strive to create an internal culture that is conducive to change. For usually that is what strategic management involves—making changes. Each strategy typically requires an individual to make a change, no matter how slight, in the way he or she performs his or her job. It often requires a reallocation of resources. Referring back to our airline example, let's assume that the strategic management team developed three tactics to be used to increase market share by 1 percent this year. Perhaps the Director of Marketing needs to place more creative and enticing advertisements. And the Director of Sales needs to hire additional salespeople. And the mechanic must keep more parts on hand to reduce the turnaround time for repairs. More planes would arrive on time, which may become a competitive advantage for the airline. This may lead more consumers to switch over to this carrier.

As can be imagined, an enormous number of people are involved in the process of executing an organization's strategies and tactics. The more they understand and believe in the organization's goals and objectives and are able to see the link from the goals and objectives to performing the strategies and tasks, the better they will perform their duties. Empowered and enlightened employees perform at higher levels of satisfaction than employees who are just told what to do with no explanation. And remember that happy employees lead to happy customers, particularly in the hospitality industry.

Once the strategies and tactics are in the process of being executed, the strategic management team should begin to monitor the results to catch any potential issues before they become problems. They also need to continually monitor the external environment to take advantage of potential opportunities and avoid possible threats. The team should be prepared to replace any strategy or tactic that may not be working. Now, this should not be performed precipitously, but with a great deal of analysis and forethought since a lot of work went into developing the strategies and tactics in the first place. However, holding onto a strategy that is just not working is counterproductive. Letting go is hard for some people to do and they may be reluctant to abandon a strategy that they themselves championed. So it often takes a team decision to change direction.

Analysis, Evaluation, and Adjustment

Most organizations perform a formal review of their annual plan at the end of a 12-month period. An informal pulse is taken throughout the year to determine the overall health of the plan. Is it working? Is it moving the organization forward? Quite often, the annual performance analysis takes place during the strategic management planning process and retreat for the following year.

Whenever the performance review takes place, it should be conducted in the most thorough manner. First, all statistics should be compiled and all reports gathered. An analysis should be conducted of what went right, what went wrong, and what could be improved in the future. Some questions that the organization may ask itself include:

- Which opportunities were taken?
- Which opportunities were lost?
- Which threats were avoided?
- Which threats were eliminated?
- Which threats were encountered?
- What resources do we need for next year?
- Which strategies and tactics worked?
- Which strategies and tactics did not work?
- Which strategies and tactics would improve with more or different resources?
- Which strategies and tactics should we expand for next year?
- Which strategies and tactics should we contract or reduce for next year?
- Which strategies and tactics should we eliminate for next year?
- Did our efforts this year help us achieve our long-term and/or short-term goals and objectives?
- Should our goals and objectives be revised for next year?
- How should our goals and objectives be modified?
- How should we change the strategic management process for next year?

Once the organization answers these questions, it will then be possible to modify current strategies and tactics still in use and develop new strategies and tactics for the following year.

Unfortunately, some organizations still fail to perform this important strategic management process on a regular basis. These organizations are the exception though and not the norm. Remember the adage, fail to plan and plan to fail. Study after study have shown that planning leads to higher revenues and ultimately to higher profits. The more strategic an organization becomes, the more competitive it becomes. And it is so very important to be prepared in our rapidly changing environment. Some of the reasons that organizations report for their failure to develop a strategic management plan include lack of resources, lack of time, or lack of knowledge. There exists an abundance of skilled strategists in the marketplace that are able to help organizations overcome all of these obstacles. And once the process has been completed the first year, it becomes increasingly easier to plan for each successive year.

The Strategic Revenue Management Process and Our RevMAP

Now that students have a basic understanding of the strategic management process, we may apply these same concepts to developing a strategic revenue management plan. We have combined the eight fundamental elements with the four primary activities, our four building blocks performed in the strategic management process, to create our RevMAP shown in Figure 11–1.

The **RevMAP** may be defined as the critical path leading to strategic revenue management. It is a roadmap to be followed in developing, executing, and evaluating the strategic plan. Each of the eight fundamental elements serves as a step in the path leading to the strategic IDEA. The eight fundamental elements plus the strategic IDEA combine to create the **strategic revenue management process**. Consider these steps to be the bricks in a yellow brick road leading to increased revenue and profitability for the organization. A road paved with gold so to speak. The revenue management team (RMT) should take each step in order to arrive at their final destination, which is strategic revenue management.

The ideal scenario is to have the revenue management team meet to develop their strategic revenue management plan prior to when the organization holds its divisional retreat. A well-conceived plan may then be presented by the division leader with the goal of obtaining the needed resources to implement the plan. The revenue management team may then adjust and modify the final plan based upon the resource commitments received by the divisional leader.

The journey begins with Step One: Customer Knowledge. The revenue management team should bring to their meeting all internal and external data gathered on the organization's past, current, and potential customers. This would include all guest history profiles and calculated assessments of total customer worth. An analysis should be conducted on the potential impact that changes occurring in consumer behavior may have on the organization's products and services. And trends should be assessed to determine whether they call for the development of new products and services or the modification of existing products and services.

The second step in the journey involves the analysis and selection of market segments. Segment production reports should be analyzed and total customer worth

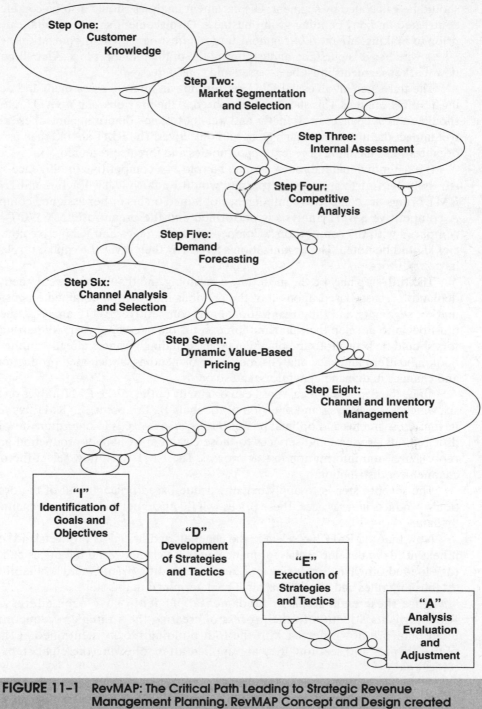

FIGURE 11-1 RevMAP: The Critical Path Leading to Strategic Revenue Management Planning. RevMAP Concept and Design created by Kimberly A. Tranter, 2006

should be calculated by segment. Displacement analyses should also be conducted on contracted and any pending group business. Displacement should also be calculated prior to making any market segment target adjustments. The organization needs to assess whether it is pursuing and capturing the optimal market mix. And all potential new market segments must be assessed and considered.

The third step involves the RMT performing an internal assessment and developing a SWOT analysis. This should be compared to the previous year's SWOT. The RMT should address changes in strengths and weaknesses and determine how these changes will impact the upcoming year's goals and objectives. The RMT should then assess the organization's handling of recent opportunities and threats presented.

If each individual had been assigned a role as a competitive intelligence specialist, then the fourth step in the journey would be fairly easy. Each member of the RMT brings the competitive intelligence obtained on his or her assigned competitor. A competitive SWOT analysis is performed and the organization's SWOT is then compared with the competitors'. Competitive advantages and distinctive competencies should be noted. The organization's SWOT is then revised to make it relative to its competitors.

The fifth step may be the most time consuming and that is the development of the demand forecast. Based upon all of the previous information obtained on customers, market segments, and the organizational and competitive SWOT analyses, the RMT must begin to develop their demand forecast for the upcoming year. All pertinent factors should be brought to the planning table, including business already on the books, booking pattern and pace analysis, major events pending, anticipated production from and changes in demand generators, and so on.

Once the demand forecast has been originally outlined, the RMT moves on to step six, which is the analysis and selection of channels. By this point, the RMT has selected its market segments and optimal mix of business, so it needs to determine how best to distribute its products and services to those customers. Channel production and cost reports are vital information in this process. The RMT must now select the optimal channels for distribution.

The seventh step is to apply dynamic value-based pricing to all of the organization's products and services. These prices will fluctuate per customer, per channel, and by date.

Now that the RMT has selected the channels and priced its products and services, it next needs to develop a plan for managing these channels and the prices and inventory loaded on each. Strategies and tactics regarding pricing, unit availability, and establishing rules and restrictions must be determined in this step.

Once these eight steps, or fundamental elements, have been addressed, the RMT turns its attention to the process of creating the strategic revenue management plan. We now refer back to the four building blocks mentioned at the start of the chapter and see how they are applied after following the eight steps in the critical path.

To recap, the RMT begins by identifying the goals and objectives of the revenue management department or division. These goals and objectives should align with the overall strategic goals and objectives of the organization. Once the goals and objectives have been identified, the RMT needs to start the process of developing strategies. The RMT must focus upon developing SMART strategies, in other words, strategies that are specific, measurable, achievable, realistic, and trackable. Just as in the larger-organization strategic planning retreat, the RMT must consider available resources in time, materials, capital, labor, and technology. The best strategies are then selected for implementation in the upcoming year. The RMT then turns to developing specific tactics for achieving these strategies. A monthly action plan calendar is created to help manage the execution of these tactics.

Now that the RMT has developed its strategies and tactics, it must usually await approval from the divisional leader before implementation and execution may take place. Since many of the people involved in implementing and executing the strategies and tactics are the same people who developed them, there are fewer obstacles to obtaining buy-in. However, all employees involved in the revenue management process should have a clear picture of the goals and objectives that the RMT wishes to achieve. They should also understand their role in achieving specific strategies and tactics and how this achievement relates to the bigger picture of organizational success.

As strategies and tactics are executed, the RMT must begin monitoring their results to catch any potential issues before they become problems. They also need to continually monitor the external environment to take advantage of potential opportunities and avoid possible threats. The team should be prepared to replace any strategy or tactic that may not be working. As the RMT members developed most of these strategies and tactics, there will probably be some opposition to abandoning these plans. Be prepared for some heated debate and discussion. When cooler heads prevail, the RMT will make the adjustments needed to achieve its larger goals and objectives.

Analysis, Evaluation, and Adjustment

The RMT should perform a formal review of their annual plan at the end of a 12 month period. An informal pulse is taken throughout the year to determine the overall health of the plan. Is it working? Whenever the performance review takes place, it should be conducted in the most thorough manner. First, all statistics should be compiled and all reports gathered. An analysis should be conducted of what went right, what went wrong, and what could be improved in the future. The questions previously presented for the organizational strategic management process may now be asked by the RMT in the course of their strategic revenue management process:

- Which opportunities were taken?
- Which opportunities were lost?
- Which threats were avoided?
- Which threats were eliminated?
- Which threats were encountered?
- What resources do we need for next year?
- Which strategies and tactics worked?
- Which strategies and tactics did not work?
- Which strategies and tactics would improve with more or different resources?
- Which strategies and tactics should we expand for next year?

Courtesy of Destination Hotels & Resorts.

T. Cook's North Patio at the Royal Palms.

- Which strategies and tactics should we contract or reduce for next year?
- Which strategies and tactics should we eliminate for next year?
- Did our efforts this year help us achieve our long term and/or short term goals and objectives?
- Should our goals and objectives be revised for next year?
- How should our goals and objectives be modified?
- How should we change the strategic management process for next year?

Once the RMT answers these questions, it will then be possible to modify current strategies and tactics still in use and develop new strategies and tactics for the following year. To recap, here is a summary of the steps to be taken in strategic revenue management process:
Begin the journey by traveling along the fundamental element steps:

- Step 1: Customer knowledge
- Step 2: Market segmentation and selection
- Step 3: Internal assessment
- Step 4: Competitive analysis
- Step 5: Demand forecasting
- Step 6: Channel analysis and selection
- Step 7: Dynamic value-based pricing
- Step 8: Channel and inventory management

The RMT now arrives at the building blocks containing the strategic IDEA. We have now added the key components involved with each building block:

"I" = Identify the goals and objectives of the Revenue Management Team
1. Gather all information obtained in the first eight steps.
2. Brainstorm possible long-term goals and objectives.
3. Brainstorm possible short-term goals and objectives
4. Select the best long-term and short-term goals and objectives based upon the current analyses.

"D" = Develop strategies and tactics to achieve the revenue management goals and objectives established above.
1. Create a list of all possible strategies to be considered.
2. Select the best strategies to pursue over the next calendar year.
3. Also develop a strategic contingency plan.
4. Develop monthly tactics for achieving these strategies and allocate appropriate resources.
5. Assign responsibility for completing the duties and tasks involved.

"E" = Execute the strategies and tactics.
1. Obtain buy-in before implementation.
2. Provide necessary resources.
3. Continually monitor for pace and results.
4. Shift efforts and resources as needed.
5. Remain prepared to activate contingency plans if needed to address changes in the environment.

"A" = Analyze, evaluate, and adjust strategies and tactics as needed.

1. Review results of the plan, paying particular attention to key result areas.
2. Determine areas of success and look for additional improvement.
3. Determine areas of failure and adjust tactics accordingly.
4. Continually adjust strategies and tactics and shift resources to obtain optimal revenues.

Now that students understand the RevMAP, it is time to review some tools, tactics, and resources available for managing the process.

SUMMARY

Most organizations perform a strategic management planning process on an annual basis. The process may be broken down into four primary activities or building blocks that we refer to as the IDEA. Goals and objectives are identified and strategies and tactics are developed during the planning process. Once all management personnel return from the planning sessions, these strategies and tactics are implemented. And then throughout the year, their progress is carefully monitored with adjustments made as needed.

This process is circular and as the organization approaches year end, it performs an analysis and evaluation of the strategies and tactics implemented over the previous 12 months. New strategies and tactics are then developed and old ones may be modified or eliminated in this ongoing process. Contingency plans must also be developed to prepare for unexpected events in the internal and external environment.

The revenue management team should also undergo a similar strategic management process. And we have developed a map for the members to follow. Each fundamental element that we previously identified has been placed as a step in the critical path leading up to the four building blocks of the strategic management process. Combined, the path and the blocks create the strategic revenue management process which we call our RevMAP.

KEY TERMS AND CONCEPTS

The following key terms and concepts were presented in this chapter. Each term and concept is also contained in the Glossary of Terms located at the end of this book:

- action plan
- circular
- contingency planning
- four building blocks
- goal
- long term
- long-term goals and objectives
- long-term strategies

- mission statement
- objective
- organizational buy-in
- RevMAP
- Short-term goals and objectives
- Short-term strategies
- SMART
- strategic management

- strategic revenue management process
- strategy
- tactics
- The IDEA
- values
- vision statement

DISCUSSION QUESTIONS

1. Discuss a situation in which you applied a planning process similar to the strategic management process described at the start of this chapter.

2. Provide an example of when an organization or team that you were on suffered from not having a contingency plan.

3. Do you know whether your department or college within the university undergoes a similar strategic planning process?

4. What are some other reasons why organizations may fail to undertake the strategic management process?

5. Think of a goal that you want to achieve by year's end. Develop a list of strategies and tactics that may help you to achieve this goal. Be prepared to share it with the class.

INTERNET EXERCISES

1. Go online and search for organizations offering strategic planning assistance.

2. Select a hospitality organization and see if you are able to find a SWOT analysis for that entity online.

Wedding Set Tarrytown House Estate & Conference Center.

CHAPTER

12

Tools, Tactics, and Resources

The objectives of this chapter are to:

- Introduce the 5Ws and an H analysis
- Apply the 5Ws and an H analysis to each of the eight steps in the RevMAP
- Present strategies and tactics to consider at each step in the journey
- Provide tools and resources available to assist the revenue management team along the way

Now that the RevMAP has been unfurled before you, it is time to review some of the aid and assistance available to help you along your journey. Many of these items have been discussed previously and some are being presented for the first time here. This chapter gathers everything together. Imagine a travel kit packed with useful tools, tactics, and resources that you will need to arrive at your final destination, in this case optimal revenue. Some items are unique to one step in the journey, while others may be used at several locations along the way. One of the universal tools available is the 5W analysis, which we have expanded to 5Ws and an H. This stands for *who, what, where, when, why, and how.* This analysis will help you navigate through the RevMAP.

Step One: Customer Knowledge

To get started, the revenue management team (RMT) may easily apply the **'5Ws and an H'analysis** and ask the following questions in an effort to better understand the organization's customers (note that these questions should be asked regarding both individuals and groups):

Who?
   Who are our past and current customers?
   Who are our potential customers, the ones we wish to acquire?

What?

What do our customers need, want, and desire?

What (or which) primary products and services do our customers buy?

What (or which) ancillary products and services do our customers buy?

What is the total customer worth of our average customer?

What (or which) products and services do our potential customers buy?

What (or which) products and services do we offer?

What trends are occurring with the potential to impact consumer buying behavior?

What (or which) new products and services could we develop to capitalize on these trends?

What (or which) products and services can be modified to add more value?

Where?

Where do we sell our products and services?

Where do our customers prefer to make their purchase (online, at a ticket window)?

Where do our potential customers make their purchases?

Where should we sell our products and services to attract our desired customers?

When?

When are our products and services in demand?

When do our customers buy (time of day, week, year)?

Why?

Why do our current customers purchase our products and services?

Why do our potential customers purchase products and services from our competitors?

How?

How far in advance do customers purchase these products and services?

How do customers make their reservations (directly, through a travel agent)?

How can we bundle together goods and services to increase the customer propensity to purchase?

How can we customize our products and services to reach various niche markets?

How can we expand this customer-centric approach?

How do customers perceive the price value of our services?

How can we change our price/value positioning?

While this list is in no way exhaustive, it is a wonderful start along the path to customer knowledge. The RMT may wish to develop a perceptual positioning map to determine where its products and services are positioned in the marketplace. And to review, the equations for calculating total customer value and total customer worth are:

$$\frac{Total\ Customer}{Value} = \frac{Perceived\ Product\ or}{Service\ Value} - \frac{Total\ Acquisition}{Cost}$$

$$\frac{Total\ Customer}{Worth} = \left(\frac{Primary}{Revenue} + \frac{Ancillary}{Revenue} - \frac{Acquisition}{Cost}\right) \times Propensity\ Y$$

Remember that total customer value is assessed from the perception of the consumer, while total customer worth is assessed from the perception of the hospitality provider.

The RMT should use all of the available resources at its disposal to determine answers to the questions posed. To begin, they should gather all of the information acquired through the organization's marketing intelligence program. An analysis of both primary and secondary data will yield the most comprehensive portrait of the organization's customers. An example of internally gathered data includes:

Guest comment cards
Guest registration cards
Segmentation sales statistics
Meal cover reports
Beverage sales reports
Season ticket holder data
Point of sale reports
Automated sales systems
Personal observation
Mystery shoppers
Listening to and speaking with the guests

The organization should also obtain information regarding consumer purchasing patterns by looking at:

Booking patterns and pace reports
Channel reports
Cancellations and no-shows
Reservation conversion percentages (the percentage of inquiries to reservations)
Comparisons to historical sales
Vendor reports

Next, the RMT should learn more about the buying habits of the market by consulting with and reviewing a variety of resources, including:

Convention and visitors bureaus
Chambers of commerce
Resort associations
Park services
Ticket agencies
AAA motor club
Travel agencies and consortia
Tourist organizations
Trade associations
Trade publications
Channel reports
Vendor reports
Retail sales reports
Local colleges and universities

Strategies and Tactics to Consider for Acquiring and Retaining Customers

Capitalize on brand equity
Create value-added products and services

Develop new products and services to meet changing consumer trends and behaviors
Enable consumers to customize their products or services
Bundle products and services to create a variety of packages

Step Two: Market Segmentation and Selection

After the RMT has gathered and reviewed all of the marketing intelligence on the market's customers, it should next proceed to break down and analyze that data by market segment. Once again, we may apply the 5Ws and an H analysis to begin:

Who?

- Who comprises the different market segments and subsegments?
- Who are our current customers?
- Whom do we wish to retain?
- Whom do we wish to acquire?

What?

- What do these customers need, want, and desire by market segment and subsegment?
- What (or which) primary products and services are purchased by each market segment and subsegment?
- What (or which) ancillary products and services are purchased by each market segment and subsegment?
- What is the average total customer worth by segment and subsegment?

Where?

- Where does each market segment and subsegment purchase its products and services?
- Where do we sell our products and services to these market segments and subsegments?
- Where should we be selling our products and services to increase our capture of desired market segments and subsegments?

When?

- When are our products and services in demand as determined by market segment and subsegment (time of day, week, year)?
- When do customers purchase (analyzed by market segment and subsegment)?

Why?

- Why do customers from each market segment and subsegment buy our products and services?
- Why do customers from each segment and subsegment buy products and services from our competitors?

How?

- How are purchases made by market segment and subsegment?
- How far in advance do the different market segments and subsegments book?
- How are reservations made per market segment and subsegment?
- How can we bundle together products and services to attract new market segments and subsegments?

- How can we increase value to different market segments and subsegments?
- How do we attract and retain new market segments and subsegments?

Once the RMT has answered these questions, it should take a long look at its responses. First, which market segments and subsegments contain the greatest total customer worth? Is the organization capable of increasing its capture of these highest-producing market segments and subsegments given the organization's current array of resources? What would be the impact of changing the current mix of business?

To answer that last question, the RMT needs to perform a displacement analysis based upon the average total customer worth of its various market segments and subsegments. It should then use this analysis to determine the organization's optimal mix of business. Some additional resources that it may wish to review when completing this assessment include:

- Market segment and subsegment reports
- Customer relationship management system data
- Database reports purchased from the major credit card agencies
- Industry publications specific to individual market segments and subsegments

Strategies and Tactics to Consider in Selecting Market Segments and Subsegments

- Create products and services to appeal to different market segments and subsegments
- Add value through additional products, services, or amenities
- Sell benefits alongside features
- Displace lower-rated business with higher-rated business
- Seek out opportunities to increase primary and ancillary spend
- Pursue the optimal mix of business

Step Three: Internal Assessment

The next step in the process is for the RMT to conduct an internal assessment and develop an initial SWOT analysis. Before it begins, the RMT must identify its competitive set. It should also develop a list of its other primary and secondary competitors. When developing the internal SWOT analysis, the organization's strengths and weaknesses should be assessed relative to the competitors. Some common strengths found in the hospitality industry are:

- Location
- Destinations serviced
- Facilities
- Amenities
- Excellent price/value perception
- Brand/image
- Reputation
- Product positioning
- Human resources
- Financial resources
- Technological resources
- Customer loyalty/repeat business

Some common weaknesses found in the hospitality industry are:

- Location
- Destinations serviced
- Facilities
- Amenities
- Poor price/value perception
- Poor brand/image
- Poor reputation
- Poor or incorrect positioning
- Weak or lacking human resource talent
- Low financial resources
- Inadequate or dated technological resources
- Little repeat business

The following is a list of common opportunities presented to the hospitality industry:

- New demand generators entering the market
- Current demand generators expanding their operations within the market
- An upswing in the economy
- New technological advances
- Increased consumer propensity to spend
- Customizable bundling of hospitality products
- New channels and more effective channels of distribution
- New opportunities for segmentation
- Increased demand for newer products and greater services
- Current supply leaving the market
- Contraction of current supply
- No scheduled renovations or expansions of existing competitive supply
- Change in ownership or operational direction of top competitor

And some potential threats faced by many hospitality organizations include:

- Terrorism
- Fear of travel
- Cost of fuel
- Weather
- A downturn in the economy
- Political upheaval
- The devaluation of currency (country specific)
- Changing consumer behavior
- Changing demographics
- Changing tastes and trends (what was hot is now not)
- Changing cultural values and mores
- Other items competing for disposable income
- Bird flu pandemic
- New supply entering the market
- Expansion of current market supply
- Planned renovation or expansion of existing competitive supply
- Change in ownership or operational direction of top competitor

In completing the internal SWOT analysis, the RMT will need to address the following questions:

Who?
- Whom do we compete with directly, that is, our competitive set?
- Whom do we compete with indirectly, that is, hospitality providers offering similar or substitutable products and services

What?
- What are our strengths?
- What are our weaknesses?
- What opportunities exist?
- What potential threats exist?

Where?
- Where do we possess a competitive advantage?
- Where do we possess a distinctive competency?

When?
- When may a strength become a weakness and vice versa?
- When will be able to reduce or eliminate our weaknesses?

Why?
- Why do our weaknesses exist?
- Why do our competitors outperform us at times?
- Why do we outperform our competitors at other times?

How?
- How can we apply our strengths to capture opportunities?
- How can we apply our strengths to deflect or eliminate threats?

Strategies and Tactics to Consider Regarding the Organization's Internal Assessment

- Use our competitive advantage and distinctive competencies in establishing higher prices for our products and services
- Capitalize on opportunities by utilizing our available resources
- Use our strengths to acquire and maintain customers
- Reallocate resources to reduce our weaknesses
- Prepare contingency plans for each major possible threat

The answers to the above questions help the RMT develop SWOT analyses for each of the organization's competitors. The completion of the competitive SWOT analyses helps the organization return and refine its own SWOT analysis. Therefore the development of an internal SWOT and competitive SWOT analyses are complementary activities. They could be performed in either order as long as the organization takes the final step of refining the internal SWOT upon conclusion of the SWOT construction process. However, we feel that most organizations know themselves better than they may know their neighbor so it is usually easier to start with internal SWOT development.

Step Four: Competitive Analysis

Once the internal assessment and SWOT analysis have been completed, the RMT should turn its attention to the competition. To begin, the RMT should gather together all of the competitive intelligence obtained by its group of specialists. It should review the primary research that it obtained as a result of its:

- Review of competitors' daily event or reader boards
- Parking lot observations
- Customer surveys
- Employment of mystery shoppers
- Vendor inquiries
- Nightly call-arounds assessing availability
- Listening to and speaking with competitors' employees
- Visiting the competitors' premises and listening to their guests

Next, the RMT should review the pertinent secondary research obtained from the following sources:

- Financial websites
- Company annual reports
- Brochures and other collateral
- Press releases
- News articles
- Business journals
- Trade publications
- Trade associations
- Marketing material
- Online databases
- Sector performance reports
- Convention and visitors bureaus
- Chambers of commerce
- Resort associations
- Park services
- Ticket agencies
- Travel agencies and consortia
- Tour operators and wholesalers
- Channel reports
- Vendor reports
- Local colleges and universities
- Guest review and comments posted on websites

Again, notice that several of these resources are sources of both market and competitive intelligence.

Information that the RMT should try to glean about their competitors from these resources includes:

- Company historical background
- Physical and online presence

- Ownership and management entities
- Analysis of key financial ratios if available
- Products and services available and pending
- Facility demand, capacity, and condition
- Corporate- and location-specific marketing initiatives
- Pricing strategies
- Distribution strategies
- Key personnel and cultural environment
- Forward-looking plans for acquisition, disposition, repositioning, and expansion or contraction

The RMT should then develop a SWOT analysis for of its primary competitors. Often from this process, the RMT may learn that it needs to adjust its competitive set. As previously stated, the organization should go back and reassess and possibly revise its own SWOT analysis. Following the development of the competitive SWOT and revision of the organization's SWOT, the RMT should apply the 5Ws and an H analysis to ask itself the following questions:

Who?

- Who are our primary competitors?
- Who are their customers?

What?

- What are their primary products and services?
- What are their ancillary products and services?
- What are their strengths?
- What are their weaknesses?
- What opportunities exist for our competitors?
- What threats exist for our competitors?
- What do they do better than us?
- What do we do better than them?
- What market segments and subsegments do they attract and why?
- What competitive advantages do they possess?
- What distinctive competencies do they possess?

Where?

- Where do they sell their products and services?
- Where do they operate?

When?

- When are their products and services most in demand (time of day, week, month, or year)?
- When do customers see them as their first choice for purchase?

Why?

- Why do we compete directly with our competitive set?
- Why do consumers purchase their products and services?
- Why do we compete directly with these organizations?

How?

- How do we compete for customers?
- How can we change our product or service mix to become more competitive?
- How can we take advantage of opportunities in advance of our competitors?

Once an organization becomes adept at creating SWOT analyses for its competitive set, it may wish to expand their analysis to secondary, or indirect, competitors.

Strategies and Tactics to Consider in Regard to Competitors

- Take advantage of price transparency by continually monitoring competitors' rates and inventory
- Use automated tools and resources whenever possible to capture competitors' rates and inventory allocation
- Monitor competitors' changes in price
- Monitor competitors' reactions to changes in our pricing strategies
- Seek out opportunities for capturing increased market share
- Develop more competitive products and services

Step Five: Demand Forecasting

The RMT must develop an exceptional understanding of the mechanics of supply and demand in its marketplace. First, it should become aware of all products and services available. It should also make a list of all items that are substitutes for these products and services. Second, the RMT needs to determine the price elasticity of demand for its products and factors that may impact that elasticity. It should understand how this elasticity impacts consumer spending and total revenue for the organization. Charts are available showing the price elasticity for many different consumer products.

Once the organization understands the mechanics of demand, they need to determine how best to manage demand:

- How should the organization control demand?
- How should the organization direct demand?
- How should the organization try to influence demand?
- How should the organization try to create demand?

Upon completing this analysis, the RMT should turn its attention to developing a demand forecast. The demand forecast is created based upon all of the data collected thus far in the first five steps. Additional historical reports to review and incorporate into the demand calendar include:

- Denials and regrets
- Lost business reports
- Cancellations
- No-shows
- Walk-ins
- Group arrival/departure and stay patterns
- Transient arrival/departure and stay patterns

Annual forecasts and 30/60/90-day forecasts are the most prevalent but many organizations now also create 7/14/21-day forecasts. Applying the 5Ws and an H analysis leads us to the following questions:

Who?

- Who has already made a reservation (business on the books)?
- Who has made inquiries into booking future dates?
- Who are the area's major demand generators?

What?

- What business is being generated by events?
- What business is anticipated from the major demand generators?
- What other elements are driving demand into the market?
- What products and services are needed to meet this demand?
- What products and services are needed to capture additional demand?
- What impact will price have on capturing demand for each market segment and subsegment on each date?

Where?

- Where is this business coming from?

When?

- When is business expected from the major demand generators?
- When does excess demand exist?
- When is additional demand needed?

Why?

- Why are customers demanding products and services from this market at this time?

How?

- How can we control, direct, influence, create, or otherwise manage demand?

Now that the RMT has a picture of demand, it needs to decide how it is going to allocate inventory to meet that demand.

Strategies and Tactics to Consider in Demand Forecasting

- Use all automated resources available to assist with the development of the forecast
- Continually monitor and adjust forecast
- Develop strategies to increase capture of demand from special events and area demand generators
- Use demand to assess proper positioning of prices and inventory

Step Six: Channel Analysis and Selection

Determining which channels through which to sell their products and services is a significant challenge to most organizations today. The abundance of traditional and electronic channels of distribution makes the choice more complex than ever before. The best place for an organization to begin is to gather some production reports. It needs to determine which channels are producing which customers. Production reports should be obtained from:

- The major global distribution systems
- The organization's central reservation office
- Central reservation systems

- The organization's proprietary website
- The merchant models
- Retail operations
- Opaque sites
- Auction sites
- Referral services
- Special-interest sites
- General Web portals
- Marketing campaigns
- Personal sales efforts
- Promotional programs
- Travel agents and consortia
- Ticket office
- Any other channels used to distribute its products and services

The next step for the RMT is to determine the distribution cost per channel. Once the production and distribution costs have been obtained, the RMT needs to determine the contribution per channel. The RMT completes the analysis by determining which channels produce the greatest total customer worth. It may then select the channels to use when allocating inventory to achieve its optimal mix of customers. Some questions the RMT may ask when performing this analysis include:

Who?

- Who books through each channel?
- Who does each channel target?
- Who else is using this channel (i.e., other competitors)?

What?

- What other products and services are being sold through this channel?
- What product or service of ours sells best through this channel?

Where?

- Where do their customers come from?
- Where do they operate (in cyberspace, brick and mortar location)?
- Where do they place their presence to attract customers?

When?

- When is this channel open for business?
- When do customers use this channel?

Why?

- Why do customers book through this channel?
- Why do competitors utilize this channel?

How?

- How are customers directed to our products and services?
- How does the channel manage its customers?

More analysis of channels will be addressed when the RMT reaches step eight.

Step Seven: Dynamic Value-Based Pricing

Establishing the right price is such a key component in optimizing revenue that the RMT needs to give this step a lot of attention. It begins by reviewing the price/value analysis performed on its products and services. What does the customer think they are worth? In value-based pricing, price is set based upon the consumer's value perception and demand for the product or service. Each customer assesses value differently. Therefore, success is based upon creating the optimal price/value relationship. Some questions that the RMT needs to address when establishing prices include:

Who?

- Who would be attracted to this product or service based upon its current price?
- Who would be attracted to this product or service if the price were lower?
- Who would be attracted to this product or service if the price were higher?
- Who else is selling similar products and services at similar prices?
- Who are our most loyal customers and what price do they pay?
- Who is paying for this purchase (the consumer or company)?

What?

- What (or which) products and services are most sensitive to changes in price?
- What (or which) products and services are our highest priced?
- What (or which) products and services are our lowest priced?
- What prices are set for similar competing products and services?
- What percentage of total spend does this purchase represent?
- What substitutes are available for immediate purchase?

Where?

- Where do our products and services currently reside in their overall life cycle?
- Where do customers buy our highest priced products and services?
- Where do customers buy our lowest priced products and services?
- Where are our competitors selling their similarly priced products and services?
- Where can we ensure price parity across channels?
- Where do customers position our products and services?

When?

- When do our customers shop?
- When do customers buy at the regular price?
- When do customers buy at discount?
- When do we need to offer volume discounts?
- When do we need to lower price to induce trial?
- When should we implement prestige pricing or conduct marketing skimming?
- When should we close out discounts?
- When should we offer best available rates?

Why?

- Why do customers buy certain products over others offered at the same price?
- Why do customers buy certain services over others offered at the same price?
- Why do we lose some customers over price?

How?

- How do customers perceive the price/value relationship of our products and services?
- How do customers perceive the price/value relationship of our competitors' products and services?
- How can we adjust price to capture an increased share of the market?
- How can we capture an increased share of the market without reducing price?
- How can we increase price without adding value?
- How can we add value to increase price?
- How do we capitalize on brand equity?
- How do we ensure customer loyalty without having to discount price?
- How do customers react to changes in price?
- How do our competitors react to changes in price?
- How do we react to our competitors' changes in price?
- How can we merchandise our products and services to increase total customer spend?

Responses to these questions will assist the RMT in developing price fences and appropriately allocating inventory. As you can see, a lot of these questions are time specific and will all depend upon forecasted demand. The RMT should also review the ingredients in its pricing alphabet soup to ensure that no ingredient in the overall pricing strategy is missing.

Strategies and Tactics to Consider with Dynamic Value-Based Pricing

- Set initial prices low to induce trial
- Set initial prices high to position products and skim the market
- Use lowered prices to increase market share
- Assess pricing strategies for frequent guest programs
- Construct price fences
- Use competitive advantages and distinctive competencies in determining price
- Price superior products higher and inferior products lower
- Maintain channel price parity and rate integrity
- Develop a proactive rather than reactive approach to pricing
- Use price to lengthen stay patterns
- Discount sparingly and carefully
- Adjust price to more accurately reflect the location of the product or service in its life cycle
- Negotiate volume business on percentage off best available rates
- Use promotional pricing to increase capture of special event-related business
- Analyze competitors' price positioning surrounding special events

Step Eight: Channel and Inventory Management

And finally, we have arrived back at our warehouse and now our revenue manager needs to allocate inventory per channel. We selected our channels in step six, and now we need to determine the levels and pricing of inventory to load into each channel. Based upon achieving our optimal business mix of customers, the RMT must allocate the appropriate amount of inventory in the appropriate channel. Thus, inventory may need to be loaded into a mix of the following channels:

- The major global distribution systems
- The organization's central reservation office
- Central reservation systems
- The organization's proprietary website
- The merchant models
- Retail operators
- Opaque sites
- Auction sites
- Referral services
- Special-interest sites
- General Web portals
- Promotional programs
- Franchise programs
- Discount clubs
- Travel agents and consortia
- Ticket office
- Group sales office
- Catering sales office
- Any other channels used to distribute its products and services

Once the inventory is loaded, it needs to be managed. Remember that the three key elements in managing inventory are:

1. Pricing
2. Unit availability
3. Purchasing rules and restrictions

The revenue manager must continually monitor booking pace and pattern and the changing demand forecast. Price fences should be constructed to maintain inventories for the appropriate customers. As demand changes, prices will need to be changed and inventory levels adjusted. Reservation content must also be updated per channel. Decisions will need to be made regarding volume discounts, duration pricing, and stay restrictions applied. Some possible stay controls that may be implemented include:

- Closed to arrival
- Minimum length of stay
- Maximum length of stay
- Must stay
- Full pattern length of stay

When no stay restrictions are implemented, inventory is said to be open for sale.

The RMT must also learn how cross-channel behavior impacts the selling of its products and services. And the RMT should develop strategies for increasing its "ownership" of customers arriving via these various channels. Continual monitoring of date, rate, and inventory is required to manage channels effectively. The organization may also wish to maintain price parity across channels. And the RMT must continually keep an eye on the rates and inventory loaded into these channels by its competitors. A final analysis is conducted using the 5Ws and an H:

Who?

- Who is buying which products and services at what prices from which channels?
- Who is choosing alternative channels when booking repeat business?
- Who is selling on the same channels that we selected?

What?

- What (or which) products and services are being purchased on each channel and at what price?
- What (or which) products and services are our competitors selling on these channels and for what prices?
- What does cross-channel behavior tell us about our customers?
- What price adjustments are needed to meet fluctuating demand and inventory?

When?

- When are customers using the various channels to purchase?
- When do we need to adjust price or inventory?
- When do we need to apply restrictions?

Where?

- Where do our customers make their purchases?
- Where do our competitors offer their products and services?

Why?

- Why do our customers purchase through this channel?
- Why do the competitors choose specific channels?

How?

- How can we manage prices and inventory more effectively across channels?
- How can we use technology to improve the process?

Strategies and Tactics to Consider for Channel and Inventory Management

- Improve and enhance website
- Develop email strategies for capturing new and repeat business
- Maximize franchise opportunities
- Develop Internet linkage strategy for connecting to other sites
- Determine search engine optimization options
- Update price, availability, and content across channels as often as needed
- Implement stay controls and other restrictions when appropriate
- Utilize available tools and resources to effectively manage channels
- Purchase new technology (hardware and software) to improve the management of channels and inventory
- Develop an electronic marketing plan
- Audit and update content (including descriptions and images) through all channels as appropriate
- Partner with a Channel Distribution Consultant

In addition to distributing products and services, many channels today offer a variety of marketing and reservation services as well. And that takes us to the topic of electronic resources.

Electronic Resources

By now, many of you are thinking that you will need a team of thousands just to address the items included in your travel kit above. This may be true if you were trying to accomplish this all manually. Fortunately, electronic resources are available to provide you solutions to managing price, channels, and inventory today. The following are a sampling of the electronic resources available for purchase today:

Market and Competitive Intelligence:

- Analysis of market penetration
- Performance data on the organization and its competitors
- Historical information on the organization and its competitors
- Competitive inventory availability reports
- Market data trend analysis and monitoring
- Market positioning
- Breakdown of arrival patterns and length of stay
- Capture of customer information
- Customer relationship management and communication tools

Demand Forecasting:

- Future booking data from the GDS
- Comparison of booking pace to competitors
- Identification of peak and weak periods to enable action to be taken early
- Identification of market demand
- Analysis of booking pace and stay patterns developing

Channel Analysis:

- Production reports across GDS and IDS
- Booking contribution by channel
- Identification of top producing channels for the market

Dynamic Value-Based Pricing:

- Rate shopping tools and reports
- Pricing opportunity alerts
- Competitive pricing change alerts
- Rate recommendation tools
- Confirmation of price parity across channels
- Pricing data per market
- Monitoring of best rate guarantees
- Length of stay rate comparisons

Channel and Inventory Management:

- Central Reservations Systems
- Tools for updating rate, inventory, and restrictions across multiple channels

- Reservation conversion improvement tools
- Value added product development

Electronic Marketing Services:

- Marketing management in the GDS and IDS
- Pay-per-click advertising
- Online merchandising opportunities
- Website design and management
- Digital media display distribution to multiple sites
- Travel agent enhanced screen display
- Headline and point of sale marketing in GDS
- Web links
- Package development and marketing
- Search engine optimization

The following is a list of just a few of the vendors that an organization may consult for these products and services:

- Blizzard Marketing
- E-Site Marketing
- EZ Revenue Management
- Google Ads
- IdeaS
- Micros/Opus
- Pegasus
- Rubicon Group
- Smith Travel Research
- SynXis
- TravelClick

Students interested in learning more about electronic distribution and channel management may wish to check out these association websites:

Hospitality Sales and Marketing Association International (HSMAI)
    Web address: www.hsmai.org
    HSMAI also offers a link to their revenue management group:
    Web address: www.revmanagement.org

American Hotel & Lodging Association (AH&LA)
    Web address: www.ahla.org

Hospitality Financial and Technology Professionals (HFTP)
    Web address: www.hftp.org

Hotel Electronic Distribution Network Association (HEDNA)
    Web address: www.hedna.org

PhoCusWright, Inc.
    Web address: www.phocuswright.com

The following are a few other association websites which may prove useful to students in gathering data needed when developing revenue management strategies:

American Gaming Association (AGA)
  Web address: www.americangaming.org

Association of Destination Management Executives (ADME)
  Web address: www.adme.org

Association of Luxury Suite Directors (ALSD)
  Web address: www.alsd.com

Club Managers Association of America (CMAA)
  Web address: www.cmaa.org

Cruise Lines International Association (CLIA)
  Web address: www.cruising.org

International Association for Exhibition Management (IAEM)
  Web address: www.iaem.org

International Association of Amusement Parks and Attractions (IAAPA)
  Web address: www.iaapa.org

International Association of Assembly Managers (IAAM)
  Web address: www.iaam.org

International Association of Conference Centers (IAAC)
  Web address: www.iacconline.org

International Association of Convention and Visitors Bureaus (IACVB)
  Web address: www.iacvb.org

International Associations of Fairs and Expositions (IAFE)
  Web address: www.fairsandexpos.com

International Council of Cruise Lines (ICCL)
  Web address: www.iccl.org

International Festivals and Events Association (IFEA)
  Web address: www.ifea.com

International Special Events Society (ISES)
  Web address: www.ises.org

International Ticketing Association (INTIX)
  Web address: www.intix.org

Meeting Planners International (MPI)
  Web address: www.mpiweb.org

National Golf Course Owners Association (NCGOA)
  Web address: www.ngcoa.org

National Indian Gaming Association (NIGA)
  Web address: www.indiangaming.org

National Restaurant Association (NRA)
  Web address: www.restaurant.org

Professional Association of Innkeepers International
  Web address: www.paii.org

Professional Convention Management Association (PCMA)
  Web address: www.pcma.org

Courtesy of Destination Hotels & Resorts.

Hamilton Park Hotel & Conference Center (exterior).

Stadium Managers Association (SMA)
  Web address: www.stadiummanagers.org

Trade Show Exhibitors Association (TSEA)
  Web address: www.tsea.org

Travel Industry Association of America (TIA)
  Web address: www.tia.org

Upon completion of the first eight steps in the RevMAP process, the RMT is now able to turn its attention to developing the strategic revenue management plan. There are four primary activities, or building blocks, involved in developing the plan, which we refer to as the **IDEA**:

I = *Identification of goals and objectives*

D = *Development of strategies and tactics*

E = *Execution of selected strategies and tactics*

A = *Analysis, evaluation, and adjustment of strategies and tactics*

It is important to remember that this activity process is circular, meaning that once the process is complete, it simply begins once again. A detailed analysis of these four steps is contained in the previous chapter. Now that students know how to navigate the RevMAP, let's turn to the legal and ethical issues surrounding the practice of revenue management and some potential bumps we may encounter along the road.

SUMMARY

Before embarking upon any journey, a traveler needs to pack a kit of supplies. Here we have assembled a travel kit containing the tools, tactics, and resources needed to get the revenue management team to their final destination, optimal revenues. One of the universal tools in this kit is the 5Ws and an H analysis which aids the travelers in getting through each step in the RevMAP. They need to pause on each of the eight steps in our critical path and ask themselves *who, what, where, when, why,* and *how.* They then turn to the other tools in their kit which will assist them in developing their strategies and tactics appropriate at each step in their journey.

While all of the work required in the revenue management process may be completed manually, this would be cumbersome and inefficient for any but the smallest organizations. Fortunately today there exist an abundance of electronic resources available for purchase, including tools for:

- Market and competitive intelligence
- Demand forecasting
- Channel analysis
- Dynamic value-based pricing
- Channel and inventory management
- Electronic marketing services

A series of association websites is provided and may prove useful to students in gathering data needed when developing revenue management strategies.

KEY TERMS AND CONCEPTS

The following key terms and concepts were presented in this chapter. Each term and concept is also contained in the Glossary of Terms located at the end of this book:

- 5Ws and an H Analysis

DISCUSSION QUESTIONS

1. Pick any of the eight steps and review the 5Ws and an H analysis questions presented. What other questions could you develop for that step?
2. Answer the questions under Step One: Customer Knowledge using your school as the organization.
3. What are some alternative strategies and tactics that you could develop for any of the eight steps?
4. Can you think of any tools to add to the travel kit?
5. Can you think of any additional websites that may be helpful in the revenue management journey?

INTERNET EXERCISES

1. Go to TravelClick's website. Review and report on the available revenue management resources found there.
2. Select any two of the general association websites and report on any revenue management-related content.

Hong Kong Airport Currency Exchange.

CHAPTER

13

Legal and Ethical Issues and Potential Bumps in the Road

Chapter Objectives

The objectives of this chapter are to:

■ Discuss the issue of price and the concept of fair price
■ Revisit the price/value relationship
■ Present two methods for increasing prices
■ Review pricing laws in place to protect consumers
■ Assess potential bumps in the road to achieving revenue management goals and objectives

Money makes the world go around . . . money can't buy happiness . . . money talks . . . money begets money . . . a fool and his money are soon parted . . . love of money is the root of all evil . . . money, money, money, money . . . MONEY!

Our ambivalence about money is well documented in music and literature. We need it, we want it, we desire it, and yet we hate the fact that we crave it. More wars have been fought over money than love. The very thought of money may stir up intense emotions within a person. So when it comes to negotiating price in the marketplace, intellect may often give way to emotions.

Byron stated that "A bargain is in its very essence a hostile transaction . . . do not all men try to abate the price of all they buy? I contend that a bargain even between brethren is a declaration of war."[1] And to obtain that bargain, two people must negotiate. The very term **negotiate** refers to the act of conferring upon or settling upon a satisfactory conclusion.

The Issue of Price

So it is no surprise that our lexicon is filled with warlike terms used to describe price. There are price controls, price concessions, price fixing, price yielding, and price wars. Whew! No wonder we become a bit emotional when we think about price.

Many hospitality professionals immediately think of the action of raising prices whenever they even hear the term *revenue management*. But as we have seen, raising the price is just one small element of the practice of revenue management. The goal of both this book and the ever-expanding leagues of revenue management professionals is to get hospitality professionals to think about revenue management as the skillful means to optimizing revenues.

To those consumers even remotely familiar with the concept, the term *revenue management* simply means higher prices at the cash register. Today, if you were to ask the average person on the street what he or she thought about the practice of revenue management, you would be greeted with a blank stare. The concept is simply unfamiliar to most Americans. However, if you asked these same people their feelings regarding raising or lowering prices to match demand, you would be barraged with a variety of responses ranging from displeased to enraged.

Revisiting the Price/Value Relationship

We need to refer back once again to our discussion on consumer perception. Remember that consumers affix a price/value relationship in their heads for the products and services that they purchase. Each individual will assess a different value to each product. Most consumers understand the principles involved in elevating price to match peak demand. For example, they understand the high price of a Super Bowl ticket. They also understand the high prices set on extremely valuable luxury items like a mansion or a yacht. They can see the value in the physical product. They also perceive that the people who are able to afford such items are not really concerned with price, and to some extent that is true. The rich are often less price-sensitive when it comes to certain items. But they may also be as miserly as Scrooge when it comes to their price sensitivity for other items.

So once an organization tries to raise prices on a familiar item, the consumer's perception of price/value is upset. In their mind they had set a certain value for the product. An increase in price will raise one element in that ratio without increasing the second element in the ratio. Price goes up, but value does not change. Remember back to our price/value teeter-totter. Now the customer either needs to mentally realign the equation making value now equal to the new price or needs to abandon the price/value relationship entirely and seek another new relationship. Once again, the availability of substitute products comes into play. For example, as movie ticket prices continued to climb, some consumers abandoned the relationship in favor of renting a movie at the video store. The cost of gas and the rental were less than the cost of a ticket at the theater and the consumer could save money too by making his or her own popcorn at home. And then came satellite television. Now the consumer abandoned the drive to the video store in favor of purchasing a pay-per-view movie at an even lower price. And that consumer could make the purchase in his or her jammies while munching on homemade popcorn.

We can also visualize this process by looking at an example of coffee. Consumers used to place a value of less than $1 on a cup of coffee. And then came the world of gourmet coffee. All of a sudden the price of a cup of coffee had gone up. So people shifted their price/value perceptions just a bit. Gourmet coffee, they thought, was worth a little bit more. Some consumers scoffed, and they still scoff at this notion. Needless to say, they are not the consumers being targeted by the marketing team at gourmet coffee world. The marketing team is targeting those consumers who easily shift their perceptions along with their additions of the various combinations continually being produced by the coffee chefs. And wait, the food scientists at gourmet coffee world have developed some very tasty, and very expensive, scones that the consumer must purchase to accompany his or her morning cup of gourmet brew. And this cycle will continue until consumers stop shifting their price/value perceptions and cease purchasing coffee from gourmet coffee world in favor of other alternatives that may not be much cheaper but that may offer better price/value in their eyes.

In the previous example, we discussed shifting consumers' price/value perception over time. When price changes occur slowly in increments, there is usually less of a hue and outcry regarding the increase. However, institute a dramatic price change and cover your ears! A virtual roar will emanate from consumers. That is what happened in 2005 when gasoline prices first approached the $3 per gallon mark. Americans were outraged! They called their senators and representatives and wanted to know what they were doing about the high prices. The senators and representatives fearing the loss of the next election went about selecting a panel to investigate the huge amounts of profits being made by the big oil companies. The government assured American consumers that they were on top of this situation and that they would soon emerge with an answer—and a resolution.

So what has happened? The congressional committee was convened and they asked a lot of questions of the executives of the huge oil producers. And the executives turned red, tugged at their ties, and looked extremely uncomfortable when trying to explain away the hundreds of billions of dollars in profits they made in one year alone. Members of Congress 'tsked tsked' the executives, shook their heads, and then went away to write their report. The executives, given a bit of a scare, lowered gasoline prices . . . temporarily. The news media reported on how lucky Americans were not to have to pay the prices being paid by their European cousins. And the reason for the increase in oil focused on diminishing reserves, the war with Iraq, and various other conflicts taking place in the Middle East. So Americans started to become resigned to the fact that they would have to just absorb these higher prices. Some of them pushed back by purchasing smaller vehicles. They were shifting their price/value perception once again. Others fought back by simply driving less miles and therefore purchasing less gasoline. But for most American consumers, the price/value perception of gasoline has just crept upward. We have accepted these new prices with very little resistance whatsoever. While Americans do not like the upward shift in price with no corresponding increase in value, we are limited by the lack of available substitutes for gasoline. We do not think that gasoline prices are fair, but so far there has been little that we could do about them.

What Is Considered to Be Fair?

That brings us to the concept of fairness. The very word *fair* conjures up a wealth of positive images. By definition, the word possesses a variety of meanings: just and honest, impartial, unprejudiced, free from discrimination, clear, straight, square, favorable, of moderately good size, and according to the rules.[2] So when consumers hear the term **fair price** they conjure up a positive price/value relationship in their heads. When they arrive at the point at which they are prepared to make the actual purchase, if the price does match this price/value perception, they often judge the price to be unfair. Whether they proceed with the purchase is based on the extent of their feelings regarding the fairness of the price. If it appears just slightly unfair, they will probably still purchase the product. If it appears quite unfair, they may purchase the product, but may never return to purchase from this merchant again. If they perceive the price to be tremendously unfair, they will refuse to complete the transaction, they may complain to the manager, and they will tell as many people as they can about this unpleasant experience.

Communication is also an important constituent in the acceptance of changes in price. Nearly everyone is aware that increasing gasoline prices are having a huge impact on the transportation industry. At first, consumers may only think of the modes of transportation they use to get from point A to point B, such as automobiles or airplanes. But soon they have come to face the reality that the increasing price of fuel is impacting many of the products that they purchase. Even at the grocery store, the impact of gasoline prices is being felt. For example, the costs of butter and flour have increased due to the increased cost to get the ingredients from the manufacturers to the bakers. This increased cost is passed along to the baker. The baker also has to pay increased prices to get his bread to market, so he passes along this increased transportation cost to the grocer. And then the grocer has to pass along this increase to the consumer.

Now consumers greatly dislike surprises when it affects their pocketbooks. So the smart grocer would prepare his consumers to anticipate increased prices due to the impact of fuel costs on the grocer's suppliers. Communicating the fact that the price of gasoline has increased the price of the ingredients that go into making a product will have the consumer decide whether to accept the new price/value relationship or seek out alternative products. However, it is very important that the consumer understands that the cause of the increased prices is not the grocer, but rather the increased cost of a barrel of oil. Therefore by effectively communicating with customers, the grocer deflects

Courtesy of Destination Hotels & Resorts.

The Driscoll Austin.

any perception of unfairness in setting his new higher prices and the resulting anger is redirected back to the originating cause of these price increases.

So when it comes to practicing revenue management, hospitality organizations must keep one eye on the bottom line and one eye on their customers. Organizations need to carefully monitor their customers' reactions to price changes and be prepared to make adjustments as needed. For it is not only about the cost of acquiring and replacing these customers, it is about the perception of the organization within the marketplace. We have all stayed away from purchases that our friends told us were a rip-off. Conversely, we have often rushed to make purchases when our friends told us about the great deal they had just found. Remember that we stated that friends and family greatly influence consumer purchases. This is particularly true when it applies to the concept of perceived fairness.

How to Increase Prices . . .

Again, this highlights the importance of knowing the wants, needs, and desires of the organization's customers and understanding their sensitivity to price as it applies to the organization's products and services. Many consumers will happily pay a higher price to receive any products or services remaining in periods of high demand. However, it is when demand is moderate that organizations must be very careful in managing their revenues. Raise prices too high too quickly and risk rapidly losing customers. Raise prices across the board and price/value perceptions may suffer when comparisons could easily be made to available substitutes. Here we present two methods of implementing price increases without causing irreparable damage to the price/value relationship.

The first method is to raise prices slowly over time. A two- or five-dollar increase every six months in the price of a guest room will be almost imperceptible to most market segments. The second method is to prepare the consumer for the price increase and convince them that the value of the product or service matches this new price level as we saw in the example with our grocer. Another example of this consumer preparation occurs whenever a facility completes a renovation. The marketing team goes into action, raving about the newest greatest facilities and increasing the excitement level as customers anticipate this new and improved product or service. So when the renovated facility reopens, the sheer newness of the renovation helps to reinforce this perception in the eyes of the consumer. Given this wonderful newness in the product or service, the increase in price appears to be totally justified.

And as the reader will learn through review of the applications chapters, there are various other methods used to increase price and revenues. Today, one of the most popular methods is to assign separate values to individual units of production and then add customized value until the value is level with the price in each targeted consumer's mind. Technology is enabling us to develop and tweak these customized relationships easily and faster than ever imagined possible. It will be left to each hospitality organization to determine how best to manage these customized relationships over the long term.

Pricing Laws to Protect Consumers

Unfortunately, not all organizations play by the rules and regulations of the marketplace. This is why laws have been enacted to protect the consumer. The first group of laws that we will address are the **antitrust laws** designed to prevent restraints on trade.

These laws were enacted in the late 1800s to protect both consumers and businesses. They prohibit behavior that is unfair and uncompetitive in nature. They also prohibit any actions that violate society's standards of ethical behavior. For example, businesses colluding to set prices artificially high would be in violation of the antitrust laws. Hospitality executives should exercise extreme caution when discussing prices for upcoming events with competitors. Sometimes the mere appearance of collusion is enough to dissuade customers from purchasing from an organization or market.

There are also laws against price gouging. **Price gouging** is defined as setting price levels much higher than what is perceived just and fair. We earlier alluded to the price gouging that occurred in some hotels in Mississippi and Louisiana following Hurricane Katrina. In these cases, price gouging was easily proved as the hotels increased their rates sometimes by 400 percent to take advantage of the lack of inhabitable hotel supply in the region. They did not care at all about the consumers. Complaints quickly poured in and the attorneys general for each state decided to press charges of price gouging against the establishments. The establishments were immediately ordered to cease their price gouging practices. In many cases, they were faced with both criminal charges and huge fines.

Currently, there are no federal laws against price gouging. However, the aftermath of 2005's devastating hurricane season has initiated several laws against price gouging at the state level. The breadth of the laws ranges from covering just essential goods and services to covering all consumer goods following a natural disaster or other physical emergency such as a dam break. However, an organization may adjust prices to reasonably cover the increased cost of providing the product or service to the consumer. An example would be a restaurant charging slightly higher prices to offset the cost of additional ice or the cost to run a generator.

Many economists disagree with the concept of setting controls of any kind on price in a free market economy. They suggest that the mechanisms of the market will put pressure on prices to fall back toward equilibrium as additional resources become available. Additionally, when prices appear to be exorbitant, consumers will seek out alternative products and services or conserve remaining resources. This may also result in many consumers shifting their demand to substitute products or services and abandoning the original product, which also creates a downward pressure on both its price and demand.

Potential Bumps in the Road

Now that we have seen how legal and ethical issues weigh upon price and the implementation of revenue management strategies and tactics, let's shift our focus to look at some of the potential problems an organization may encounter when trying to follow the RevMAP. Both internal and external environmental factors may impact the entire strategic revenue management planning process.

The first major issue is that of organizational buy-in. If the decision makers within the organization do not understand or believe in the concept of revenue management, the possibility of properly implementing a strategic revenue management plan is greatly diminished. There is still a significant population of hospitality executives who think that revenue management is only about increasing and placing controls on prices. They have no idea how to properly manage channels and inventory or develop products and services that may best meet the needs, wants, and desires of their customers. In fact, they may not even be able to identify their customers or why they buy. Some executives may lack a thorough understanding of economic principles or have an aversion to learning about new technological innovations. And whenever a person is challenged regarding his or her level of knowledge, defensive mechanisms usually kick in. So, often the less a person understands a concept, the more he or she will resist its implementation. Whenever buy-in is lacking within an organization, obtaining necessary resources becomes a major struggle.

Let's recap the basic resources needed to implement a strategic revenue plan. First, there is the need for the appropriate levels of personnel. Many of us know of General Managers who would rather have the reservation telephone lines be lit up with a dozen calls holding than hire one additional reservation agent at $8 per hour. This simply does not make sense. If that reservation agent makes just one sale that day of a theater ticket at $75, a hotel room at $125, or an airline seat at $300, he or she has more than paid for her $64 daily wage and most likely paid for the daily cost of her benefits as well. And if you think about it, that agent is easily going to handle many more purchases in one day. One of the first struggles faced by the revenue management team is acquiring the appropriate number of personnel to effectively activate a revenue optimization program.

Another problem arises with the level of experience and skill set of the personnel that the organization shifts over to the revenue management role. Many of these associates are given daily tasks to perform, such as report generation, without being properly trained to understand the big picture. They don't know what they are looking for, so the organization should not be surprised when they don't find it. Training, training, and more training is necessary to enable anyone to perfect his or her own job. The greater the skill set, the more valuable will be the information an individual generates. And the more competent and confident associates become, the more they contribute to the overall organizational goals and objectives.

When it comes to human resources, some sectors of the hospitality industry have also been known to be penny wise and pound foolish. This means that they will pay lower wages rather than forking out a few more dollars to attract and retain the best talent. The hospitality industry has one of the highest turnover rates among both management and line-level employees of any industry. Much of this can be tracked directly back to poor recruitment, selection, and training practices. Lesser qualified people are hired at lower wages and not trained properly in the beginning, leading to incompetence, eroding confidence, and eventual disillusionment or dismissal.

Another factor impacting the turnover rate in hospitality is the long and unusual hours worked. We are a 24/7 industry and variances in demand do not always lend themselves to the optimal staffing levels at all times. So hospitality industry employees rapidly experience periods of burnout. Slowly, this situation is starting to change. The echo boomers and the millennial generation are seeking better work/life balances then their baby boomer parents. Burnout is a serious risk to the revenue management effort. Revenue management is a cerebral process, requiring long periods of analyzing numbers and data. Several people should therefore be drafted to the team in an effort to both alleviate the potential for burnout and to obtain different insights into capturing additional revenue opportunities. Obtaining a variety of diverse perceptions and opinions will also enable an organization to best satisfy its wide array of guests.

A related but slightly separate issue arises when determining the appropriate level of technological support to be allocated to the revenue management team. Again, there is a personnel issue to consider. Is the revenue management effort at this location large enough to dedicate one technical specialist to the team full-time? Or does the revenue management team call upon the **Information Technology (IT) Department** only when needed? Depending upon the size of an organization, the IT Department may range from one computer technician onsite to a full division comprised of computer technicians, information analysts, programmers and developers, and strategic system designers. Does the organization's current IT team possess the knowledge, skills, and abilities to assist the revenue management team in linking to the GDS and IDS? Does the organization have to wait and consult its corporate office whenever it wishes to implement even small changes? Are the individual business units involved with developing information technology strategies? And most importantly, does the IT team know how to expand the organization's ability to capture additional customers through the various channels?

One of the most time-consuming aspects of the revenue management process is managing inventory across multiple channels. Once again, technology plays a significant role here. Does the organization possess the proper hardware and software to quickly adjust prices and inventory across multiple channels? Is the technology advanced enough to alert the revenue management team to changes in demand requiring adjustments to be made in rate or inventory? Is management providing the proper budgetary support to enable the revenue management team to obtain the tools and resources that it needs to be most effective?

Most of the potential obstacles that we just addressed come down to one major element and that is money. If the organization does not properly budget for the tools and resources needed by the revenue management team to be successful, results will likely suffer. This may lead back to the decision makers using the team's failure as a confirmation of the decision makers' original doubts and justification for their lack of support. This could easily become a vicious circle as the revenue management team does not receive adequate resources, so they do not perform at the optimal level, leading to additional erosion of support and even less resources the second time around.

Some other potential obstacles facing the RMT include extremely rapidly changing conditions, never-before experienced conditions, and extremely adverse conditions. An example of rapidly changing conditions may be the economic demise of a major market demand generator as was the case in the demise of the dot-com organizations. A dramatic fall in the stock market would be another example. Events are occurring faster than the RMT is able to respond. Prices adjusted from yesterday are obsolete today. The opportunity to sell additional inventory came and went in under a day. One day airline passengers were allowed to board a plane carrying shampoo in their carry-on bag and the next day they were not.

An example of a never-before experienced condition is the situation the country faced on September 11 and the days following the terrorists attacks. The United States had never experienced a domestic disaster of this magnitude, so most people and organizations reacted with numbed silence. Once the shock wore off, their entire world had changed. What was once certain was now uncertain. Consumer behavior deviated from pattern and Americans struggled to define this new existence.

And finally an example of extremely adverse conditions would be the conditions following any of the recent major natural disasters. Whenever natural disasters occur, the landscape will change in both physical and metaphorical terms. The rules have changed. Expectations have changed. Propensity and purpose of purchase are altered completely. Some landscapes take years to recover and some may never return to their predisaster state.

The Richardson Dallas Lobby.

Sometimes problems will arise from other departments within the organization. The first potential area of conflict arises between the Sales Department and the RMT. Many times a salesperson may spend months or years cultivating a customer and when that customer decides to finally make a purchase, that purchase is declined by the RMT. Naturally, this frustrates and disillusions the salesperson who may now see the RMT as his or her enemy and an obstacle to his or her success. Salespeople are very territorial about their customers, so it takes a great effort and a lot of communication to develop a working relationship to get everyone thinking on the same page. In some cases, it will just never happen. The hurt runs too deep and war zones are created. If this scenario arises, it should quickly be addressed. If no resolution is possible, a realignment of personnel and resources may be required to achieve the organization's revenue management goals and objectives.

Some problems that arise in the general strategic management process often rear their ugly heads in the strategic revenue management process as well. For example, some people who do not understand the process or dislike the process will hope that it will fail. These are the people who just love to say, "See, I told you so." They prefer the status quo and would like nothing more than for everything to remain exactly as it is today. Sometimes they are so adverse to change that they will sabotage a process to ensure that it will fail. Keep in mind that fear of the unknown masquerades as aversion to change. This may be more common in regard to revenue management too due to the high application of technological tools and resources. This again brings us back to the importance of obtaining buy-in and taking the time to properly train all associates to enable them to achieve their responsibilities in a comfortable and confident manner.

If the organization does not hire a dedicated revenue management team, but instead adds revenue management tasks to the list of duties being performed by the Director of Sales, Reservations Manager, or Front Office Manager, many strategies and tactics may simply go unimplemented. This occurs when the selected personnel are too busy accomplishing their primary tasks to have any time to focus on the revenue management effort. In this scenario, revenue management is given a subordinate role and will never achieve its potential as a strategic management process.

Another problem results from the failure to regularly review, monitor, and adjust tactics as shifts in the external and internal environments occur. Opportunities may be lost or threats may be encountered. An organization should make a concerted effort to regularly review the results of its strategies and tactics. This is best accomplished through the use of daily duties and meeting attendance as previously outlined. And while some organizations are great at obtaining and reviewing the results, they fall short on implementing needed changes. Again, some individuals will be adverse to change, some will be territorial if the failing strategy or tactic was one that they proposed and continue to hang on to, and some may lack a sense of urgency regarding implementing a needed change.

And finally, some organizations simply do not know where to start. They have not drafted their RMT since there are no players in their organization who have ever previously played the game. These organizations are fortunate in that they are at least aware of their need to get into the game. Fortunately, there are ample tools and resources today to help them get started. Hopefully, this book will provide the spark for them to begin. For everyone who is involved, or is about to become involved, in revenue management, we have polished off our crystal ball and provided a glimpse into the future in our next chapter.

SUMMARY

Money causes people to act and react in the most emotional manner. Revenue management is often equated with raising rates. But as we have seen, that is only one small element in the practice of strategic revenue management. However, it is very important for revenue management professionals to understand the market dynamics of increasing prices.

There are several legal and ethical issues surrounding price, including antitrust legislation and state laws against price gouging. These laws were designed to protect consumers and businesses alike. Organizations must learn to manage their rates both within the law and with one eye on the consumer.

Strategic revenue management development and implementation often face obstacles to achievement. These potential bumps in the road include lack of organizational buy-in, lack of resources, poor funding, inadequate or untrained personnel, and lack of available time to properly implement strategies and tactics. In addition, today's RMT faces extremely rapidly changing conditions, never-before experienced conditions, and extremely adverse conditions. And some organizations simply do not know where to start. And the best place to begin is with our RevMAP.

KEY TERMS AND CONCEPTS

The following key terms and concepts were presented in this chapter. Each term and concept is also contained in the Glossary of Terms located at the end of this book:

- antitrust laws
- fair price
- Information Technology (IT) Department
- negotiate
- price gouging

DISCUSSION QUESTIONS

1. Do you feel that raising prices to meet demand is fair? Why or why not?
2. Provide one example of a price increase that you feel is fair. Provide one example of a price increase that you feel is unfair.
3. In what other ways could an organization go about raising prices?
4. Have you ever experienced any examples of price gouging personally? If so, please explain.
5. What other potential bumps in the road can you foresee for revenue managers?

INTERNET EXERCISES

1. Go online and check to see if your state has enacted any price gouging laws. Report your findings.
2. Go online and search for any organizations announcing price increases. Did they make the announcement themselves? Or was it a result of a news story? How do you think that this price increase will go over with consumers?

REFERENCES

1. Byron, George Gordon Noel. Letter, July 14, 1821. *Born for Opposition: Byron's Letters and Journals*, vol. 8, ed. Leslie A. Marchand, Cambridge: Harvard University Press, 1978.

2. Webster's New World College Dictionary, 4th ed. Wiley, 2002

A Seat with a View.

CHAPTER

Crystal Ball

![Chapter Objectives]

The objectives of this chapter are to:

- Explore how the Internet has impacted pricing and the tracking of market segments
- Identify how customers' usage of the Internet may impact revenue management practices in the future
- Discuss other key developments that are shaping the application of revenue management principles
- Speculate on future enhancements in revenue management systems and marketing intelligence research and resources
- Discuss how the revenue management professional may take advantage of these new changes and what new knowledge, skills, and abilities might be required to achieve success

What might the future hold for revenue management? With the changes brought about by the continuing evolution of the Internet, technological enhancements, new distribution relationships, and changing consumer expectations, the practice of revenue management undoubtedly will be required to adapt. Although difficult to predict with certainty, several trends are emerging that may hint at what those future adaptations may look like. In this chapter, we will explore these trends and provide insights into how these trends may shape the discipline of Revenue Management. You will also have the opportunity to let your imagination take you into your own future and speculate on what you may see when you arrive there. Finally, we will explore what skill sets you may wish to develop to better prepare yourself for this new tomorrow. Now, let's buckle up, it's going to be an exciting ride!

A Brief Look Back . . .

Let's start by taking a look back in time and examine what the Internet has done to pricing over the past several years. As previously discussed, price fences are established to segment customer types. Following the economic slowdown in 2001, which was accelerated by the precipitous drop in demand following the events of 9/11, providers of hospitality products and services were desperate to fill guest rooms. Many saw Internet travel sites as a way to reach value-conscious customer segments, so they offered discounted rates to attract **incremental business** (guests that would not stay with them otherwise), while preserving what was remaining of their higher-rated business segments. One significant pricing fence that existed during these early times of the Internet was the limited use of the Internet itself.

Compared to today, far fewer Internet users were online, and of those online, fewer still were willing to purchasing much of anything. Clearly, hoteliers saw this channel of distribution as a safe place to discreetly move perishable inventory. What happened?

These Internet channels of distribution became very popular very quickly. As more and more people heard of the great values to be had online, adoption rates rose meteorically to the point where these channels were no longer discreet, but rather mainstream contributors of significant volumes of business. Once the domain of leisure travel, business travelers began to use these same Internet intermediaries to make travel arrangements and caused segment tracking on the part of suppliers to become very challenging as the lines of definition that once existed between these very different types of travelers became blurred.

The Internet also allowed the average consumer, for the first time, to easily see travel suppliers' pricing structures. In the past, travelers needed to rely heavily on the expertise of travel agents to decipher the cryptic rate codes and associated rules in the GDS systems. The pricing transparency offered by the Internet combined with the new volume of business coming through these channels at the time forced hospitality providers to rethink their revenue management strategies. How did they respond?

Many adopted the practice of price parity across channels. This meant that a prospective guest who called their local travel agent, the organization directly, the chain 800#, clicked on the property or chain website, or other online intermediary would get the same quote for the same hospitality product or service available over the same dates. In the same way that pricing strategies were impacted, the blurring of segmentation also meant that hospitality providers needed to rethink how they tracked and reported customer types. Many organizations abandoned the idea of attempting to segment their transient (individual) customers into corporate and leisure travelers, but instead favored tracking midweek (Sunday through Thursday) production and weekend (Friday and Saturday) production in order to identify trend information and measure the effectiveness of their marketing efforts.

Searching the Internet

With the unprecedented volume of online content available, consumers are seeking ways to filter out irrelevant search returns and ensure that what they receive is meaningful and tailored specifically to their unique interests. Searches as we know them today will likely look very different tomorrow. Imagine a search engine such as Google, MSN, or Yahoo! tracking your online behavior—the websites you visit, how long you stay on those sites, what specific pages you go to, what types of transactions you make online, what you download, what you share with friends or relatives. Perhaps too, this information would be augmented and refined through a special "just for me" page, where you could build your own profile and specify your individual interests based on the range of options provided. In addition, it is now possible for suppliers of online content to access profile data on you based on your off-line expenditures (more on this later). Now imagine this same search tool using information about you to serve up highly filtered and customized content automatically based on your historical online habits, your online profile, and your offline spending patterns. Or better yet, instead of wading through pages and pages of websites, imagine this search engine returning the exact websites you are most likely to need based on your identified interests at that time.

A good example of this would be, say, a search for "Paris Hilton." If your demonstrated interests related to fragrances, glamour, fashion, actors, or celebrities, you probably wouldn't be very interested in knowing that there is a Hilton Hotel located close to the Eiffel Tower on Avenue de Sufferen in Paris, France. On the other hand, if you were identified as having an interest in traveling to Europe based on your more recent online searches and yesterday's credit card purchase at your local luggage store, you probably would be very interested to know that this hotel exists. In addition, you may also want to know what other accommodation choices may exist in the vicinity, what airlines will take you to Paris from your current location (as this too can be easily determined based on from which point you access the Internet), how to get to the hotel from Charles de Gaulle International Airport, and what sort of sightseeing activities are available over the planned dates of your stay.

Revenue managers of tomorrow will be challenged to think through how they can take advantage of this medium to reach the right travelers at just the right time by providing both relevant content and the right offers in order to optimize both primary and ancillary revenues. We identified "Customer Knowledge" as our first fundamental element in the development of a revenue management strategy. Tomorrow we may have the ability to take this definition to a whole new level. Can you think of any downsides to this level of customer knowledge? Will the right to privacy be challenged? If a travel supplier has access to this type of customer insight, how do you think they may be able to use it effectively and not negatively impact their relationship with a prospective or existing customer?

Another way that individuals are using the Internet to obtain relevant content is through online collaboration. The proliferation of blogs (Weblogs), since becoming popular in 1999, plus websites such as Igo Ugo and Tripadvisor now allows individuals to both learn and share feedback on specific travel-related providers and experiences from around the globe. For example, site visitors or subscribers can quickly and easily learn what others liked and didn't like about their recent visit perhaps to San Francisco based on these posted reviews and comments. As these types of sites continue to grow in popularity, it is can be reasonably foreseen that likeminded individuals would be interested in learning from, and sharing with, their peers. For example, as a student planning this year's spring break, you would probably prefer to hear what other students had to say about a hotel they selected for their spring break trip to Miami last year. Certainly, you may learn something from the opinions shared by a regular business traveler to that city, but it is highly likely that this road warrior may not be looking for the same types of things that would be meaningful to you on your vacation.

All of this means that the revenue manager of tomorrow will be better able to assess the value that a given customer segment places on their product or services by closely monitoring these sites. In addition, they may be able to discover new opportunities and customer types.

For example, a hotel may be surprised to find out that private pilots flying into the local airport like to stay with them because of their proximity to a popular aviation museum, the free breakfast that is offered, and the shuttle service offered within a five-mile radius of the hotel. An astute revenue manager would recognize the opportunity to develop a uniquely priced pilot's package complete with admission tickets to the local aviation museum. They could also collaborate with the sales staff to call on the **fixed base operations (FBOs),** those companies operating out of the local airport, and work with their website developer to enable sales of the package online complete with relevant "links" from other sources to broaden the exposure.

As you can see, the role of tomorrow's revenue manager may incorporate different elements than what is traditionally contemplated by many organizations today. It will also demand a different skill set, including an in-depth knowledge of marketing, e-commerce, and direct sales.

Enabling technology, such as **RSS (really simple syndication) feeds,** will also allow travelers to select customized content views that will be highly personalized and updated, in real time, as new opportunities and offers are made available. Many people use RSS feeds today, but don't even realize it. For example, you may have a "My Yahoo!" account that allows you to customize your personal home page to include top news stories, weather from your home town, and movie times for shows at the theatre down the street. RSS is the technology behind the scenes that allows for this level of customization. What does this mean to those in the Revenue Management discipline?

It means that for the first time, suppliers will be able to communicate electronically, in real time, with anyone interested in receiving their content. Special offers, promotional opportunities, public relations initiatives and more can be readily distributed in a moment's notice. Need to sell some last-minute seats on a certain flight or for an event? Send out an exceptional deal to RSS subscribers to stimulate last-minute (opportunistic) demand. It is not unreasonable to surmise that, in the not too distant future, passengers of an airline could subscribe to an RSS feed that will allow them to select a destination of their choice, in the requested travel dates and times and subsequently receive an individualized offer along with alternatives (depending upon the flexibility of the travelers' schedule) directly from the airline.

Tomorrow's technology will evolve to allow these airlines to recognize the potential lifetime value of a particular passenger and offer value in terms of pricing and/or services on a highly individualized basis. Branding, loyalty, experience, and passenger relationships will all be enhanced as a result. This will most likely signal the need for suppliers to once again reestablish or redefine market segmentation and pricing strategies as we rapidly move toward the reality of a market segment of a single individual.

Dynamic packaging (meaning travel components, supplier services and/or destination services that are bundled together) based on the individual selections made by a traveler is just one more trend that will likely continue to gain momentum in the years ahead. Dynamic packaging will require enhanced communication between airlines, car rental companies, lodging providers, event centers, golf operations, bicycle shops, restaurants, sightseeing tour companies, flower shops, and more. People will want *what* they want, *when* they want it, and *how* they want it. The next time you are waiting for an elevator with the button already lit, watch who comes up beside you and presses the button again to make sure that you pressed the button properly and that the elevator is really coming to take them up. This sounds a lot like Sally from the movie, doesn't it? All that this means really is that people want to feel as though they have some degree of control over their lives. With time and other constraints being placed on us from home, work, or school pressures, it's nice to know that we have some freedom to shape our environment and experiences. This is particularly true when it comes to planning all types of travel. Revenue managers of the future will need to recognize this trend to maximize the revenue opportunities for their employer. This could be simply a matter of disclosing rate availability over different sets of dates to allow travelers to select the travel times that best suit their needs and budget. It could also mean that extra efforts need be made to widen the breadth of experiences that are offered through a single point of sale—such as an airline's website for example.

Can customization go too far? The next time you are at Starbucks, observe the people who are in line. You may see customers at the front of the line standing looking up at the choices on the board as they are ordering. This may mean that they are "inexperienced" at quickly and efficiently ordering coffee or perhaps they are trying to remember what their friend had asked them to pick up. In either case, they are probably aware of the person behind them breathing down their neck, you know, the impatient one from the elevator. They are also likely wishing that there were fewer choices from which to select. The same holds true for distributors of travel-related services. There is probably a point of diminishing returns where too much choice will actually hurt the firm's revenue potential. The secret is in thoroughly understanding your customers and serving up solutions that best meet their expectations.

Just as technology will impact how customers interact with travel suppliers, suppliers too will benefit from enhanced tools and systems that will help them to meet the demands of this changing landscape. The calculations related to the value associated with taking a particular booking at a particular time, the probability of converting a higher-rated piece of business at a later date, or the decision as to which inventory restrictions to place on which product categories to optimize availability for anticipated future demand seems like a daunting task. In reality, manual tools and processes can be developed to aid in making sound business decisions. In fact, many suppliers have been successfully operating in a manual environment for years. Obviously, the mental gymnastics involved in making optimal decisions consistently over time in an ever-changing environment is nearly impossible without the aid of technology.

While many software systems exist today that enable suppliers to make informed revenue management decisions based on sophisticated mathematical algorithms, these too will undoubtedly evolve. Some of the companies in this space include Integrated Decisions and Systems Inc., Opus2 Revenue Technologies, Pros Revenue Management, Easy Revenue Management Systems, and Optims, to name a few. Some of these systems will incorporate competitors' pricing strategies into their calculations and use this to provide recommendations, not only regarding inventory restrictions and rate controls, but to formulate pricing by individual customer and/or segment.

Systems and technology will never replace the role of a revenue manager, but rather help make an effective revenue manager that much better. Other elements essential to making a revenue management initiative a success, such as management buy-in, a strong enterprise-wide revenue management culture, defined processes, good communication, market knowledge and product positioning, will remain unchanged.

Products and services related to competitive intelligence will also continue to grow and improve. Smith Travel Research based near Nashville, Tennessee, is a firm that has been tracking hospitality industry performance since 1988. Using their "STR®" report, a property can benchmark their own historical performance on a monthly basis against a specific competitive set, their market, or an entire region. Since that time, Smith Travel Research has continued to add to its product offerings to include such tools as airport statistics, lodging supply and pipeline reports, and market trend reports, which allows subscribers to view performance benchmark measures on a day-to-day basis and by broad customer segment (group, leisure individual, and corporate individual). To see a sample report, access www.smithtravelresearch.com and click on browse all products. Enter a city and a list of available reports pops up. Students may scroll through and view sample reports without subscribing to the service. Smith Travel Research will likely expand its offerings to allow hotels and resorts to benchmark their performance in non–room-related revenue outlets. Golf- or spa-related revenue benchmarking may be an example of the types of data products that may exist in the future that don't exist today.

> Another company that provides revenue management tools to organizations is TravelCLICK. "TravelCLICK was originally established to provide key data and statistics for a variety of applications including central reservations, GDS performance benchmarking and marketing. Since that time, the company's vision has evolved to become much more. Today, TravelCLICK helps hotels drive demand, increase conversion and generate higher revenue through integrated distribution technology and marketing solutions. Its Hotelligence and Hotelligence FuturePace reports allow hotels to easily benchmark their historic and future GDS performance against a selected competitive set. While RateVIEW enables properties to 'shop' competitors'

rates and changes made to those rates over time. TravelCLICK is also pioneering an intriguing approach to improving manual pricing. Its rate recommendation tool, RateADVISOR, merges competitive pricing intelligence with the sophisticated mathematical algorithms by IDeaS to provide hotels with a suggested 'optimal' rate. TravelCLICK's tool set fits naturally into a hotel's ongoing revenue management process."[1]

As the future unfolds, these types of creative relationships between service providers will continue to develop. Again, it is important to establish a fundamentally sound revenue management strategy and process by following the RevMAP concept introduced earlier and then to properly integrate the best products and services available at the time that will complement your strategy. Buying advanced products and services without first identifying a sound strategy and process could do more harm than good.

We can speculate that in the future customer satisfaction levels and revenue management will become more closely tied. For example, in the past, if a restaurant patron didn't like their experience due, let's say, to a rude server, the establishment may risk losing a customer. Perhaps in addition this patron may tell his or her handful of friends about this server's transgressions and the establishment may lose the opportunity to serve them too. At worst, the patron may happen to have been a food critic and may have a loyal following of readers in the local paper who will follow his or her advice not to eat at that restaurant. If they are fortunate, the establishment may have been given the opportunity to correct the situation before it got out of hand and temper the potential damage that would otherwise be caused.

In the era of online collaboration, however, the damage may not be limited to a group of friends or a local paper, but a bad review could be instantaneously broadcast to millions worldwide. Many will choose not to eat at this establishment based on these prior bad reviews despite the restaurant's best marketing efforts. Revenue managers of the future will need to have a clear picture of the establishments' online reputation in order to appropriately price products and services relative to their competitors. The role of a revenue manager may need to expand in the future in some cases to include the development of service training standards and measurement. Hold on! You may be thinking "isn't that the responsibility of operations?" Technically, the answer is "yes", in theory; however, the title of this book includes the words ". . . for the real world." You will find that, in the real world, most business organizational structures are more "organic" than not—meaning that not everything fits neatly into a box based on role and title. Some responsibilities such as identifying new revenue opportunities or improving customer satisfaction should be shared. The extent to which these shared responsibilities are executed successfully within an organization depends upon the culture of that organization. The culture of that organization is driven by leadership—not necessarily the boss—but the norms that have been championed, established, and measured or rewarded. Even a revenue manager new to his or her role in an organization can have a dramatic impact on aspects that go beyond what is contained in his or her official job description. As roles change, so will

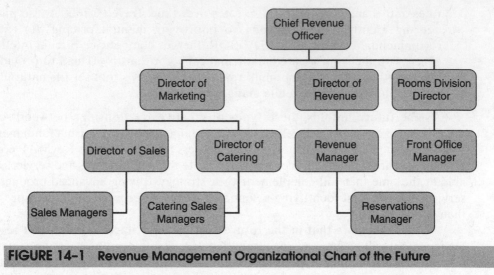

FIGURE 14-1   Revenue Management Organizational Chart of the Future

Note: The Chief Revenue Officer would report directly to the General Manager.

organizational charts. We have included one possible organizational chart of the future in Figure 14–1.

In this scenario, our Chief Revenue Officer reports directly to the General Manager. And then reporting directly to the Chief Revenue Officer are the Director of Marketing, Director of Revenue, and Rooms Division Director. We feel that this organizational chart may more accurately reflect the reporting structure of the future.

And exactly what should go into a revenue managers' job description given the speed at which the above trends are shaping how we think about this relatively new role? That is definitely a difficult question to answer as it depends on many factors as you have already discovered; however, we can explore some of the skill sets that would be helpful to develop as you contemplate how the future role of a revenue manager may appear. The skills, experience, and knowledge previously identified are summarized below, as they will be enduring:

- Communication
- Leadership
- Direct sales (preferably in your chosen industry sector)
- Reservation sales
- Distribution management
- Finance
- Analytical aptitude (a course in logic may be helpful)
- Economics

Courtesy of Lisa Marie Parker.

Princeville, Kauai, Hawaii.

- Marketing
- E-commerce
- Sociology
- Psychology

In addition, there are some "soft skills" that can be developed or inherent talents that can be honed that will help the revenue manager to remain effective in the future, regardless of current trends or demands. Below is a partial list of what those may look like:

- Drive (self-starter)
- Passion (motivation and energy)
- Detail orientation (patience and diligence)
- People skills (leadership and communication)
- Sales skills (persuasion)
- Ability to synthesize (develop a comprehensive understanding of a situation)
- Creativity (imagination)
- Curiosity (driven to seek answers to questions)
- Calculated risk taking (push the envelope to discover or create new possibilities)

There are many more trends and industry developments that we have not explored in this book that will continue to shape the future of this exciting field. Suffice it to say that once you have read this textbook, you will have a much better understanding of some of the fundamentals associated with this discipline and you can then review the stories contained in Chapter 1 with a new-found perspective and appreciation. The application chapters that follow will serve to hone your newly obtained knowledge even further. The field of revenue management is exciting, dynamic, challenging, and rewarding. Professionals skilled in the practice and application of revenue management principles will be in great demand in the years ahead. And, the journey has just begun.

SUMMARY

This chapter outlines the impact that the Internet has had on pricing and market segmentation definitions and explores ways in which this medium may impact the travel industry in the future. We continue by speculating on how revenue management systems, research, and intelligence resources are likely to be enhanced in the future and conclude by reexamining which skills and experiences will assist revenue management professionals in being effective.

KEY TERMS AND CONCEPTS

The following key terms and concepts were presented in this chapter. Each term and concept is also contained in the Glossary of Terms located at the end of this book:

- dynamic packaging
- fixed base operations (FBOs)
- incremental business
- RSS (really simple syndication) feeds

DISCUSSION QUESTIONS

1. Where do you see revenue management heading as a profession?
2. How do you believe customization will change in the next five years?
3. Look into your crystal ball and share what you see.

INTERNET EXERCISE

Go online and review any of the tools mentioned in this chapter. Do you feel this would be useful in your work? How so?

REFERENCE

1. TravelClick's website, accessed March 18, 2007, http://www.travelclick.net.

Seagrove at L'Auberge Del Mar Resort and Spa.

CHAPTER

15

Applications in Lodging and Food and Beverage

Chapter Objectives

The objectives of this chapter are to:

■ Explore the application of revenue management techniques in lodging and food and beverage establishments

■ Consider several scenarios, strategies, and tactics for the Lofty Pines Lodge, an elegant mountain ski resort

■ Consider several scenarios, strategies, and tactics for Chic B'tique, a hip and happening new city-center hotel

■ Consider several scenarios, strategies, and tactics for Scrumptious!, a fine-dining restaurant

In this chapter we are going to embark upon a journey using our RevMAP to venture to scenic locations along the way. We will apply the knowledge gained thus far to envision an effervescent stream rushing toward a pot of gold waiting just around the next bend in the road leading to our destination. Let's begin our journey by taking a quick trip to the mountains.

The Lofty Pines Lodge and Ski Resort

The first snow of the year has just dusted the trees along the Rocky Mountain Front Range. For millions of people that means just one thing. Time to wax the skis! And to thousands of others, it means time to polish up the snowboard! So the first stop in our journey will be the top of Mount Powder for a weekend stay at The Lofty Pines Lodge and Ski Resort.

The Lofty Pines Lodge has resided at the top of Mount Powder since the early 1960s. It is a traditional ski lodge, built with rough hewn timber beams and rugged boulders. Hearing the crush of stones under the wheels as the SUV pulls up in the drive, one has the feel of arriving at a classic European ski resort. The lobby smells of crisp mountain air, pine resin, and a musky woodsy smoke. The well-burnished baby-soft leather sofas beckon the traveler to plop down before the crackling fire. Spa brochures sit atop an imposing concierge desk placed in front of the French doors opening onto the terrace. And laughter, accompanied by a subtle clink of crystal, emanates from the doorway leading to a cozy slope-side lounge. Immediately, the traveler appreciates the lush accommodations of this luxury mountain retreat.

Hopefully, the reader is now imagining being curled up in front of the fire, sipping a hot chocolate or hot apple cider. Wonderful! In each of our scenarios, we will attempt to transport you to the scene to help you to use visual imagery to envision the possible revenue opportunities present at that location. We will present the facts and then some possible revenue management strategies and tactics that may be implemented at that destination. To begin, here is some additional information on the Lofty Pines Lodge:

Physical facilities:

- 268 guest rooms, including eight deluxe suites
- One fine-dining restaurant, called the Embers (naturally)
- One breakfast café, called the Lift
- One lounge, called Après
- 18,000 square feet of meeting space
- A full-service spa
- Beauty salon
- Business center
- Ski rental shop
- Gift shop
- Alpine garden
- Indoor/outdoor pool
- Located within a two-hour drive of Denver
- Transportation possible via automobile, private plane, or resort shuttle

Products and services available:

- Guest rooms (kings, double queens, and suites)
- Meeting rooms
- Conference services
- Catering services
- Breakfast
- Lunch
- Dinner
- Snacks
- Room service
- Cocktails
- Fireside entertainment in the evening
- Full range of spa services
- Salon services
- Ski rentals
- Discounted lift tickets

- Shuttle service to village
- Concierge
- Valet

Abbreviated SWOT Analysis for the Lofty Pines Lodge

Strengths: Reputation, location, facilities, amenities, service, new spa

Weaknesses: No brand affiliation, remote location

Opportunities: Increase capture of Front Range skiers, great snow forecast, spa grand opening

Threats: Lack of snow potential, high gas prices

Competitors: Total room supply for the resort area is 1,909 guest rooms. Only one other facility contains a full service spa, but several contain comparable meeting space.

Time period used for analysis: October 1st through November 15th (a shoulder season)

Booking pace and pattern: Slow for weekdays; high demand for Saturday nights. Saturday nights are already 70 percent sold out.

Channels currently used: Lodge website, merchant models, direct mailings to travel agents, Small Luxury Ski Resort Association (referral service), direct sales efforts, ski resort association central reservation system

Guest room price range for time period: $199 to $385 for king and double queen; $425 to $595 for suites. Price is per room per night.

Overview

During this time period, the resort traditionally sells out on Saturday nights. In the early weeks of October, Saturday nights are filled with color tour visitors. **Color tour visitors** or **color tourists** are the phrases used to describe visitors who travel up to the mountains to view the changing aspen leaves and other fall foliage. Once the leaves and snow both begin to fall, Saturday nights are filled with early-season skiers. Color tours are often enjoyed by couples. Early-season skiers and snow boarders are usually younger and more price sensitive or extremely avid enthusiasts who may not be as sensitive to price. The early season also attracts families with children who take advantage of the off-season prices for lessons and lift tickets.

What are some possible strategies and tactics that may be applied during this time period to optimize revenues?

1. First, inventory should be immediately closed to arrival for Saturday-night stays. This will force guests to book a two-night weekend stay instead. The strategy here is to increase average length of weekend stay. The tactic is closing Saturday to arrivals.

2. Consider instituting a three-night minimum stay for the two weekends that the aspen leaves are anticipated to peak. Guests could stay Thursday, Friday, and Saturday or Friday, Saturday, and Sunday nights. Rates should be maximized for these two weekends, but price may be hidden by creating an enticing color tour package. The lodge could bundle a king guest room for three nights, deluxe breakfast for two at the Lift each morning, one complimentary hot stone massage per person, beverage coupons for use in the lounge, a picnic lunch on Saturday,

and discounted rates at the area jeep rental agency. The price for this package is $1,500 per couple. The strategy here is to maximize revenues from peak color tour weekends. The first tactic is to implement a three-night minimum stay requirement. Another tactic is to develop an all-inclusive three-night stay package for couples to increase both primary and ancillary revenues.

3. The sales department could try to solicit additional small meetings to help fill the lodge midweek. They could develop an autumn package to attract more price-sensitive groups who cannot afford to stay at the lodge during peak seasons. The strategy here is to fill dates of soft demand. The tactic is to solicit price-sensitive midweek group business.

4. The lodge could offer deeply discounted guest room rates on Sunday and Monday nights to attract young price-sensitive skiers and boarders. Students have more flexible schedules enabling them to ski midweek. However, these Sunday-night discounts would not be available on the two peak color tour weekends. The strategy is to drive ski and board demand to softer periods of occupancy. The tactic is to offer discounts on dates of low demand.

5. Packages could be developed for Halloween and the weekends in November to attract families. Depending on the snow, the package could include a double queen room for Friday and Saturday nights, continental breakfast for the family on Saturday and Sunday, two-day unlimited ski passes for four, discounted ski pass for additional children, six hours of ski lessons, and discounted movie passes to the local theater. The price of the package is $999 for a family of four. The strategy is to capture price-sensitive families. The tactic is to create a family friendly package for slower-demand weekends.

6. The lodge may also decide to utilize additional channels or provide incentives in current channels to move more inventory during the shoulder season. It may purchase headline marketing in the GDS, offer travel agents 20 percent commission for all rooms arriving Sunday through Wednesday, and create and advertise Monday snowboard specials in the Front Range entertainment newspapers. The strategy is to increase production from selected channels. The tactics are to market to travel agents, offer incentives to travel agents, and reach young skiers and boarders.

What other strategies and tactics could the lodge develop to capitalize on opportunities to increase revenues? Which strategies could be developed to reduce or minimize potential threats?
This is a perfect place for the reader to take a moment to think about other possible opportunities facing the lodge during this time period.

Possible Results

Scenario #1

We stated that the lodge was already 70 percent booked for Saturdays. That leaves about 80 rooms available on each Saturday night. Let's assume that there are six Saturday nights between October 1 and November 15. So 80 times six equals 480 rooms left to sell on Saturday nights. We will assume that just half of these rooms will be sold now that a two-night minimum stay is required for guests wishing to stay over Saturday night. That leaves us with 240 rooms. Since Saturday nights are the

Skamania Lodge Forest View.

evenings of highest demand, let's also assume that the average rate for these nights is $330. If the 240 rooms were sold for one night only, total revenue would be $79,200. But now the revenue will be doubled, as guests who want to stay over Saturday night are required to book two nights. So total revenue generated is now $158,400. This one stay restriction for one night per week for just six weeks generated over $79,000 in additional revenue!

Ah, but the reader will object that some of these people would have stayed for two nights anyway. This is true! So let's say that just half of them would not have stayed for two nights. That still means that the length of stay restriction added $39,500 in revenue!

But wait, there is another factor to consider here and that is total customer worth. We are only looking at guest room revenue in this example. But there are additional ancillary revenue opportunities presented when extending a guest's length of stay. This includes money spent for food and beverage, spa services, and gift purchases. And acquisition cost was minimal as it only required the addition of a stay restriction being placed across all channels.

Scenario #2

First, we already know that we have 80 rooms left on each Saturday. We are targeting two weekends. Again, let's just assume that half of the Saturday-night rooms remaining are sold. Since a three-night minimum is required, that would mean that we would sell an additional 40 rooms for three nights over each of those weekends. 120 room nights times two weekends equals 240 room nights. Since these are the peak weekends, we determined the average rate to be the maximum at $385 per night. Multiplying 240 room nights times $385 generates a total of $92,400.

Let's assume that we sell an additional 10 packages each over the course of these two weekends. 20 packages times $1,500 equals $30,000. This revenue represents a combination of primary and ancillary revenue since the price is based upon the total elements of the package. If we add the package revenue to the three-night minimum revenue, we arrive at a total of $122,400.

Let's contrast that to not applying the restrictions or bundling the products. If the lodge sold 50 rooms for just two nights on each of these weekends, these additional 200 room nights would generate total room revenue of $77,000 at the average rate of $385. Ancillary revenues would add to this total, but in all probability the total revenues spent over these six days would be less than the $122,400 generated from the packages and length of stay restrictions.

Scenario #3

In this case, let's assume that the sales department was able to book Monday through Thursday meetings for three of the six weeks. One group needs 50 rooms for three nights arriving on Monday. The other two groups need 25 rooms per night for three nights also arriving on Monday. These total up to an additional 300 room nights. Since these groups are price sensitive, we will assume that the average room rate is $200. So 300 room nights times $200 represents an additional $60,000 in revenue.

We have only considered room revenue in this example. However, it should be noted that ancillary revenues per person are often substantial in the meetings market. Total group revenues include meeting facilities, food and beverage, audio-visual, entertainment, and possibly lift tickets. If these expenditures are calculated at just 25 percent of the room revenue, these three meetings would add total ancillary revenues of $15,000. So our total revenue generated from these small meetings would represent an additional $75,000 to the hotel. But also remember that group bookings have higher acquisition costs due to the personalized nature of the selling process and that this needs to be calculated when determining the worth of groups.

Scenario #4

In this scenario, let's assume that an additional 10 rooms are sold each Sunday and Monday night for six weeks. This represents an additional 120 room nights. Even if rates were slashed in half from the lowest rate of $199, this would generate an additional $12,000 in revenue. In reality, the rate would probably be set higher, let's say $139. Multiplying $139 by 120 equals an additional $16,680 in revenue. A few carefully placed ads in local entertainment newspapers may be enough to generate this additional business quite inexpensively.

These skiers and boarders would also spend money on food and beverage, lift tickets, and possible ski rentals. These ancillary revenue streams would need to be added to determine total revenue generated.

Scenario #5

This scenario adds the element of multiple occupancies per room. Using an average room rate of $250, the total elements of the package added up to a retail price of $1,040.

Courtesy of Destination Hotels & Resorts.

Beverage Service at Tarrytown House Estate and Conference Center.

A retail price of $999 was set instead to help generate sales. In this case, we will assume that the lodge sells 10 family packages each for two weekends. These 20 packages will generate an additional $19,980 in revenue. The lodge also added value to this package by including discounted movie tickets. In most cases, these tickets would be obtained in trade. The hotel and movie theater may exchange products and services of similar value. For example, the hotel would provide a free weekend package in exchange for 75 movie passes. There is usually increased ancillary revenue generated from rooms containing multiple occupants, which is another consideration to think about when developing package strategies.

Scenario #6

In the final scenario, any rooms booked from these channels would generate additional revenue to the lodge. The additional revenue would more than offset the additional channel expenditures needed to generate the business.

We next travel down from the mountain to examine the revenue opportunities for a boutique hotel located in the heart of the city.

Chic B'tique

A major nationwide hotel company has added a new brand to its portfolio. Known as Chic B'tiques, these classic upscale high-rise hotels are all located in major urban areas. As a cab whizzes up to the curb, the bellman swoops down to open the door. Upon emerging from the cab, the guest is greeted by the doorman standing under a classic black canopy. But as the beveled glass doors swing open, the guest realizes that all comparisons to standard downtown hotels are gone.

For the Chic B'tique is a whirl of sensory delights. First, there is the sound. Guests enter the hotel through a stone archway glistening with streaming water cascading down the granite sides and disappearing apparently to the level below. Almost imperceptible New Age music whispers in the background.

Next there are the lights, or lack of them. The lobby is washed in various colored lighting seemingly streaming from the ceiling and disappearing once again to an imaginary level below. Not a single lighting fixture in visible. A mood of playfulness is present in the pastel hues of childhood, all cotton candy and lemonade. And suddenly, the lights all change, entirely altering the mood. Now the lights are bold, energizing reds and flame-like oranges. And a few minutes later, they change again to cool off the lobby, bathing it in soft sheets of blue and lavender.

By now totally enraptured, the guest begins to notice a scent as she makes her way to the kiosk to check in. At first, it smells like bubblegum to match the childlike mood of the pastel lights. But as the guest walks further and the lights change from soft to bright, the scent also changes from bubblegum to peppermint. Intrigued by this creative use of aromatherapy, the guest smiles as the smell of peppermint fades away to the calming scent of lavender to match the changing mood of the lighting.

Fascinated with her first two minutes inside the hotel, the guest anxiously anticipates what surprises might await her in her guestroom. She quickly checks into her room via a kiosk and heads to the elevators that will take her to her floor. She is startled with her first step into the elevator as the floor is an aquarium filled with stunning colored fish. "How cool is this?" she thinks to herself as she turns to smile at the next guest who enters and expresses a small gasp of surprise.

The tumbler clicks in the door and she pushes it aside in a rush to see what awaits her inside. First, her eyes and nose are immediately drawn to a huge bouquet of flowers centered on a small table in front of the balcony. "How did they know my favorite flowers?" she thought as she kicked off her shoes. Immediately, she felt the plush pile of the luxurious carpeting reaching up to embrace her tired toes. And then she saw the treats. Her favorite Godiva chocolates placed on a delicate china plate next to a snifter of Chambord on the nightstand. "They know me so well," she thought as she grabbed the remote and sunk down on the feather bed to relax from a long day of travel.

Here are some facts about the Chic B'tique:

Physical facilities:

- 688 guest rooms and 19 suites
- 18 floors
- One fine-dining restaurant, called Anise
- One casual-dining outlet, called Sparkle
- One lounge, called Spritz
- 29,000 square feet of meeting space
- Business center
- Health club on the top floor with rooftop pool
- Helipad
- Gift shop
- In the center of downtown Metropolis

Products and services available:

- The ultimate in personalized service
- Guest rooms (kings, double queens, and suites)
- Free parking for overnight guests
- Conference services
- Catering services
- Breakfast
- Lunch
- Dinner
- Snacks
- 24-hour room service
- Cocktails
- Evening entertainment in the lounge
- Business center services
- Free wireless access anywhere on premises
- Automobile rental desk
- Airport shuttle
- Concierge
- Valet

Abbreviated SWOT Analysis for the Chic B'tique

Strengths: Downtown location, cool new product buzz, latest technological innovations installed, hip energized staff, brand affiliation, free parking for overnight guests, abundant meeting space, outstanding products and services in outlets.

Weaknesses: Sensory elements may be too busy or annoying; environment may be unfamiliar and uncomfortable to silver-haired seniors; lack of brand recognition in the leisure market.

Opportunities: Convention center six blocks away, offices of most Fortune 500 companies located within five-mile radius, adjacent to opera house and performing arts center, within two miles of baseball field, football stadium, hockey rink, and basketball center all housing national franchises; two blocks from light rail station; convenient airport; temperate climate.

Threats: Traffic congestion, new supply entering the market, increasing gas prices impacting group travel market.

Competitors: Total room supply for metro area is 39,600 guest rooms. Downtown supply of 5,280 guest rooms. Several new similar brands opening within next 18 months.

Time period used for analysis: April 1 to May 31 (peak meeting season).

Booking pace and pattern: Heavy arrivals on Sunday and Monday nights; nearly sold out midweek, little to no weekend business. Some slowing surrounding the last weekend in May due to Memorial Day holiday.

Channels currently used: All franchise services including CRS, hotel website, tie-in with all Metropolis Convention & Visitors Bureau and convention center marketing and websites, hotel link placed in state tourism office website and CRS, all merchant models, GDS marketing, direct sales efforts, placement of inventory with select retail operators, referral service, and listing on high-technology websites.

Guest room price range for time period: Sunday through Thursday $225 to $450 for king or double queen, suites start at $1,250. Weekend (Friday and Saturday nights) $185 to $295, suites starting at $650.

Overview

The two peak periods for downtown Metropolis hotels are late spring and mid-fall. Conferences, conventions, and corporate meetings are attracted to Metropolis due to its clean and safe downtown area and easy access to the airport. In addition, the airport is served by a variety of national carriers offering moderate fares from most major cities. Sunday nights and Monday nights are busy with arrivals. The hotel is close to being sold out on Tuesdays and Wednesdays. Thursday runs about 70 percent full, while Friday and Saturday nights are nearly empty.

What are some possible strategies and tactics that may be applied during this time period to optimize revenues?

1. The hotel is obviously doing well despite its lack of brand recognition during the middle of the week. Demand is high during this time period, so the hotel may wish to consider raising rates to displace lower-rated business with higher-rated business. The strategy is to reposition rates based upon demand. The tactic may be to increase midweek rates in periods of high demand.
2. The hotel should immediately close out arrivals for Tuesday nights. This would force guests to book at least two nights. The hotel may also place stay restrictions on Wednesday night. The strategy is to optimize allocation of midweek inventory. One tactic is to close out arrivals on Tuesday night. Another tactic would be to require a three-night stay that would include Wednesdays.
3. Chic B'tique is obviously *not* the first choice of leisure travelers coming to the downtown area for the weekend. First, it should check its weekend pricing against its competitors. If the pricing is in line, then the problem most likely lies with the sales and marketing effort. So they could temporarily reduce prices to induce trial. The hotel should consider creating weekend packages. The strategy here is to increase weekend revenues. The first tactic is to reduce rates to induce trial. The second tactic is to create value-added packages to capture new weekend business.
4. The hotel should carefully monitor its market mix during the midweek to ensure that it is optimizing revenues. It should perform a total customer worth analysis on its different market segments. Then it should replace business generating lower total customer worth with that business generating higher total customer worth. The strategy is to optimize revenues during peak season. One tactic could be to have the salespeople focus their efforts on the more lucrative corporate business market, including both groups and high-end locally negotiated rates.
5. The hotel possesses a significant "wow" factor upon entry. People who enter the lobby are momentarily stunned by the sensory environment. The hotel features an award-winning fine-dining restaurant named Anise and a funky lounge named Spritz that offers cutting-edge entertainment. The hotel needs to market these outlets to increase capture of the local market. The impression left upon these

local guests will help develop a reputation within the local community for both the hotel and its outlets. The strategy is to increase foot traffic to increase brand recognition in the local market. One tactic would be to market the superb reviews that Anise has received from the local food critic in the city's *Dining Out* magazine. Another tactic would be to feature the top local bands in Spritz on Friday and Saturday nights. A third tactic could be to create an outstanding Sunday brunch in Sparkle to draw in more couples and families.

6. And the hotel could join forces with a local charity to help raise money for a cure or a solution to a community problem. The strategy here is twofold: first, become a good corporate citizen while fundraising for a cause, and second, instill a sense of pride and purpose in the hotel's employees. Tactics would include a variety of activities to raise money for a cure or resolution to the problem.

What other strategies and tactics could the Chic B'tique develop to increase revenues?
Take a moment to consider some alternative options.

Possible Results

Scenario #1
The hotel originally feared that its lack of brand recognition would hurt its occupancy during the peak meeting season. However, due to superior marketing efforts, the hotel's name is present in all channels appealing to various market segments over this time period. Thus the hotel needs to reassess its value in the eyes of its customers. Where do its customers currently perceive the hotel as being positioned. Due to the high occupancy and lack of rate resistance, there appears to be an opportunity to raise rates. While it may be too late to capture a tremendous amount of additional revenue during this two-month time period, the hotel should look at other periods of similar demand, particularly the mid-fall meetings market to determine opportunities to increase rates to generate higher revenues.

For example, we know that the hotel nearly sells out on Tuesdays and Wednesdays during this time period. Assuming there are nine Tuesdays and nine Wednesdays during that time period, this means that 18 nights are nearly sold out. In this example, we will only concern ourselves with the standard rooms and not the suites. If 95 percent of the hotel's 688 rooms sell out, that represents 654 rooms per night. Multiply 654 rooms by 18 nights and the result is a total of 11,772 room nights. If the hotel raised the rate of these room nights by just $10, this would generate an additional $110,772 in revenue to the hotel. And if it raised rates by just $20 per room per night, that small increase would generate nearly a quarter of a million dollars more in revenue in just a two-month period!

Scenario #2
The revenue manager should consider applying restrictions on periods of high demand. Again, it is not enough to look at the current month. He or she must look out for a minimum of 12 months and even longer regarding convention business. A formal strategy should be to optimize revenues for the entire year. Price and inventory must be continually assessed for all future dates on a daily basis and adjustments should be made alongside fluctuations in demand. The hotel should ensure that it is accurately

tracking booking pace and pattern so that it may continually refine its strategies and tactics on an ongoing, continual basis.

Numerically, if the hotel is able to capture 10 additional rooms on Tuesday nights that would represent an additional 90 rooms during this time period. If the average daily rate for Tuesday nights was $400, this restriction would generate an additional $4,000 per night and $36,000 in room revenue over the two-month period. But remember, that is only in room revenue. Those additional 90 rooms sold would also generate ancillary revenue in the food and beverage outlets and other areas of the hotel.

Scenario #3

The hotel really needs to immediately generate some weekend business. So the first plan of action is to reduce rates for the next few weekends. This rate reduction should be marketed as a special short-term offer to the local market using drive-time radio spots, entertainment newspapers, and perhaps fliers distributed to the downtown office buildings. It should also be offered on select channels throughout the Internet distribution system.

Next, the Marketing Department should develop a strong relationship with the Marketing Departments of the opera house and the performing arts center. Together they should assess opportunities to cross sell their products and services. The hotel may wish to bundle an opera-night package including a Saturday night stay for two, wine and cheese reception preceding the performance, two tickets to the opera, dinner for two in Anise after the performance, a horse-drawn carriage ride following dinner, and Sunday brunch in Sparkle the next day. One package could include a standard room, while another could include a suite. The price for the standard package may be $495, while the suite package may be priced starting at $795. These prices represent substantial discounts from the total price of the individual elements, creating the perception of good value in the minds of the guests. The hotel rooms make money, the hotel outlets make money, the opera house makes money, the carriage operator makes money, and the guest saves money. A win-win situation for all.

The same concept could be applied to the performing arts center. In both scenarios, the hotel should consider ways to extend the package to two nights. Perhaps one night of opera and the other night attendance at a play.

And the hotel should remain alert to any additional opportunities to package weekends during this time period. The marketing team should ensure that the hotel is participating in all possible downtown event tie-ins, including advertising, promotion, and creative packaging. Perhaps a winemaking convention is being held in the convention center. The hotel may be able to convince convention attendees to extend their stay over the weekend by offering a series of classes and lectures featuring local wine experts, a visit to the local vineyard, and a sampling of the local wines.

Again, let's take a quick look at the numbers. If the hotel sold 10 opera packages for each of the nine Saturday nights in the time period, that means that it would sell a total of 90 packages. 90 packages at $495 equals total revenue of $44,550. It is easy to see how just a few packages may substantially increase the total revenues, both primary and ancillary, of any hotel property.

Scenario #4

Many students would assume that hotels surrounding a convention center would be filled with convention business and be ecstatic about it. While that may have been true in the past, as more and more hotels implemented revenue management techniques, it became apparent that this business while plentiful, was not always the best business to book.

For example, corporate group business often commands a higher room rate than convention business. And a corporate meeting will usually generate a higher total amount of additional revenues in food and beverage, audio-visual, and conference services. Most often, corporate meetings are held entirely onsite at the hotel during the day, with some evening events held off-premises. Convention business is just the opposite. Convention attendees spend most of their day at the convention center, returning to the hotel only in the evening. So the hotel must make sure that it is not displacing the higher revenue generating corporate group business with the lower revenue generating convention business.

And individual business travelers often are used to paying higher rates than may be acceptable to a person attending a convention. It is vital that the hotel perform analyses regarding both the total customer worth of their segments and changes in revenue streams as a result of displacement. The details of each conference or convention being held at the center that requires guest rooms should be carefully analyzed. How many rooms are needed, are the attendees price conscious, and are most meals available at the center during the course of the convention? Is there any affiliated business available to capture for the preceding weekend or the weekend following the convention? The hotel should select the business that optimizes revenues for all outlets within its operation, not just rooms.

Once again, a numerical example here may help illuminate this scenario. A convention is in town this week and the majority of the convention attendees are arriving on Sunday night and staying for three nights. Continental breakfast and a full luncheon banquet are provided at the convention center each day. Attendees are on their own for dinner. The hotel rate for the convention attendees is $249 per night. The Chic B'tique anticipates selling 100 rooms to attendees of this convention. So this represents 100 rooms for three nights for a total of 300 room nights. At a rate of $249, this equals a total of $74,700 in total rooms revenue. The hotel assumes that it may capture a few of the attendees for dinner on one of the nights, so it projects receiving an additional $1,000 in dinner revenue. And a few attendees may decide to have a heartier breakfast at the hotel, so figure in another $300. In total, this group of conventioneers may generate approximately $76,000 to the hotel.

However, the hotel has a chance to book a corporate meeting over this same time period. The meeting planner states that she needs 85 rooms for three nights, meeting space for 100 each day, and the following meal service each day for three days: continental breakfast, lunch, and midmorning and midafternoon breaks. She is also planning one awards dinner with entertainment on the last evening. She will need all audio-visual equipment to be provided by the hotel. The meeting is a training and recognition event for the company's top salespeople. She is looking for a room rate under $300. What would this piece of business be worth?

First, the meeting planner requires a total of 85 rooms for three nights, which equals 255 room nights. The negotiated room rate is $289. This represents a total of $73,695 in room revenue. The reader may be tempted to stop here since the convention business will generate more room revenue. Also, there are 15 more guests in the hotel per night with the convention business, which may represent more opportunity for ancillary revenue right? Not so fast. Let's take a look at the corporate meeting revenue first. We have determined that the meeting would generate $73,695 in room revenue. So let's now add food and beverage revenues to this equation. Two meals and two breaks per day could be estimated at approximately $38 per person per day. Multiply that times 85 people for three days and the total is $9,660. Then add the awards dinner for another $3,230. And entertainment costs $1,750 for the evening. The total rental for the meeting rooms is minimal based on the room block, so let's just add another $500. And the three day charge for audio-visual amounts to another $750. Add it all up, and this one corporate meeting is worth a total of $89,585. So, in reality, the corporate meeting would generate an additional $15,890 in direct revenue, plus free up an additional 15 rooms for three nights that would generate even more revenue.

An important note needs to be added here. The above example does not represent total customer worth as we did not consider all possible ancillary revenues, omitting, for example, cocktails served in the lounge or at the awards banquet and merchandise sales at the gift store. And we also did not subtract the cost of acquiring the convention attendees or the corporate meeting in this equation. Instead, we kept this as a simpler example to point out the importance of looking at all revenues generated by a particular piece of business rather than just considering the primary revenues generated.

Scenario #5

If it were possible, the hotel's staff wishes that it could grab every single passerby off the street and pull them in to see the hotel. However, since this is not physically possible, the hotel will invite them to stop in to visit the outlets through the use of careful advertising placement and special promotions. The desired result of this strategy is to simply get more local residents in to see the hotel. The goal is to generate some word-of-mouth marketing buzz that will help position the hotel as the coolest place to stay in the local market.

Scenario #6

This is another strategy that speaks to the hotel's positioning. Adopting a charity is a quick and effective means of public relations that also helps position the hotel within the community. And this strategy helps not only the hotel; it enables its staff to feel good and it helps the charitable organization raise funding. For example, the hotel's General Manager may feel very strongly about retinal cancer as his father lost his eyesight from this disease. Or the Director of Marketing serves on the board of the Dumb Friends League, and is passionate about controlling the pet population. Or the Food & Beverage Director is involved with *Share our Strength*, an organization of food professionals who work to help alleviate hunger in the community.

The hotel should select one or more charities or causes that it feels it is best able to support with its available resources. It should develop an event in conjunction with the charity that may be held during periods of soft demand. For example, the hotel could host an *Envision the Cure* dinner and local celebrity auction. The admission price may be an old pair of eyeglasses that could be recycled. Guests would be able to bid on the opportunity to be *seen* having brunch with that celebrity the following morning. The dinner would be a feast for the eyes, with vibrantly colored china and entrées. Rooms would be available at a special rate for all those wishing to stay over and enjoy the following day's brunch. Then all revenue generated from the event

Vernadero Restaurant at The Royal Palms.

would be donated to finding a cure for retinal cancer. Or on a more modest level, the hotel could hold a wag-n-wash pet grooming event on the roof of its parking facility to raise money for the local animal shelter. All of these charitable activities increase the associates' level of pride in the facility and help position the hotel as a good neighbor in the eyes of the community.

Scrumptious!

A new restaurant has opened up in downtown Metropolis near the convention center called *Scrumptious!* Arriving guests are greeted by a valet and ushered through an alcove in the stone façade leading to the entrance partially hidden from the street. The hostess then leads the couple across the gleaming mahogany floor to a semicircular booth set discretely in one corner. Wall sconces and small table lamps create a soft ambient glow. The thick starched napkins and linen tablecloths lend an air of formality to the establishment.

Waiters in multicolored vests, jazz playing softly in the background, and a whimsical menu add a lighter, more mischievous element to the experience.

The menu features the standard favorites updated with a creative flair. A rich selection of prime steaks is matched with unique creations from the sea. And the delectable desserts alone lend credence to the restaurant's name.

Off to the left of the dining room resides a warm and inviting banquet room. The dichotomy of architectural design adds interest to the room. French doors, a heavy stone fireplace, and big bay windows make the room enticing for wedding receptions, parties, and family birthday celebrations. The room is set for an event of elegance, with early arriving guests lingering near a carving station in anticipation of the succulent slices of beast to come.

Located to the right of the dining room is a small, yet festive lounge. Two tops circle the half moon bar located in the room's middle. Stools and a mahogany rail ring the room. Tucked in one corner is a microphone, evident of the previous night's entertainment. Scents of fine wine and 20-year-old scotch waft through the air, competing for space with a variety of perfumes.

Physical facilities:

- 80-seat restaurant
- 36-seat lounge
- 1,900 square foot banquet room
- 16-seat terrace patio outside banquet room

Products and services:

- Lunch
- Dinner
- Cocktails
- Banquets
- Entertainment
- Open six days per week

Abbreviated SWOT Analysis for Scrumptious!

Strengths: Downtown location, quality of product, great reputation.

Weaknesses: No chain affiliation, less hip location than competitors.

Opportunities: Increase capture of conventioneers, book more events, increase lunch business from surrounding offices.

Threats: Cost of ingredients, lack of fresh local seafood, increased fuel costs.

Competitors: Other similarly positioned restaurants within walking distance of the convention center.

Time period used for analysis: June 1st through July 15th.

Booking pace and pattern: Individual dinner reservations made in the week for the week. Banquets booked 3 to 6 months out. Social events booked from 1 to 12 months in advance. Local walk-in business for lunch.

Channels currently used: Restaurant website, advertisements in the convention center and bureau publications, radio spots, link on state's Restaurant Association website, membership in the Downtown Metropolis Partnership, included in AAA travel guide and *Zagat Dining Guide*, advertisements in local newspapers.

Prices: Lunch entrées range from $12 to $18; dinner entrées start at $26.

Overview

The restaurant is new and is currently very busy. How long this initial excitement will last is up for speculation. Will the restaurant become a tried and true favorite or just be a passing flash in the pan?

What are some possible strategies and tactics that may be applied during this time period to optimize revenues?

1. To begin, the restaurant needs to determine an integrated strategy to capture increased business from the convention center. It is already advertising in the official convention publications, so it needs to address alternative means of catching the attention of attendees. Since most conventions run during business hours, a significant portion of this increased business would occur over lunch. Convention attendees often want to grab a quick lunch so that they may return to check messages and call the office. So the restaurant should develop a limited express luncheon menu that may be served in the lounge and out on the terrace. The menu could be printed on express tickets to be placed in the convention attendee's welcome packets. It could also set the banquet room with additional seating when large conventions are in town. The strategy is to increase capture of business generated by conventions at the center. Tactics are to create express luncheon menus, promote the express luncheon menu tickets through welcome bag distribution, and provide seating alternatives to service increased covers.

2. The restaurant has a wonderful banquet room that will seat approximately 150 people using banquet round tables. This is the size of an average wedding. Its downtown location makes the restaurant convenient to numerous churches where the ceremony may be held. An abundance of hotel rooms are available within walking distance to house out-of-town guests. And horse-drawn carriage rides are available nightly. The average cost of a wedding is also quite substantial today, making wedding receptions good business to obtain. And *Scrumptious!* also sounds so appropriate for a wedding reception. Written on a reception invitation, the name would immediately conjure up images of a multitiered wedding cake covered in billowy icing. Since brides book well in advance, any strategy would take a few months to produce results. One way to increase wedding business is to advertise in local church newsletters. The event coordinator for the restaurant may also want to attend local bridal shows to develop relationships with wedding industry suppliers who may provide referrals. The strategy is to increase the restaurant's share of the wedding market. Tactics include church newsletter advertising and bridal show attendance to generate referrals.

3. In addition to pursuing the wedding market, the event coordinator should also try to capture holiday parties booked by local offices. Nearly every company plans an all-employee party at the holidays. Most firms actually reserve their space before the beginning of summer. Last-minute bookers know that they will pay higher prices. The event coordinator should first solicit evening parties in the range of 150 people for Friday and Saturday nights between Thanksgiving and December 22. These are the nights of peak demand so every effort should be

made to maximize capacity to optimize revenue. The event coordinator should next pursue Friday holiday luncheons occurring within those same dates. Another possibility is to create a Sunday holiday brunch for smaller offices or to host the holiday employee parties of other restaurants whose employees work in the evening. And special discount packages should be developed to shift demand to other nights of the week. The strategy here is to increase capture of holiday party business. Tactics include maximizing revenues on hot dates and shifting demand to other times and dates to generate additional revenues.

4. The restaurant should also develop a preferred luncheon customer program to increase capture from local offices and generate repeat business. Program members would receive special incentives, such as a free dessert on his or her birthday and percentage discounts during periods of low demand. The strategy here is to increase capture of local office luncheon business. The tactic used is developing a frequent diner program to generate new and repeat business over lunch.

5. The restaurant's lounge jumps during happy hour. However, it starts emptying out by 8 PM. So the restaurant has booked entertainment to extend the stay of happy-hour customers and to attract later arrivals. A second midnight happy hour was instituted from 11:30 to 12:30 to capture late-night theater and opera goers. The strategy is to increase late-night beverage sales. The tactics are to use entertainment and an additional late-night happy hour to attract new customers.

What other strategies and tactics could the restaurant develop to increase revenues? Which strategies could be developed to reduce or minimize potential threats?
As before, the reader should take a moment to consider strategies needed to capitalize on opportunities and reduce or eliminate threats.

Possible Results

Scenario #1

Let's assume that the restaurant is able to capture just four (one four top table) additional conventioneers to purchase lunch on Mondays, Tuesdays, and Wednesdays for 20 weeks out of the year. That would represent an additional 240 luncheon patrons. If the average luncheon entrée purchased cost $15, this would represent an increase in revenue of $3,600.

Now, remember that the conventioneers are visiting from out of town. Being unfamiliar with the city, they may return to Scrumptious! for dinner, or to enjoy a drink and some entertainment. Thus, there is the opportunity to capture ancillary evening revenue as well.

Scenario #2

The average American wedding now approaches $25,000 in cost. The most significant expense is usually the cost of the reception. We know that the banquet room will hold about 150 people. If the bride selected a sit-down meal rather than hors d'oeuvres, the cost of the food alone may appear staggering to some. Catering prices are frequently set higher than individual dinner menu prices. To illustrate, let's assume that the minimum entrée for an evening reception is $36 per person. Multiply this by 150 people and dinner alone costs $5,400. Add in a wedding cake at an average

The Richardson Dallas Elegant Weddings.

price of $900, with another $225 cake-cutting fee and a champagne toast to the happy couple at $4 per person for $600 and we are now up to $7,125. And that is even before the open or hosted bar. Depending upon the age of the average guest, the bar cost could range from a quarter of the food cost to nearly matching it. In our scenario, we will assume a hosted bar for the first hour generates $1,200 and a cash bar open for another two hours generates $1,800 more in beverage sales.

And don't forget the flowers, candles, gift table decorations, and ice carving which we will price at another $2,250. Totaling up these figures, we see that our average 150-person wedding generates $12,375 in revenue. Our pastry chef actually creates the wedding cake in-house. Remember Scrumptious! is known for its desserts. Saturday is the number one choice for weddings. Although there are 52 Saturdays in a year, some dates are just not very hot for weddings such as Christmas Day or New Year's Day. These days are not very well attended, so many brides select alternative dates. Thus, we will assume that there are 50 good Saturdays in a year on which to book a wedding. If the restaurant books one 150-person wedding on each of the 50 Saturdays, total revenue generated would be $618,750.

Catering weddings is a serious affair. Organizations that host wedding receptions often become experts in the process. Those organizations that just book an occasional wedding often run into unexpected problems. To maximize this effort, the event coordinator should try to book weddings at times other than just Saturday evenings. Guests enjoying themselves at a wedding reception often transfer these positive feelings to the venue. Weddings may actually generate future lunch or dinner business from the wedding guests as well.

Scenario #3

This is a simple example to consider. First, let's assume that the program entices just one birthday diner to come over for lunch on his or her special day. Naturally, the birthday boy or girl will not be coming alone, but will probably be accompanied by friends and relatives. But even if they just come for lunch in pairs that would result in two additional luncheons being sold per day. The restaurant is open 6 days per week, which represents 312 days per year. Multiply that 312 by the two diners and the result is 624 additional meals. If the average birthday lunch check for two is $36, this represents an additional $22,464 in revenue. That buys a lot of birthday cake!

Scenario #4

In this scenario, we are only going to consider theater goers on Friday and Saturday night. We are going to assume that this market segment is not overly price sensitive when it comes to alcoholic beverages, but instead possesses quite discriminating tastes. Since their beverages are considered top shelf, most establishments do not offer discounts on these drinks. Let's assume that 20 theater patrons on Friday and 30 patrons on Saturday decide to pop into the restaurant for a bit of refreshment following the performance. That represents 50 additional customers per weekend. If their average beverage cost $8.50, this represents $425 in beverage sales over the two nights. Multiply that $425 in revenue by 52 weekends and you arrive at $22,100 in additional beverage revenue annually. And, naturally, many of these customers will stay for the entertainment and end up purchasing more than one drink, so total revenue will be a bit higher.

The purpose of the applications in this chapter is to illustrate to the reader how implementing just a few strategies and tactics may generate substantial increases in revenue. Now that we have reviewed a few examples in the lodging and dining sectors, let's turn our attention to opportunities in the sports, entertainment, and event sectors of the hospitality industry.

SUMMARY

In this chapter we explored the application of revenue management techniques regarding the products and services of three hospitality providers: a mountaintop lodge, a city center boutique hotel, and a fine-dining restaurant. Each organization was briefly examined in terms of its customers, market segments, partial internal SWOT analysis, forecasted demand for the time period, prices, and channels used for distributing inventory. Various scenarios were presented in which the organization could implement strategies and tactics to drive revenues. Possible results were presented to demonstrate the impact of these potential strategies and tactics.

KEY TERMS AND CONCEPTS

The following key terms and concepts were presented in this chapter. Each term and concept is also contained in the Glossary of Terms located at the end of this book:

- color tour visitors or color
  tourists

DISCUSSION QUESTIONS

1. What additional opportunities may face each of these facilities?
2. What additional threats may face each of these facilities?
3. What other strategies and tactics could you develop for the Lofty Pines Lodge?
4. What other strategies and tactics could you develop for the Chic B'tique?
5. What other strategies and tactics could you develop for *Scrumptious!*?

EXPERIENTIAL EXERCISE

Get into groups of two and select another type of lodging or food and beverage facility. Personally visit the facility and conduct a similar analysis and determine possible strategies and tactics that may be used to optimize revenues.

INTERNET EXERCISES

1. Go online and find packages available in October that are similar to the ones offered for Lofty Pines Lodge. Do you see any opportunities to increase revenues? Please explain.
2. Select a boutique hotel in the city nearest your school and review the different rate tiers and packages available online during the peak meeting season for that area. Does it appear the hotel is optimizing revenues? Please explain.
3. Select a fine-dining restaurant in your area. What channels, traditional and electronic, do they use to promote the facility? Are there any other opportunities to increase revenues? Please explain.

Red Rocks by Air.

CHAPTER

16

Applications in Sports, Entertainment, and Event Management

Chapter Objectives

The objectives of this chapter are to:

■ Explore the application of revenue management techniques in sports, entertainment, and event management

■ Consider several scenarios, strategies, and tactics for the Granite Palace football stadium

■ Consider several scenarios, strategies, and tactics for Tunes amphitheater

■ Consider several scenarios, strategies, and tactics for Metropolis Convention Center

Our journey continues using our RevMAP to enter the world of sports, entertainment, and events. Once again we are seeking that elusive pot of gold waiting just around the bend in the road leading to these new destinations. Let's resume our journey by venturing to the Granite Palace on game day just before kickoff.

Granite Palace

One of less than 40 major football stadiums in the United States, the Granite Palace is considered to be the epitome of innovative football facilities. Since opening three years ago, the facility has also become the site to hold cutting-edge events and corporate training retreats. Cocktail parties are even held in the team locker rooms on non–game days as the locker room is unbelievably luxurious. A permanent camera has been installed to capture a fan's picture in front of what appears to be the locker of their favorite player. They just type in the player's name on a keyboard, stand on a dot, and say "cheese" while pressing the remote control. And it has become THE place to be on game day. Let's see why . . .

Fans are ushered into the stadium grounds by exiting the freeway ramp and entering a multicolored tunnel that sets the tone for a day of fun. Emerging from the tunnel into the massive parking lot, a car full of fans immediately sees the smoking steam

267

emitting from the tailgate grills and smells the scents of charcoal, grilling burgers, sizzling brats, and freshly opened beer. It is game day and the festivities have just begun. As the fans pile out of the car, they hear the thump, thump, thump of the 70s rock and roll music emanating from the parking lot speakers. Nothing like a little Led Zeppelin to get the blood moving of this primarily baby boomer-aged crowd.

They fire up the grill and put up their flag. For they are members of the tailgate club, which provides them special privileges and prizes. The "Gater Patrol" strolls the parking lot in search of groups of tailgate club members having the most fun. They also look for the group cooking with the most unusual or intriguing ingredients. And they select the tailgate that they would most like to dine from that day. That last prize could go to either tailgate club members or general fans as it is such a special distinction. These three winning groups will win tickets to watch the next home game from the box seats of the Champions' Club.

The horn blows across the speakers signaling time for the fans and revelers to head to their seats to prepare for kickoff. The thump of the rock and roll music is replaced with the thump of trunks and SUV hatchbacks shutting as the groups pack up their parties. Grabbing their tickets, they head toward the Palace.

The fans start upon a long path winding up and around a small mounded hill. Perched atop is the Granite Palace, majestic in its presence above the approaching sea of fans. Just as Dorothy approaching the door to the Emerald City, first-time visitors and fans draw in their breath when they cross the threshold for the first time. For this is the ultimate in football-viewing experience and there is a palpable excitement in being a part of it. For the die-hard fans, it is being a part of the team's history. They can say they were there when the Hail Mary pass was thrown . . . and caught to win the play-off game. And they were there for the overtime win during the Super Bowl. They consider themselves to be alumni and this is their alma mater. And they are just so thrilled to be a part of it. They pick up a program, grab a quick beer, and head to their seats.

Physical facilities:

- 85,000 seats of which 25,000 are reserved by season-ticket holders
- 8,950 club seats
- 125 luxury suites
- Home of a National Football League franchise
- Natural-grass playing surface
- 250,000 square feet of event space
- 525 concession stand points of sale
- Video boards for projecting corporate images
- Souvenir store
- 9,800 parking spots onsite, 18,750 in adjacent lots
- 100 spots for RV parking
- 626 television monitors
- Two upscale restaurants
- Media room

Products and services available:

- Game-day tickets
- Season tickets

- Club-level tickets
- Annual luxury suite contracts
- Meetings and events
- Full catering and conference services
- Concession food and beverage
- Dinner served in fine-dining restaurants each evening, closed Tuesdays
- Team merchandise in souvenir store
- Tailgate club
- Tented tailgate dining and rest area
- Game programs kiosks
- Children's play area
- Daily tours
- Fully compliant with the Americans with Disabilities Act guidelines

Abbreviated SWOT Analysis for the Granite Palace

Strengths: New state-of-the-art facilities, within walking distance of downtown, abundance of onsite and adjacent parking, great service, winning team, sold out regular seat season tickets.

Weaknesses: Demand but no additional supply of season tickets, lack of cover during inclement weather, higher cost to maintain natural grass, perceived high food and beverage prices.

Opportunities: Capture additional business from playoff games, secure contract with another sports team such as a soccer team, increase capture of meetings and events business.

Threats: Losing season with loss of fan loyalty, competing sports and events occurring during the same time, inclement weather, and loss of the segment of local fans preferring to watch the game from large-screen televisions at home.

Competitors: All other local activities occurring at the same time that appeal to the same customer base and compete for the same dollar, including other team sports, events at entertainment venues, amusement parks, movie premieres, or local fairs and festivals.

Time period used for analysis: Traditional fall football season.

Booking pace and pattern: Annual contracts for all luxury suites, club seats contracted for groups typically 90 to 120 days prior to game day, renewal by season-ticket holders 6 months prior to opening day, individual game-day tickets available starting the last week in July.

Channels currently used: Franchise ticket office, team website, ticket brokers and services such as Ticketmaster, merchant models, opaque and auction sites, booster club sales, resale market presented through newspaper and various fan websites.

Price Range:

   Tickets: (Based on 10 home games)

      Single game: $38 to $90 regular seat: $210 to $340 club seats

      Season tickets: $375 to $900 regular seats: $2,100 to $3,400 club seats

   Parking:

      Per car, truck, or SUV: $200 to $500 for season pass

      Game Day: $10 for adjacent lot and $20 for onsite parking

      RV Parking: $600 to $1,000 season pass: $40 on game day in adjacent lot

Overview

Metropolis has had a winning team for the past 20 years. Many loyal fans watched the construction of this new sports palace with an eye for finally obtaining the chance to purchase a season ticket. The team has 10,000 more seats in this facility, of which they added 3,000 to the season-ticket pool. All 25,000 season tickets have been sold out since opening day at the Granite Palace and a five-year waiting list has already developed. The stadium is sold out for all home games, although some fans will not show up in cases of inclement weather.

What are some possible strategies and tactics that may be applied to next year's football season and off-season to optimize revenues?

1. The first and most obvious choice is to raise ticket prices. Unlike other stadiums which were funded by local taxes and must adhere to local governmental restrictions on ticket prices, the Granite Palace was funded entirely by private funds provided by the team owner's family. So the franchise is free to raise prices as long as they remain in line with National Football League standards. All 25,000 season tickets are sold out with a five-year waiting list. So the first place to capture additional ticket revenues is from the season ticket holders. The strategy here is to increase ticket revenues. The tactic is to raise season-ticket prices.

2. Club seats are considered to be more of an upscale purchase than regular-seat tickets. Therefore it is likely that fans who purchase club seats are less price sensitive than regular ticket purchasers. So once again, the franchise should consider raising ticket prices, this time for club seats. The strategy here is to increase ticket revenues. The tactic is to raise club-seat season-ticket prices.

3. The stadium features 525 concession points of sale. However, there is the perception of high prices for food and beverage items available. The stadium could offer children's portions, which would appeal greatly to families. It could also reduce the portion size of certain other items and reduce the price accordingly. Offer a medium-sized nacho instead of jumbo nachos for example. Presentation is part of the challenge here. When food is properly wrapped smaller portions may actually appear larger. Also the concessionaire could offer drink sizes by the ounce, which may be perceived as greater value for the dollar than if sized as small, medium, or large. The concessionaires could also bundle together items into sports-fan packages. The packages would be priced lower than the sum of their parts, which would then be perceived as a value to the fan. The strategy is to increase concession revenue. The tactics are to offer children's portions and smaller portions for reduced prices, develop new sizes that are perceived to be values, and bundle items together and sell value-added packages.

4. Parking is also a significant revenue generator for the stadium. While there is ample parking in the adjacent lot, it is quite a bit of a hike to actually reach the stadium. So the stadium may consider charging higher prices for the onsite parking spots. It may also use an odd dollar amount to provide fans with a few dollars in change with which to buy a program or other concession item available at each of the stadium entrances. Raising the onsite parking rate would also enable stadium management to increase the adjacent parking as it would still appear to be a bargain. The strategy here is to increase parking revenue. The tactics are to

raise parking prices for both lots. A side effect of raising the prices to an odd amount may be to generate additional purchases of programs and merchandise at the stadium entrances.

5. The sales and marketing department could step up its solicitation of group business to help fill the facility in the off-season. It may want to consider attracting high school proms, parties for family reunions, and corporate training events that use the field for team-building exercises.

6. The stadium may consider constructing a retractable dome to reduce the effects of inclement weather. The strategy here is to create a year-round environment within the stadium. The tactic is to build a retractable dome roof.

What other strategies and tactics could the football franchise and stadium develop to capitalize on opportunities to increase revenues? Which strategies could be developed to reduce or minimize potential threats?

This is a good place to pause and discuss alternative strategies and tactics that the team or stadium management could develop and implement in an effort to drive revenues.

Possible Results

Scenario #1

Currently the stadium maintains 25,000 reserved seats for season-ticket holders. There is an average of 10 home games per season. The average season price paid per seat is $625. Total annual revenue for these season tickets is $15,625,000. Now let's assume that they raise the price of each season ticket by just $50. That would represent an additional $1,250,000 a year in season-ticket revenues. But they may lose some season-ticket holders due to this price increase, right? Possibly, but most season-ticket holders would look at this price increase on a per game basis. Paying just $5 more per game really does not seem too high, at least as long as the team is winning. Besides, we noted that there is already a five-year waiting list for season tickets. Most season-ticket holders would not give up their coveted tickets for a mere $50. And if some did resist and not renew their tickets then the price increase would have the effect of displacing some lower-rated fans with some higher rated fans.

Scenario #2

We know that single game club seats range from $210 to $350 per ticket. Increasing these prices just $15 so that the range is $225 to $365 probably will not have any significant impact on sales. In fact $225 seems to make more sense than $210, don't you agree? Remember that the stadium has 8,950 club seats. Raising prices $15 per game will yield an additional $134,250 per game or $1,342,500 per season.

Scenario #3

The key point to remember here is that there are 525 sales points at which fans may purchase food and beverage. When prices were perceived to be too high, parents may have ordered a larger drink and just shared it with a child. Or Mom ordered one large hot dog and tore it into two hopefully equal pieces to enable her two small children to share it. Now, if priced appropriately, Mom may decide to buy both children a new mini hot dog wrapped in a biscuit—a pig in a biscuit so to speak. It saves any bickering and will probably decrease any mess on the children's clothing. Mom may also decide to order a small nacho. In the past, she would just share a large nacho with Dad. But he wants a burger today and a small nacho seems reasonable, so Mom decides to purchase both. Or Mom and Dad stop at the concession stand and see a family fan pack offering a burger, nachos, two small pigs in a biscuit, and four small drinks at a total price less than if they ordered all of the items separately. So they order the package and Dad orders an extra medium drink. More food and beverage is actually sold due to this perception of price/value. Americans just hate to pass up a bargain. Let's just say that five of these family fun packages are sold at a price of $19 each at every one of the concession points of sale on game day. That would translate into concession revenue of $49,875. This is just 2,625 family fan packages in a stadium seating 85,000 so it is probably very realistic, if not rather understated. The difference between the package revenue and what the family would have spent normally to share nachos and hot dogs represents an increase in revenue to the concessionaires.

Scenario #4

In this case, let's think about what would happen if we set the new price for onsite parking at $26, a $6 increase over the current price per game. Many people will probably just stuff the $4.00 in change into their pockets rather than reopen their wallets. And for some reason, Americans can often feel these four orphaned bills burning a hole in their pockets so they spend them the first chance they get. In this case, the stadium hopes that they will spend them on programs and merchandise sold at the stadium entrances. With 9,800 onsite parking spaces, this additional revenue would add up to $58,800 on each game day. With 10 home games that represents more than a half a million dollars! And if adjacent parking was raised by $5 to $15 per spot and that was multiplied by 18,750 spots, the total additional revenue per game day would be $93,750. This would represent $937,500 per season! Remember, that there are 85,000 seats in the stadium so it is likely that any fan resisting the price increase would just be replaced by a fan looking for a parking spot.

Scenario #5

Here, let's look first at proms. If the stadium is able to book two proms per night using their two largest event spaces for three Saturday nights in May, that would equal six proms. If the average attendance at each prom is 400 students, that equals 2,400 students or approximately 1,200 couples. At a price of $40 per couple for an evening of dining and dancing, that would represent $48,000.

The sales and marketing team could capture one-day team-building events for local corporations. Let's assume that they are able to sell two events per day, staggering the time spent on the actual field between morning and afternoon. Let's also assume that the peak days for selling these team-building sessions are Tuesday, Wednesday, and Thursday and that there are approximately 35 weeks per year based on availability and weather that the sales team is able to sell these sessions. So six sessions per week times 35 weeks equals 210 team-building sessions over the course of the year. If that average session accommodates 100 corporate employees at a cost of $99 per employee per day, this would equal $9,900 per session. Multiplied by 210 sessions, this would equal

Courtesy of Rod Tanaka—www.tanakaphoto.net

Guitar Close-up.

$2,079,000. This is just a simplistic example. In the real world these sessions could vary tremendously in size as could the price per employee.

Scenario #6

The additional revenue realized from adding a retractable dome would be twofold. First, the team needs to determine how many seats remain unoccupied during games played in inclement weather. An average value would need to be assigned to these vacant seats. For example, do season-ticket holders show up no matter the weather, or are they the first to stay home on blustery game days since they already have tickets for the rest of the season? And then the amounts of any ancillary spend lost when these ticket holders stayed at home would need to be added. Second, stadium management must determine how many additional events the sales and marketing team would be able to sell if weather was not an issue. Combined, these calculations would total the additional revenue that could be anticipated from building a retractable roof.

Our next destination has no retractable roof as its patrons prefer being under the moon, the sun, or the stars . . .

Tunes, A Lyrical Bowl

Fans have been sitting in line for over three hours awaiting the opening of the gates to Tunes, an outdoor amphitheater. Two young couples stand up and stretch as they hear the crowd begin to rustle. "Here they come," someone shouts as security figures unlatch the gates. The crowd peacefully inches forward through the gates and starts descending the stone stairs to a series of landings below. Each landing leads to a different section of seating. Built into the side of a gently sloping hill, this amphitheater gives the impression of having been chiseled by the gods in a prior millennium. In actuality, it is a modern marvel of engineering, being built by a group of rock and roll enthusiasts. The group was comprised of a landscape architect, a structural engineer, a sound engineer, and a part-time musician and liberal arts major who all attended college in the early 1970s. Tunes opened in the early 80s and has been jamming ever since. Fans look out over the stage to the glistening lights of the city below. The sound surrounds and cocoons fans nestled into the hillside. It is a beautiful, magical place in which to listen to tunes under the stars.

Physical facilities:

- 7,800 seats
- 3,600 parking spaces
- Concession stands
- Covered stage
- Retail souvenir shop
- Merchandise kiosks
- 1000 space remote parking lot located two miles below

Services:

- Concerts
- Special events department
- Catering services
- Concessionaire services
- Merchandise sales
- Professional photographer
- Amphitheater tours
- Parking
- Shuttle to remote lot
- Fully compliant with the Americans with Disabilities Act guidelines

Abbreviated SWOT Analysis for Tunes, A Lyrical Bowl

Strengths: Facilities, sound quality, mystique, established fan base.

Weaknesses: Too small to attract major band tours, weather can be a factor, stone stairs are sometimes hard for children and seniors to negotiate. Limited parking with no other nearby lots.

Opportunities: Expand entertainment offerings to meet the needs of a more diverse population, use venue for nonmusical events such as weddings and services.

Threats: Weather, other indoor venues, more high-tech facilities.

Competitors: All area music venues and large outdoor sporting venues that may be used for hosting concerts and events.

Time period used for analysis: Summer.

Booking pace and pattern: Depends entirely on the artist.

Channels currently used: Tunes' website, ticker brokers, each band's website, eBay.

Prices: Seats range from $49 to $99, each depending upon location. Each seat is acoustically phenomenal, but some offer better lines of sight than others. Parking is $20 per car onsite lot, $10 for the remote lot.

Overview

Tunes attracts a lot of big name acts who enjoy playing this unique hillside venue. All ages seem to enjoy attending shows here, so concerts range from classical to rock. The site is very popular for wedding ceremonies and for couples renewing their vows. In recent years, it has also become increasingly popular as a site for large motivational speaker seminars.

What are some possible strategies and tactics that may be applied by Tunes during the summer to optimize revenues?

1. Tunes management should consider increasing ticket prices for the bands in hottest demand. The strategy here is to optimize ticket revenue. The tactic is to increase prices for the hottest bands.
2. Management should consider raising the prices of the top 10 percent of the seats. The strategy here is to optimize ticket revenue. The tactic is to increase the price of the best seats.
3. Management should consider adding some unique niche bands during dates of soft demand. The strategy here is to increase ticket sales. The tactic is to fill periods of low demand.
4. The venue should aggressively market wedding ceremonies and renewal of vows. The strategy is to increase special event revenue. The tactic is to attempt to capture more wedding receptions and vow renewals.
5. The venue could also increase the price of parking. The strategy here is to optimize parking revenue. The tactic is to raise prices for both onsite and remote lots.
6. The venue should continue to market to motivational speakers as a great place to energize groups. The strategy here is to increase daytime revenues. The tactic is to increase capture of motivational speaking market.

What other strategies and tactics could Tunes use to capitalize on opportunities to increase revenues? Which strategies could be developed to reduce or minimize potential threats?

This is a good spot to take a brief break and consider other opportunities facing the amphitheater during this time period.

Possible Results

Scenario #1

If they just raised rates $2 per ticket on sold out nights this would generate an additional $15,600 per concert. And if the venue sold out entirely two nights per week over the summer that would equal 24 sold out nights. Therefore, if we multiply $15,600 by 24 the result is $374,400 in additional revenue.

Scenario #2

The top 10 percent of the seats would represent 780 seats. If these seats were raised by $15, this price increase would generate an additional $11,700 on sold out nights. Again, based upon 24 sold out nights per summer, this action would increase revenues by $280,800. These seats could be marketed as having a premium due to their superior sound and sight lines.

Scenario #3

Some niche bands have huge followings, but these followings may only be large enough to fill the amphitheater once in a while. So if the venue could book just one of these niche acts every other week in the summer, this would represent six special concerts. If each concert sold 5,000 tickets with an average price of $49, this would represent $1,470,000!

Scenario #4

The special events team should increase its capture of the wedding and vow renewal markets by attending bridal shows, making personal sales calls on bridal shops, and sending brochures to all couples listed in engagement announcements in the local newspaper. If these ceremonies are priced at $500 each and two are booked per week, this would represent $12,000 over the summer.

Scenario #5

If the venue increased the price of parking to $25 on site, this would generate additional revenue of $18,000 per show. If remote parking was increased to $15, this would generate another $5,000 in new revenue if the show were sold out. Combined, these $5 increases would generate an additional $23,000 in parking revenues on sold out nights.

Scenario #6

If the venue were able to sell out with a motivational speaker seminar at a price of $99 per ticket, this would represent $772,200 in revenue. If the venue could sell out with motivational speakers just once per month in the summer this would generate an additional $2,316,600 in revenue! Wow! Do you have Tony Robbins' number? Don't forget to subtract the speaker's fee from the total revenue anticipated.

Sometimes, these events are just too big for an amphitheater or they require an indoor venue. So let's return to Metropolis to take a look at their new convention center.

Courtesy of Destination Hotels & Resorts.

The Richardson Dallas Conference Room.

Metropolis Convention Center

Leaping from the light rail car, the kids lead the way while motioning for Mom and Dad to hurry up. They are headed inside the Metropolis Convention Center to do some serious shopping. They have tickets to this weekend's consumer electronics show and they just cannot wait to see all of the new gadgets and toys that they will need to add to their gift request list this year. This is the first day of the show and they do not want to miss a thing.

Inside the center, they pick up an exhibitors' map and head straight to the main exhibit hall upstairs. The kids literally bound up the escalator and run to the hall in their hurry to get to the first booth. Out of breath, their eager eyes scan the merchandise while the exhibitor asks them if they want to sign up for a free drawing. "Uh-huh," they both utter as they continue scanning the new products before them. Behind them Dad, their home chef, is looking on the exhibitor map for the newest kitchen gadgets while Mom is searching her map for new electronic office tools. Everyone agrees to hook back up at the entrance in two hours when they intend to grab a bite for lunch.

Laughingly, and yet lovingly, referred to as MC^2, the Metropolis Convention Center was opened in 2006 to great fanfare. Declared by the meeting world to be the most innovative and user-friendly center in the United States, the center has not failed to please all whom have entered. Located at the edge of downtown, the center has added a new dimension to the city's skyline. Its foam-coated circular architecture makes the center appear almost embraceable from a distance, like a big soft pillow. This is precisely the image the architects intended as they wanted pedestrians seeing the center to view it as a soft and pleasant place to visit. And hotels love the analogy and play off the pillow image in all of their convention advertising and marketing campaigns. The center is the largest in a six-state region. The center tries to keep the exhibit space booked with trade and consumer shows and attempts to fill the remaining space with meetings and social events.

Physical facilities:

- 750,000 square feet of contiguous exhibition space
- 250,000 square feet of unobstructed meeting space in 176 rooms
- Two 36,000 square foot ballrooms, each divisible into thirds
- 6,800-seat theater
- 1,875-space parking garage
- Another 2,700 spaces within six block radius
- Two permanent three meal a day restaurants open show days
- Two cocktail lounges open 11 AM to 11 PM on show days
- Retail shops ring the exterior perimeter

Services:

- Full-service catering services
- Full conference services
- Onsite electrical and telecommunications technician
- Onsite computer technician and audio-visual contractor
- Light rail station stop on west side

Abbreviated SWOT Analysis for the Metropolis Convention Center

Strengths: New innovative facility, ample space for accommodating 80 percent of all conventions held in the United States, location in Metropolis which is considered to be a safe and clean town for conventions, adequate hotel accommodations nearby.

Weakness: In a less populated area near the middle of the country, so flights from each coast tend to be a bit high. Also the center will not realize its full potential until it is open a few years as meeting planners book so far in advance and only a few wanted to book the first year in the center for fear of construction delays.

Opportunities: The wonderful publicity surrounding its opening has intrigued meeting planners, so the sales team has the opportunity to book a significant amount of business.

Threats: Other centers, other locations, increasing cost of jet fuel impacting airline tickets, terrorism, the economy.

Competitors: All other convention centers in the country, all smaller venues in and around Metropolis for the smaller-sized business.

Time period used for analysis: April through June, peak convention months for Metropolis.

Booking Pace and Pattern: Large trade shows 5 to 10 years out, large consumer shows three to five years out, smaller shows' booking pattern varies by size. Only social business such as proms and charity balls are booked 12 to 24 months out.

Channels currently used: Joint venture for all marketing activities with the Convention and Visitors Bureau, proprietary website, tickets for consumer shows sold online through ticket brokers.

Rates: Each group rate is negotiated individually with a salesperson. Price depends on amount of space needed, food and beverage requirements, local hotel usage, and potential traffic.

Overview

The center was built to drive tourism revenues into Metropolis. The center enjoys an excellent mix of trade and consumer shows. Trade shows are most often closed to the general public but they also often generate the highest revenue. Most consumer shows are held over the weekend, but some larger shows extend over two weeks.

What are some possible strategies and tactics that may be applied during this time period to optimize revenues for the center?

1. First of all, since this is peak season, the sales team must make sure that it has booked the business representing the highest total customer worth to both itself and the city. The strategy here is to optimize peak-season revenues. The tactic is to select the business generating the highest total customer worth.

2. Second, the sales team should make sure that it is optimizing use of the convention and meeting facilities. Perhaps one trade association needs one half of the center. The sales team should endeavor to find another group or two groups to fill the other half of the center during this time period. The strategy is to optimize space sales. The tactic is to fill any remaining space with smaller events.

3. Third, the center should heavily promote its theater to all trade and consumer shows. Many shows have educational elements involved and this theater would

allow the event planners to also make revenue by adding in seminars, lectures by industry leaders, and certification programs applicable within their industry. The strategy is to increase show revenues by selling the theater. The tactic is to market the theater as a revenue generator to the show organizer.

4. Fourth, the center needs to find avenues for filling its soft holiday weekends during the peak season. Easter and Memorial Day both fall during the April through June peak convention season for Metropolis. Holidays are often the kiss of death for business travel. Most people do not like to travel for business over the holidays. In this case, the week before Easter is usually soft as many Christians take at least half of the day off on Good Friday, shortening the work week. And since Memorial Day falls on a Monday, the rest of that week is usually weak when it comes to business travel. So the center sales team should either seek out some consumer shows with great potential local draw during these holiday weeks, or it should work with the city to develop a unique annual event to draw in business to the downtown. The strategy is to fill soft demand periods. The tactic is to solicit or develop unique consumer shows appealing to the local market.

5. The center should use the size and flexibility of its two ballrooms to capture the most lucrative social and charitable events. The ballrooms are able to seat 3,000 each or 1,000 per section. This seating capacity is based on seating 10 people around a 72-inch round table. The strategy here is the optimize ballroom revenues. The tactic is to seek the most lucrative social and charitable events anticipating 1,000 or more guests in attendance.

What other strategies and tactics could the Metropolis Convention Center use to capitalize on opportunities to increase revenues? Which strategies could be developed to reduce or minimize potential threats?

Take a moment to think about other possible opportunities facing the center during this time period.

Possible Results

Scenario #1

First, most convention centers are built specifically to support tourism to an area. So the Metropolis Convention Center always needs to consider the impact that any show booked there has on local hotel room supply. The center needs to book large conventions that need substantial convention space as well as significant numbers of hotel rooms. The center should conduct a series of displacement analyses and also calculate total customer worth per segment both to itself and to the city as a whole.

Conventions represent substantial revenue to any city. So it is incumbent on the center's sales team to optimize the revenues generated by the facility for the city as a whole. Local restaurants, cabs, shops, and conference related services benefit in addition to the hotels. These all need to be added to determine total customer worth.

Scenario #2

Some shows wish to have a facility all to themselves during the dates covering their actual events. If they do not physically fill all available space, they may either buy the remaining space or they must be prepared to have other events occurring during the same time. They may be more open to other events occurring on the dates that they set up or tear down. There are not enough of these huge "run of the house" shows to fill every single center in the United States on every single day of the year. So many shows have become accustomed to sharing centers with other groups over the same dates. The key here is to make each group feel as if they are the only, or at least the most important, group in house at that time. That is achieved by careful planning and skillful management of logistics.

So filling the convention center is like putting together a jigsaw. The better able the sales team is to fill in all pieces of the larger picture over a given time, the more revenues will be generated over those same dates.

Scenario #3

In this instance, the center stands to make additional revenue for each day that it sells the theater. If the theater is priced at $10 per seat and the center sells just half the seats for an event, this represents $34,000 in revenue that day. Or the center could rent it at a flat rate, perhaps only $10,000 if needed by a large convention. The convention organizer would be able to add the theater for lectures, seminars, or certification which adds value to the convention in the mind of convention attendees. So in this case both the center and the convention organizer make additional revenues.

Scenario #4

Many centers actually "**go dark**" during holiday weeks. In other words, they shut their doors, turn down the heat or air conditioning, and turn off the lights. Remember also that the center has fixed costs that it must pay regardless of whether it is open or closed. So any business booked during these weeks would generate additional revenue to both the center and the city.

Scenario #5

Metropolis is a pretty good sized town, so there are quite a few events that command attendance of 1,000 people or more. Many of these are annual awards or charitable galas. Also several local colleges require space the size of one of the ballrooms for their annual commencement ceremonies. And brides planning receptions of 700 or larger find it difficult to find adequate ballroom space in local hotels.

Let's assume that the average dinner price is $29. If the sales team was able to book one 2,000 person gala in one ballroom and one 800 person wedding reception in a section of the other ballroom, this would generate total revenue of $81,200. If this were possible just half of the year, we would multiply this amount by 26 weeks to arrive at $2,111,200 in revenue.

Now that we have reviewed a few examples in sports, entertainment, and events, let's turn our attention to opportunities in the cruise, spa, and luxury recreational vehicle (RV) resort sectors.

SUMMARY

In this chapter we explored the application of revenue management techniques regarding the products and services of three hospitality providers: a football stadium, a musical amphitheater, and a convention center. Each organization was briefly examined in terms of its customers, market segments, partial internal SWOT analysis, forecasted demand for the time period, prices, and channels used for distributing inventory. Various scenarios were presented in which the organization could implement strategies and tactics to drive revenues. Possible results were presented to demonstrate the impact of these potential strategies and tactics.

KEY TERMS AND CONCEPTS

The following key terms and concepts were presented in this chapter. Each term and concept is also contained in the Glossary of Terms located at the end of this book:

• go dark

DISCUSSION QUESTIONS

1. What additional opportunities may face each of these facilities?
2. What additional threats may face each of these facilities?
3. What other strategies and tactics could you develop for the Granite Palace?
4. What other strategies and tactics could you develop for Tunes?
5. What other strategies and tactics could you develop for Metropolis Convention Center?

EXPERIENTIAL EXERCISE

Get into groups of two and select another type of sports, entertainment, or event venue. Personally visit the venue and conduct a similar analysis and determine possible strategies and tactics that may be used to optimize revenues.

INTERNET EXERCISES

1. Go online and see how many different seat prices are available at the stadium housing your favorite football team. Do you see any opportunities to increase revenues? Please explain.
2. Go online and find the ticket price for a favorite artist playing at a favorite venue. Do you see any opportunities here to increase ticket prices? Please explain.
3. Go online and find the website of the largest convention center in your area. Report on the products and services available. Do you see any opportunities to capture increased revenue at the center? Please explain.

Aqua Dolce Tub at Royal Palms.

CHAPTER

17

Applications in Cruise, Spa, and Luxury RV Resorts

Chapter Objectives

The objectives of this chapter are to:

- Explore the application of revenue management techniques in the leisure sector
- Consider several scenarios, strategies, and tactics for Skimmer Cruises
- Consider several scenarios, strategies, and tactics for Coachman's Seaside Paradise luxury RV resort
- Consider several scenarios, strategies, and tactics for Quiescence Spa Retreat

The third leg of our journey leads us to some wonderful leisure activities involving relaxing waters. Again, we need to apply our RevMAP to help us find the pot of gold waiting at each of these destinations. Let's begin by following the smell of the salty air . . .

Skimmer Cruises

The cab slowly inches through the bustling activity surrounding the dock. Our couple exits the cab and peers straight ahead into a wall of white. As they tilt back their heads and strain their necks skyward they are able to see the Skimmer logo splashed across the ship's bow. They squeeze each other's hand in excitement and then gather up their luggage and camera gear purchased just for this adventure. They are about to board Skimmer's newest vessel, the Sea Lion, for a seven-day cruise of the Gulf of Alaska.

Once aboard, they drop their bags in their ocean-view suite and emerge deck side. After grabbing two ice-cold tropical drinks from the passing waiter, the weary couple drop into two awaiting deck chairs. Ah, time to relax. The heavy scented rum, the warm September afternoon sun, and the gentle rocking of the ship soothes them slowly into a restful slumber. Muffled in their subconscious is the sound of a horn announcing the ship's departure from the shore. Here are some of the ship's features that the couple may be dreaming about:

Physical facilities:

- 110,000 tons
- 989-feet long
- 1,388 interior and ocean view staterooms, plus 149 suites
- Four restaurants and seven lounges
- 24-hour room service
- Live entertainment nightclub
- 70s discotheque
- Casino
- Three pools
- A variety of hot tubs and sauna
- Fully equipped gymnasium
- Spa and hair salon
- Putting green
- Game room
- Gift shops

Services:
Included in per person price:

- Accommodations
- Three meals per day
- Use of all shipboard recreational facilities
- Use of aromatherapy room in the spa
- Nightly entertainment
- Basic Kids' Club activities
- $100 in shipboard credit

Services available for an additional fee:

- Shore excursions
- Photographs
- Yoga and exercise classes
- Cooking and wine seminars
- Kids' club lessons (i.e., swimming, snorkeling)
- Spa and salon treatments

Products and services not included in price:

- Airfare to and from Vancouver, British Columbia
- Alcoholic beverages, juices, and soft drinks
- Taxes, gratuities, and governmental fees

Abbreviated SWOT Analysis for the Skimmer Sea Lion

Strengths: Newest vessel in line, full-service cruise ship, popular ports of call, excellent food and beverage quality and service.

Weaknesses: New cruise line facing some brand unfamiliarity, new staff with little prior training, high fuel and operating costs, limited storage for provisions.

Opportunities: Still huge untapped first-time cruiser market, bundling of products and services to create new packages, add new ports of call, capture group cruises.

Threats: Weather, terrorism, shipboard illnesses, fuel costs, running out of food and beverage provisions, the economy.

Competitors: All other cruise lines that travel to the same ports and cruise lines that travel to different ports, land-based travel destinations in the same region.

Time period used for analysis: The month of September.

Booking pace and pattern: Seven-day cruises are booked traditionally three to six months prior to departure. About 10 percent of passengers, primarily discount seekers, book within 30 days of departure.

Channels currently used: Skimmer Cruise website, links to all cruise associations, merchant models, opaque and action sites, GDS headlines and advertising, wholesale and retail packages sold to travel agent market, airline tie-ins, destination tourism offices, advertising in all travel and trade associations and publications.

Stateroom prices: (per seven-day cruise) $1,399 for interior stateroom, $1,719 for ocean-view stateroom, and $2,900 for a suite.

Overview

September is one of the peak months of the year for cruise tours of Alaska. A vast array of wildlife is abundantly present, the weather is mild, and the changing colors of the foliage provide for amazing scenery. Numerous cruise lines offer tour packages to Alaska during this time period. Airlines offer some reduced rates for weekend departures since the summer vacation season is past and most children are back in school. Skimmer Cruises has contracted with a variety of local hospitality suppliers for day excursions along the coast, including jeep tours, fly fishing, wildlife photography, and panning for gold.

What are some possible strategies and tactics that may be applied by the Skimmer Sea Lion during this time period to optimize revenues?

1. First, Skimmer cruises should shop its competitors and determine whether its prices are positioned properly for the month of September. The cruise line's marketing department decided to utilize a market penetration strategy when it first launched the Sea Lion in March. It should reassess its price positioning to see if there is an opportunity to now start raising prices.
2. The Sea Lion's marketing team should develop senior-citizen fall-foliage packages. This is one of the older generation's preferred seasons to travel precisely because most children are back in school. The pace is a bit slower and the weather is temperate and perfect for viewing wildlife among the changing leaves.
3. The marketing team should also consider developing other packages, including a couple's package, a honeymoon package, photography package, poker tour

package, group cruises, and spa packages. They should also offer family packages for those families who travel during the fall.

4. Since fewer families vacation in September, this may be a good time to offer more adult oriented theme cruises. For example, the Sea Lion could host a Gold Rush Poker Tournament offering substantial prizes that would be broadcast on the cable poker network. Marketed correctly, this could become an annual event.

5. The cruise ship could change one of its food outlets to an upscale brand or celebrity chef showcase. Dinners in this facility would not be included in the package price.

What other strategies and tactics could the Sea Lion develop to capitalize on opportunities to increase revenues? What strategies could be developed to reduce or minimize potential threats?

Take a moment to consider other possible opportunities and threats facing the Skimmer Sea Lion during this time period.

Possible Results

Scenario #1

The Sea Lion originally set its prices low to induce trial by first-time cruisers and to encourage seasoned cruisers to experience the new vessel. While this strategy was

Courtesy of Lisa Marie Parker.

Port of Barcelona.

extremely successful upon launch, the cruise line would now like to start raising its prices to more correctly position the Sea Lion as an upscale cruising experience. So the pricing department has been carefully examining the price and positioning of its main competitors and feels that fall is the right time to reposition the Sea Lion. First, they feel that there should be a broader price spread between the regular staterooms and the suites. So it decides to raise the price of the suites by $750 each to $3,650, which is similar to the suite prices of its closest competitors. Remember that there are 149 suites onboard. So if the Sea Lion sails with just half of its suites sold, this increase in suite prices would generate an additional $55,875 in revenue.

Since this is a popular month for Alaskan cruises, let's assume the ship sets sail with 75 percent of its rooms sold, and 50 percent of its suites. Remember that the ship has 1,388 staterooms, so if 75 percent are sold that would equal approximately 1,041 staterooms. So if the Sea Lion raises the prices on both its interior and ocean-view staterooms by $100 each, this would generate an additional $104,100 per cruise. Add in the additional $55,875 in revenue generated by the increased suite rates and the total is now $159,975 per seven-day cruise.

Scenario #2

First, think back to our discussion of generational marketing in Chapter 4. The silver-haired seniors have high levels of disposable income to spend. They also like comfort and convenience. So organizations that develop a fall foliage package that offers comfort and convenience will most likely capture an additional slice of this disposable income. For example, the Sea Lion could package a seven-day fall foliage tour that includes airfare to and from Vancouver, ocean-view rooms and suites, all meals included, a photography lesson and development package, shore excursions for viewing wildlife, morning stretching sessions, and evening massage treatments in the spa. The price of the package should be less than the combined retail price of its components in order for the passengers to perceive it as a value. Remember that the airlines are offering lower fares in September, so it will be easy for the cruise line to purchase special discounted fares to build into this package. Let's assume that the fall foliage package is priced so that it increases total revenue per passenger by $1,000 and that the Sea Lion sells 250 of these packages per seven-day cruise. Multiply that $250,000 by the four weeks in September and the Sea Lion just generated an additional $1 million in revenue!

Scenario #3

The marketing team should offer as many packages as it feels are feasible to sell to raise revenues in September. But also keep in mind that acquisition costs are involved in attracting customers. So the Sea Lion should conduct a segment analysis and determine which segments provide the greatest total customer worth for each particular cruise in each month. It should then develop packages that are the most likely to sell and that will generate the most revenue in the month of September.

Scenario #4

There are numerous advantages to hosting a shipboard poker tournament. First, the television network would most likely kick in the prize purse. The tournament would showcase the Sea Lion and provide the cruise line with outstanding television coverage. This coverage would attract future cruise passengers who are also gaming enthusiasts. And the combination of the tournament participants and their fans would most likely generate traffic in the ship's casinos and entertainment venues. This is especially important if half of the ship is filled with silver-haired seniors on a fall foliage tour.

Scenario #5

The ship could try to increase its ancillary revenues by leasing one of its restaurants to a celebrity chef as do many of the casinos in Las Vegas. The price for dinner in this establishment would not be included in the price. Thus, all revenues generated from this restaurant would be considered additional ancillary spend.

Courtesy of Destination Hotels & Resorts.

Royal Palms T. Cook's Outdoor Fireplace.

Our silver-haired seniors had a wonderful time on their cruise. But winter is just around the corner, so it is time for them to head south. They return home from their cruise, take a few months off for the holidays and then fire up the RV for some serious touring.

Coachman's Seaside Paradise

There once was a time when the term *recreational vehicle* (RV) meant a silver bullet occupied by the grandparents or a popup camper being hauled by the family station wagon. Times have drastically changed in RV-land but this fact is still a relatively well-kept secret. Instead of Dad backing up the camper onto an old broken cement slab in a campground that smelled of sewer and stagnant water, with a rusted swing set off in one corner, today he is driving through the gates of a luxury RV resort. Let's take a look . . .

Ron and Sandy have just retired and purchased a new $175,000 motorcoach. This year they leave their home in Michigan to travel to the gulf coast of Florida. For they have also purchased a lot in Coachman's Seaside Paradise located just outside of Naples. Coachman's Seaside Paradise is a gated community featuring 150 waterside RV lots facing either the lake or the Gulf of Mexico. Boat docks are located adjacent to all lakeside lots and an expansive beach and fishing pier jutting out into the Gulf are easily accessed by all residents of the park.

As they pull up through the gates, they see the beautifully landscaped lake off to one side. Blue herons stroll through the reed-filled marsh while black swans glide across the glassy still waters. To the left, a few late golfers rush to complete the last two holes in the orange glow of the final rays of sunlight. The motorcoach rounds the bend and the couple approaches their lot overlooking the Gulf of Mexico. The sun looms as the cavernous mouth of a glaring jack-o-lantern as it sets slowly on the horizon. They pull into their porte-cochere and Ron quickly hooks up the water and utility supply lines to their home away from home. They pull out a few lawn chairs and sip iced tea as they watch the sun finally set.

The next morning they arise early and head out on their bikes for a quick tour around the resort. They need to formally check in since they arrived late last night. They visit the welcome center and receive their winter resident packets containing all the passes they will need for use of the various recreational facilities available onsite. They get back on their bikes and resume their ride, stopping when they reach the resort clubhouse to grab some breakfast. They pick up the event calendar for the day and see that there is a snowbird welcome barbecue that evening that they decide to attend. A **snowbird** is a person who travels south for the winter. So Sandy heads over to the spa for a quick pedicure, while Ron hooks up with some of the buddies he met last year for a round of golf. They will meet up on the beach for a walk later this afternoon. This is the changing face of today's new RV resorts. And they are popping up all over the nation as America rediscovers the fun of hitting the road in a home. Let's recap what the Coachman's Seaside Paradise has to offer:

Physical facilities:

- Secure, gated community
- 150 lakeside or Gulf-side lots, located on the Gulf of Mexico near Naples, Florida

- Lots available for sale or rent
- Utility hookups, including satellite television
- Porte-cochere featuring built-in grill, small refrigerator, and outdoor dining table
- 18-hole championship golf course
- Full-service spa and salon
- Clubhouse with restaurant, lounge, and meeting space
- Healthcare clinic onsite
- Onsite grocer, pharmacy, dry cleaning, and gasoline station
- Lakeside marina
- Fishing pier
- State-of-the-art fitness center with indoor/outdoor pools
- Tennis courts and shuffleboard courts

Services:

- Breakfast, lunch, and dinner available in clubhouse
- Individual golf and league play
- Full range of spa and salon services
- Nightly happy hour
- Weekend entertainment
- Meal delivery service
- Prescription delivery service
- Daily and overnight excursions to nearby attractions
- Weekly dental clinic
- Marina services
- Bait and lures available for sale
- Complete range of housekeeping services available
- All landscaping maintenance included

Abbreviated SWOT Analysis for Coachman's Seaside Paradise

Strengths: Location, clean, upscale facilities, full range of amenities.
Weaknesses: High price, continually changing resident pool, low occupancy in summer months.
Opportunities: Partner with other resorts to offer lot sharing similar to unit interchange in the timeshare industry, growing popularity of RVing in baby boomer population.
Threats: Hurricanes, condominium-based retirement resorts, the high price of gasoline, and the economy.
Competitors: All other forms of retirement and rental lodging.
Time period used for analysis: Late October through late April.
Booking pace and pattern: An RV resort is operated like a condominium resort. So owners purchase their lots and whenever they are not in residence the resort association retains the right to rent the lot. Therefore, the owners must declare their anticipated usage pattern once a year. Amendments to this schedule are made with advance notice. Vacant lots are rented on a nightly, weekly, or

monthly basis. Nightly rentals are often drive-ins that occur without reservation. These are RV travelers who hear of the resort when they are nearby and decide to try it out for a night. Only Class A and Class C motorcoaches are permitted in the resort.

Channels currently used: Direct real estate sales onsite, advertising in upscale travel publications and special-interest magazines, brochure distribution at major RV dealers, tie-ins with all state and local tourism organizations, direct mail to travel agents and database lists, and discount coupons for nightly rentals placed in retirement publications.

Sales and rental prices: Lots start at $195,000 and increase to over $495,000 for ownership. Annual association dues of $35,000 are assessed for each lot. Nightly rentals start at $75 per lot and increase to $225 for premium lots adjacent to the Gulf.

Overview

The resort is 80 percent sold out. The real estate office anticipates selling the remaining lots over the next 18 months. Most owners occupy their lots from mid-December through mid-March. Many extend these stays by one month on either side, so they arrive in November and depart in April. Approximately 20 percent of the lot owners are full-time resort residents. Whenever the owner is not in residence, the resort association attempts to rent the lot to generate additional revenue.

What are some possible strategies and tactics that may be applied by the resort for the upcoming year?

1. First, the resort should consider raising its sales prices on the remaining lots. Naples is a high-demand resort location and waterside lots are always at a premium. The strategy is to optimize real estate sales revenue. The tactic is to increase lot prices.

2. The resort association should consider offering courses and classes to generate ancillary sales. For example, it could offer cooking courses with local celebrity chefs. It may also offer golf or tennis lessons. The strategy is to increase ancillary revenues. The tactic is to offer a variety of learning opportunities for a small fee each.

3. The resort should consider partnering with other RV resorts to offer reciprocal stay agreements. These reciprocal rights could either be extended along with the ownership deed to the lot at Coachman's Seaside Paradise or be charged as an additional annual assessment. The strategy is to increase revenues from owners. The tactic is to provide reciprocal stay rights with other RV resorts.

4. The sales and marketing team should focus upon capturing extended-stay business during the off season. **Extended-stay business** is defined as business that generates seven or more nights stay. Rather than spend the bulk of its marketing dollars on nightly stays, the sales and marketing team should seek out longer-term weekly, monthly, or quarterly business. The strategy is to optimize off-season rentals. The tactic is to target and attract extended-stay travelers during the off-season.

5. The resort should develop golf and spa packages that it could sell in the off-season to more price-sensitive RV owners. The strategy here would be to increase off-season rentals. The tactic is to design and market golf and spa packages to more price-sensitive market segments during periods of low demand.

What other strategies and tactics could the resort develop to capitalize on opportunities to increase revenues? Which strategies could be developed to reduce or minimize potential threats?

Once again, take a few moments to think about other opportunities and threats facing the resort.

Possible Results

Scenario #1

Assuming there are 30 lots left, raising the sales prices by $35,000 each would generate an additional $1,050,000. The reduced supply will increase demand, which in turn will enable the real estate sales office to increase the prices. To optimize revenues, the salespeople should determine the value of each of the remaining lots and price them accordingly. If they increased the price of the least desirable lots by $35,000 and kept increasing prices with the increased value of each lot, the total revenues generated would be substantially higher than $1 million.

Scenario #2

For purposes of example, let's say that the resort offered classes two days a week from December through March. Monday cooking classes are attended by about 85 people and there are 10 golfers enrolled in Thursday golf lessons. If the cooking classes were priced at $20 per person and were available for 16 weeks, they would generate additional revenues of approximately $27,200. If golf lessons were priced at $40 per person, they would generate additional revenues of $6,400.

Scenario #3

There are several possible approaches to generating additional revenues from reciprocal agreements. First, the resort could ask potential buyers if they were interested in these reciprocal arrangements. Those who were could purchase these privileges for say another $25,000 up front and $250 per week per year. Or, they could just enter a pay-as-you-go plan at a cost of $1,000 per week per year. Since many lot owners are retirees, they may spend 12 weeks or more on the road each year. In this case, it would behoove them to purchase the reciprocal privileges up front to save money in the long run. Those not interested in reciprocal arrangements would not be assessed any fees or additional charges. The weekly reciprocal assessment charge is split 50/50 between the two resorts to maintain the program's quality. Remember that there are still 30 lots left to sell. If the purchasers of 10 of these lots decided to enter the first reciprocal arrangement, they would pay the $25,000 at closing, which would represent an additional $250,000 to the resort. If they used just two weeks per year at the reciprocal resort, the Coachman's Seaside Paradise would receive an additional $250 in fees from each or $2,500 in total. So we are now up to $252,500 in the first year. If purchasers of another 10 lots decided to accept the pay-as-you-go reciprocal agreement and also spent two weeks per year at the reciprocal resort, Coachman's would receive an additional $1,000 in fees from each or $10,000 in total. So added to the first group, this totals $262,500 in additional revenues. And naturally, it could offer pay-as-you-go privileges to all of the owners who purchased their lots before the reciprocal agreement was entered.

Scenario #4

It is much more cost effective to target travelers who stay for 7 to 30 nights than it is to target travelers just staying for one night. In most cases, the acquisition cost of capturing seven single-night stays is higher than the acquisition cost for one traveler staying seven nights. The sales and marketing team should very carefully monitor the channel production reports it receives. It should also evaluate its total customer worth per market segment. Ideally, the sales and marketing team should strive to capture long-term stays from the segments representing the highest total customer worth.

Scenario #5

The marketing team could develop one-week golf packages, one-week spa packages, and one-week golf and spa packages for couples that would be sold in the

Courtesy of Destination Hotels & Resorts.

Alvadora Relaxation Room at the Royal Palms.

shoulder seasons and the off-season. For example, the golf package could include a seven-night stay on a lakeside lot, one round of golf per day, two golf lessons, and lunch for two each day in the clubhouse. Pricing this package at $699, would be a perceived price value. If the resort sold just two of these packages per week for 30 weeks of the year, the resort would generate an additional $41,940.

The resort may wish to develop a golf and spa package for its silver-haired senior couples. The package could include a seven-night stay on a Gulf-side lot, one round of golf per day, two golf lessons, two spa treatments per day, and lunch for him at the clubhouse and lunch for her at the spa each day. Sound stereotypical? Possibly, but remember that we are speaking about the silver-haired seniors here. This package could be priced at $1,750. Again, if the resort sold just two of these packages per week for 30 weeks of the year, the resort would generate an additional $105,000.

Speaking of spas, let's make one more stop on our journey by dropping in for a day of pampering at a destination spa located in the Arizona desert.

Quiescence Spa Retreat

Once again our journey begins with our traveler being dropped off at the spa's entrance, this time by the local jeep shuttle service. After a short but dusty ride from the airport, just the sound of the entrance fountain's babbling waters made her parched mouth swallow. It takes a moment for her eyes to adjust from the bright sun of the desert heat to the cool darkness of the lush oasis before her. The thick adobe walls, moist green plants, and gentle misters make the lobby feel 20 degrees cooler than the outdoors. As she checks into the spa, a gentle soul slides up beside her and swiftly scurries off with her bags. A unique blend of calming sound fills the air. She hears a combination of chimes, and birds and water along with the hiss of the misters and a low murmuring chant emanating from a tented recess in the garden. She immediately begins to feel the day's travel stress melting from her shoulders. Now, if she could just get to her room to plunge into a nice cool bath . . .

The door to her cabana was ajar and her bags had been laid just inside. Although slippers had been placed on the mat, the cool tile of the floor looked more inviting. As she kicked off her shoes, she spotted the tall iced tea next to a welcome note on the fireplace mantel. She was at first startled by the presence of the fireplace as she was still flushed with heat outdoors. But then she remembered she was in the desert and a chill often descends after dark. She grabbed the glass and went into the bath. A few moments later she would wash off the dust of the day in a cool bath anointed with special herbs and essence. Her week of total relaxation had begun.

Physical facilities:

- 28 cabanas located in the Sedona desert
- In-room tranquility tubs
- Outdoor dining room
- Tropical gardens
- Hiking paths
- Aromatherapy room

- Water therapy room
- Outdoor swimming pool
- No television, telephones, or communication devices
- State-of-the-art spa

Services:

- Hydrotherapies
- Massage therapies, including traditional Swedish, Thai, Deep Tissue, Hot Stone, and floor Shiatsu, hand, foot, facial, and cranial
- Reflexology
- Herbal body wraps
- Mud baths
- Paraffin therapy
- Facials and exfoliating peels
- Depilatory waxing
- Manicures and pedicures
- Haircuts, styling, highlights, and color
- Body Composition Analysis
- Nutritional Counseling
- Yoga and Pilates sessions
- Personal trainer

Abbreviated SWOT Analysis for Quiescence Spa Retreat

Strengths: Beautiful facilities, great location, well-trained staff, superb reputation.
Weaknesses: Limited in size, remote location for travel, no brand affiliation, desert heat.
Opportunities: Increased interest from new market segments, increased availability of charter air services from each coast, potential for room tie in with the larger resorts, add new products and services, develop support services to take home.
Threats: New competition coming from hotel spas, cheaper day spas growing in number and location.
Competitors: Other major spas in the desert region, spas in area hotels, day spas.
Time period used for analysis: The upcoming year.
Booking pace and pattern: Most packages purchased three to six months out with the exception of gift packages which are good for one year. Three- or seven-day packages are the most popular. Individual night stays are only accepted during off-peak demand periods.
Channels currently used: All major spa publications, women's magazines, merchant models, retail travel agents, opaque channels, direct mailings to high-income travel segments obtained from credit card database, website links with state and area tourism and resort associations.
Package prices per person: High season: Three-night package for $2,990; Seven-day package for $5,950. Low season: Three-night package $1,950; Seven-day package for $4,900. Price includes accommodations, meals, personal trainer, nutrition counselor, and two spa services per day. Guests staying at nearby hotels may purchase a la carte spa services ranging in price from $100 to $425 each.

Overview

The Quiescence has been open as a desert oasis since the 1940s, so it has the feel of the classic spa resorts seen in the movies. But the equipment and technology transform it into a cutting-edge body-sculpting facility. Due to its reputation and undeniably stunning location, the spa operates at 85 percent occupancy year round. The owners have just completed a total renovation of both the cabanas and the main spa facilities. They are meeting with their management team next week to determine their strategic management plan for next year.

What are some possible strategies and tactics that may be developed by the spa to optimize revenues next year?

1. First, with the continued high demand and recently completed renovation, the spa should consider raising its rates across the board for its packages. The strategy is to increase revenue from packages. The tactic is to raise prices for all packages available.

2. The spa should analyze its individual treatment prices and comparison shop its competitors. It may wish to price items just slightly above the next best area spa now that the Quiescence has been renovated. The strategy is to increase revenues from individual spa treatments. The tactic is to set prices slightly above its nearest competitor.

3. The spa should plan a Grand Re-Opening event and marketing campaign. It should send all previous guests an invitation to revisit the spa retreat with a promise of a special gift upon their return. The Quiescence should develop a special keepsake in honor of this event. The strategy is to capitalize on its

Aqua Dolce Villa Spa at the Royal Palms.

Courtesy of Destination Hotels & Resorts.

renovation and increase revenues. The tactic is to contact previous guests and entice them back.

4. With its new state-of-the-art facilities, the spa may be able to displace lower-rated package business with higher-rated business. The strategy here is to increase revenues from packages. The tactic here is to capture additional higher-rated packages.

5. The spa should take advantage of its Re-Grand Opening to obtain a series of special features written by spa and travel writers invited to visit the retreat. The strategy here is to capitalize on its renovation by obtaining free publicity. The tactic is to get articles written by travel and spa writers.

What other strategies and tactics could Quiescence use to increase revenues? Take a moment to meditate on this question.

Possible Results

Scenario #1

Let's assume that the spa raised prices by $200 per night across the board. Remember that the retreat has 28 cabanas and operates at 85 percent occupancy. So multiplying 28 times 365 days equals 10,220 room nights. At 85 percent this equals 8,687 room nights. At $200 more each per room per night, this price increase would generate an additional $1,737,400 in revenue. It should try to maximize any rate increase this year following the extensive renovation. But even if the owners got cold feet and raised the prices only by $100 per night, this would generate an additional $868,700 in revenue.

Scenario #2

In this case, let's assume that the spa sells five treatments to local residents and three treatments to guests of area hotels each weekday. So that is eight treatments per day. If the spa raises its prices just $10 on each of these treatments, that would generate $80 more per day. Multiplied by five days per week and 52 weeks in the year, this generates an additional $20,800 in revenue.

Scenario #3

The spa decides to run the Grand Re-Opening special for three months. If they are able to capture 100 previous guests each month this would total 300 extra guests over the 90-day period. If each of these guests purchased the three-night package for the new price of $3,590, this promotion would generate an additional $1,077,000 in package revenues.

Scenario #4

In this case, all marketing activities should be focused on securing more seven-day packages then three-day packages in both the high and low seasons. For our purposes here, we will consider all weeks high season with the exception of the 12 off-season weeks from June 1 to August 31. If the spa was able to capture just two more seven-day packages at the new prices during the 40 high-season weeks, this would generate an additional $588,000. And if it captured two more seven-day packages each week in the 12 weeks in the low season this would generate an additional $151,200. Combined, capturing just two more seven-day packages at the new higher rates each week of the year would generate an additional $739,200 in revenue.

Scenario #5

Business generated by good press is sometimes hard to track. So the spa should try to tack on special promotions to any stories authored by writers placing articles in spa and travel magazines. A special promotion is usually one which states "mention this ad to receive . . ." or "mention promotional code 123 when making reservations," or something to that effect. This enables the spa to track the results of the good press they received.

Now that we have reviewed a few examples of applying revenue management strategies and tactics in the cruise, spa, and luxury RV resort segments, let's turn to analyzing applications in golf, gaming, and theme parks.

SUMMARY

In this chapter, we explored the application of revenue management techniques regarding the products and services of three hospitality providers: a cruise ship, a luxury RV resort, and a spa retreat. Each organization was briefly examined in terms of its customers, market segments, partial internal SWOT analysis, forecasted demand for the time period, prices, and channels used for distributing inventory. Various scenarios were presented in which the organization could implement strategies and tactics to drive revenues. Possible results were presented to demonstrate the impact of these potential strategies and tactics.

KEY TERMS AND CONCEPTS

The following key terms and concepts were presented in this chapter. Each term and concept is also contained in the Glossary of Terms located at the end of this book:

- extended-stay business
- snowbird

DISCUSSION QUESTIONS

1. What additional opportunities may face each of these facilities?
2. What additional threats may face each of these facilities?
3. What other strategies and tactics could you develop for Skimmer Cruises?
4. What other strategies and tactics could you develop for Coachman's Seaside Paradise?
5. What other strategies and tactics could you develop for Quiescence Spa Retreat?

EXPERIENTIAL EXERCISE

Get into groups of two and select another type of hospitality facility or a hospitality provider of products and services made for rest and relaxation. If possible, make a personal visit to the facility and sample a product or service. Conduct a similar analysis and determine possible strategies and tactics that may be used to optimize revenues.

INTERNET EXERCISES

1. Go online and find a cruise package available during the fall months. Do you see any opportunities to increase revenues with this package? Please explain.

2. Go online and find the website of a luxury RV resort. Are there any opportunities to increase revenue at this resort? Please explain.

3. Go online to a spa resort website. Report on the products and services available. Do you see any opportunities to capture increased revenues at the spa? Please explain.

Ocean Hammock Resort Golf Course.

CHAPTER

Applications in Golf, Gaming, and Theme Parks

Chapter Objectives

The objectives of this chapter are to:

■ Explore the application of revenue management techniques to golf courses, gaming establishments, and theme parks
■ Consider several scenarios, strategies, and tactics for the Crags Oceanside Golf Resort and Spa
■ Consider several scenarios, strategies, and tactics for the Desert Snow Castle Resort Casino
■ Consider several scenarios, strategies, and tactics for the Childhood Classics Theme Park

The final leg of our journey takes us on some unique recreational experiences. As always, we need to apply our RevMAP to help us find the pot of gold waiting at these final destinations. Let's begin by looking for a tiger in the woods . . .

The Crags Oceanside Golf Resort and Spa

Squeezed between the rocky cliffs high above the battering ocean is a narrow green with its tattered flag being continually whipped by the unrelenting winds. The fairway slopes down the knoll and disappears behind a crop of boulders. The golfer pulls up the neck of his windbreaker, replaces his club in his bag, and starts the descent toward the final hole below.

Just beyond the 18th hole lies the clubhouse of this quaint little golf resort that the locals simply call the Crags. Founded by a family from Scotland who missed the beauty of St. Andrews, the Crags has been home to international golf competitions since the mid-1950s. Golf in its best tradition is played here. One can smell the woodsy scents of tweedy caps, leather polish, and freshly mown grass near the caravans of carts in the drive. Entering the clubhouse, a golfer pauses to stroke the woolen sweater vest carefully folded on a round mahogany table set up just outside the pro shop. He joins his foursome and heads out to the immaculately groomed course still glistening with just a hint of last night's frosty dew. The sun is quickly melting any remnants of moisture and the group is just about to tee off.

Later, the group returns for a bit of refreshment at the 19th hole, in other words, to grab the traditional drink at the clubhouse. Since the wind has kicked up and the clouds are hanging ominously low, they decide to skip the terrace and go inside to the tavern. The warmth of the paneled retreat greats them accompanied by the blended aroma of fine brandy, cigars, and a wood fire. The foursome nestles into sturdy wing-back chairs to recount the play of the day.

Physical facilities:

- 18 holes of golf along the ocean coast
- Driving range
- The course is reserved for members only on the weekend and open to the public on Monday through Thursday
- Clubhouse with restaurant, tavern, rentals, and retail merchandise
- Indoor event space and permanent outdoor tent
- Golf carts with global positioning systems onboard
- Full-service spa
- Barber shop and salon
- Media room
- Golf clinic with video recording of swing and putting techniques

Services:

- Breakfast
- Lunch
- Dinner
- On-course drink and snack carts
- Cocktails
- Saturday-evening social events
- Catering
- Event-planning services
- Full range of spa products and services
- Haircutting and styling
- Golf merchandise ranging from clubs to shoes
- Golf cart rental
- Golf lessons
- Video analysis of swing and putting performance

Abbreviated SWOT Analysis for the Crags Oceanside Golf Resort and Spa

Strengths: Location and upscale reputation, moderate climate, challenging course.
Weaknesses: No play in the winter months, sometimes tee times delayed due to frost on the greens, somewhat stodgy reputation.
Opportunities: Create or capture additional tournament play, attract more women and younger golfers, fill slower times with corporate outings, increase share of event and reception business.

Threats: Drought conditions, bad weather, newer and cheaper courses in the area, the economy.

Competitors: Several new golf courses are in the planning stages along the coast, the area's less-expensive municipal courses.

Time period used for analysis: September and October.

Booking pace and pattern: In the week for the week for members, within the month for weekday tee times made by the general public, three to six months for tournaments and corporate groups.

Channels currently used: Clubhouse telephone and website, direct mail to members, advertising in area publications, annual spread in *Golf Digest* with tear-out information card, tie-ins with local hotels and tourism organizations.

Prices: Per 18 hole round of golf:

   Annual memberships: $75,000 annually and $25 per member per round.

   Corporate memberships: $150,000 annually and $45 per employee per round.

   Nonmembers: Foursomes before noon and after 5 PM: $360; Midday: $240.

Cart rental included with membership. Nonmember fee $15 per day.

Lessons and video analysis: $65 per hour.

Club rentals: $35 per day.

Overview

It is difficult, if not impossible, to get a tee time before 11AM at the Crags during the summer. Play slows down a bit in the fall, with significantly more tee times available early in the week. This is a popular course for conducting business and many of the local corporations maintain corporate memberships. Visitors to the neighboring hotels and resorts are able to purchase rounds of golf within a resort and recreation package sold by both the properties and the club. Regardless of the season, Saturdays are booked solid. In the summer, the clubhouse tent is a popular location for wedding receptions and family reunions. Seventy percent of the golfers playing the course are men over the age of 40.

What are some possible strategies and tactics that may be applied by golf course management during this time period to optimize revenues?

1. First, the club needs to shift excess demand to the less busy tee times in the middle of the day. Special incentives could be offered during weekdays in the fall and discounts could be offered midday year round to local residents. The strategy here is to shift demand to slower time periods. The tactics are to offer incentives or discounts in the local market.

2. The club needs to capture more women players. Perhaps start a league on Sunday or Monday afternoons. They should make the clubhouse more comfortable for women by adding ladies apparel in the pro shop, providing women-only golf clinics, and offering mid-afternoon refreshments on the terrace. The club could also create a *green tea* package combining a round of golf with a treatment at the spa. The strategy here is to increase capture of women golfers. The tactics are to form a women's golf league, change the environment from its current old boys' club ambience, and develop a golf and spa package.

3. The club needs to increase its capture of both leisure and business travelers staying at local hotels. It should design a more attractive package and increase its

Courtesy of Destination Hotels & Resorts.

Golf Course and Cart at Skamania.

commission to the local hotels and resorts to induce the front office and sales departments to sell more packages. The strategy here is to increase capture of visiting golfers. The tactic is to create and aggressively market packages with the local hotels and resorts.

4. Since many of the club's members are getting on in years, it is time for the club to start soliciting new members. One way to attract young golfers is to offer discounted golf lessons and clinics to local high schools and colleges. The club may also choose to sponsor a local school golf team to garner additional recognition in the local community. And it could develop a junior golf league. The strategy is to attract and capture younger golfers. The tactics include providing discounted golf lessons and clinics, sponsoring a local school golf club, and developing a junior golf league.

5. The catering department needs to find new sources of meeting and event business during the week. It may create an annual fall tournament. It should also consider instituting a Sunday brunch which could be offered to groups who wish to reserve the tent. The catering department must also make sure that it is optimizing its wedding reception revenues on its peak summer dates. The strategy is to increase catering revenues. The tactics include adding a fall golf tournament, creating a Sunday brunch for individuals and groups, and optimizing revenues from summer weddings.

What other strategies and tactics could the Crags develop to capitalize on opportunities to increase revenues? What strategies could be developed to reduce or minimize potential threats?

Students may wish to consult friends or family members who play golf to help them develop alternative strategies and tactics for the club to use to increase revenues.

Possible Results

Scenario #1

In the first instance, let's assume that the club turns away just two groups each morning due to lack of early morning tee times. If it were able to capture these groups by offering additional incentives for a midday round of golf on Mondays through Thursdays in September and October, this would result in a significant increase in revenue. For example, let assume that the club is able to capture two more foursomes each day for four days a week by offering free cart and club rental, one free beer or soft drink per player from the beverage carts on the course, and one free round of beverages in the tavern after the round. The retail price of this package would be at least $320. But the club offers a $100 discount, pricing this package at $220. This is lower than the normal price of $240 before the cart, clubs, or beverages. So this is definitely a perceived value. Multiply these eight rounds per week by approximately eight weeks in the months of September and October and this adds up to 64 more rounds of golf. Sixty-four rounds at $220 will generate $14,080 in additional revenue. Not bad for a cart, some clubs, and a few beers!

Scenario #2

First, if the beginning season of the women's golf league attracted just four foursomes, two of which were composed of members and two of which were composed of nonmembers, this would generate additional revenues per day of $920 during peak golf time and $680 during nonpeak times. Multiply that by five months of golf (approximately 20 weeks) and this league would generate additional revenues of $18,400 golfing during peak hours or $13,600 golfing during midday hours. Most likely, the club would offer discounted prices to the league, but you get the general idea.

Second, offering a *green tea* golf and spa package would drive additional women into the club for an afternoon of golf, spa treatments, and camaraderie. One package could be priced per nonmember foursome with a midday tee time at $599. The same package for members would be priced at $399 per foursome. If just 10 packages were sold per week, five at each price, this would generate an additional $4,990 per week, $19,960 per month, and $99,800 over the 20-week golf season.

Scenario #3

In this case, let's assume that the golf club offers the hotels and resorts a commission of $25 for each golf package sold. Some properties permit the clerks or salespeople selling the package to retain the $25 as a bonus. Others collect the $25 and use the funds to pay for the annual holiday party for associates. In either case, the hotel properties are delighted to be able to offer this additional recreational opportunity to their guests while also adding to their own revenue streams. So imagine what would happen if the course doubled the commission to $50!

If all local hotels and resorts combined sell just one peak time package six days per week (remember Saturdays are usually booked) and one midday package each day of the week, that represents an additional 13 packages per week. Using nonmember prices, the six peak time packages would generate $2,160 per week and the midday packages would generate $1,680 per week. Combined, this is $3,840 per week. Subtract the commissions paid to the hotel and this still represents an additional $3,190 in revenue per week. Multiply that time 20 weeks and the packages generate an additional $63,800 in revenue per season to the club. Most likely at double the commission, the staffs of the hotels and resorts would work even harder to sell these packages, and the revenues would at least double to over $125,000 per season!

Scenario #4

Both teenagers and schools are usually a bit strapped for cash. In fact, the cost of equipment, lessons, and a round of golf precludes many young people from even learning the game. To attract this segment, the club is going to have to offer incentives. First, it should reduce its rates for junior league golfers. These younger golfers have more stamina and seem to thrive in the heat, so all junior league play would take place in the late midday during the week. If just four foursomes joined the first year and played each Tuesday and Thursday afternoon, this would represent eight rounds of golf each week. If these rounds were priced at 50 percent off the midday fee of $240, each round of golf would cost $120 or just $30 per player for nonmembers. So eight rounds times $120 equals $960 per week. Then multiplying $960 times a 20 week season and these four foursomes would generate an additional $19,200 to the club.

Many parents are also very receptive to paying for lessons for their children to help them to excel in sports. A discounted golf lesson and clinic could be made available to local children at a cost of $20 per lesson. However, lessons would only be offered in the evenings on Sundays and Mondays on the driving range. If just five children signed up for each night, that would generate an additional $100 per night or $200 per week. Once again multiplied by the 20 weeks in the golf season, these lessons would generate an additional $4,000 in revenue.

And the publicity and benefits of sponsoring the local school golf team is priceless to the club and its members.

Scenario #5

Let's begin our analysis of this scenario by focusing on the fall golf tournament. We must keep in mind that we will be displacing normal play during this period, so regular rounds of golf will have to be factored out of this final equation. Let's assume that the club was fortunate enough to get a celebrity **pro-am** (professional paired with an amateur) tournament in support of a major charity. The tournament is scheduled for the last week in September. A dozen foursomes have signed up during this inaugural year of the tournament. The cost to register each foursome is $1,000 with 75 percent of the fees going to charity and the other 25 percent going to the club for tournament operations. So the registration fees alone would generate $12,000, of which $9,000 would go to the charity and $3,000 would go to the club. Spectator tickets could be sold for $50, this time with 50 percent going to the charity and the other half going to the club. If 500 tickets are sold each day for two days, this would generate an additional $25,000 each for the charity and the club. And all food and beverage and retail revenues would remain the property of the club. The benefits of sponsoring this type of tournament are threefold. First, the club helps support a major charity; second, it generates a small amount of additional revenue; and third, it obtains outstanding publicity and media coverage. If the event grows in size and stature over the years, the club may even be able to capture revenues from any television broadcasts of the tournament.

Next let's take a look at the possible revenues that may be generated by a Sunday brunch. First, let's assume that the brunch is priced at $28.75 per person and that the clubhouse would serve 160 covers per Sunday. That alone represents $4,600 in revenues. But let's add an average of another 56 covers from private group brunches held in the tent and that adds another $1,610. Combined, this revenue adds up to $6,210 per Sunday. Multiply this by the 20 weekends in the season and these Sunday brunches would add up to nearly $125,000 in additional revenues.

And finally, let's quickly assess the potential from Friday- and Saturday-night weddings at the club during the summer, which is the peak wedding season. The tent holds 208 guests. So if the catering department only accepted full sit-down dinners or buffets priced at $39 per person with a minimum of 200 guests and sold out each Friday and Saturday during the season, this would represent 40 weddings at $7,800 or total revenue of $312,000 in just food alone. Add beverage service, the cake, flowers, candles, favors, and a champagne toast and those wedding reception revenues would easily surpass half a million dollars.

Speaking of tournaments, let's travel on to Las Vegas, where competition takes place every day . . .

Courtesy of Destination Hotels & Resorts.

Brunch at the Royal Palms.

The Desert Snow Castle Resort Casino

At first, visitors to the mega resort do a double take. What! Snow in the desert? But it is 120 degrees in the shade! Precisely! This is why our developers decided to create a winter wonderland right in the middle of this huge neon oasis of sand.

A family of four pulls up between the bellmen flanking the circular drive. The children have been pressing their noses against the windows since leaving the airport. Their eyes whirled wildly around the lights and scenes of the passing Las Vegas Strip. Their gaping lips left steaming circles of condensation on the glass. "We're here!" shouts Dad as everyone quickly piles out of the car.

The huge oaken doors to the castle are slowly pulled back by the doormen to reveal a huge glistening ice sculpture just inside the door. The children run up to watch the pink and purple streams of a magical liquid rush down and around luge-like tracks carved into the ice. A snow maiden stands to one side and asks the children if they would like to taste a sample. Mom nods her approval and the snow maiden dips a snow cone into one of the streams and the magical potion turns the ice in the cup a beautiful shade of pink. She hands this to one child while she dips the other snow cone into the stream of purple. This cup she hands to the other child. Dad is thrilled that the children are occupied while he ushers the family toward the front desk.

But wait, the front desk is made entirely of ice! Lights imbedded in the ice give it a soft blue glow, making its outline more visible to the guests. A plastic mat has been laid across the top of the ice to enable guests to set down their wallets and sign the guest register. As Dad is confirming the room arrangements, the kids peer around the corner to see what other frosty delights lay before them. A low "whoa" escapes as the older child spots the snow slopes in the atrium. And appearing to be speeding straight toward them is a snowboarder racing down the 30-floor mound of fresh-blown snow. He screeches to a halt and turns to race under an overhanging mound of snow which hides a glass express elevator rushing children back to the top. The children shuffle a little closer and start to circle the snow mountain before them. Suddenly, they see a toboggan full of children swoop and whirl down the other side. The riders all tumble out with a thunderous glee at the bottom. They brush themselves off and also rush to disappear under a wall of snow. Creeping still further, the children are startled by the roar of an avalanche crashing down yet another side of this seemingly imaginary mountain. Little children giggle as they are tossed and turned inside this bundle of snow. All of a sudden Dad calls out to follow him and off they go . . .

Physical facilities:

- 5000 guest rooms, including 10 penthouse apartments
- 300,000 square foot casino
- 25 restaurants
- 24-hour room service
- 35 lounges
- 5 nightclubs
- Sports betting parlor
- High rollers club
- 8,000 seat state of the art concert venue
- 250,000 square feet of meeting space
- Tram stop connecting to the Strip

- 100 retail shops
- Indoor 30 floor high mountain of snow
- A variety of winter activities and rides on the snow mountain
- Full-service spa and salon

Services:

- Just about anything that is legal . . .

Abbreviated SWOT Analysis for the Desert Snow Castle

Strengths: Unique theme, escape from the heat, great family facilities, cool environment for singles and couples, great casino, outstanding state of the art conference facilities, easy access to the Strip, the full menu of amenities and services.

Weaknesses: The sheer number of children may be a turn-off to older and single patrons, the cost to keep the ice flowing and snow blowing in the desert, continual turnover of hourly employees as is customary in gaming towns.

Opportunities: Capture more families, attract guests looking for something new, steal conference business from the neighboring resorts, and create awareness among high rollers.

Threats: Drought conditions, competing cities, increasing fuel costs, the economy.

Competitors: All local Las Vegas resorts, resorts in other gaming towns, riverboat gambling, major theme parks outside of gaming districts.

Time period used for analysis: July.

Booking pace and pattern: Varies greatly by market segment. Nearly every market segment is captured.

Channels currently used: Every single electronic channel of distribution is utilized to fill this mega resort. In addition, the resort maintains a huge marketing budget for print and television advertising, and sends out staggering amounts of direct mail each year. Tie-in with children's television programming and movie promotions.

Prices: Rooms range from $99 to $9,000 for deluxe suites and hundreds of packages are available to attract every single type of traveler. The penthouses are priced separately or reserved on a complimentary basis for high rollers.

Overview

The Desert Snow Castle is the new kid on the block, so it is receiving a tremendous amount of publicity both here and abroad. Alongside the airline industry, the gaming industry has the most sophisticated automated revenue management systems in the hospitality industry. In fact, the gaming industry has nearly perfected the concept of developing a marketing segment of one—and that is you! The advanced technology of the gaming industry is able to capture every bit of information regarding your tastes, your actions, and your preferences. They are able to customize an entire vacation with a single click of a button on a computer. They are the kings of bundling products and services quickly to create new and exciting packages customized just to please you.

Before we begin our analysis, we need to define one market segment here, that of the high roller. A **high roller**, also known as a **whale**, is a gambler who wagers large amounts of money, often in the millions of dollars. The casinos usually lavish amenities on high rollers to capture their gaming business.

What are some of the immediate strategies and tactics that may be applied during the month of July to optimize revenues at the Desert Snow Castle?

1. First and foremost is to focus on families. And while there really is no off-season for Las Vegas, the month of July is one of the least desirable due to the extreme heat. Since this is a winter playground in the desert, the resort should first target families from other desert communities in California and Arizona within drive time, enticing them to beat the heat. And most school-aged children are off in the month of July. The strategy is to increase business in July. The tactic is to focus on desert families within drive time.

2. Las Vegas hosts a variety of tournaments, perhaps the hottest of which right now is poker. The resort could continue the cool winter theme in an ice academy of poker. Patterned leaded crystal that looks like ice could be used as tabletops and clear block supports could project soft lights from below. In fact, corporate sponsorship logos could be projected on the center of these tables for televised events. Snow maidens could serve as the beverage wait staff. The strategy is to capture more revenues from poker. The tactics are to capture increased tournament business and corporate sponsorships.

3. The uniqueness of the venue would attract meetings and conference planners seeking a change. And the attendees may be more likely to bring their families to this child-friendly resort. The strategy is to increase group meeting and conference business but also capture extended weekend stays involving spouses and children. The tactic is to provide an exciting new alternative venue to seasoned meeting professionals.

4. The resort could host a Christmas in July festival entirely based upon the theme of Dr. Seuss' *How The Grinch Stole Christmas!*[1]. The village of Whoville could be set up in the atrium surrounding the mountain of snow which has been crowned Mt. Crumpet. Max, the Grinch's dog, would be available for pictures with the kids. And children could pile into a giant sleigh that rushes down the mountain to provide gifts to all of the Whos down below. The strategy is to capture additional family business. The tactic is to create a unique event appealing to children and their baby boomer parents in the middle of summer.

The following two strategies do not apply only specifically to July, but are worth mentioning here to provide students with some additional examples of revenue-generating activities in the gaming segment:

5. Naturally, just like all of the other resort casinos, the Desert Snow Castle would create a frequent-player card. Only this time, every day that a guest played he or she would be entered into a monthly drawing to win a free ski trip to Switzerland. The strategy is to capture repeat transient business. The tactic is to increase play among frequent players.

6. And finally, the Desert Snow Castle could create a new high rollers club entitled the Cool as Ice Club. Special packages would be developed to deliver these high rollers to outstanding casino resorts throughout the world in the middle of each

Courtesy of Destination Hotels & Resorts.

Cinnamon Beach Pool at Night.

resort's winter. The goal of club members would be to wager in every single location on every single continent in its winter season. The strategy is to develop an incentive to appeal to the high rollers. The tactic is to make a unique club most appealing to high rollers who like to travel internationally.

Possible Results
Scenario #1

Let's say that the resort was able to attract another 100 families to the resort this first summer from just California and Arizona. And let's further assume that each family drives to Las Vegas and spends a total of $1,750 over three nights and four days. Therefore, these additional 100 families would generate $175,000 in increased revenue to the resort.

Scenario #2

In this case, let's assume that the resort was able to capture a major playoff round in the biggest international poker tournament. Between players, fans, poker vendors, corporate sponsors, and the media, let's assume that the resort sells 1,000 rooms for this tournament. And then let's assume that the average length of stay is three nights. The tournament rate is $199 per night. So these 3,000 room nights would generate $597,000 in room revenue alone. Factor in double that amount per day for food, beverage, gaming, and entertainment and the revenue generated is now $1,791,000 over these three days. And we haven't even calculated in the revenues generated by corporate sponsorships and television broadcast rights.

Scenario #3

The resort would benefit from additional group business and any pre- or post-conference stays occurring over the weekends. Also, substantial ancillary revenue would be generated from the multiple occupancy in each guest room.

Scenario #4

This is a unique promotion for not only children who love the Grinch but also for their baby boomer parents who are still able to hear the resonating voice of Boris Karloff singing in the original animated television special[2]. Wow, Boris Karloff and Jim Carrey[3], now that's a dichotomy of spirit!

The Grinch package would be based on two adults and two children and could contain a two-room suite for four nights (there are three afternoons of festivities planned), breakfast each morning with another character from the book, private showing of both the original televised version and the feature length film, a special chapter reading one night performed by Jim Carrey, a visit with Santa to provide this year's Christmas list, a "come as your favorite character" costume party, a framed duel photograph of each child in costume and on the sled with Max (the Grinch's dog), and a special bag of toys to take home. The price per package would be $1,957 in honor of the year the book was published. And don't forget lunches, dinners, and any wagers placed by Mom and Dad add up to more ancillary revenue. Assuming that this package was available Monday through Thursday for four weeks in July and that 250 packages were sold per week, this would amount to 1,000 packages in total. At a price of $1,957, the Grinch package alone would generate $1,957,000! My, but that would buy a lot of roast beast!

Scenario #5

Hopefully, the incentive of possibly winning a free ski trip to Switzerland is enough to lure players away from the other casinos, even if only briefly. If 100 frequent players just stopped in each day and dropped $20 that would amount to $2,000 per day or $60,000 in one month. These revenues would definitely exceed the cost of the trip to Switzerland, particularly since the Desert Snow Castle would most likely obtain all of the elements in the package in trade!

Scenario #6

Snob appeal is the name of the game here. And also stiff competition among the well-to-do. How many high rollers can actually say they have played on every continent? And even fewer can honestly state that they have played on every continent during its winter. Now that's bragging rights . . .

Since we are on the topic of fun, let's end our journey at our final destination, a theme park that is nicknamed Munchkenland!

Childhood Classics Theme Park

Grimm's Fairy Tales[4], *The Cat in the Hat*[5], *Charlotte's Web*[6], *The Wizard of Oz*[7], *Charlie and the Chocolate Factory*[8], *Bambi*[9], and *Harry Potter and the Sorcerer's Stone*[10] . . . The mere mention of these classic books in children's literature whisks one's mind to earlier times—times spent slumped in a rocker pushing bare toes across a painted wooden porch while lost in the stories of other places and other faces. A magical time, a magical place, a time to imagine.

The developers of Childhood Classics Theme Park wished to transport the children back to this simpler time. A time when children used their imaginations to conjure up images more fantastic than movies. A time when words on a page were more powerful than the most stupendous special effects. So they decided to design a park based around the places tucked deep in the recesses of their memories.

Children enter the park and are immediately greeted by Bambi[9] and her mother. The animated versions speak to the children while each child is given a tiny plush fawn to stroke in delight. Out jumps the Cat in the Hat[5] to lead them on their way. They wander into Dr. Seussland where they meet all kinds of familiar characters. They ride in spinning teacups and catch fish in a bowl and put on all kinds of silly hats.

Willy Wonka[8] next takes the lead guiding the children into a wonderful garden planted with lollypops. They are able to hold a cup under the chocolate fountain until it is filled to the brim. And they chomp on special gobstobbers that turn their mouths lime green!

Willy waves them goodbye and they are greeted by Wilbur, a most likeable pig. He takes them to his home in the barn where they are offered salutations from Charlotte. She is sitting so gently on the threads of her web. The children bid Wilbur and Charlotte[6] goodbye, and suddenly out falls the scarecrow to take them to Munchkenland[7] where they will have lunch. The older children rub their hands with glee since they know that the flying monkeys and the scary broom stick ride around the witch's castle are awaiting right after they eat.

Physical facilities:

- 50 rides
- Emerald City Hotel
- 22 food and beverage outlets
- Meeting pavilion
- Ample parking and onsite shuttles
- Shuttles to downtown
- Nightly fireworks display
- Souvenir shops and bookstores containing all of the classics
- Fully compliant with the Americans with Disabilities Act guidelines

Services:

- Open May 15 through Halloween Night
- Park opens at 8AM and closes at midnight
- Group sales and events department
- Full catering and conference services
- Meals available during all park hours
- Shuttle to car from park entrance
- Online retail outlet

Abbreviated SWOT Analysis for Childhood Classics Theme Park

Strengths: Strong appeal with parents and grandparents, gentle rides for younger children and scary rides for older children, international character recognition.
Weaknesses: Less appeal for older teenagers, perception of less high-tech action rides.

Opportunities: Packages and groups, evening attractions and shows to appeal to the older teenage demographic.

Threats: Competition from other entertainment venues, character licensing issues, weather, injuries, high gasoline prices and the economy.

Competitors: No other major theme parks within one day's drive but numerous smaller venues featuring rides and petting zoos for young children. The park competes with all other forms of entertainment for their guest's dollar.

Time period used for analysis: May 15 through October 31.

Booking pace and pattern: Most tickets are bought in the week for the week with the exception of groups which book 30 to 90 days out.

Channels currently used: Park website, discounted tickets through local grocery store chain, ticket brokers, merchant models, packages with local hotels and tourism organizations, television advertising, paycheck stuffers given to local corporations, community print and radio news sources, church newsletters.

Ticket prices: Online discount for general admission $36.99, general admission 12 and over $46.99, children aged four to eleven $25.99, and children under three free. General admission season tickets are $50 each. Groups of 10 or more $32 per ticket when purchased online at least two days in advance. Parking is $15.

Overview

Children's Classic Theme Park is a one-of-a-kind experience located in the Black Forest. Families drive from surrounding states or fly in on vacation to spend a few days with the numerous rides and attractions based on classic children's books. There is something for everyone at this park. There are gentle rides for the toddlers, wild rides for the teens and 'tweens, romantic rides for the parents, and relaxing rides for the grandparents. A concert series runs in the evenings throughout the summer. Classical music concerts are held each Sunday in the park's gardens. And a wide variety of food and beverage outlets are available offering an array of items broad enough to suit any palate. Special events may be booked in the park ranging from a child's 5th birthday bash to the grandparent's 50th anniversary picnic.

What are some possible strategies and tactics that may be applied this season at the park to optimize revenues?

1. First, the park may consider raising the price of online tickets. Currently there is a $10 spread between the cost of online tickets and those purchased at the park. The park should reduce this price spread. The strategy here is to increase ticket revenues. The tactic is to raise online prices.

2. The park should consider substantially increasing the price of its season tickets. There is only a $3 spread currently between the cost of one day's general admission ticket and a season pass. The strategy here is to increase ticket revenues. The tactic is to raise season-pass prices.

3. The sales department should solicit more group business. It should focus on increasing the amount of intergenerational group bookings from family reunions, anniversaries, engagement parties, and birthday bashes. The strategy here is to increase group business. The tactic is to develop family event packages.

4. The sales department should also try to solicit more youth groups interested in having some traditional clean fun. The sales department should offer special packages and discounts to church youth groups and camp and scout outings.

5. In the fall months, the park should try to book school field trips to the park. This could be designed as a special treat to young children just starting school and unhappy to be away from home for the day. It may enable the children to bond with each other and take away some of the fear involved with just starting school.

6. And of course, the park should plan for special Halloween festivities. Parents would be delighted to bring their young children to trick or treat in the safer environment of the park. And older children could have a blast at a Boo Bash or Monster Mash Bash dance and haunted house. The strategy is to increase fall revenues. The tactics are to plan an early evening trick or treat street for the younger children and a dance and haunted house later in the evening for the older children.

Take a few last moments to consider other possible opportunities and threats facing the park during this time period.

Possible Results

Scenario #1

The $10 differential between booking online and purchasing a ticket at the park represents an unnecessarily high incentive to online purchasers. Let's consider what may occur if the price differential was cut in half to $5. If 1,000 visitors a day come to the park with online tickets, this additional $5 would generate $5,000 per day in additional revenue. That's $35,000 more per week and $150,000 more per month!

Scenario #2

Currently, there is just a three-dollar spread between the purchase of a single-day pass and a purchase of a season pass. There appears to be no rationale for this low season-pass

The Lodge at Ocean Hammock Pool.

Courtesy of Destination Hotels & Resorts.

pricing. So the park needs to raise its season-pass pricing. If the park raises the price of a season pass to $75, the pass more than pays for itself in just two visits. If 100 season-pass holders visit the park per day, this extra $25 would generate $2,500 in additional revenue each day.

Scenario #3

If the sales department could book just one family outing for 25 people each on Saturdays and Sundays, these events would generate a total of $1,600 in additional revenue each weekend in just ticket prices. Add in souvenirs, parking, and food and beverage service, and the total revenues would at least double if not triple.

Scenario #4

In this case, let's assume that most of the children in these youth groups are between the ages of 8 and 11. The normal admission price for children of this age would be $25.99. The park could consider discounting these tickets to $20 for groups of 15 or more children. If one youth group containing 25 children was booked each day, this would generate an additional $500 per day, $3,500 per week, and $15,000 per month.

Scenario #5

The park could develop a special package for classes comprised of kindergarteners and first graders. A three-hour visit could be prepared for the kindergarteners at a cost of maybe $6 per child. A five-hour visit including lunch could be prepared for first graders at a cost of $10 per child. Many schools would send a busload or two of students and make this a joint field day for several classes. If 64 first graders visited the park, that would represent an additional $640 in revenue to the park before they purchased any treats or souvenirs on their own. The park may wish to take photographs and offer online purchases of the final portfolio to parents.

Scenario #6

In this example, let's assume that the park sets prices at $10 with a discounted price of $15 for two children to trick or treat. All candy could be donated by local merchants to help the community enjoy a safer Halloween. If 200 children attended at an average price of $8 that would represent $1,600 in revenues to the park. And that is before any food or beverage purchases made by the parents as they tag along.

The price could be a set $10 for the older children. This would include admittance to the dance, witches brew punch and spider web cookies, and the entrance fee for the haunted house. If 250 teenagers came to the festivities, this would generate an additional $2,500 for the evening. And that is not counting the money spent by the ghosts trying to win stuffed animals for their favorite goblins that evening!

So, as you can see, there are many opportunities to increase revenues involved in nearly every recreational activity imaginable. It just takes a little time and creativity to come up with unique and enchanting ways of enticing those dollars out of our wallets.

SUMMARY

In this chapter, we explored the application of revenue management techniques to the products and services of three hospitality providers: a golf course, a resort casino, and a theme park. Each organization was briefly examined in terms of its customers, market segments, partial internal

SWOT analysis, forecasted demand for the time period, prices, and channels used for distributing inventory. Various scenarios were presented in which the organization could implement strategies and tactics to drive revenues. Possible results were presented to demonstrate the impact of these potential strategies and tactics.

KEY TERMS AND CONCEPTS

The following key terms and concepts were presented in this chapter. Each term and concept is also contained in the Glossary of Terms located at the end of this book:

- high roller
- pro-am
- whale

DISCUSSION QUESTIONS

1. What additional opportunities may face each of these facilities?
2. What additional threats may face each of these facilities?
3. What other strategies and tactics could you develop for the Crags Oceanside Golf Resort and Spa?
4. What other strategies and tactics could you develop for the Desert Snow Castle Resort Casino?
5. What other strategies and tactics could you develop for the Children's Classics Theme Park?

EXPERIENTIAL EXERCISE

Get into groups of two and select another type of recreational facility or a hospitality provider of recreational products and services. Personally visit the facility and conduct a similar analysis and determine possible strategies and tactics that may be used to optimize revenues.

INTERNET EXERCISES

1. Go online and find a golf package available during the fall months. Do you see any opportunities to increase revenues with this package? Please explain.
2. Go online and find a summer resort casino package in Las Vegas that is oriented toward families. Are there any opportunities to increase revenue with this package? Please explain.
3. Go online to a theme park website. Report on the products and services available. Do you see any opportunities to capture increased revenues at the park? Please explain.

REFERENCES

1. Geisel, Theodor Seuss. *How the Grinch Stole Christmas!*, New York: Random House, 1957.
2. *Dr. Seuss' How the Grinch Stole Christmas!*, Chuck Jones and Theodor (Dr. Seuss) Geisel, Metro-Goldwyn-Mayer, Inc., 1966.
3. *Dr. Seuss' How the Grinch Stole Christmas!*, Ron Howard, Universal Studios, 2000.
4. Grimm, Jacob and Wilhelm. *Kinder und Hausmärchen (Children's and Household Tales)*, 1812
5. Geisel, Theodor Seuss. *The Cat in the Hat*, New York: Random House, 1957.
6. White, E.B. *Charlotte's Web*, New York: HarperCollins, 1952.
7. Baum, Frank. *The Wizard of Oz*, Chicago: G.M. Hill, 1900.
8. Dahl, Roald. *Charlie and The Chocolate Factory*, New York: Knopf, 1964.
9. Salten, Felix. *Bambi*, New York: Simon & Schuster, 1928.
10. Rowling, J.K. *Harry Potter and the Sorcerer's Stone*, New York: Scholastic, 1998.

Glossary of Terms

(4) four building blocks see **IDEA**.

4Ps of marketing product, price, place, and promotion.

5Ws and an H analysis applying the questions *who, what, where, when, why, and how* to an analysis of a subject.

90-day forecast a forecast extending 90 days into the future.

acquisition cost this term may apply to either a customer or an organization. To a customer, acquisition cost may include intrinsic costs, such as price, and extrinsic costs such as the time it takes to make the purchase and the cost of gasoline it requires to get to and from the store. To an organization, acquisition cost means the cost of acquiring the customer, including the costs of marketing, the costs of taking reservations, and the costs of actually serving the guest.

action plan a calendar used for planning and assigning tasks to be completed over the course of a year.

Airline Reservation System also known as an ARS. An automated system for taking airline reservations.

ancillary purchase a supplementary or additional purchase made in a series of transactions.

antitrust laws laws designed to prevent restraints on trade. These laws were enacted in the late 1800s to protect both consumers and businesses. They prohibit behavior that is unfair and uncompetitive in nature. They also prohibit any actions that violate society's standards of ethical behavior.

ARS see Airline Reservation System.

auction site a website on which the price of a product or service is determined by the winning bid. Examples are Priceline and Luxury Link.

average channel contribution value determined by dividing the total revenue generated by the channel by the total number of transactions it completed.

average daily rate also known as ADR. Calculated by dividing rooms revenue by the number of rooms sold.

B2B business-to-business e-commerce.

B2C business-to-consumer e-commerce.

baby boomers a generational marketing term. Born between the years of 1946 and 1964, the baby boomers are not only the largest generational segment at nearly 78 million members, they are also the most powerful in terms of both wealth and propensity to spend.

best available rate the lowest rate per room available to the general public on a given night.

best-rate guarantee program program that guarantees that the consumer will receive the best rate from the organization. If a consumer can find a better price than the one posted on the organization's website, the organization will match that price.

booking pace refers to the pattern and tempo (rate) of receipt and acceptance of advanced reservations.

brand equity the value generated by a brand.

branding placing an identifying mark or logo on a product produced by a specific organization or associating that brand with a service performed by that organization.

brick and mortar store the local building that houses a retail establishment.

bundling combining products and services to create a package.

C2C consumer-to-consumer e-commerce.

cannibalization the concept of a customer leaving a higher-rated market segment to jump over a fence and gobble up lower-priced products or services offered by the same provider to other lower-rated market segments.

capacity the amount of space that can be filled.

central reservation office also known as CRO. Automated reservations system that take reservations for all properties within an organization.

central reservation system also known as CRS. An automated reservation system for booking several travel components, including air, car, and hotel room.

ceteris paribus economic term meaning all things being equal.

channel refers to the source of the booking.

channel contribution the revenue generated from a single transaction.

channel contribution percentage a percentage calculated by dividing the channel's total revenue by the total revenue produced by all channels.

channel production the number of transactions generated by channel.

channels of distribution avenues that have developed to bring the buyer and seller together. These channels act as distribution outlets through which the sellers offer their products and services for sale to their customers. Channels may be electronic or non-electronic. Whereas the source of a reservation used to be referred to as the source of business, today all sources of business may be tracked via both market segment and the channel that generated the business.

circular moving in a circle. Once a circular process is complete, it simply begins once again.

closed or closed out inventory is no longer available for sale.

closed to arrival means that the customer cannot arrive on that date no matter their intended length of stay.

color tour visitors or color tourists the phrases used to describe visitors who travel up to view the changing color of the fall foliage. Also referred to as fall foliage toursists.

commission the percentage or flat fee above the selling price that goes to an intermediary that must also be added to the cost of distribution. Also known as a load.

competitive advantage that component of an organization's operation in which it excels or maintains an advantage over its competitors.

competitive intelligence the practice of conducting primary research and analyzing secondary research to understand the characteristics of the competition.

competitive intelligence specialist an individual assigned to monitor a competitor.

competitive set an organization's primary direct competitors. If your facility is sold out, a direct competitor would be the facility that your customer would select next.

competitor a rival with whom one competes.

complements used here to describe two products or services where an increase in cost of one item will cause a decrease in demand for another item. When the increase in the price of one good causes a decrease in the quantity demanded of another good, all things being equal, the goods are considered to be complements of one another. The general rule for complementary goods or services is that the price of one good or service and the demand for the other good or service will move in the opposite directions.

compression a situation that occurs whenever an activity or event forces demand to be pressed outward to the surrounding areas. Pressure placed on a market as a result of demand.

constrained demand demand that is held back or confined by rules, restrictions, and availability. An example of constrained demand would be trying to book a flight using your frequent-flier mileage.

contract binding agreement that specifies rates, terms, anticipated volume, minimum usage, and effective dates.

contingency planning planning for unexpected events and changes either in the internal or external environment.

conversion rate the number of calls converted from inquiry to sale. This number is usually expressed as a ratio by dividing the number of reservations booked over the number of reservation calls received.

core competencies the central activities that an organization performs well and that differentiate it from other firms.

cost-based method of pricing using this method, the organization calculates the overall cost of producing the product or service. Then they simply add a markup or percentage increase to arrive at a selling price.

cost of goods sold direct expenses in producing a good for sale. This includes variable costs but does not include indirect fixed costs such as rent, advertising, or office equipment.

CRO see central reservation office.

cross-channel behavior behavior that occurs when a customer accesses more than one channel when making a purchase.

CRS see central reservation system.

customer-centric approach any marketing or operational effort focused on the needs, wants, and desires of an organization's customers.

customer relationship management also referred to as CRM. Strategies and tactics developed to acquire and retain customers.

cut-off date the date that all unconfirmed reservations will be released to general inventory for resale.

data mining the process of continually digging deeper into the data captured by a marketing intelligence system.

decline stage the stage of the product or service life cycle in which sales of the product or service are flat or falling. Both volume and prices continue to fall. Newer products or services are competing directly for customers. Unchecked decline will ultimately lead to the death of a product or service. The producer either needs to innovate or evaporate.

demand the amount of a good or service that a purchaser is willing and able to buy for any given price at any given time.

demand drainer an activity or event that causes demand to decrease.

demand forecasting the act of estimating, calculating, and predicting consumers' demand for products and services in the future.

demand generator an organization or event that drives customers into a marketplace. An activity or entity that produces demand.

demography the study of the characteristics of a population. Common characteristics considered include age, gender, marital status, education, occupation, income, race, religion, and nationality.

denial a response that occurs when a facility is not able to accommodate a guest due to unavailability of product or service at that price.

discount price leadership applies to an organization setting the lowest rate in the market.

discounting the practice of offering special reductions in price.

displacement replacing one customer for another.

displacement analysis an analysis conducted to determine the total customer worth of competing pieces of business. The piece of business generating the highest total customer worth would be chosen in most cases.

distinctive competency an operational element which an organization performs so well or possesses so uniquely that it distinguishes the organization from its competitor.

distressed inventory inventory that an organization is having difficulty selling.

distribution cost the cost of getting a product or service to market.

dynamic packaging a new customer-centric approach to packaging. Hospitality providers may vary the products and services bundled in a package to suit the needs of the individual consumer.

early adopters consumers who strive to be the first to try any new product or service.

e-commerce the coming together of buyers and sellers on the Internet.

economies of scale an economic concept that means the more of a product or service that is produced, the lower its per unit cost of production.

elastic an economic term. Whenever a 1 percent change in price causes more than a 1 percent change in quantity supplied or demanded, the elasticity calculation will result in a number greater than 1. When this occurs, we say that the supply or demand is elastic. In this case, the quantity demanded or supplied is very sensitive to price.

electronic distribution the selling of hospitality products and services via the computer. Think of these basically as electronic warehouses in which a person may conduct one-stop shopping for a variety of hospitality products and services.

environmental scanning constantly monitoring and assessing the external environment to spot changes and emerging trends.

equilibrium *see* **market equilibrium**.

extended stay business business that generates seven or more nights stay.

fair price a positive price/value relationship; a just and honest price.

finite not unlimited; once the last unit of the item is utilized, that item will cease to be available in the future.

first-level adopter an organization which tries out new innovations first, before those innovations are mass-produced or disseminated to the market.

FIT foreign or free independent traveler.

fixed costs costs that do not change with a change in the activity of a business. Rent is a fixed cost.

fixed base operations (FBOs) those companies operating out of the local airport.

flash report a daily report completed to recap the previous day's business.

folio a record of in-house charges made by the guest since arrival.

food and beverage cost controller a person who audits the price and inventory on all food and beverage purchases and makes recommendations for cost savings whenever feasible.

forecasting the act of estimating, calculating, or predicting conditions in the future.

forecasts predictions of the future. Various time periods may be used, including short-term 3 to 5 day forecasts, 90-day forecasts, mid-term forecast covering 10 to 14 days, monthly, and 12-month forecasts.

free sell anytime rooms are needed by the wholesaler outside of those originally blocked, those rooms are considered to be sold based upon free space, in other words free sell. A wholesaler may also enter into a free-sell agreement with a hotel that states that any time rooms are available, and the hotel is interested in taking a reservation at the wholesale rate, the reservation will be accepted. In this case, no rooms are specifically reserved, or blocked, for the wholesaler. They are simply purchased freely, based upon availability.

frequent-traveler programs programs designed to reward loyal patronage and induce repeat business.

full pattern length of stay restriction an arrival-based restriction on a guest's stay. It may allow a guest to stay for 1, 2, 4, or 7 nights but not for 3, 5, or 6 nights, for example.

GDS see global distribution system.

Generation X a generational marketing term referring to those people born between 1965 and 1976. They are sometimes referred to as the baby busters, since as a group they only number 45 million, a huge slowdown from the birth rates generated by their grandparents.

Generation Y a generational marketing term. The echo boomers, also known as the baby boomlets. This population is defined as those nearly 72 million people born between 1977 and 1994. They are the children of the younger population of baby boomers. As a group, the echo boomers are almost as large in population as the baby boomers.

global distribution systems systems offering the inventory of multiple carriers and various suppliers of hospitality products and services. A computerized reservation system facilitating the sale of hospitality products and services primarily to organizational buyers, such as travel agents. The four major global distribution systems (GDS) today are SABRE, Amadeus, Gallileo, and Worldspan.

go dark when a venue shut its doors, turns down the heat or air conditioning, and turns off the lights.

goal an end for which to strive. A desired outcome.

graying of America refers to the fact that Americans are living longer and a significant portion of the population is now pushing past the age of 40.

gross margin revenue minus cost of goods sold (COGS).

gross margin percentage a percentage calculated by subtracting cost of goods sold from revenue and dividing that number by revenue and multiplying the result by 100.

group business business that involves more than two individuals coming together for a common reason.

growth stage this is the second stage in the life cycle of a product or service. Volume sold increases, which in turn generates economies of scale in production.

high roller a gambler who wagers large amounts of money. The casinos usually lavish amenities on high rollers to capture their gaming business. Also known as a **whale**.

IDEA I = Identification of goals and objectives
D = Development of strategies and tactics
E = Execution of selected strategies and tactics
A = Analysis, evaluation, and adjustment of strategies and tactic.

IDS see Internet Distribution System.

incentive pay additional pay for upselling products and services.

incremental business guests the organization would not otherwise obtain.

induce trial to entice customers to try out new products or services.

inelastic an economic term. Whenever a 1 percent change in price causes less than a 1 percent change in the quantity supplied or demanded, the elasticity calculation will result in a number less than 1. When this occurs, we say that the supply or demand is inelastic. In this case, the quantity supplied or demanded is not very sensitive to price.

inferior goods goods that decrease in demand with increases in consumer income. The more a consumer's income rises, the less that person will purchase of the inferior good.

Information Technology (IT) Department depending upon the size of an organization, the IT Department may range from one computer technician onsite to a full division comprised of computer technicians, information analysts, programmers and developers, and strategic system designers.

Internet distribution system (IDS) the electronic system that facilitates purchases of hospitality products and services by consumers. It is comprised of a variety of components, each falling into one of the following eight categories:
1. Proprietary site (individual unit and/or CRS)
2. Merchant model
3. Retail operation
4. Opaque site
5. Auction site
6. Referral service
7. Special interest or niche site
8. General Web Portal.

introductory stage the first phase in the life cycle of products and services. This is when the product or service is brand new and only the most adventurous consumers are poised to purchase.

inventory products or services made available for sale through various channels of distribution.

inventory management the process of controlling the units and availability of products and services across various channels of distribution.

last available room if a contract with Company B states availability is based upon 'last available room,' that means if a traveler from Company B shows up at the last minute and wants to purchase the last remaining room in inventory, he or she would be able to occupy that room at the established negotiated rate.

law of demand an economic law that states that the quantity of a good or service demanded by buyers tends to increase as the price of that good or service decreases, and tends to decrease as the price increases, all things being equal.

law of supply an economic law that states that as price rises, the quantity supplied increases and as the price falls, the quantity supplied decreases.

load the percentage or flat fee above the selling price that goes to an intermediary that must also be added to the cost of distribution. Also referred to as a **commission**.

load factor the percentage of seats sold (common airline term).

locally negotiated rates corporate negotiated rate business, often referred to as LNR.

long term defined here as more than one year.

long-term goals and objectives usually defined as goals and objectives spanning more than one year.

long-term strategies broad and far-reaching strategies planned for usually over one year.

lost business business that had considered an organization's products or services, but in the end decided against purchasing.

loyalty program programs whose members are rewarded either by receiving reduced rates or by increased value, such as added amenities. Some programs provide both reduced rates and added amenities. In addition, most programs contain a point reward system for each purchase. Guests are eligible for prizes or free travel components after accumulating a certain number of points.

managing demand the act of controlling, directing, influencing, and creating consumer purchasing propensity for a specific point in time.

market any place, real or virtual, in which a buyer and seller may come together to exchange goods and services.

market equilibrium a situation that occurs when the quantity supplied is exactly equal to the quantity demanded at that point in time.

market penetration the act of capturing additional market share. Also a marketing strategy in which the organization sets its price lower than its competitors' in an effort to create a better price/value perception in the minds of consumers and lure the consumers away from the competition. These lower prices are only temporary. Once the organization has captured a healthy market share, it will adjust price to displace lower-rated business with higher-paying customers. These lower introductory prices also have the effect of dissuading other potential entrants into the market.

market segmentation the practice of dividing a market into smaller specific segments sharing similar characteristics.

market share that percentage share of an overall market captured by an individual organization.

market skimming a marketing strategy in which an organization sets prices high to create the perception of value and position the product or service higher in the minds of consumers. They would use this high price/value perception to capture, or skim, the top-paying customers from their competitors.

marketing the process of satisfying the wants, needs, and desires of customers.

marketing intelligence practice of conducting primary research and analyzing secondary research to understand the characteristics of a market.

mature stage the time when nearly every consumer has purchased the product or service and it is no longer considered to be a hot item.

maximum length of stay restriction a stay restriction that permits a guest to stay only a certain number of nights.

merchandising the strategic selling and packaging of products and services.

merchant model the familiar online travel site, the third-party website.

meta search engines referral sites that scour other sites for the best price or deal.

midterm forecast a forecast generally covering 10 to 14 days into the future.

millennials a generational marketing term. Children born after 1994, children born at the turn of the century, this time the turn of a new millennium.

minimum length of stay restriction a restriction that dictates how many nights a person checking in on the night that has this restriction must stay.

mission statement a statement that reflects the current state of the business.

multiplier effect a term meaning that for every dollar that a traveler spends in direct costs to reach a destination, some multiple of that amount will be spent on total products and services during that traveler's visit.

must-stay restriction a restriction that applies to all reservations that stay over on the night on which this restriction is placed, including those guests arriving on that night. Guests must stay and pay through this date.

negotiate refers to the act of conferring upon or settling upon a satisfactory conclusion.

net rate also referred to as the wholesale rate. A rate that is often 20 to 30 percent or more off the retail rate.

niche a small, specific market.

niche sites websites that target small, specific subsegments of the market.

objective a target at which to aim.

occupancy the percentage of the hotel's rooms sold last night.

occupancy percentage a percentage calculated by dividing the total number of rooms occupied by the total number of rooms available.

off-season a season facing the lowest demand; also referred to as a weak or valley season.

online store a retailer's website.

onward distribution the conveyance of rates, inventory, and content to various channels through the GDS or through the Internet via switching mechanisms.

opaque channel a website on which either the price or the product is hidden to the customer. Examples of opaque sites are Hotwire and Travelocity packages.

open for sale inventory that is available for purchase, usually without restrictions.

opportunity cost the cost of taking any action is the loss of opportunity of taking any alternative action given the same time and resources.

organizational buy-in support and belief in the process or idea by members of an organization.

pace refers to a unit of time measurement.

pay per click fee a small fee assessed each time a consumer clicks to access a specific website.

peak season a season with the highest demand.

per diem per day.

perceived value the value of a product or service as perceived by the consumer that may include material value and quality, benefits received from ownership or usage, and esteem associated with the product or service.

perceptual positioning map a map that illustrates the price/value relationship and perceived positioning of several properties, usually direct competitors, within a market.

perfectly elastic an economic term. In the very rare case in which the supply or demand of a good would change without a change in price, the supply or demand of that good would be considered to be perfectly elastic.

perfectly inelastic An economic term. In the other rare case in which the quantity supplied or demanded does not change at all in response to a change in price, the supply or demand of that good is considered to be perfectly inelastic. Numerically, this would be equal to zero (zero divided by the change in price).

perishable a term meaning that if a product or service is not sold in a given time (a day, a night, a week) that product cannot later be sold. An example is an airline seat. Once the plane takes off, the seat cannot be stored for sale later.

perishable inventory products or services that possess the possibility of spoilage or loss.

Food is a perishable commodity. A hotel room and an airline seat are also perishable products. An empty airline seat on a flight cannot be stored for another flight. Once the airplane takes off, the revenue from an empty seat is lost forever. The same analogy applies to a hotel room that remains vacant for the evening.

pick-up the number of rooms sold. Or the number of units that have been confirmed as sold within that block.

place where a product or service is sold and relates to channels of distribution. One of the 4Ps of marketing.

portal a website gateway designed to provide access to other websites and services.

positioning the physical and mental perceptual placement of a product or service in a customer's mind.

prestige pricing a strategy of using high price to elevate the positioning of an organization's products and services and increase the perceived value to the consumer.

price the value that consumers exchange for the acquisition of products and services.

price elasticity of demand calculated by taking the absolute value of the percentage change in the quantity of a good demanded and dividing that by the percentage change in the price of that good.

price elasticity of supply calculated by taking the absolute value of the percentage change in quantity of a good supplied and dividing that by the percentage change in the price of that good.

price fences rules and regulations constructed to prohibit customers from leaping from one segment to another in an attempt to receive a lower rate. By placing restrictions on these offers, travel suppliers create a barrier, or fence, around these uniquely flexible travelers.

price fencing setting up rules and restrictions regarding the eligibility of an individual to purchase products and services at a specific price.

price gouging setting price levels much higher than what is perceived just and fair. Some hotels in the south substantially raised their rates during the days immediately following Hurricane Katrina. This was considered to be price gouging, which is illegal.

price leader an organization that leads the market in price.

price leadership applies to the organization setting the highest rates in the market.

price parity the practice of maintaining consistent prices across all channels of distribution.

price transparency the ability to observe prices. The Internet has made price transparency a feature of all products and services offered online.

primary purchase the main purchase made during a single or series of transactions.

primary research research designed and conducted by an organization for its own purposes.

pro-am professional paired with an amateur.

product refers to the goods and services presented for sale. One of the 4Ps of marketing.

promotion the methods used to market the products or services. One of the 4Ps of marketing.

promotional pricing a pricing strategy established to increase capture of date-specific demand.

PMS see property management system.

propensity to purchase a consumer's probability of purchasing an organization's products and services in the future.

Propensity Y future propensity to purchase.

property management system also known as a PMS. A computerized system used to manage the inventory of products and services available at a single location.

proprietary being owned and operated by that entity.

prosumer a term coined by Alvin Toffler to refer to a customer that was part producer and part consumer of the desired product or service. A second meaning for the term *prosumer* has increasingly appeared in discussions of consumer behavior. This reference combines the word *professional* with the word *consumer* to arrive at the alternative definition of prosumer—that of a professional consumer.

rack rate full rate. In earlier days, many hotels had a key rack behind the front desk. Perched above the rack was a sign stating the night's room rate. Walk-in guests would be offered that rate upon check-in. Thus the term *rack rate*.

rate integrity the maintenance of consistent prices for similar purchase conditions.

referral sites also known as **meta search engines**, these are websites that scour other sites for the best price or deal.

regret a response that occurs when the facility has the product or service available, but the customer chooses not to buy based upon price or some other factor. Regrets often indicate an imbalance in the price/value relationship.

repositioning to change the positioning of a product or service within a marketplace.

reservation an arrangement between a buyer and a seller to hold a product or service in advance of purchase on a promised intention of future purchase made by the buyer.

reservation conversion percentage the percentage of reservations that progress from inquiry level to final sale.

reservation call statistics statistics that include the number of calls received, number of calls answered, and the number of calls converted from inquiry to sale.

retail operator a firm that sells products and services of various hospitality providers at the prices set by the providers. A retail operator may maintain both an online presence and brick and mortar stores.

retail travel agent a travel professional who sells travel products and services directly to the public.

revenue management the act of skillfully, carefully, and tactfully managing, controlling, and directing capacity and sources of income, given the constraints of supply and demand.

revenue management team (RMT) those individuals who participate in the strategic revenue management process.

RevMAP the critical path leading to strategic revenue management.

RevPAR refers to revenue per available room and is calculated by dividing the actual room revenue by the number of rooms available.

room night a statistic calculated by multiplying one room times one night. A guest booking one room for three nights would be said to generate three room nights.

RSS (really simple syndication) feeds enabling technology that allows travelers to select customized content views that will be highly personalized and updated, in real time, as new opportunities and offers are made available. Many people use RSS feeds today, but don't even realize it. For example, you may have a "My Yahoo!" account that allows you to customize your personal home page to include top news stories, weather from your home town, and movie times for shows at the theater down the street. RSS is the technology behind the scenes that allows for this level of customization.

run of house the best available rates will be available for all room types. When a customer is given the run of the house, they are guaranteed the best available rate through the last room sold.

secondary research work conducted and published by other organizations.

secondary competitors these are organizations that also compete with a firm for a portion of that firm's customers, but they may do so indirectly.

short-term goals and objectives targets for the upcoming year.

short-term strategies plans of action to be achieved in the upcoming year.

short-term 3 to 5-day forecast a forecast that extends 3 to 5 days into the future.

shortage a situation that occurs when the quantity demanded exceeds the quantity supplied. There are more buyers than there are goods or services at this price at this point in time.

shoulder season a time of year immediately before or after a peak or weak season.

silver-haired seniors a generational marketing term. Comprised of all individuals born prior to 1946.

SMART S = Specific
M = Measurable
A = Achievable
R = Realistic
T = Trackable.

SMERFE a market segment comprised of social, military, educational, religious, fraternal, and entertainment business.

snowbird a person who travels south for the winter.

special-interest website also known as a niche site. This is a website that targets a small, specific subsegment of the market.

stakeholder anyone with an interest in an activity, entity, or event.

stay the number of nights a guest occupies a specific product, whether it is a hotel room, a cruise berth, or a campground space.

stay controls duration rules and restrictions that may apply to arrival dates, departure dates, and minimum length of stay.

stay pattern a pattern that can cover the individual's arrival day, number of nights' stay, and departure day for the guest.

strategic management the process of developing, implementing, and evaluating strategies that enable an organization to achieve its objectives.

strategic revenue management process the eight fundamental elements plus the strategic **IDEA** combine to create the RevMAP.

strategy *how* the organization plans to achieve a goal or objective.

substitutes an economic term. If the price of one item goes up causing the increase in the demand for another similar item, those two items are referred to as substitutes for one another. The general rule for substitute goods or services is that the price for one and the demand for the other will both move in the same direction.

supply the amount of a good or service that a seller is willing and able to sell for any given price at any given time.

surplus a situation that occurs when the quantity supplied exceeds the quantity demanded. There is greater supply of the good or service than may be sold at this price at this point in time.

switch a single electronic connection through which a hospitality provider must pass first before being connected to the GDS. There are just two switches operating today that connect the entire hospitality industry, Pegasus (originally known as THISCO—the hotel industry switch company) and Wizcom (which was originally developed to connect select car rental companies to the GDS systems).

SWOT analysis an assessment of an organization's strengths, weaknesses, opportunities, and threats.

tactics skillful methods used to achieve desired results. Tactics are the action steps taken to fulfill a strategy.

third-party website they serve as an intermediary, in other words a third party, between the consumer and the hospitality product or service providers who comprise the other two parties.

total acquisition cost may apply to either a customer or an organization. To a customer, total acquisition cost may include intrinsic costs, such as price, and extrinsic costs, such as the time it takes to make the purchase and the cost of gasoline it requires to get to and from the store. To an organization, total acquisition cost means the cost of acquiring the customer, including the costs of marketing, the costs of taking reservations, and the costs of actually serving the guest. So the perceived product or service value must be equal to or exceed the total acquisition cost to produce total value to the consumer.

total cost cost summation calculated by adding together fixed and variable cost.

total customer value Perceived Product or Service Value − Total Acquisition Cost.

total customer worth (Primary Revenue + Ancillary Revenue − Acquisition Cost) × Propensity .

total spend the amount of primary and ancillary revenue that is spent per customer.

tracking reports statistical reports that should be analyzed to determine where the organization's business is emanating from to seize any potential opportunities arising from the appearance of new customers and new segments.

transient an individual traveling, dining, attending a game or performance, or staying alone. A temporary individual hospitality customer.

unconstrained demand naturally occurring demand that occurs in the absence of restraints and restrictions.

unit elasticity an economic term. A measurement of elasticity which occurs when a 1 percent change in price results in exactly a 1 percent change in the quantity supplied or demanded. This measure of elasticity numerically equals 1.

valley season a season facing the lowest demand; also known as a weak season.

value-based pricing in this scenario the organization needs to focus upon the value placed by the customer on the product or service. Next, the organization needs to equate that value to a specific price. A price/value relationship then develops in which the price must be equal to or less than the value placed upon that product or service by a consumer to generate a sale.

values the principles by which the organization operates. Values include being responsible corporate citizens and active protectors of the environment.

variable costs costs that change in direct proportion to a change in the activity of a business. Fuel is a variable cost.

variance report a report upon which any deviation between forecast and actual production is recorded.

VFR visiting friends and relatives.

vision statement a statement that reflects what the business desires to become.

wash factor a predetermined percentage of usage based upon historical data and experience.

weak season a season facing the lowest demand; also referred to as a valley season.

whale also known as a high roller; a gambler who wagers large amounts of money. The casinos usually lavish amenities on high rollers to capture their gaming business.

wholesale rate also referred to as the net rate. A rate that is often 20 to 30 percent or more off the retail rate.

wholesale tour operator travel professional who creates travel packages to be sold to travelers directly or through travel agencies at a discount.

wholesaler a person who purchases individual travel components at a discount based upon volume, and repackages the components and sells them to a consumer on a retail basis, either directly through the wholesale organization or via a travel agent or tour operator.

worth   the sum value of the customer to the organization.

yield   refers to the amount of revenue received by the airline for each mile flown per passenger (also known as passenger mile).

yield management   the precursor to what we now refer to as revenue management. A formalized method of managing and controlling revenue.

Index